Excel

Get the Results You Want!

Year 7 Mathematics Practice Tests

Lyn Baker

PASCAL PRESS

Reprinted 2021, 2023 (twice), 2025

ISBN 978 1 74125 634 5

Pascal Press
PO Box 250
Glebe NSW 2037
www.pascalpress.com.au

Publisher: Vivienne Joannou
Project editor: Rosemary Peers
Edited by Rosemary Peers
Answers checked by Peter Little
Typeset by Kim Webber
Printed by Vivar Printing/Green Giant Press

The publisher thanks the Royal Australian Mint for granting permission to use Australian currency coin designs in this book.

Contents

NUMBER AND ALGEBRA

Squares and Index Notation

Computations with Integers

Fractions

Decimals

Percentages

Money

Ratio and Rates

Algebra, Equations and Coordinates

MEASUREMENT AND GEOMETRY

Length, Area and Volume

Geometric Reasoning

Introduction

- The main purpose of this book is to provide students with **extensive test and exam practice** at all levels in Year 7, in the topics they cover in class. This way students will be given the test and exam practice they require to be fully prepared to excel at their class tests and exams.
- This book covers all the topics in **Year 7 Australian Curriculum Mathematics.**

The following features will help students excel in their class tests and exams:

- This book is a **workbook** that students can write in, ensuring that they have all their tests, exams and working in one place. This is invaluable when revising for topic tests and exams—no lost pages or notes.
- Each unit of work has a **pretest**. The pretests have been designed to check that students have the necessary skills for each section of work and this has determined their position in the book.
- The **main tests** all have **three sections**: Part A has multiple-choice questions, Part B has short-answer questions and Part C consists of questions that require some working out.
- The main tests also have three different **levels of difficulty**.
  - **Level 1** tests are the easiest. They should determine whether a student has a basic understanding of the topic.
  - **Level 2** tests are aimed at the average student. Those who do well in these tests will have a solid grasp of the content of the topic.
  - **Level 3** tests are the most challenging. They are aimed at good students and should determine whether they have a thorough knowledge of the content and are able to apply that knowledge.

  Together these different tests can also be used as carefully **graded exercises** for revision.
- Some tests have been designed as **non-calculator tests**, allowing an examination of students' ability to work with whole numbers, fractions and decimals, without the use of a calculator. This is an integral part of the Year 7 course.
- Other tests in these topic areas are specifically **calculator allowed** to make sure students are also familiar with the working and limitations of calculators. It is assumed that students will have access to a calculator but in most cases the use of a calculator will not be essential.
- There are **five yearly examination papers**. There is one at each level specifically designed to be done without a calculator, plus two that are calculator allowed.
- **Answers** to all questions are provided at the back of the book.
- Note that the **innovative test and exam format** of this book can be used both as a means of assessing students' knowledge and understanding, and also to provide comprehensive revision of the course.

There are four titles in the series:

Squares and Index Notation

PRETEST

Time allowed: 15 minutes **Total marks: 16**

					Marks
1	Which of these is divisible by 5?				
	(A) 234	(B) 324	(C) 543	(D) 345	1
2	Which of these is a multiple of 7?				
	(A) 17	(B) 42	(C) 43	(D) 177	1
3	Which of these numbers is prime?				
	(A) 12	(B) 13	(C) 14	(D) 15	1
4	What number, multiplied by itself, is 36?				
	(A) 4	(B) 6	(C) 8	(D) 9	1
5	Which of these is a square number?				
	(A) 8	(B) 12	(C) 16	(D) 20	1
6	Nine multiplied by itself is:				
	(A) 3	(B) 18	(C) 72	(D) 81	1
7	Which has factors of both 2 and 5?				
	(A) 7	(B) 12	(C) 35	(D) 980	1
8	Which of these numbers is composite?				
	(A) 1	(B) 5	(C) 35	(D) 53	1
9	How many factors must a prime number have?				
	(A) 0	(B) 1	(C) 2	(D) more than 2	1
10	Which is **not** a multiple of 11?				
	(A) 33	(B) 77	(C) 222	(D) 374	1
11	Which is equal to 24?				
	(A) $2 \times 2 \times 2 \times 3$	(B) $2 \times 3 \times 3 \times 3$	(C) $2 \times 2 \times 3 \times 3$	(D) $3 \times 3 \times 3 \times 3$	1
12	If a number is divided by one of its factors the result **must** be:				
	(A) a whole number	(B) a fraction	(C) prime	(D) composite	1
13	Which is a common factor of 18 and 24?				
	(A) 6	(B) 9	(C) 12	(D) 72	1
14	Which is a common multiple of 3 and 4?				
	(A) 7	(B) 12	(C) 28	(D) 34	1
15	What is the highest common factor of 12 and 48?				
	(A) 3	(B) 6	(C) 12	(D) 24	1
16	What is the lowest common multiple of 5 and 10?				
	(A) 5	(B) 10	(C) 15	(D) 50	1

Total marks /16

LEVEL 1 TEST

PART A

Time allowed: 40 minutes

Marks

1 $5^2 =$

(A) 10 (B) 25 (C) 52 (D) 55 [1]

2 $\sqrt{64} =$

(A) 2 (B) 4 (C) 8 (D) 16 [1]

3 $3 \times 3 \times 3 \times 3 =$

(A) 3×4 (B) 2×3^2 (C) 4^3 (D) 3^4 [1]

4 $10^4 =$

(A) 1000 (B) 10 000 (C) 100 000 (D) 10 101 010 [1]

5 $2^3 =$

(A) 5 (B) 6 (C) 8 (D) 9 [1]

6 $5 + 4^2 =$

(A) 21 (B) 13 (C) 29 (D) 81 [1]

7 $\sqrt[3]{1} =$

(A) 0 (B) $\frac{1}{3}$ (C) 1 (D) 3 [1]

8 $\sqrt{25} - \sqrt{9} =$

(A) 2 (B) 3 (C) 4 (D) 5 [1]

9 $5^3 =$

(A) 5×3 (B) $5 + 3$ (C) $3 \times 3 \times 3 \times 3 \times 3$ (D) $5 \times 5 \times 5$ [1]

10 48 expressed as a product of its prime factors is:

(A) 6×8 (B) $2 \times 2 \times 2 \times 2 \times 3$ (C) $2 \times 3 \times 4$ (D) $2 \times 3 \times 2 \times 3 \times 2$ [1]

11 $5 \times 7 \times 5 \times 5 \times 7 \times 5 \times 7 =$

(A) 5×7^7 (B) 35^7 (C) $5^3 \times 7^4$ (D) $5^4 \times 7^3$ [1]

12 $2^2 + 3^2 =$

(A) 13 (B) 17 (C) 25 (D) 36 [1]

13 $3 \times 2^2 =$

(A) 12 (B) 18 (C) 34 (D) 36 [1]

14 Which is the best estimate for $\sqrt{50}$?

(A) 5 (B) 6 (C) 7 (D) 8 [1]

15 Which is **not** divisible by 3?

(A) 675 (B) 495 (C) 855 (D) 935 [1]

PART B Write answers only in the space provided.

16 $6^2 =$ ______________ [1]

17 $\sqrt{100} =$ ______________ [1]

18 Write $7 \times 7 \times 7 \times 7 \times 7 \times 7$ in index form. ______________ [1]

19 Write 11^4 in expanded form. ______________ [1]

20 Write 42 as the product of its prime factors. ______________ [1]

21 $2^5 =$ ______________ [1]

22 $\sqrt[3]{27} =$ ______________ [1]

23 Write $2 \times 2 \times 3 \times 3 \times 3$ in index form. ______________ [1]

24 Between which two whole numbers does $\sqrt{40}$ lie? ______________ [1]

25 Given that $2025 = 3 \times 3 \times 3 \times 3 \times 5 \times 5$, what is the value of $\sqrt{2025}$? ______________ [1]

PART C Show all working.

26 a Briefly explain why 26415 must be divisible by 5. [1 mark]

____

____

b What is the sum of the digits of 26415? [1 mark]

____

c Explain why 26 415 must be divisible by 9. [1 mark]

____

____

d Briefly explain why 26415 must be divisible by 45. [1 mark]

____

____

e When 26 415 is divided by 45 the result is the prime number 587. Write 26415 as the product of its prime factors. [1 mark]

____

27 a Write 18 as the product of its prime factors. [1 mark]

____

____

b Use the result from **a** to find 18^2. [2 marks]

____

28 a Complete factor trees for:
i 60 [2 marks] **ii** 75 [2 marks]

b What is the highest common factor of 60 and 75? [1 mark]

____

c What is the lowest common multiple of 60 and 75? [2 marks]

____

____

Total marks /40

LEVELS 2 AND 3 TEST — PART A

Time allowed: 40 minutes

Question	Marks
1 $32^2 =$ (A) 1024 (B) 904 (C) 964 (D) 9664	1
2 $2^3 \times 5^4 =$ (A) 5000 (B) 1000 (C) 25 000 (D) 10 000 000	1
3 $\sqrt{3969} =$ (A) 57 (B) 63 (C) 67 (D) 73	1
4 Which is divisible by 3? (A) 8572 (B) 4805 (C) 2378 (D) 5217	1
5 200 expressed as a product of its prime factors in index form is: (A) 2×10^2 (B) $2^2 \times 5^3$ (C) $2^3 \times 5^2$ (D) $(2 \times 5)^3$	1
6 A number is divisible by both 48 and 98. Which of these numbers might it **not** be divisible by? (A) 12 (B) 14 (C) 16 (D) 18	1
7 $\sqrt{547}$ lies between which two whole numbers? (A) 21 and 22 (B) 22 and 23 (C) 23 and 24 (D) 24 and 25	1
8 $5 \times 2^4 =$ (A) 10 000 (B) 1000 (C) 160 (D) 80	1
9 A number must be divisible by 9 if its digits: (A) add to a multiple of 9 (B) add to a factor of 9 (C) multiply to a multiple of 9 (D) multiply to a factor of 9	1
10 $\sqrt{36 + 64} =$ (A) 10 (B) 14 (C) 50 (D) 70	1
11 $3^2 + 4^2 =$ (A) 14 (B) 25 (C) 49 (D) 169	1
12 $2^3 \times 3^2 \times 4^2 =$ (A) $2^5 \times 3^2$ (B) $2^6 \times 3^2$ (C) $2^7 \times 3^2$ (D) $2^8 \times 3^2$	1
13 Which of these numbers is divisible by both 5 and 6? (A) 735 (B) 432 (C) 820 (D) 780	1
14 If $192 = 3 \times 2^*$, what is $3 \times 10^*$? (A) 3000 (B) 30 000 (C) 300 000 (D) 3 000 000	1
15 Which of these is **not** equal to the others? (A) 2^8 (B) 4^4 (C) 8^3 (D) 16^2	1

Squares and Index Notation Non-calculator (Levels 2 and 3 Test)

PART B Write answers only in the space provided.

16 What is the square of 9? ______________ [1]

17 Write 600 as the product of its prime factors in index form. ______________ [1]

18 Find $\sqrt[3]{1000}$. ______________ [1]

19 What number could be expressed as $2^4 \times 5^5$? ______________ [1]

20 Given that $1936 = 2^4 \times 11^2$ find $\sqrt{1936}$. ______________ [1]

21 What is the highest common factor of 48 and 64? ______________ [1]

22 $21^2 =$ ______________ [1]

23 What is the sum of 2^6 and 6^2? ______________ [1]

24 Find $\sqrt{625}$. ______________ [1]

25 Find the value of $\sqrt{\dfrac{100-64}{\sqrt{25-9}}}$. ______________ [1]

PART C Show all working.

26 a Write 28 as the product of its prime factors. [1 mark]

____

b Use the result from **a** to find 28^2. [2 marks]

____

27 The square of any whole number is always one less than the average of the squares of the numbers one less than and one more than that whole number. Use this fact to find 147^2 given that $146^2 = 21\,316$ and $148^2 = 21\,904$. [2 marks]

____

____

____

28 a Complete a factor tree for 324. [1 mark]

b Write 324 as the product of its prime factors in index form. [1 mark]

____

c Find $\sqrt{324}$. [2 marks]

____

29 a Write 216 as the product of its prime factors. [1 mark]

____

b Find $\sqrt[3]{216}$. [2 marks]

____

30 Find the lowest common multiple of 504 and 540. [3 marks]

____

____

____

____

____

Total marks /40

LEVEL 2 TEST PART A

Time allowed: 40 minutes

Marks

1 $\sqrt{5329} =$

Ⓐ 67 Ⓑ 73 Ⓒ 77 Ⓓ 83 — 1

2 $7 \times 3 \times 3 \times 7 \times 3 \times 7 \times 3 \times 7 \times 3 =$

Ⓐ 3×7^9 Ⓑ $3^5 \times 7^4$ Ⓒ $(7 \times 3)^9$ Ⓓ $7^5 \times 3^4$ — 1

3 $5^7 =$

Ⓐ 16 807 Ⓑ 117 645 Ⓒ 78 125 Ⓓ 390 625 — 1

4 $\sqrt[3]{4096} =$

Ⓐ 64 Ⓑ 36 Ⓒ 24 Ⓓ 16 — 1

5 $\sqrt{64} + \sqrt{225} =$

Ⓐ 17 Ⓑ 19 Ⓒ 21 Ⓓ 23 — 1

6 $\sqrt{350}$ lies between which two whole numbers?

Ⓐ 17 and 18 Ⓑ 18 and 19 Ⓒ 19 and 20 Ⓓ 20 and 21 — 1

7 $6 + 3^5 - 2^2 =$

Ⓐ 9 Ⓑ 735 Ⓒ 245 Ⓓ 59 045 — 1

8 $\sqrt{144 + 1225} =$

Ⓐ 27 Ⓑ 37 Ⓒ 47 Ⓓ 57 — 1

9 In the number 2^3, 2 is called the:

Ⓐ base Ⓑ index Ⓒ power Ⓓ exponent — 1

10 Which is **not** a prime factor of 3705?

Ⓐ 5 Ⓑ 13 Ⓒ 17 Ⓓ 19 — 1

11 $23^2 + 264^2 =$

Ⓐ 265^2 Ⓑ 267^2 Ⓒ 275^2 Ⓓ 287^2 — 1

12 What is 4896 expressed as the product of powers of prime numbers?

Ⓐ $2^4 \times 3^2 \times 51$ Ⓑ $2^5 \times 3 \times 51$ Ⓒ $2^4 \times 3^3 \times 17$ Ⓓ $2^5 \times 3^2 \times 17$ — 1

13 Which statement is correct? I $2^5 \times 3^5 = 6^5$ II $\sqrt{9} \times \sqrt{16} = \sqrt{9 \times 16}$

Ⓐ I only Ⓑ II only Ⓒ both I and II Ⓓ neither I nor II — 1

14 $5^3 + 3 \times 2^4 =$

Ⓐ 173 Ⓑ 2048 Ⓒ 1421 Ⓓ 294 499 921 — 1

15 If $400 = 2^{\nabla} \times 5^{\bullet}$ then $5^{\nabla} \times 2^{\bullet} =$

Ⓐ 2500 Ⓑ 12 500 Ⓒ 5000 Ⓓ 25 000 — 1

PART B Write answers only in the space provided.

16 Find the square of 64. ______________ [1]

17 Find the value of 7^4. ______________ [1]

18 Find $\sqrt{6889}$. ______________ [1]

19 Evaluate $\sqrt[3]{79\,507}$. ______________ [1]

20 Express 588 as the product of powers of its prime factors. ______________ [1]

21 What number can be expressed as $2^3 \times 3^4 \times 5 \times 7^2$? ______________ [1]

22 Find $\sqrt{4596}$ giving the answer to the nearest whole number. ______________ [1]

23 Find the value of $5^3 - 7 \times 2^6 + 11 \times 3^4$. ______________ [1]

24 Evaluate $\dfrac{\sqrt{3264^2 + 8927^2}}{2 \times 17^2 + 3^3 \times 7^2}$. ______________ [1]

25 Find the value of $\dfrac{\sqrt[3]{745^2 - 713^2}}{\sqrt{745^2 - 713^2}}$. ______________ [1]

PART C Show all working.

26 Write $2^5 \times 2^3$ in:

a expanded form [1 mark]

____

b simplest index form [1 mark]

____

27 a Find $\sqrt{9^3}$. [1 mark]

____

b Is $(\sqrt{9})^3 = \sqrt{9^3}$? Justify your answer with appropriate calculations. [1 mark]

____

28 Explain why $4^3 = 2^6$. [1 mark]

____

29 a Is $\sqrt{1089 + 3136} = \sqrt{1089} + \sqrt{3136}$? Justify your answer. [2 marks]

____

b Is $\sqrt{1089 \times 3136} = \sqrt{1089} \times \sqrt{3136}$? Justify your answer. [2 marks]

____

30 a Express 95 256 as the product of its prime factors in index form. [2 marks]

____

b Express 111 132 as the product of its prime factors in index form. [2 marks]

____

c What is the highest common factor of 95 256 and 111 132? [1 mark]

____

d What is the lowest common multiple of 95 256 and 111 132? [1 mark]

____

Total marks /40

Computations with Integers

PRETEST

Time allowed: 15 minutes **Total marks: 15**

Marks

1 718 + 92 =

(A) 800 (B) 810 (C) 780 (D) 880 [1]

2 Which are in ascending (from lowest to highest) order?

(A) 510, 5009, 527, 5207 (B) 5009, 510, 5207, 527

(C) 5009, 510, 527, 5207 (D) 510, 527, 5009, 5207 [1]

3 The product of 2 and 8 is:

(A) 6 (B) 4 (C) 10 (D) 16 [1]

4 728 is equal to:

(A) 7 + 2 + 8 (B) 70 + 20 + 80 (C) 700 + 20 + 8 (D) none of these [1]

5 If 7 × 4 = 14 + ☆, then ☆ =

(A) 2 (B) 8 (C) 17 (D) 14 [1]

6 The number two hundred and five thousand and seventy-six is:

(A) 25 076 (B) 205 076 (C) 20 576 (D) 25 760 [1]

7 The sum of 6 and 2 is:

(A) 3 (B) 4 (C) 8 (D) 12 [1]

8 5642 ÷ 7 =

(A) 86 (B) 806 (C) 860 (D) 8006 [1]

9 Four sets of six stamps is the same as eight sets of ☆ stamps. ☆ =

(A) 12 (B) 10 (C) 3 (D) 2 [1]

10 563 – 75 =

(A) 418 (B) 488 (C) 498 (D) 518 [1]

11 Zac has 12 marbles. Bella has eight more marbles than Zac and five less than Celia. How many marbles does Celia have?

(A) 25 (B) 15 (C) 9 (D) 23 [1]

12 57 + 121 + 378 is closest to:

(A) 540 (B) 550 (C) 560 (D) 570 [1]

13 A group of five friends shared 255 cards equally. How many cards did each get?

(A) 51 (B) 53 (C) 55 (D) 56 [1]

14 If Olivia had seven more eggs she would have five dozen eggs. How many eggs does she have?

(A) 67 (B) 57 (C) 43 (D) 53 [1]

15 Mia has 24 toy cars and trucks. She has 10 more cars than trucks. How many toy trucks does Mia have?

(A) 7 (B) 10 (C) 14 (D) 17 [1]

Total marks /15

Computations with Whole Numbers Non-calculator

LEVEL 2 TEST — PART A

Time allowed: 40 minutes

Question	Marks
1 The answer to 867 divided by 43 would be closest to: Ⓐ 15 Ⓑ 20 Ⓒ 25 Ⓓ 30	1
2 Which is correct? Ⓐ $7 + 8 = 8 + 7$ Ⓑ $7 - 8 = 8 - 7$ Ⓒ $7 + 8 = 8 - 7$ Ⓓ $7 - 8 = 8 + 7$	1
3 Which is **not** equal to $17 \times 85 + 15 \times 17$? Ⓐ 17×100 Ⓑ 100×17 Ⓒ $17 \times (85 + 15)$ Ⓓ $17 \times 85 + 15$	1
4 If $283 = 17 \times 16 + 11$ then $283 \div 17 =$ Ⓐ $16\frac{11}{16}$ Ⓑ $17\frac{11}{16}$ Ⓒ $16\frac{11}{17}$ Ⓓ $17\frac{11}{17}$	1
5 Which does **not** have the same value as 35×66? Ⓐ 33×70 Ⓑ 30×77 Ⓒ 55×42 Ⓓ 95×22	1
6 $94 \times 93 =$ Ⓐ $94 \times 100 - 94 \times 6$ Ⓑ $94 \times 100 - 7 \times 94$ Ⓒ $94 \times 100 - 7 \times 93$ Ⓓ $94 \times 100 - 93 \times 6$	1
7 Which of the symbols +, –, × or ÷ could replace ☆ in 129 ☆ 73 = 73 ☆ 129 and make a true statement? Ⓐ + only Ⓑ + or × only Ⓒ + or – only Ⓓ × or ÷ only	1
8 Which of these gives the same value as $2 \times 5 \times 7 \times 3$? Ⓐ $(2 \times 5) \times (7 \times 3)$ only Ⓑ $2 \times (5 \times 7 \times 3)$ only Ⓒ $2 \times (5 \times 7) \times 3$ only Ⓓ all of these	1
9 57×18 is the same as: Ⓐ $57 \times 9 \times 2$ Ⓑ $57 \times 10 + 8$ Ⓒ $50 + 7 \times 18$ Ⓓ $50 \times 10 + 7 \times 8$	1
10 Which of these has the same value as $144 \div 12 \div 6 \div 2$? Ⓐ $(144 \div 12) \div (6 \div 2)$ Ⓑ $144 \div (12 \div 6 \div 2)$ Ⓒ $144 \div (12 \div 6) \div 2$ Ⓓ none of these	1
11 Which does **not** give the same result as 733×48? Ⓐ $733 \times 24 \times 2$ Ⓑ $6 \times 733 \times 8$ Ⓒ $3 \times 18 \times 733$ Ⓓ $4 \times 733 \times 12$	1
12 Given that $641 \div 74 = 8\frac{49}{74}$, then $641 =$ Ⓐ $(8 + 49) \times 74$ Ⓑ $8 + 49 \times 74$ Ⓒ $8 \times 49 + 74$ Ⓓ $8 \times 74 + 49$	1
13 $103 \times 37 - 3 \times 37 =$ Ⓐ 100×37 Ⓑ 100×34 Ⓒ 103×34 Ⓓ $103 \times 34 \times 37$	1
14 Which is **not** equal to 89×56? Ⓐ $100 \times 56 - 11 \times 56$ Ⓑ $50 \times 89 + 6 \times 89$ Ⓒ $56 \times 13 \times 3$ Ⓓ $7 \times 89 \times 8$	1
15 Which of the symbols +, –, × or ÷ could replace ☆ in (12 ☆ 6) ☆ 2 = 12 ☆ (6 ☆ 2) and make a true statement? Ⓐ + only Ⓑ + or × only Ⓒ + or – or × Ⓓ all of them	1

Computations with Whole Numbers Non-calculator **(Level 2 Test)**

PART B Write answers only in the space provided.

16 $5 \times 79 \times 2 =$ ______________ 1

17 $107 \times 62 - 7 \times 62 =$ ______________ 1

18 $4 \times 9 \times 8 \times 3 \times 0 \times 7 \times 5 =$ ______________ 1

19 If $378 \div 29 = 13\frac{1}{29}$, what is $378 \div 13$? ______________ 1

20 Find 99×28. ______________ 1

21 $322 + 784 + 678 =$ ______________ 1

22 $37 \times 863 - 36 \times 863 =$ ______________ 1

23 $4 \times 73 \times 25 =$ ______________ 1

24 $6 \times 213 + 4 \times 213 =$ ______________ 1

25 If $413 \div 32 = 12\frac{29}{32}$, what is $416 \div 32$? ______________ 1

PART C Show all working.

26 Determine whether these statements are true or false:

a $19 + 18 + 17 + 16 = 17 + 19 + 16 + 18$ 1 mark

____

b $(72 \div 6) \times 2 = 72 \div (6 \times 2)$ 1 mark

____

c $95 \times 8 + 7 \times 95 = 15 \times 95$ 1 mark

____

d $(8 \times 12) \div 3 = 8 \times (12 \div 3)$ 1 mark

____

27 a Find $10 \times 23 + 2 \times 23$. 1 mark

____

b What is the result when 284 is divided by 23? 1 mark

____

c What is 23×13? 1 mark

____

28 a Find $100 \times 87 + 2 \times 87$. 1 mark

____

b Find 87×103. 1 mark

____

c Find 112×87. 1 mark

____

29 Find:

a 947×99 1 mark

____

b 947×98 1 mark

____

30 Given that $78 \times 69 = 5382$:

a what is the value of 79×69? 1 mark

____

b what is the value of 78×68? 1 mark

____

c what number between 5400 and 5500 is divisible by 78? 1 mark

____

Total marks /40

Integers Non-calculator

LEVELS 1 AND 2 TEST — PART A

Time allowed: 40 minutes

Marks

1 Which of these numbers is the largest?

(A) –7 (B) –11 (C) –3 (D) 2 — 1

2 What number is found at the position marked by the arrow?

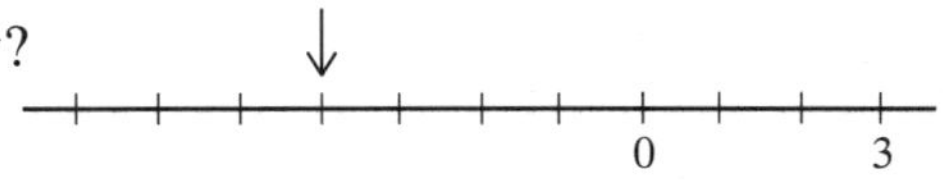

(A) –4 (B) –3 (C) –2 (D) –1 — 1

3 Which is **not** correct?

(A) –3 > –2 (B) –5 < 1 (C) 4 > –7 (D) –8 < –6 — 1

4 –3 + 7 =

(A) 3 (B) 4 (C) –4 (D) –10 — 1

5 5 – 8 =

(A) 3 (B) –3 (C) –13 (D) 13 — 1

6 Which of these numbers is the smallest?

(A) –12 (B) –8 (C) 5 (D) –2 — 1

7 Which arrow shows the position of –16?

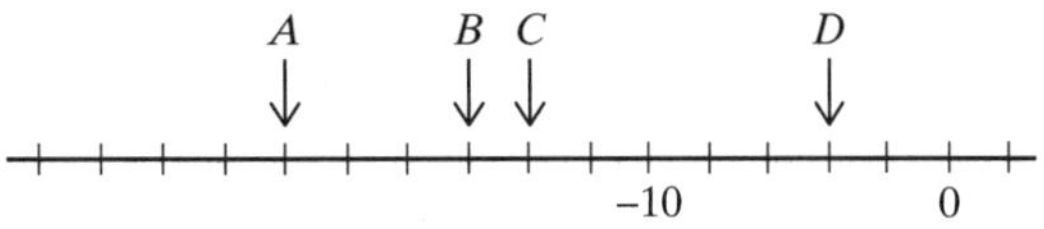

(A) A (B) B (C) C (D) D — 1

8 –6 – 4 =

(A) 2 (B) –2 (C) 10 (D) –10 — 1

9 –11 + 5 =

(A) –6 (B) 6 (C) –16 (D) 16 — 1

10 Which numbers are in ascending order?

(A) 0, –2, 5, 7, –9 (B) –2, –9, 0, 5, 7 (C) 0, –2, –9, 5, 7 (D) –9, –2, 0, 5, 7 — 1

11 9 – –3 =

(A) 6 (B) –6 (C) 12 (D) –12 — 1

12 4 + (–7) =

(A) 3 (B) –3 (C) 11 (D) –11 — 1

13 –5 – –8 =

(A) –13 (B) –3 (C) 3 (D) 13 — 1

14 At 8 am the temperature was –3 °C. It was 1 °C at 9 am. The change is a:

(A) fall of 2° (B) rise of 2° (C) fall of 4° (D) rise of 4° — 1

15 The temperature in a freezer was –6 °C. When next checked, the temperature had fallen by 3°. What was the new temperature?

(A) –2° (B) –3° (C) –9° (D) –18° — 1

PART B Write answers only in the space provided.

16 –3 + 7 = ______________ 1

17 5 – 9 = ______________ 1

18 –8 – 6 = ______________ 1

19 –2 – 10 = ______________ 1

20 –20 + 4 = ______________ 1

21 Show the position of –7 on the number line. 1

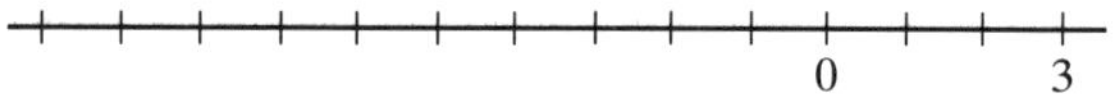

22 Write the integers –6, –10, 4, –8, 2, 0 and –5 in ascending order. ______________ 1

23 3 – –7 = ______________ 1

24 –5 + (–6) = ______________ 1

25 –4 – –2 = ______________ 1

PART C Show all working.

26 Find the value of:

a –3 – 6 + 2 1 mark

____

b 4 – 9 – 10 1 mark

____

c –4 + 7 – 3 1 mark

____

d –11 + 8 – 21 1 mark

____

27 a What temperature is shown on this thermometer? 1 mark

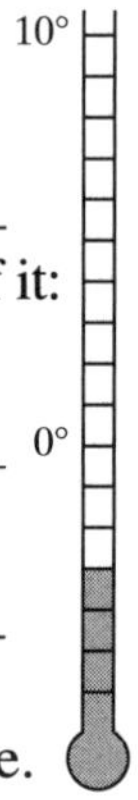

____

b What would be the temperature if it:

i rose by 2°? 1 mark

____

ii instead dropped by 6°? 1 mark

____

c Two hours later the temperature is 8°. Briefly describe the change. 1 mark

____

____

28 Some children played a game where they got 1, 2 or 3 points for getting questions right but lost those points if they were wrong.

a Billy's score is –5. What will his score be if he gets a 3-point question wrong? 1 mark

____

b Mary's score is –4. What will her score be if she gets a 3-point question right? 1 mark

____

c Cody's first five questions are worth 1, 3, 2, 2 and 3 points in that order. What is his score if he gets both of the 3-point questions wrong but the others right? 1 mark

____

d Does it matter in what order Cody answers the questions? 1 mark

____

29 a Briefly explain what a bank balance of –$1200 would mean. 1 mark

____

____

b Ella's bank balance was –$1200 and she withdrew another $230. What is her new balance? 1 mark

____

c If, instead, Ella had placed $570 in the bank what would her new balance be? 1 mark

____

Total marks /40

LEVELS 2 AND 3 TEST — PART A

Time allowed: 40 minutes

Marks

1 13 – 25 =

Ⓐ 12 Ⓑ –12 Ⓒ –13 Ⓓ –38 [1]

2 Consider these statements: I –17 < –9 II –17 > 8 Which is correct?

Ⓐ both I and II Ⓑ neither I nor II Ⓒ I but not II Ⓓ II but not I [1]

3 –23 – 4 =

Ⓐ –19 Ⓑ –27 Ⓒ 19 Ⓓ 27 [1]

4 –17 – –43 =

Ⓐ –26 Ⓑ 26 Ⓒ –60 Ⓓ 0 [1]

5 40 + (–29) =

Ⓐ 11 Ⓑ –11 Ⓒ 69 Ⓓ –69 [1]

6 12 ÷ 3 – 9 =

Ⓐ 2 Ⓑ –2 Ⓒ –5 Ⓓ 5 [1]

7 Which number is found at the position of the arrow?

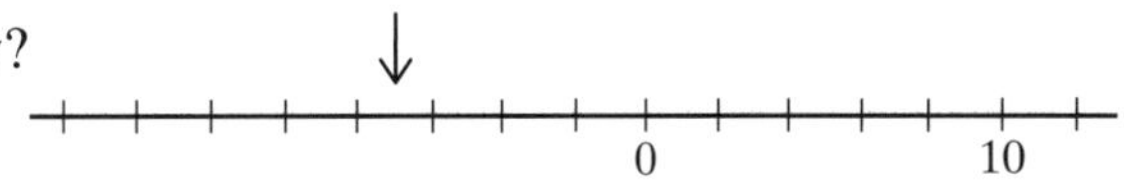

Ⓐ $-3\frac{1}{2}$ Ⓑ $-1\frac{1}{2}$ Ⓒ –3 Ⓓ –7 [1]

8 –16 – –37 =

Ⓐ 21 Ⓑ –21 Ⓒ –53 Ⓓ 53 [1]

9 3 – 2 × 4 =

Ⓐ –4 Ⓑ –5 Ⓒ 4 Ⓓ 5 [1]

10 –12 + 5 × 3 =

Ⓐ 3 Ⓑ 21 Ⓒ –3 Ⓓ –21 [1]

11 –3 + 7 – 2 – 8 =

Ⓐ –6 Ⓑ –10 Ⓒ –20 Ⓓ 0 [1]

12 4 × 7 – 3 × 10 =

Ⓐ 160 Ⓑ 2 Ⓒ –2 Ⓓ 250 [1]

13 –8 – 6 ÷ 2 =

Ⓐ –5 Ⓑ –7 Ⓒ –9 Ⓓ –11 [1]

14 The temperature in New York was –9 °C and it was 7° colder in Detroit. What was the temperature in Detroit?

Ⓐ 2 °C Ⓑ –2 °C Ⓒ –12 °C Ⓓ –16 °C [1]

15 What is the sum of –5 and –7?

Ⓐ 12 Ⓑ 2 Ⓒ –2 Ⓓ –12 [1]

PART B Write answers only in the space provided.

16 –2 + 5 – 8 – 6 = ______________ 1

17 Write 15, –3, –8 and 0 in ascending order. ______________________________ 1

18 5 – 3 × 7 = ______________ 1

19 –8 – 4 × 3 = ______________ 1

20 Show the position of –23 on the number line. 1

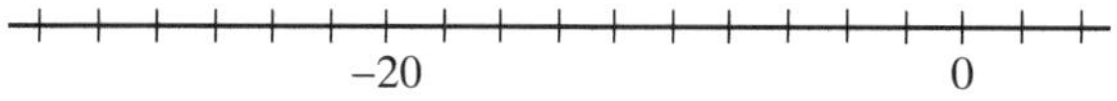

21 6 – 9 – 3 – 5 = ______________ 1

22 –11 + (–5) – –3 = ______________ 1

23 12 ÷ 4 – 7 = ______________ 1

24 Which of the numbers –18 and –37 is the larger? ______________ 1

25 13 – –6 + 8 – –4 + (–2) = ______________ 1

PART C Show all working.

26 The table shows the maximum and minimum temperatures, in degrees Celsius, recorded one day in several places in Canada.

Place	Montreal	Ottawa	Quebec	Toronto
Max.	–2	–1	–5	0
Min.	–12	–13	–16	–10
Place	Halifax	Churchill	Yellowknife	
Max.	2	–20	–11	
Min.	–5	–24	–25	

a What was the lowest temperature overall? 1 mark

____

b What was the lowest maximum temperature? 1 mark

____

c What was the highest minimum temperature? 1 mark

____

d What is the difference between the maximum and minimum temperatures in Quebec? 1 mark

____

e Which place had the largest difference between the maximum and minimum temperatures and what was that difference? 2 marks

____

____

f What was the difference between the highest and lowest maximum temperatures? 1 mark

____

g The forecast maximum for Quebec was –1 °C. Briefly explain how the maximum differed from that forecast. 1 mark

____

h Another city had a difference of 11° between its maximum and minimum temperatures. If the minimum was –13 °C, what was the maximum? 1 mark

____

27 An account had a balance of –$576.

a An amount of $318 was withdrawn from the account. What was the new balance? 1 mark

____

b Then an amount of $432 was deposited into the account. What was the balance then? 1 mark

____

c Finally an amount of $629 was deposited. What was the final balance? 1 mark

____

28 On a quiz show contestants start with 20 points and gain 5 points if they get a question correct and lose 5 points if they get one wrong.

a Pip answered 25 questions but got 15 wrong. What was Pip's final score? 1 mark

____

b Charles got 13 questions right but 17 questions wrong. What was Charles's score? 1 mark

____

c Elsie finished the show with a score of –10. If she got 6 questions right, how many did she get wrong? 1 mark

____

Total marks /40

LEVEL 2 TEST PART A

Time allowed: 40 minutes

Marks

1 –2486 + 9473 =

(A) –6987 (B) 6987 (C) 11 959 (D) –11 959 1

2 –42 183 – 156 753 =

(A) 198 936 B 114 570 (C) –114 570 (D) –198 936 1

3 Which of these numbers is the smallest?

(A) –21 372 (B) 5104 (C) –38 516 (D) –56 482 1

4 Subtracting –17 is the same as:

(A) adding –17 (B) adding 17 (C) subtracting 17 (D) none of these 1

5 Which number is shown by the arrow?

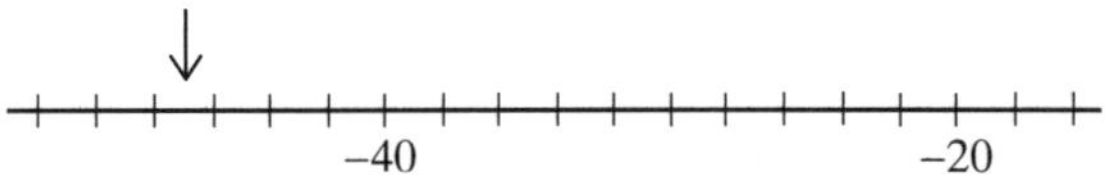

(A) –43.5 (B) –43 (C) –45 (D) –47 1

6 The difference between –87 and 59 is:

(A) 146 (B) –146 (C) 28 (D) –28 1

7 –39 + (–48) – –175 =

(A) –262 (B) –166 (C) 88 (D) 184 1

8 68 – 19 × 14 =

(A) –686 (B) –198 (C) 198 (D) 686 1

9 Which is **not** equal to 37 – 65?

(A) –65 + 37 (B) –37 + 65 (C) 37 + (–65) (D) –65 – –37 1

10 312 – –618 – 2453 =

(A) –1523 (B) –2759 (C) 2147 (D) 3383 1

11 Which arrow shows the number –11?

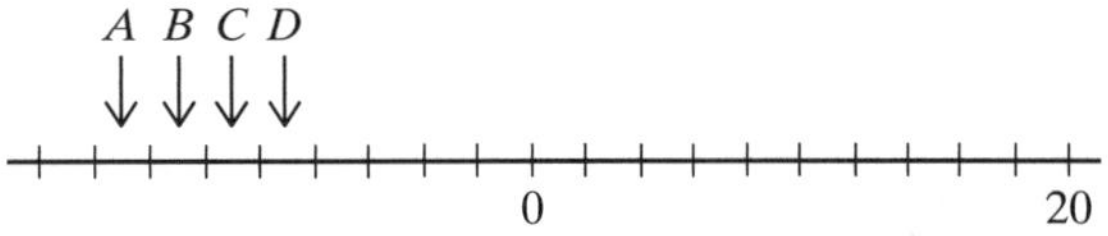

(A) A (B) B (C) C (D) D 1

12 Which is correct?

(A) –37 > –28 (B) –63 < –89 (C) 75 < –94 (D) –49 > –81 1

13 Which numbers are in ascending order?

(A) –312, –956, –1348 (B) –817, 543, –211

(C) –628, –419, –73 (D) –940, –1260, 359 1

14 7812 – 9723 + 6482 – 12 869 =

(A) –8298 (B) –21 262 (C) 4476 (D) –1816 1

15 Which is correct?

(A) 9 – 17 > –12 + 5 (B) –16 + 11 > 14 – 19

(C) 24 + (–72) > –13 – 38 (D) 42 – –96 < –82 + 219 1

PART B Write answers only in the space provided.

16 –95 – 138 + 672 = ______________ [1]

17 17 – 300 + 186 = ______________ [1]

18 95 – 7 × 28 = ______________ [1]

19 69 + (–104) = ______________ [1]

20 –836 – –412 = ______________ [1]

21 Write in ascending order: –915, –728, 1004, 57, –866, –23. ______________ [1]

22 What is the sum of –212, –873, –496 and –1040? ______________ [1]

23 What number is 27 more than –15? ______________ [1]

24 What is the average of 39, –416 and –67? ______________ [1]

25 By how much does –62 exceed –125? ______________ [1]

PART C Show all working.

26 Which of –231 and –213 is the larger and by how much? [2 marks]

____

____

27 a Is [39 + (–28)] + (–45) = 39 + [(–28) + (–45)]? [1 mark]

____

b Is [57 – (–42)] – –17 = 57 – [–42 – –17]? [1 mark]

____

c Briefly explain the results of parts **a** and **b**. [1 mark]

____

28 Briefly explain any similarities or differences between 47 + (–58) and 47 – 58. [1 mark]

____

____

29 Is –23 – –18 ≥ –16 + 11? Justify your answer. [2 marks]

____

____

30 a In the Fahrenheit scale of temperatures the freezing point is 32 °F. How many degrees below freezing is a temperature of –19 °F? [1 mark]

____

b What is the difference between a temperature of –5 °F and –13 °F? [1 mark]

____

c Is the difference between –5 °C and –13 °C the same? Explain your answer. [1 mark]

____

d The maximum recorded temperature at Daisyville was 43 °C and the minimum was –7 °C. What is the difference between the maximum and minimum? [1 mark]

____

e The temperature in Lilydale is –11 °C. How many degrees will the temperature need to rise to reach the forecast maximum of 26 °C? [1 mark]

____

31 A tall building has 47 floors, eight of which are below ground level. The first floor is the name given to the floor above ground level.

a Ali catches the lift from the thirty-second floor to five floors below ground level. How many floors did the lift go down? [1 mark]

____

b Kahlia gets on the lift at the fourth floor below ground level and gets off twenty-nine floors above. On what floor did Kahli get out of the lift? [1 mark]

____

Total marks /40

Fractions

PRETEST

Time allowed: 15 minutes **Total marks: 13**

Marks

1 What fraction is shaded?

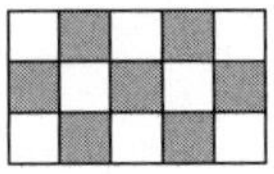

(A) $\frac{1}{2}$ (B) $\frac{7}{8}$ (C) $\frac{7}{15}$ (D) $\frac{2}{5}$ 1

2 Which is **not** equivalent to $\frac{3}{4}$?

(A) $\frac{5}{6}$ (B) $\frac{6}{8}$ (C) $\frac{15}{20}$ (D) $\frac{300}{400}$ 1

3 What is $\frac{60}{100}$ in simplest form?

(A) $\frac{6}{10}$ (B) $\frac{1}{40}$ (C) $\frac{2}{3}$ (D) $\frac{3}{5}$ 1

4 $\frac{5}{9} + \frac{2}{9} =$

(A) $\frac{7}{9}$ (B) $\frac{7}{18}$ (C) $\frac{7}{81}$ (D) $\frac{10}{81}$ 1

5 $6\frac{1}{2} + 4\frac{1}{2} =$

(A) $10\frac{1}{2}$ (B) 11 (C) $10\frac{3}{4}$ (D) $11\frac{1}{4}$ 1

6 $\frac{7}{10} - \frac{1}{2} =$

(A) $\frac{3}{4}$ (B) $\frac{3}{5}$ (C) $\frac{2}{5}$ (D) $\frac{1}{5}$ 1

7 What is $\frac{1}{8}$ of 40?

(A) 4 (B) 5 (C) 6 (D) 7 1

8 Two pies are shared equally between six people. What fraction of a pie does each person get?

(A) $\frac{1}{6}$ (B) $\frac{1}{12}$ (C) $\frac{1}{3}$ (D) $\frac{1}{2}$ 1

9 Which is **not** the same as $1\frac{1}{2}$?

(A) $\frac{3}{2}$ (B) $1\frac{5}{10}$ (C) $1\frac{2}{4}$ (D) $1\frac{4}{6}$ 1

10 $2\frac{4}{7} + 3\frac{3}{7} =$

(A) $6\frac{1}{2}$ (B) 6 (C) $5\frac{1}{2}$ (D) 5 1

11 $1\frac{1}{4} - \frac{3}{4} =$

(A) $\frac{1}{2}$ (B) $\frac{3}{4}$ (C) $\frac{5}{8}$ (D) $1\frac{1}{2}$ 1

12 $\frac{1}{4} + \frac{5}{8} =$

(A) $\frac{7}{8}$ (B) $\frac{1}{2}$ (C) $\frac{3}{4}$ (D) $\frac{3}{16}$ 1

13 $\frac{7}{8} - \frac{3}{4} =$

(A) $\frac{1}{2}$ (B) $\frac{1}{4}$ (C) $\frac{1}{8}$ (D) 1 1

Total marks /13

LEVEL 2 TEST PART A

Time allowed: 40 minutes

Marks

1 What is the highest common factor of 24 and 36?

(A) 4 (B) 8 (C) 12 (D) 24 — 1

2 What is the lowest common multiple of 12 and 15?

(A) 30 (B) 60 (C) 120 (D) 180 — 1

3 What is $\frac{32}{72}$ in simplest form?

(A) $\frac{4}{9}$ (B) $\frac{3}{7}$ (C) $\frac{2}{3}$ (D) $\frac{1}{40}$ — 1

4 What is $5\frac{3}{7}$ as an improper fraction?

(A) $\frac{15}{7}$ (B) $\frac{22}{7}$ (C) $\frac{38}{7}$ (D) $\frac{56}{7}$ — 1

5 What is $\frac{41}{8}$ as a mixed numeral?

(A) $1\frac{5}{8}$ (B) $5\frac{1}{8}$ (C) $5\frac{3}{8}$ (D) $3\frac{5}{8}$ — 1

6 Which is **not** equivalent to $\frac{3}{7}$?

(A) $\frac{9}{49}$ (B) $\frac{24}{56}$ (C) $\frac{6}{14}$ (D) $\frac{33}{77}$ — 1

7 Which fraction is found at the position marked by the arrow?

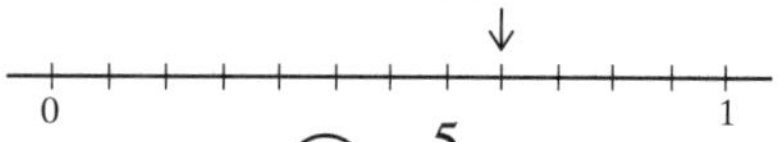

(A) $\frac{7}{12}$ (B) $\frac{2}{3}$ (C) $\frac{8}{11}$ (D) $\frac{5}{8}$ — 1

8 Which is equivalent to $\frac{18}{30}$?

(A) $\frac{23}{35}$ (B) $\frac{25}{40}$ (C) $\frac{33}{55}$ (D) $\frac{44}{75}$ — 1

9 Which arrow shows the position of $1\frac{3}{4}$?

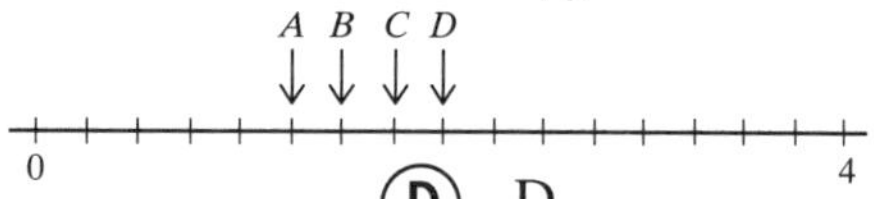

(A) A (B) B (C) C (D) D — 1

10 Which fraction is greater than $\frac{1}{7}$?

(A) $\frac{1}{8}$ (B) $\frac{2}{15}$ (C) $\frac{8}{56}$ (D) $\frac{3}{20}$ — 1

11 Which fraction is the smallest?

(A) $\frac{2}{3}$ (B) $\frac{5}{9}$ (C) $\frac{7}{12}$ (D) $\frac{11}{18}$ — 1

12 Which fraction is found at the position marked by the arrow?

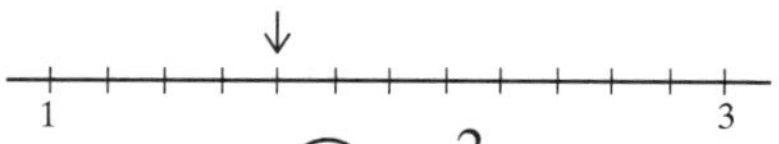

(A) $1\frac{7}{10}$ (B) $1\frac{7}{12}$ (C) $1\frac{4}{5}$ (D) $1\frac{2}{3}$ — 1

13 Which fraction is the greatest?

(A) $\frac{7}{16}$ (B) $\frac{5}{12}$ (C) $\frac{3}{8}$ (D) $\frac{19}{48}$ — 1

14 Which fraction is found at the position marked by the arrow?

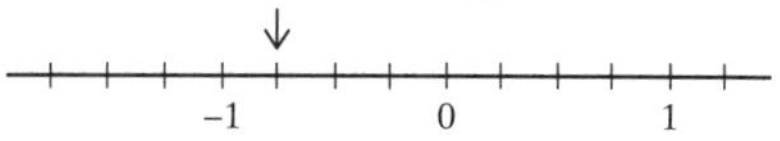

(A) $-1\frac{1}{4}$ (B) $-1\frac{3}{4}$ (C) $-\frac{1}{4}$ (D) $-\frac{3}{4}$ — 1

15 Which would be equivalent to $\frac{\blacksquare}{\Delta}$?

(A) $\frac{3+\blacksquare}{3+\Delta}$ (B) $\frac{3-\blacksquare}{3-\Delta}$ (C) $\frac{3\times\blacksquare}{3\times\Delta}$ (D) $\frac{3\div\blacksquare}{3\div\Delta}$ — 1

PART B Write answers only in the space provided.

16 Write $\frac{16}{24}$ in simplest form. ______________ 1

17 Write $2\frac{5}{7}$ as an improper fraction. ______________ 1

18 Mark the position of $2\frac{3}{10}$ on the number line. 1

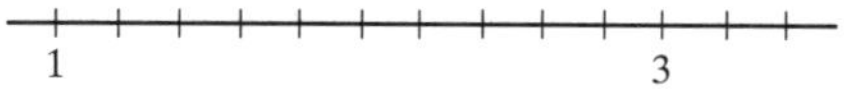

19 Write $\frac{11}{3}$ as a mixed numeral. ______________ 1

20 Which of $\frac{4}{5}$ and $\frac{3}{4}$ is the larger? ______________ 1

21 Mark the position of $-\frac{2}{3}$ on the number line. 1

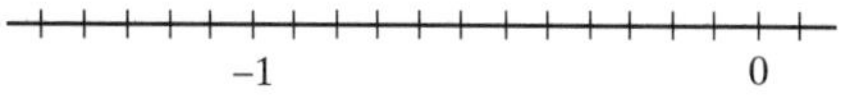

22 What is the lowest common denominator for the fractions $\frac{3}{8}$ and $\frac{3}{28}$? ______________ 1

23 Write $\frac{30}{4}$ as a mixed numeral in simplest form. ______________ 1

24 Which of $\frac{2}{3}$, $\frac{5}{8}$ and $\frac{7}{12}$ is the smallest? ______________ 1

25 What fraction is found at the position marked by the arrow? 1

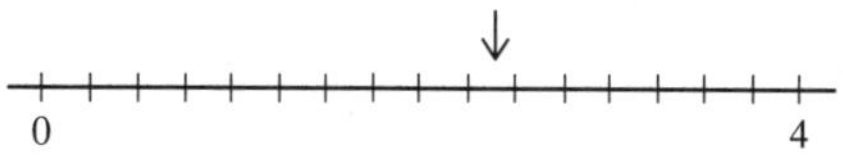

PART C Show all working.

26 a What is the lowest common multiple of 16 and 20? 1 mark

____

b Which of $\frac{9}{16}$ and $\frac{11}{20}$ is the larger? Justify your answer. 1 mark

____

____

27 Label the fractions found at the indicated places on the number line. 3 marks

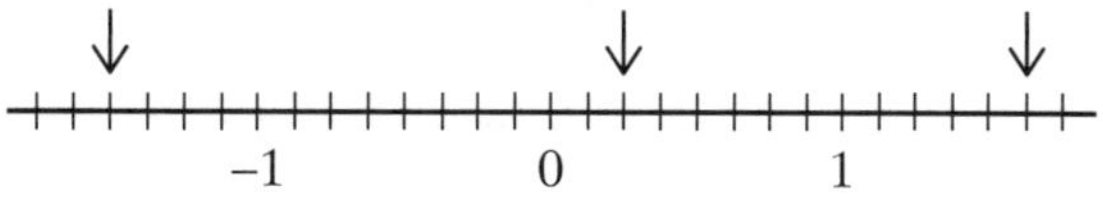

28 Write $\frac{4}{5}$, $\frac{5}{7}$, $\frac{7}{10}$ and $\frac{26}{35}$ in order from lowest to highest. 2 marks

____

____

29 a Write $3\frac{2}{5}$ as an improper fraction. 1 mark

____

b Add 4 to both the numerator and denominator of the improper fraction from part **a** and then change to a mixed numeral in simplest form. 1 mark

____

c Is the answer to part **b** $3\frac{2}{5}$? Explain why or why not. 1 mark

____

30 Find equivalent fractions for $\frac{7}{8}$ and $\frac{5}{6}$ with the same (lowest common) denominator. 2 marks

____

____

31 Carefully mark the position of $-\frac{1}{4}$, $\frac{3}{5}$ and $1\frac{2}{3}$ on the number line. 3 marks

Total marks /40

LEVEL 2 TEST

PART A

Time allowed: 40 minutes

Marks

1 What is two parts of 10?

(A) $\frac{1}{8}$ (B) $\frac{1}{5}$ (C) $\frac{1}{20}$ (D) $\frac{1}{4}$ [1]

2 What fraction is 20 minutes of an hour?

(A) $\frac{1}{3}$ (B) $\frac{1}{5}$ (C) $\frac{1}{6}$ (D) $\frac{2}{5}$ [1]

3 Ron got 21 questions out of the 30 questions in a test correct. What fraction did Ron get correct?

(A) $\frac{7}{10}$ (B) $\frac{2}{3}$ (C) $\frac{11}{15}$ (D) $\frac{3}{5}$ [1]

4 About what fraction of a year is 4 months?

(A) $\frac{1}{4}$ (B) $\frac{1}{3}$ (C) $\frac{2}{5}$ (D) $\frac{1}{15}$ [1]

5 What fraction is 40 cents of a dollar?

(A) $\frac{4}{9}$ (B) $\frac{1}{3}$ (C) $\frac{2}{5}$ (D) $\frac{2}{3}$ [1]

6 There are 12 oranges and three apples in a bowl. Apples make up what fraction of the fruit?

(A) $\frac{1}{2}$ (B) $\frac{1}{3}$ (C) $\frac{1}{4}$ (D) $\frac{1}{5}$ [1]

7 Twenty-five seconds is what fraction of a minute?

(A) $\frac{1}{4}$ (B) $\frac{5}{12}$ (C) $\frac{3}{8}$ (D) $\frac{3}{20}$ [1]

8 What fraction of a day is 6 hours?

(A) $\frac{1}{4}$ (B) $\frac{1}{3}$ (C) $\frac{1}{2}$ (D) $\frac{1}{10}$ [1]

9 What fraction is 900 mL of a litre?

(A) $\frac{9}{1000}$ (B) $\frac{9}{100}$ (C) $\frac{9}{10}$ (D) none of these [1]

10 In a class, three students are absent and 15 are present. What fraction of the class is absent?

(A) $\frac{1}{5}$ (B) $\frac{1}{6}$ (C) $\frac{1}{9}$ (D) $\frac{3}{5}$ [1]

11 What fraction of a metre is 65 cm?

(A) $\frac{16}{25}$ (B) $\frac{3}{5}$ (C) $\frac{11}{20}$ (D) $\frac{13}{20}$ [1]

12 There are five white and two black buttons in a box. Black buttons make up what fraction?

(A) $\frac{1}{2}$ (B) $\frac{1}{5}$ (C) $\frac{2}{5}$ (D) $\frac{2}{7}$ [1]

13 What fraction of \$50 is 5c?

(A) $\frac{1}{10}$ (B) $\frac{1}{100}$ (C) $\frac{1}{1000}$ (D) $\frac{1}{10\,000}$ [1]

14 Of some balloons, nine are red, five are white and six are blue. What fraction is blue?

(A) $\frac{1}{3}$ (B) $\frac{2}{7}$ (C) $\frac{3}{7}$ (D) $\frac{3}{10}$ [1]

15 What fraction is 50 metres of a kilometre?

(A) $\frac{1}{19}$ (B) $\frac{5}{19}$ (C) $\frac{1}{20}$ (D) $\frac{1}{200}$ [1]

PART B Write answers only in the space provided. Give all fractions in simplest form.

16 What fraction of an hour is 45 minutes? ______________ [1]

17 What fraction of two dollars is 25 cents? ______________ [1]

18 A basket holds 14 white and 6 green pegs. What fraction of the pegs is green? ______________ [1]

19 What fraction of 120 is 75? ______________ [1]

20 What fraction of a day is 8 hours? ______________ [1]

21 A packet holds 24 biscuits. Sam ate three of the biscuits. What fraction remains? ______________ [1]

22 What fraction of 2 m is 60 cm? ______________ [1]

23 Fiona had 18 toy cars. She gave two to Kelly and four to Kim. What fraction does she still have? _____ [1]

24 What fraction of a kilogram is 750 g? ______________ [1]

25 What fraction of a tonne is 600 kg? ______________ [1]

PART C Show all working.

26 Amy sat for a test that was made up of two sections.

a In the first section Amy got five of the 15 questions wrong. What fraction did she get correct? [1 mark]

____

b In the second section Amy got 20 of the 25 questions correct. What simple fraction is that? [1 mark]

____

c What fraction of the questions in the test did Amy get correct? [1 mark]

____

27 Stella set out to drive to Greendale, a distance of 450 km.

a After 2 hours, Stella had driven 150 km. What fraction of the journey had she completed? [1 mark]

____

b Stella stopped for lunch after another 50 km. What fraction of the journey had she then completed? [1 mark]

____

c At her last stop Stella had 90 km left to travel. What fraction of the journey was completed then? [1 mark]

____

28 Stu earned $1400 last week.

a From that amount Stu paid $280 in tax. What fraction did he pay in tax? [1 mark]

____

b Stu paid $350 in rent. What fraction of his weekly earnings did he pay in rent? [1 mark]

____

c Stu spent $315 on food, $235 paying bills and $150 on other things. What fraction of his pay did he spend on these altogether? [1 mark]

____

d The remainder of Stu's money was saved. What fraction did he save? [2 marks]

____

____

29 A bowl held 13 red, 12 green and 10 black jelly beans.

a Black jelly beans made up what fraction of those in the bowl? [1 mark]

____

b Dan ate five red jelly beans. What fraction was then black? [1 mark]

____

c Dan then ate another two jelly beans. The fraction of black jelly beans then in the bowl was the same as it was originally. What colour were the two jelly beans? [2 marks]

____

____

Total marks ___ / 40

LEVEL 1 TEST PART A

Time allowed: 40 minutes

Marks

1 $\frac{2}{7}+\frac{3}{7}=$

Ⓐ $\frac{5}{14}$ Ⓑ $\frac{5}{7}$ Ⓒ $\frac{6}{7}$ Ⓓ $\frac{6}{49}$ [1]

2 $\frac{1}{2}+\frac{1}{3}=$

Ⓐ $\frac{1}{5}$ Ⓑ $\frac{1}{6}$ Ⓒ $\frac{2}{5}$ Ⓓ $\frac{5}{6}$ [1]

3 $1\frac{1}{2}+2\frac{1}{4}=$

Ⓐ $3\frac{1}{8}$ Ⓑ $3\frac{1}{4}$ Ⓒ $3\frac{3}{4}$ Ⓓ $3\frac{5}{8}$ [1]

4 $\frac{9}{10}-\frac{7}{10}=$

Ⓐ $\frac{1}{5}$ Ⓑ $\frac{3}{10}$ Ⓒ $\frac{2}{5}$ Ⓓ $\frac{1}{20}$ [1]

5 $1-\frac{2}{9}=$

Ⓐ $\frac{4}{9}$ Ⓑ $\frac{5}{9}$ Ⓒ $\frac{7}{9}$ Ⓓ $\frac{8}{9}$ [1]

6 $5\frac{7}{11}-2\frac{4}{11}=$

Ⓐ $3\frac{3}{11}$ Ⓑ $3\frac{3}{22}$ Ⓒ $2\frac{3}{11}$ Ⓓ $2\frac{3}{22}$ [1]

7 $3\frac{5}{8}+4\frac{3}{8}=$

Ⓐ $7\frac{1}{2}$ Ⓑ $7\frac{3}{4}$ Ⓒ 8 Ⓓ $8\frac{1}{2}$ [1]

8 $\frac{5}{12}+\frac{5}{12}=$

Ⓐ $\frac{5}{6}$ Ⓑ $\frac{5}{12}$ Ⓒ $\frac{5}{24}$ Ⓓ $\frac{25}{144}$ [1]

9 $\frac{1}{5}+\frac{3}{8}=$

Ⓐ $\frac{3}{13}$ Ⓑ $\frac{4}{13}$ Ⓒ $\frac{13}{40}$ Ⓓ $\frac{23}{40}$ [1]

10 $\frac{5}{7}-\frac{1}{2}=$

Ⓐ $\frac{4}{5}$ Ⓑ $\frac{4}{9}$ Ⓒ $\frac{2}{7}$ Ⓓ $\frac{3}{14}$ [1]

11 $\frac{5}{6}+\frac{1}{3}=$

Ⓐ $\frac{2}{3}$ Ⓑ $\frac{5}{9}$ Ⓒ $1\frac{1}{9}$ Ⓓ $1\frac{1}{6}$ [1]

12 $2\frac{7}{9}+3\frac{4}{9}=$

Ⓐ $5\frac{11}{18}$ Ⓑ $6\frac{2}{9}$ Ⓒ $6\frac{1}{3}$ Ⓓ $6\frac{11}{18}$ [1]

13 $8\frac{1}{3}-3\frac{2}{3}=$

Ⓐ $4\frac{1}{3}$ Ⓑ $4\frac{2}{3}$ Ⓒ $5\frac{1}{3}$ Ⓓ $5\frac{2}{3}$ [1]

14 $\frac{2}{7}+\frac{2}{3}=$

Ⓐ $\frac{2}{5}$ Ⓑ $\frac{4}{21}$ Ⓒ $\frac{20}{21}$ Ⓓ $1\frac{2}{5}$ [1]

15 $8\frac{2}{7}-3\frac{5}{7}=$

Ⓐ $4\frac{4}{7}$ Ⓑ $4\frac{3}{7}$ Ⓒ $5\frac{4}{7}$ Ⓓ $5\frac{3}{7}$ [1]

Adding and Subtracting Fractions Non-calculator **(Level 1 Test)**

PART B Write answers only in the space provided. Give all fractions in simplest form.

16 $\frac{1}{2} + \frac{1}{5} =$ ________ [1]

17 $\frac{7}{8} - \frac{1}{4} =$ ________ [1]

18 $1\frac{2}{5} + 4\frac{3}{5} =$ ________ [1]

19 $6 - \frac{3}{8} =$ ________ [1]

20 $\frac{1}{6} + \frac{1}{4} =$ ________ [1]

21 $\frac{5}{9} + \frac{1}{3} =$ ________ [1]

22 $5\frac{5}{6} - 1\frac{1}{6} =$ ________ [1]

23 $\frac{3}{10} + \frac{5}{8} =$ ________ [1]

24 $\frac{1}{7} - \frac{1}{8} =$ ________ [1]

25 $\frac{5}{9} + \frac{3}{4} =$ ________ [1]

PART C Show all working.

26 Find, giving the answers as mixed numerals (where necessary) in simplest form:

a $5\frac{2}{3} + 4\frac{7}{10}$ [2 marks]

b $\frac{1}{4} + \frac{1}{5} + \frac{1}{6}$ [2 marks]

c $9\frac{1}{2} - 5\frac{2}{3}$ [2 marks]

d $\frac{5}{6} + \frac{3}{5} - \frac{2}{3}$ [2 marks]

27 Nelly worked for $3\frac{1}{4}$ hours on Monday, $5\frac{1}{2}$ hours on Tuesday, $1\frac{3}{4}$ hours on Wednesday and $4\frac{1}{4}$ hours on Thursday.

a How many hours did Nelly work altogether on those four days? [1 mark]

b How many hours did Nelly work on Friday if she worked a total of $20\frac{1}{2}$ hours altogether over the five days? [1 mark]

28 Cows were allowed to graze on $\frac{1}{3}$ of a paddock one day. The next day the cows were given another $\frac{1}{4}$ of the paddock.

a In total, what fraction of the paddock did the cows have on the second day? [1 mark]

b On the third day the cattle were allowed on the whole paddock. What fraction of the paddock had not been grazed on either of the two previous days? [1 mark]

29 Four friends invested some money in a business. Jed put in $\frac{1}{4}$ of the money and his twin Ned put in $\frac{2}{5}$. Sam contributed $\frac{1}{3}$ of the money and Micky put in the rest.

a What fraction did the twins together put in? [1 mark]

b What fraction did Micky put in? [2 marks]

Total marks /40

LEVEL 2 TEST — PART A

Time allowed: 40 minutes

Marks

1 $\frac{1}{10}+\frac{7}{10}=$

(A) $\frac{2}{5}$ (B) $\frac{4}{5}$ (C) $\frac{2}{25}$ (D) $\frac{7}{20}$ 1

2 $\frac{1}{4}+\frac{2}{3}=$

(A) $\frac{2}{7}$ (B) $\frac{3}{7}$ (C) $\frac{1}{6}$ (D) $\frac{11}{12}$ 1

3 $\frac{3}{5}-\frac{1}{2}=$

(A) $\frac{2}{3}$ (B) $\frac{1}{5}$ (C) $\frac{1}{10}$ (D) $\frac{1}{3}$ 1

4 What is the sum of $\frac{1}{5}$ and $\frac{1}{6}$?

(A) $\frac{1}{11}$ (B) $\frac{1}{30}$ (C) $\frac{11}{30}$ (D) $\frac{11}{56}$ 1

5 $7-3\frac{5}{8}=$

(A) $3\frac{3}{8}$ (B) $3\frac{5}{8}$ (C) $4\frac{5}{8}$ (D) $4\frac{3}{8}$ 1

6 Which is **not** equal to $\frac{3}{4}$?

(A) $1-\frac{1}{4}$ (B) $\frac{1}{2}+\frac{1}{6}$ (C) $\frac{7}{8}-\frac{1}{8}$ (D) $\frac{5}{12}+\frac{1}{3}$ 1

7 $\frac{5}{9}+\frac{5}{6}=$

(A) $\frac{2}{3}$ (B) $1\frac{4}{9}$ (C) $1\frac{7}{9}$ (D) $1\frac{7}{18}$ 1

8 By how much does $\frac{3}{4}$ exceed $\frac{2}{3}$?

(A) $\frac{1}{12}$ (B) $\frac{1}{7}$ (C) $\frac{1}{4}$ (D) $\frac{1}{3}$ 1

9 $1\frac{2}{3}+1\frac{4}{5}=$

(A) $2\frac{2}{5}$ (B) $2\frac{3}{4}$ (C) $3\frac{8}{15}$ (D) $3\frac{7}{15}$ 1

10 Dee wants to add $\frac{3}{8}$ and $\frac{7}{12}$. What is the lowest common denominator?

(A) 4 (B) 12 (C) 24 (D) 96 1

11 $3\frac{5}{9}+6\frac{4}{9}=$

(A) $9\frac{1}{2}$ (B) 10 (C) $10\frac{1}{2}$ (D) $10\frac{1}{9}$ 1

12 What must be added to $\frac{7}{8}$ to give $1\frac{1}{2}$?

(A) $\frac{3}{8}$ (B) $\frac{5}{8}$ (C) $\frac{7}{16}$ (D) $2\frac{3}{8}$ 1

13 $\frac{3}{10}+\frac{2}{5}=$

(A) $\frac{1}{3}$ (B) $\frac{2}{3}$ (C) $\frac{7}{10}$ (D) $1\frac{1}{10}$ 1

14 $\frac{5}{8}+\frac{2}{3}=$

(A) $\frac{7}{11}$ (B) $\frac{7}{24}$ (C) $1\frac{5}{24}$ (D) $1\frac{7}{24}$ 1

15 $3\frac{3}{4}-\frac{5}{6}=$

(A) $2\frac{11}{12}$ (B) $3\frac{1}{12}$ (C) $3\frac{1}{5}$ (D) $2\frac{4}{5}$ 1

PART B Write answers only in the space provided. Give all fractions in simplest form.

16 $6 - 2\frac{1}{2} =$	____________	1
17 $2\frac{1}{4} + 3\frac{3}{4} =$	____________	1
18 $\frac{1}{4} + \frac{1}{5} =$	____________	1
19 $\frac{5}{12} + \frac{1}{12} =$	____________	1
20 $\frac{2}{5} + \frac{3}{8} =$	____________	1
21 $8\frac{3}{7} - 3\frac{5}{7} =$	____________	1
22 $\frac{7}{10} + \frac{3}{5} =$	____________	1
23 $3\frac{5}{8} + 4\frac{3}{4} =$	____________	1
24 $7\frac{2}{5} - \frac{4}{5} =$	____________	1
25 $9\frac{1}{2} - 2\frac{2}{3} =$	____________	1

PART C Show all working.

26 Find, giving answers in simplest form:

a $\frac{7}{12} - \frac{5}{9}$ 2 marks

b $2\frac{4}{5} + 5\frac{2}{3}$ 2 marks

c $7\frac{2}{9} - 3\frac{7}{12}$ 2 marks

27 Hannah has two paddocks. One is $6\frac{7}{10}$ ha and the other is $5\frac{3}{4}$ ha. How much land is that altogether? 2 marks

28 Milly ate $\frac{2}{5}$ of a pie and Molly ate $\frac{1}{4}$ of the same pie.

a How much of the pie did they eat altogether? 1 mark

b What fraction of the pie is left? 1 mark

c Who ate the most? 1 mark

d What is the difference between the amounts they ate? 1 mark

29 Ned painted one-third of his fence on Monday, two-fifths of the fence on Tuesday and the rest on Wednesday.

a What fraction of the fence did he paint on Wednesday? 2 marks

b On which day did he paint the most? 1 mark

Total marks /40

Adding and Subtracting Fractions Non-calculator

LEVEL 3 TEST PART A

Time allowed: 40 minutes

	Marks
1 $\frac{3}{5}+\frac{1}{9}=$	
(A) $\frac{2}{7}$ (B) $\frac{3}{14}$ (C) $\frac{24}{45}$ (D) $\frac{32}{45}$	1
2 $\frac{5}{6}-\frac{1}{12}=$	
(A) $\frac{2}{3}$ (B) $\frac{3}{4}$ (C) $\frac{11}{12}$ (D) $\frac{1}{2}$	1
3 Tony needs to subtract $\frac{11}{28}$ from $\frac{23}{56}$. What is the lowest common denominator?	
(A) 7 (B) 28 (C) 56 (D) 1568	1
4 What is the sum of $\frac{3}{4}$ and $1\frac{1}{3}$?	
(A) $1\frac{4}{7}$ (B) $1\frac{11}{12}$ (C) $2\frac{1}{12}$ (D) $2\frac{1}{4}$	1
5 $\frac{1}{2}+\frac{1}{3}+\frac{1}{4}=$	
(A) $\frac{11}{12}$ (B) $\frac{5}{6}$ (C) $1\frac{1}{12}$ (D) $1\frac{1}{6}$	1
6 $5\frac{2}{3}+4\frac{3}{5}=$	
(A) $9\frac{5}{8}$ (B) $9\frac{14}{15}$ (C) $10\frac{4}{15}$ (D) $10\frac{9}{15}$	1
7 What fraction must be added to $\frac{3}{4}$ to give $\frac{5}{6}$?	
(A) $\frac{1}{3}$ (B) $\frac{1}{24}$ (C) $\frac{1}{8}$ (D) $\frac{1}{12}$	1
8 $2\frac{3}{4}-\frac{4}{7}=$	
(A) $2\frac{5}{28}$ (B) $2\frac{11}{28}$ (C) $1\frac{27}{28}$ (D) $1\frac{1}{11}$	1
9 Waseem ate $\frac{3}{5}$ of a pizza and Wally ate $\frac{1}{4}$ of the same pizza. What fraction remains?	
(A) $\frac{5}{9}$ (B) $\frac{1}{10}$ (C) $\frac{1}{20}$ (D) $\frac{3}{20}$	1
10 $7\frac{1}{2}-2\frac{2}{3}=$	
(A) $5\frac{1}{6}$ (B) $5\frac{5}{6}$ (C) $4\frac{1}{6}$ (D) $4\frac{5}{6}$	1
11 $\frac{7}{20}+\frac{11}{35}=$	
(A) $\frac{93}{140}$ (B) $\frac{47}{70}$ (C) $\frac{19}{28}$ (D) $\frac{18}{55}$	1
12 $\frac{2}{5}-\frac{\Delta}{60}=\frac{1}{12}$. What number must be placed in the triangle to make this correct?	
(A) 19 (B) 13 (C) 7 (D) 1	1
13 What is the difference between $\frac{5}{8}$ and $\frac{5}{9}$?	
(A) $\frac{1}{5}$ (B) $\frac{5}{72}$ (C) $\frac{13}{72}$ (D) $\frac{17}{72}$	1
14 $2\frac{3}{4}+5\frac{3}{14}=$	
(A) $7\frac{25}{28}$ (B) $7\frac{27}{28}$ (C) $8\frac{1}{7}$ (D) $8\frac{1}{3}$	1
15 $8\frac{1}{6}-3\frac{5}{9}=$	
(A) $4\frac{11}{18}$ (B) $4\frac{7}{18}$ (C) $4\frac{4}{15}$ (D) $4\frac{2}{3}$	1

Adding and Subtracting Fractions Non-calculator (Level 3 Test)

PART B Write answers only in the space provided. Give all answers in simplest form.

16 $\frac{3}{5} - \frac{1}{10} =$ ____________ [1]

17 $\frac{5}{8} + \frac{5}{6} =$ ____________ [1]

18 Subtract two-fifths from three-quarters. ____________ [1]

19 $1\frac{1}{2} + 4\frac{3}{20} =$ ____________ [1]

20 $13 - 2\frac{7}{11} =$ ____________ [1]

21 $\frac{7}{15} - \Delta = \frac{1}{3}$ $\Delta =$ ____________ [1]

22 $2\frac{3}{4} - 1\frac{2}{3} =$ ____________ [1]

23 $\Delta - \frac{3}{4} = \frac{7}{8}$ $\Delta =$ ____________ [1]

24 $\Delta + \frac{5}{12} = 1\frac{1}{4}$ $\Delta =$ ____________ [1]

25 $19\frac{3}{4} - 5\frac{5}{8} =$ ____________ [1]

PART C Show all working.

26 Find, giving answers in simplest form:

a $2\frac{5}{12} + 5\frac{7}{15}$ [2 marks]

b $9\frac{1}{3} - 2\frac{4}{5}$ [2 marks]

c $\frac{5}{8} + \frac{2}{3} - \frac{3}{4}$ [2 marks]

d $2\frac{4}{5} - 1\frac{1}{3} - \frac{1}{2}$ [2 marks]

27 $\frac{5}{8}$ of the balloons in a bunch are red and $\frac{1}{3}$ are blue. What fraction are neither red nor blue? [2 marks]

28 Sally bought $3\frac{1}{5}$ m of canvas and used $2\frac{2}{3}$ m to make an awning.

a How much canvas did Sally have left? [1 mark]

b Sally then wants to make a cushion cover that needs $\frac{3}{4}$ of a metre of canvas. Does she have enough left to make the cover? How much more does she have or does she need? [2 marks]

29 Joh made three cakes to take to a party. The cakes were all the same size and the same shape but they each had different flavours. $\frac{3}{4}$ of the chocolate cake was eaten as was $\frac{2}{3}$ of the banana cake and $\frac{3}{5}$ of the vanilla cake. If the remaining pieces of the cakes were put together, what fraction of a whole cake remained uneaten? [2 marks]

Total marks ___ / 40

LEVEL 1 TEST

PART A

Time allowed: 40 minutes

Marks

1 What is $\frac{1}{3}$ of 216?

(A) 62 (B) 68 (C) 72 (D) 78 — 1

2 What is $\frac{3}{5}$ of 60?

(A) 35 (B) 36 (C) 45 (D) 46 — 1

3 What is the reciprocal of $2\frac{3}{5}$?

(A) $2\frac{5}{3}$ (B) $\frac{5}{13}$ (C) $\frac{13}{5}$ (D) $5\frac{2}{3}$ — 1

4 $5 \times \frac{2}{5} =$

(A) $\frac{10}{25}$ (B) $\frac{2}{25}$ (C) 2 (D) $\frac{25}{2}$ — 1

5 $\frac{3}{7} \times \frac{1}{10} =$

(A) $\frac{3}{70}$ (B) $\frac{4}{70}$ (C) $\frac{3}{17}$ (D) $\frac{4}{17}$ — 1

6 $8 \div \frac{1}{2} =$

(A) 4 (B) 6 (C) 12 (D) 16 — 1

7 $\frac{1}{5} \times \frac{1}{6} =$

(A) $\frac{1}{11}$ (B) $\frac{2}{11}$ (C) $\frac{1}{30}$ (D) $\frac{1}{15}$ — 1

8 $\frac{1}{12} \div 3 =$

(A) $\frac{1}{4}$ (B) $\frac{1}{9}$ (C) $\frac{1}{15}$ (D) $\frac{1}{36}$ — 1

9 $\frac{1}{2}$ of $\frac{7}{8} =$

(A) $\frac{7}{16}$ (B) $\frac{4}{7}$ (C) $\frac{3}{8}$ (D) $1\frac{3}{4}$ — 1

10 $15 \div \frac{2}{3} =$

(A) $22\frac{1}{2}$ (B) $\frac{1}{10}$ (C) 25 (D) 10 — 1

11 $\frac{3}{5} \times \frac{5}{6} =$

(A) $\frac{1}{4}$ (B) $\frac{1}{3}$ (C) $\frac{1}{2}$ (D) $\frac{1}{5}$ — 1

12 $\frac{1}{3} \div \frac{1}{4} =$

(A) $\frac{1}{12}$ (B) $\frac{3}{4}$ (C) $1\frac{4}{7}$ (D) $1\frac{1}{3}$ — 1

13 $\frac{3}{5} \times \frac{10}{21} =$

(A) $\frac{2}{7}$ (B) $\frac{1}{3}$ (C) $\frac{5}{21}$ (D) $3\frac{1}{2}$ — 1

14 $\frac{2}{3} \div \frac{3}{4} =$

(A) $\frac{1}{2}$ (B) 2 (C) $1\frac{1}{8}$ (D) $\frac{8}{9}$ — 1

15 $\frac{2}{5} \times \frac{4}{7} =$

(A) $\frac{6}{35}$ (B) $\frac{8}{35}$ (C) $\frac{1}{2}$ (D) $\frac{2}{3}$ — 1

Multiplying and Dividing Fractions Non-calculator (Level 1 Test)

PART B Write answers only in the space provided.

16 $\frac{1}{3} \times \frac{1}{4} =$ ______ [1]

17 $\frac{2}{5} \div 2 =$ ______ [1]

18 $\frac{3}{4} \times 4 =$ ______ [1]

19 $2 \div \frac{1}{9} =$ ______ [1]

20 What is the reciprocal of $\frac{4}{5}$? ______ [1]

21 $2 \times 3\frac{1}{2} =$ ______ [1]

22 $\left(\frac{1}{3}\right)^2 =$ ______ [1]

23 $\frac{2}{3} \div \frac{1}{2} =$ ______ [1]

24 $\frac{4}{5} \times \frac{3}{8} =$ ______ [1]

25 $\frac{5}{9} \div \frac{3}{2} =$ ______ [1]

PART C Show all working.

26 Find, giving answers as mixed numerals (where appropriate) in simplest form:

a $1\frac{2}{3} \times \frac{3}{5}$ [2 marks]

______

______

b $2\frac{1}{4} \times 3\frac{1}{2}$ [2 marks]

______

______

c $4\frac{1}{2} \div \frac{2}{9}$ [2 marks]

______

______

d $3\frac{3}{5} \times 4\frac{4}{9}$ [2 marks]

______

______

e $1\frac{3}{4} \div 1\frac{2}{3}$ [2 marks]

______

______

27 A packet contains 60 tablets. Iris must take $\frac{1}{2}$ a tablet every day.

a How long will a packet last? [1 mark]

______

b Iris has enough tablets left to last 28 days. How many tablets does she have left? [1 mark]

______

28 One litre of a particular paint covers 12 m^2. What area will $2\frac{1}{2}$ L cover? [1 mark]

______

______

29 Simone worked $6\frac{3}{4}$ hours on Monday.

a One-third of that time was spent at the reception desk. How many hours did Simone spend at the reception desk? [1 mark]

______

b On Tuesday, Simone worked $\frac{8}{9}$ of the amount of time she worked on Monday. How many hours did Simone work on Tuesday? [1 mark]

______

Total marks ___ / 40

LEVELS 2 AND 3 TEST

PART A

Time allowed: 40 minutes

Marks

1 $\frac{2}{3} \times \frac{3}{5} =$

(A) $\frac{2}{5}$ (B) $\frac{1}{3}$ (C) $\frac{3}{4}$ (D) $\frac{1}{6}$ 1

2 $6 \div \frac{1}{3} =$

(A) 2 (B) 3 (C) 9 (D) 18 1

3 $\frac{2}{3}$ of \$120 is:

(A) \$75 (B) \$80 (C) \$90 (D) \$100 1

4 $\frac{5}{8} \div \frac{2}{5} =$

(A) $\frac{1}{4}$ (B) 4 (C) $\frac{16}{25}$ (D) $1\frac{9}{16}$ 1

5 What is the product of $\frac{5}{6}$ and $\frac{5}{8}$?

(A) $\frac{25}{48}$ (B) $\frac{3}{4}$ (C) $1\frac{1}{3}$ (D) $1\frac{11}{24}$ 1

6 $3\frac{3}{5} \div 6 =$

(A) $\frac{3}{5}$ (B) $\frac{1}{20}$ (C) $1\frac{1}{10}$ (D) $1\frac{2}{3}$ 1

7 $\frac{7}{8}$ of 1.12 m is:

(A) 0.98 m (B) 1.08 m (C) 0.96 m (D) 0.84 m 1

8 $8 \times 4\frac{1}{2} =$

(A) $32\frac{1}{2}$ (B) 36 (C) 18 (D) 8 1

9 How many times does $3\frac{1}{2}$ divide into $\frac{2}{3}$?

(A) $2\frac{1}{3}$ (B) $\frac{3}{7}$ (C) $5\frac{1}{4}$ (D) $\frac{4}{21}$ 1

10 $2\frac{3}{4} \times 5 =$

(A) $10\frac{3}{4}$ (B) $5\frac{3}{4}$ (C) $13\frac{3}{4}$ (D) $\frac{11}{20}$ 1

11 $1\frac{1}{2} \times 2\frac{1}{4} =$

(A) $2\frac{1}{8}$ (B) $2\frac{3}{8}$ (C) $3\frac{1}{8}$ (D) $3\frac{3}{8}$ 1

12 $2\frac{1}{4} \div \frac{1}{4} =$

(A) $8\frac{1}{4}$ (B) 9 (C) $\frac{1}{9}$ (D) $1\frac{7}{9}$ 1

13 $1\frac{1}{4} \div \frac{3}{4} =$

(A) $\frac{15}{16}$ (B) $1\frac{3}{16}$ (C) $1\frac{2}{3}$ (D) 1 1

14 $2\frac{1}{2} \div 1\frac{3}{4} =$

(A) $\frac{7}{10}$ (B) $3\frac{1}{2}$ (C) $1\frac{3}{7}$ (D) $2\frac{2}{3}$ 1

15 $3\frac{2}{5} \times 3\frac{3}{4} =$

(A) $9\frac{3}{10}$ (B) $9\frac{8}{15}$ (C) $12\frac{3}{4}$ (D) $17\frac{3}{4}$ 1

Multiplying and Dividing Fractions Non-calculator **(Levels 2 and 3 Test)**

PART B Write answers only in the space provided.

16 What is $\frac{3}{4}$ of $\frac{2}{3}$? ______________ [1]

17 $\left(\frac{1}{5}\right)^2$ = ______________ [1]

18 $\frac{3}{8} \times \frac{4}{5}$ = ______________ [1]

19 $4 \div \frac{2}{3}$ = ______________ [1]

20 What is $\frac{3}{7}$ of 42 kg? ______________ [1]

21 $\frac{6}{7} \div \frac{5}{6}$ = ______________ [1]

22 $10 \times \frac{3}{5}$ = ______________ [1]

23 $\frac{5}{8} \div 10$ = ______________ [1]

24 $1\frac{1}{2} \times \frac{3}{5}$ = ______________ [1]

25 $3\frac{1}{2} \times 1\frac{1}{4}$ = ______________ [1]

PART C Show all working.

26 Find, giving answers in simplest form:

a $6\frac{2}{5} \times 4\frac{3}{8}$ [2 marks]

____

____

b $2\frac{7}{10} \div 1\frac{1}{5}$ [2 marks]

____

____

c $\frac{3}{7} \times \frac{1}{4} \times \frac{14}{15}$ [2 marks]

____

____

d $\frac{7}{8} \times \frac{3}{4} \div \frac{1}{2}$ [2 marks]

____

____

27 Karen had $4\frac{1}{2}$ m of material and used $\frac{2}{3}$ of it to make a dress.

a How much material did Karen use for the dress? [1 mark]

____

b Karen used $\frac{1}{3}$ of the material that she then had left to make a bag. How much material did she have left after making the bag? [2 marks]

____

____

28 The list of ingredients to make 24 biscuits includes one and a half cups of flour, one-third of a cup of sugar and half a cup of cream. Lisa wants to make $1\frac{1}{2}$ times the amount in the recipe.

a How many biscuits does Lisa want to make? [1 mark]

____

b How much flour, sugar and cream will Lisa need? [3 marks]

____

____

____

Total marks /40

LEVEL 2 TEST

PART A

Time allowed: 40 minutes

Marks

1 What is $\frac{3}{4}$ of 24?

(A) 15 (B) 16 (C) 18 (D) 21 [1]

2 What is $\frac{16}{36}$ in simplest form?

(A) $\frac{1}{3}$ (B) $\frac{8}{18}$ (C) $\frac{1}{21}$ (D) $\frac{4}{9}$ [1]

3 Which is the greatest?

(A) $\frac{5}{12}$ (B) $\frac{7}{24}$ (C) $\frac{1}{3}$ (D) $\frac{3}{8}$ [1]

4 What fraction is found at the position shown by the arrow?

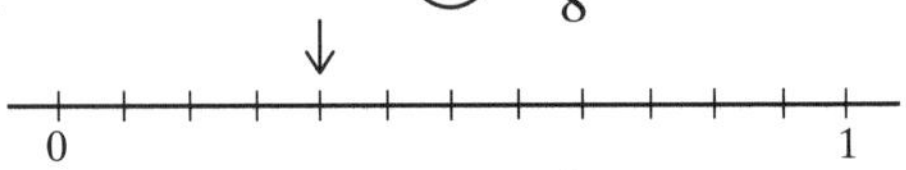

(A) $\frac{1}{2}$ (B) $\frac{1}{3}$ (C) $\frac{1}{4}$ (D) $\frac{1}{6}$ [1]

5 What is $3\frac{2}{5}$ as an improper fraction?

(A) $\frac{11}{5}$ (B) $\frac{10}{5}$ (C) $\frac{16}{5}$ (D) $\frac{17}{5}$ [1]

6 What is the reciprocal of $\frac{4}{9}$?

(A) $1\frac{1}{4}$ (B) $2\frac{1}{4}$ (C) $1\frac{3}{4}$ (D) $3\frac{1}{9}$ [1]

7 What is $\frac{32}{5}$ as a mixed number?

(A) $6\frac{2}{5}$ (B) $6\frac{3}{5}$ (C) $5\frac{4}{5}$ (D) $7\frac{3}{5}$ [1]

8 $\frac{1}{2} \times \frac{1}{3} =$

(A) $\frac{1}{6}$ (B) $\frac{1}{5}$ (C) $\frac{2}{5}$ (D) $\frac{2}{3}$ [1]

9 $\frac{1}{2} + \frac{1}{3} =$

(A) $\frac{1}{5}$ (B) $\frac{1}{6}$ (C) $\frac{2}{5}$ (D) $\frac{5}{6}$ [1]

10 $\frac{3}{4} \div 2 =$

(A) $\frac{3}{8}$ (B) $\frac{1}{2}$ (C) $1\frac{2}{3}$ (D) $1\frac{1}{2}$ [1]

11 $2\frac{3}{4} + 3\frac{3}{4} =$

(A) $5\frac{3}{4}$ (B) $6\frac{1}{4}$ (C) $6\frac{1}{2}$ (D) $6\frac{3}{4}$ [1]

12 $\frac{4}{5} \times \frac{3}{7} =$

(A) $\frac{7}{12}$ (B) $\frac{1}{5}$ (C) $\frac{12}{35}$ (D) 1 [1]

13 $\frac{5}{9} - \frac{1}{2} =$

(A) $\frac{2}{9}$ (B) $\frac{1}{18}$ (C) $\frac{4}{7}$ (D) $\frac{1}{6}$ [1]

14 $12 \div \frac{2}{3} =$

(A) 8 (B) 9 (C) 16 (D) 18 [1]

15 $\frac{3}{5} \div \frac{1}{2} =$

(A) $\frac{3}{10}$ (B) $\frac{2}{5}$ (C) $1\frac{1}{5}$ (D) $1\frac{3}{10}$ [1]

PART B Write answers only in the space provided.

16 What is half of one-half? ________________ 1

17 Simplify $\frac{25}{35}$. ________________ 1

18 What is the reciprocal of $2\frac{1}{3}$? ________________ 1

19 Show the position of $1\frac{1}{3}$ on the number line. 1

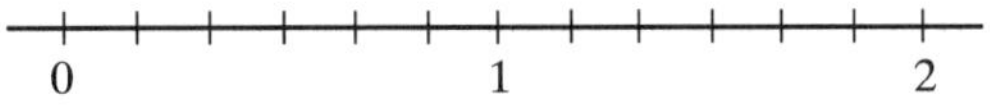

20 Complete: $\frac{3}{4} = \frac{}{48}$. 1

21 Find $\frac{3}{4} \div \frac{1}{4}$. ________________ 1

22 What is $\frac{3}{8}$ of $\frac{4}{5}$? ________________ 1

23 What must be added to $1\frac{7}{8}$ to give 4? ________________ 1

24 $8 \times 1\frac{3}{4} =$ ________________ 1

25 $\frac{3}{4} - \frac{1}{3} =$ ________________ 1

PART C Show all working.

26 Consider the fractions $\frac{2}{3}$, $\frac{5}{8}$ and $\frac{7}{12}$.

a What is the lowest common denominator of the fractions? 1 mark

____

b Arrange the fractions in order from lowest to highest. 2 marks

____

____

27 Find, giving answers in simplest form: 2 marks

a $\frac{3}{8} + \frac{5}{6}$

____

____

b $2\frac{3}{5} - 1\frac{1}{2}$ 2 marks

____

____

c $1\frac{1}{4} \times 1\frac{4}{5}$ 2 marks

____

____

d $\frac{5}{6} \div \frac{2}{3}$ 2 marks

____

____

28 A recipe to make about 24 biscuits uses $\frac{1}{3}$ cup sugar in the base and $\frac{1}{4}$ cup sugar in the filling.

a How much sugar does it use altogether? 1 mark

____

b Suresh wants to make about 60 biscuits. How much sugar should he use in the base? 2 marks

____

____

c How much sugar should he use in the filling? 1 mark

____

Total marks /40

LEVEL 2 TEST PART A

Time allowed: 40 minutes

Marks

1 What is $\frac{3}{4}$ of $1\frac{2}{3}$?

(A) $1\frac{1}{3}$ (B) $1\frac{1}{4}$ (C) $1\frac{1}{2}$ (D) $\frac{9}{20}$ 1

2 $2\frac{5}{6} + 7\frac{3}{8} =$

(A) $10\frac{1}{6}$ (B) $9\frac{5}{24}$ (C) $10\frac{5}{24}$ (D) $9\frac{1}{6}$ 1

3 $5\frac{2}{3} \times 3\frac{4}{5} =$

(A) $15\frac{8}{15}$ (B) $15\frac{2}{5}$ (C) $21\frac{2}{5}$ (D) $21\frac{8}{15}$ 1

4 $72 \div \frac{2}{3} =$

(A) 48 (B) 68 (C) 88 (D) 108 1

5 What fraction can be multiplied by $\frac{4}{7}$ to give $\frac{5}{14}$?

(A) $\frac{5}{8}$ (B) $1\frac{3}{5}$ (C) $\frac{10}{49}$ (D) $\frac{1}{2}$ 1

6 $5\frac{1}{3} - 2\frac{4}{5} =$

(A) $2\frac{7}{15}$ (B) $2\frac{8}{15}$ (C) $3\frac{7}{15}$ (D) $3\frac{8}{15}$ 1

7 How many lengths of $1\frac{1}{4}$ m can be cut from a $8\frac{1}{2}$ m length?

(A) 5 (B) 6 (C) 7 (D) 8 1

8 $5\frac{2}{3} \div 3\frac{4}{5} =$

(A) $1\frac{28}{57}$ (B) $2\frac{1}{2}$ (C) $1\frac{7}{8}$ (D) $6\frac{1}{45}$ 1

9 What is the sum of $4\frac{3}{4}$ and $2\frac{7}{8}$?

(A) $7\frac{1}{4}$ (B) $7\frac{3}{8}$ (C) $7\frac{5}{8}$ (D) $7\frac{1}{2}$ 1

10 $6\frac{5}{8} \div ☆ = 9\frac{1}{4}$. What fraction does ☆ represent?

(A) $\frac{53}{74}$ (B) $1\frac{21}{53}$ (C) $2\frac{5}{8}$ (D) $61\frac{9}{32}$ 1

11 $1\frac{2}{3} + \frac{5}{8} - 2\frac{1}{6} =$

(A) $\frac{1}{2}$ (B) $\frac{1}{8}$ (C) $\frac{1}{4}$ (D) $\frac{1}{3}$ 1

12 What is the product of $\frac{5}{8}$ and $9\frac{3}{5}$?

(A) $5\frac{7}{8}$ (B) 6 (C) $6\frac{3}{8}$ (D) $9\frac{3}{8}$ 1

13 What is the difference between $6\frac{5}{12}$ and $4\frac{9}{10}$?

(A) $1\frac{29}{60}$ (B) $2\frac{29}{60}$ (C) $1\frac{31}{60}$ (D) $2\frac{31}{60}$ 1

14 What fraction can be divided by $4\frac{3}{7}$ to leave $2\frac{1}{2}$?

(A) $1\frac{27}{35}$ (B) $\frac{35}{62}$ (C) $8\frac{3}{4}$ (D) $11\frac{1}{14}$ 1

15 What is the average of $\frac{3}{4}$, $\frac{2}{3}$ and $\frac{5}{6}$?

(A) $\frac{3}{4}$ (B) $\frac{2}{3}$ (C) $\frac{5}{6}$ (D) $1\frac{25}{36}$ 1

PART B Write answers only in the space provided.

16 $3\frac{2}{5} + 4\frac{5}{6} =$ ______________ 1

17 $7\frac{1}{2} - 5\frac{4}{5} =$ ______________ 1

18 $6\frac{2}{3} \times 1\frac{3}{4} =$ ______________ 1

19 $\frac{7}{8} \div 2\frac{1}{3} =$ ______________ 1

20 What fraction of $\frac{3}{4}$ is $\frac{2}{3}$? ______________ 1

21 What is $\frac{5}{8}$ of a million? ______________ 1

22 Sue ate $\frac{2}{3}$ of a pie and Kim ate $\frac{1}{4}$ of it. What fraction remains? ______________ 1

23 What fraction of $2\frac{1}{4}$ hours is $\frac{3}{4}$ of an hour? ______________ 1

24 Show the position of $1\frac{2}{3}$ on this number line. 1

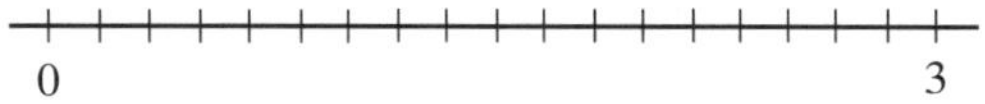

25 $\left(1\frac{1}{2}\right)^2 =$ ______________ 1

PART C Show all working.

26 a Elise has $10\frac{1}{2}$ bales of hay in her shed. She gives $\frac{1}{3}$ of the bales to her 14 calves. How many bales does she have left? 1 mark

____

b Of the hay given to the calves, they each got an equal share. How much hay did each calf get? 1 mark

____

27 Paul recorded the rain he received one week.

Rainfall (millimetres)						
Monday	Tuesday	Wednesday	Thursday	Friday	Saturday	Sunday
$2\frac{1}{2}$	7	$4\frac{3}{4}$	$5\frac{1}{4}$	$6\frac{1}{2}$	$3\frac{3}{4}$	$8\frac{3}{4}$

a What was the total rainfall for the week? 1 mark

____

b What was the average daily rainfall? 1 mark

____

c How many more millimetres of rain fell on Friday than on Wednesday? 1 mark

____

d What was the difference between the highest amount and the lowest? 1 mark

____

e On the following Monday the rainfall was $3\frac{1}{2}$ times what it was on the Monday in the table. How much rain fell on that following Monday? 1 mark

____

28 A fence post is 180 cm long.

a One-fifth of the post is placed in the ground. What height will the post reach above the ground? ______________ 1 mark

b A stay is attached to the post one-third of the distance from the top of the post to the ground. At what height above the ground is the stay attached? ______________ 1 mark

c What fraction of the whole post is between the ground and the stay? 1 mark

____

29 a Alice worked $9\frac{1}{3}$ hours on Monday. Any time over $7\frac{1}{2}$ hours is overtime. How many hours overtime did Alice work on Monday? 1 mark

____

b On Tuesday, Alice worked for $5\frac{3}{4}$ hours. How much longer, in hours and minutes, did Alice work on Monday than on Tuesday? 2 marks

____

c Alice worked for a total of $35\frac{1}{3}$ hours over five days. She worked for an equal amount of time on each of the remaining days. How long did she work on each of those days? 2 marks

____

Total marks /40

Decimals

PRETEST

Time allowed: 15 minutes **Total marks: 16**

					Marks
1	In the number 12.3456 the place value of the 4 is:				
	(A) hundredths	(B) tenths	(C) thousandths	(D) units	1
2	0.3 + 0.7 =				
	(A) 0.37	(B) 0.10	(C) 0.73	(D) 1.0	1
3	0.004 × 10 =				
	(A) 0.0040	(B) 0.0004	(C) 0.04	(D) 0.104	1
4	Rounded to the nearest 5 cents, $57.27 is:				
	(A) $57.05	(B) $57.30	(C) $57.20	(D) $57.25	1
5	0.2 – 0.06 =				
	(A) 0.04	(B) 0.6	(C) 0.14	(D) 0.16	1
6	146.28 ÷ 2 =				
	(A) 73.14	(B) 73.28	(C) 146.14	(D) 144.28	1
7	Rounded to the nearest million, 867 243 is:				
	(A) 1 million	(B) 8 million	(C) 9 million	(D) none of these	1
8	26.5 × 100 =				
	(A) 2605	(B) 2650	(C) 0.265	(D) 0.2605	1
9	10 999 rounded to the nearest ten is:				
	(A) 10 990	(B) 11 000	(C) 11 910	(D) 10 100	1
10	3.12 + 0.047 =				
	(A) 3.1247	(B) 3.059	(C) 3.59	(D) 3.167	1
11	13.78 ÷ 100 =				
	(A) 0.1378	(B) 1.378	(C) 137.8	(D) 1378	1
12	The value of 101 × 67 is closest to:				
	(A) 6900	(B) 6800	(C) 6700	(D) 6600	1
13	0.02 ÷ 10 =				
	(A) 0.2	(B) 0.5	(C) 0.002	(D) 0.005	1
14	545 273 rounded to the nearest ten thousand is:				
	(A) 540 000	(B) 545 000	(C) 550 000	(D) 555 000	1
15	0.004 ÷ 8 =				
	(A) 0.002	(B) 0.005	(C) 0.0002	(D) 0.0005	1
16	Which decimals are in order from lowest to highest?				
	(A) 0.3, 0.0325, 0.035	(B) 0.3, 0.035, 0.0325	(C) 0.035, 0.0325, 0.3	(D) 0.0325, 0.035, 0.3	1

Total marks /16

LEVEL 2 TEST PART A

Time allowed: 40 minutes

Question	A	B	C	D	Marks
1 $0.2 \times 0.3 =$	Ⓐ 0.5	Ⓑ 0.6	Ⓒ 0.05	Ⓓ 0.06	1
2 $723.85 \div 9.5$ is the same as:	Ⓐ $72\,385 \div 95$	Ⓑ $7.2385 \div 95$	Ⓒ $7238.5 \div 95$	Ⓓ $72.385 \div 95$	1
3 $1.1 \times 1.2 =$	Ⓐ 1.32	Ⓑ 13.2	Ⓒ 12.12	Ⓓ 13.12	1
4 $0.8 \div 0.2 =$	Ⓐ 0.4	Ⓑ 0.04	Ⓒ 0.004	Ⓓ 4	1
5 $0.005 \div 0.1 =$	Ⓐ 0.5	Ⓑ 0.05	Ⓒ 0.005	Ⓓ 0.0005	1
6 $0.04 \times 0.001 =$	Ⓐ 40	Ⓑ 0.004	Ⓒ 0.0004	Ⓓ 0.000 04	1
7 $15 \div 0.3 =$	Ⓐ 50	Ⓑ 5	Ⓒ 0.5	Ⓓ 0.05	1
8 $3.3 \times 0.03 =$	Ⓐ 0.0099	Ⓑ 0.099	Ⓒ 0.99	Ⓓ 990	1
9 $4 \times 0.25 =$	Ⓐ 10	Ⓑ 1	Ⓒ 0.1	Ⓓ 0.01	1
10 $0.15 \times 0.02 =$	Ⓐ 0.3	Ⓑ 0.03	Ⓒ 0.003	Ⓓ 0.0003	1
11 $0.213 \times 200 =$	Ⓐ 0.004 26	Ⓑ 426	Ⓒ 4.26	Ⓓ 42.6	1
12 $66.6 \div 0.006 =$	Ⓐ 111	Ⓑ 1110	Ⓒ 11 100	Ⓓ 0.0111	1
13 $2.02 \times 0.4 =$	Ⓐ 80.8	Ⓑ 8.08	Ⓒ 0.808	Ⓓ 0.0808	1
14 $10 \div 0.8 =$	Ⓐ 12.5	Ⓑ 1.25	Ⓒ 80	Ⓓ 0.08	1
15 $30 \times 1.12 =$	Ⓐ 336	Ⓑ 33.6	Ⓒ 3.36	Ⓓ 0.336	1

PART B Write answers only in the space provided.

16 $0.0007 \times 0.008 =$ ________________ [1]

17 $0.9 \div 0.3 =$ ________________ [1]

18 $21.2 \times 0.2 =$ ________________ [1]

19 What is the product of 1.1 and 0.04? ________________ [1]

20 Divide 6.28 by 0.002. ________________ [1]

21 $156.73 \times 0.01 =$ ________________ [1]

22 $3.55 \div 0.5 =$ ________________ [1]

23 $0.0003 \div 0.03 =$ ________________ [1]

24 $0.0036 \div 0.0004 =$ ________________ [1]

25 $0.6 \times 0.0005 =$ ________________ [1]

PART C Show all working.

26 Find:

a $0.2 \times 0.4 + 0.6 \times 0.3$ [2 marks]

____

____

b $0.36 \div 0.3 \times 0.07$ [2 marks]

____

____

c 37.8×2.3 [2 marks]

____

____

d $1.3725 \div 0.08$ [2 marks]

____

____

27 A particular container holds 0.3 L of oil.

a How many times should the container be filled in order to measure 1.8 L of oil? [1 mark]

____

b Gary fills the container 3.5 times. How much oil did Gary measure altogether? [1 mark]

____

28 **a** How many pieces of ribbon 0.08 m long can be cut from a length of 1.6 m? [1 mark]

____

b How many fewer pieces of ribbon 0.1 m long could be cut from the 1.6 m length? [1 mark]

____

29 Mel divided 16.8 by 0.02. She should have multiplied the decimals instead.

a What answer did Mel get? [1 mark]

____

b What should the answer have been? [1 mark]

____

c What could Mel multiply her answer by to get the correct answer? [1 mark]

____

Total marks /40

Rounding Off   Calculator Allowed

LEVEL 2 TEST   PART A

Time allowed: 40 minutes

Marks

1 Which of these symbols means 'approximately equal to'?

Ⓐ $\approx$ Ⓑ $\neq$ Ⓒ $\equiv$ Ⓓ $\parallel$ [1]

2 To the nearest unit, 9.5555 is:

Ⓐ 9   Ⓑ 9.556   Ⓒ 9.6   Ⓓ 10   [1]

3 When rounded to one decimal place, 13.26 becomes:

Ⓐ 132.6   Ⓑ 13.2   Ⓒ 13.3   Ⓓ 13.6   [1]

4 When written correct to two decimal places, 1.583 67 is:

Ⓐ 1.58   Ⓑ 1.67   Ⓒ 1.37   Ⓓ 1.59   [1]

5 To the nearest tenth, 423.1243 is:

Ⓐ 420   Ⓑ 423.1   Ⓒ 423.12   Ⓓ 423.124   [1]

6 Rounded to one decimal place 0.34 and 0.59 become:

Ⓐ 0.3 and 0.5   Ⓑ 0.3 and 0.6   Ⓒ 0.4 and 0.5   Ⓓ 0.4 and 0.6   [1]

7 When rounded to three decimal places 0.4157 becomes:

Ⓐ 4.157   Ⓑ 0.415   Ⓒ 0.416   D 0.420   [1]

8 To the nearest thousandth, 0.068 79 is:

Ⓐ 0.1000   Ⓑ 0.070   Ⓒ 0.069   Ⓓ 0.0688   [1]

9 When rounded to one decimal place, 16.95 becomes:

Ⓐ 16.9   Ⓑ 16.10   Ⓒ 16.0   Ⓓ 17.0   [1]

10 To the nearest hundredth, 222.2222 is:

Ⓐ 200   Ⓑ 222.22   Ⓒ 222.222   Ⓓ none of these   [1]

11 $\frac{7}{9} = 0.\dot{7}$. What is $\frac{7}{9}$ correct to two decimal places?

Ⓐ 0.70   Ⓑ 0.80   Ⓒ 0.77   Ⓓ 0.78   [1]

12 Rounded to three decimal places, 2.6479 is:

Ⓐ 2.650   Ⓑ 2.647   Ⓒ 2.657   Ⓓ 2.648   [1]

13 When rounded to two decimal places, 5.997 is:

Ⓐ 6.00   Ⓑ 5.99   Ⓒ 5.98   Ⓓ none of these   [1]

14 $2279 \div 3333 = 0.683\,768\,376\,837\,68\ldots$ What is this answer correct to three decimal places?

Ⓐ 0.683   Ⓑ 0.684   Ⓒ 0.768   Ⓓ 0.377   [1]

15 Using a calculator $\sqrt{37} = 6.082\,7625\ldots$ What is $\sqrt{37}$ correct to two decimal places?

Ⓐ 6.08   Ⓑ 6.09   Ⓒ 6.10   Ⓓ 6.83   [1]

Rounding Off Calculator Allowed (Level 2 Test)

PART B Write answers only in the space provided.

16 What is 3.275 correct to one decimal place? ________________ 1

17 Write 64.5782 correct to two decimal places. ________________ 1

18 Round 218.3475 to the nearest tenth. ________________ 1

19 What is 56.4029 to three decimal places? ________________ 1

20 Write 111.8946 to two decimal places. ________________ 1

21 Round 6258.4983 to the nearest hundredth. ________________ 1

22 What is 10.045 to one decimal place? ________________ 1

23 What does 15.4188 become when written correct to three decimal places? ________________ 1

24 To the nearest thousandth 51 496.735 69 is? ________________ 1

25 Write 0.003 4621 correct to four decimal places. ________________ 1

PART C Show all working.

26 Write 0.037 59 to:

a the nearest hundredth 1 mark

____

b three decimal places 1 mark

____

27 Write 13.994 correct to:

a the nearest unit 1 mark

____

b one decimal place 1 mark

____

c two decimal places 1 mark

____

28 a Write correct to one decimal place:

i 3.78 1 mark

____

ii 19.8675 1 mark

____

iii 25.495 1 mark

____

b Find the sum of the three numbers that are the answers to part **a**. 1 mark

____

c Find the sum of 3.78, 19.8675 and 25.495 and then round the answer to one decimal place. 1 mark

____

d Which of the answers to parts **b** or **c** is the more accurate answer? Briefly explain why. 1 mark

____

29 a Write 17.264 895 431 correct to:

i two decimal places 1 mark

____

ii three decimal places 1 mark

____

b Write the answer to part **ii** of part **a** correct to two decimal places. 1 mark

____

c Explain why the answer to part **b** is not the same as the answer to part **i** of part **a**. 1 mark

____

Total marks / 40

Mixed Decimals Non-calculator

LEVEL 2 TEST PART A

Time allowed: 40 minutes

					Marks
1	$0.2 + 0.03 =$				
	(A) 0.5	(B) 0.05	(C) 0.23	(D) 0.006	1
2	When rounded to two decimal places, 3.1784 is				
	(A) 3.17	(B) 3.18	(C) 3.20	(D) 0.17	1
3	$0.04 \times 0.02 =$				
	(A) 0.8	(B) 0.08	(C) 0.008	(D) 0.0008	1
4	$16.247 \div 100 =$				
	(A) 0.162 47	(B) 0.016 247	(C) 162.47	(D) 1624.7	1
5	$8.48 \div 0.4 =$				
	(A) 21.2	(B) 2.12	(C) 0.212	(D) 0.0212	1
6	$6 - 2.7 =$				
	(A) 4.7	(B) 4.3	(C) 3.7	(D) 3.3	1
7	$5.3 + 4.8 =$				
	(A) 9.11	(B) 9.1	(C) 10.11	(D) 10.1	1
8	$0.006 \times 10\,000 =$				
	(A) 0.006 0000	(B) 0.6	(C) 6	(D) 60	1
9	$0.3 \times 11.1 =$				
	(A) 0.333	(B) 3.33	(C) 33.3	(D) 333	1
10	$15 \div 0.005 =$				
	(A) 0.003	(B) 300	(C) 3000	(D) 30 000	1
11	If $1973 \times 6842 = 13\,499\,266$ what is 19.73×684.2?				
	(A) 134.992 66	(B) 1349.9266	(C) 13 499.266	(D) 134 992.66	1
12	What is $0.\dot{6}$ rounded to three decimal places?				
	(A) 0.666	(B) 0.667	(C) 0.676	(D) 0.777	1
13	$0.021 \div 0.003 =$				
	(A) 70	(B) 7	(C) 0.7	(D) 0.007	1
14	$0.4 \div 0.005 =$				
	(A) 80	(B) 8	(C) 0.08	(D) 0.008	1
15	$200 \times 0.03 =$				
	(A) 600	(B) 60	(C) 6	(D) 0.0600	1

PART B Write answers only in the space provided.

16 $0.7 + 0.8 =$ ______________ 1

17 $0.3 \times 0.04 =$ ______________ 1

18 $18.9 \div 0.03 =$ ______________ 1

19 What is 47.95 rounded to one decimal place? ______________ 1

20 $562.375 \times 0.0001 =$ ______________ 1

21 $3.4 - 0.8 =$ ______________ 1

22 $0.006 \div 0.2 =$ ______________ 1

23 $7.23 \div 0.6 =$ ______________ 1

24 $300 \times 0.03 =$ ______________ 1

25 $1300 \div 0.000\,01 =$ ______________ 1

PART C Show all working.

26 Find 12.32×0.004 giving the answer correct to two decimal places. [2 marks]

____

____

27 Find:

a $0.3 \times 0.5 + 0.6 \times 0.2$ [2 marks]

____

____

b $1.47 \div 0.7 \times 0.2$ [2 marks]

____

____

c $100 - 3.7 \div 0.04$ [2 marks]

____

____

28 a A 2.4 m timber plank can be cut into how many lengths of 0.8 m? [1 mark]

____

b If, instead, the plank is cut into 0.6 m lengths, how many more lengths will there be? [1 mark]

____

29 A box holds 20 packets of biscuits. Each packet weighs 0.24 kg.

a What is the total weight of the contents of the box? [1 mark]

____

b Each packet holds 12 biscuits. What is the weight, in kilograms, of each biscuit? [1 mark]

____

30 Three bags hold seed. One holds 0.75 kg, one has 0.705 kg and one has 0.075 kg.

a What is the total weight of the three bags? [1 mark]

____

b What is the difference in weight between the lightest and heaviest bags? [2 marks]

____

____

Total marks /40

LEVEL 2 TEST PART A

Time allowed: 40 minutes

Marks

1 $0.6 \div 0.5 =$

Ⓐ 0.3 Ⓑ 0.03 Ⓒ 0.12 Ⓓ 1.2 [1]

2 What is the product of 7.65 and 0.25?

Ⓐ 7.9 Ⓑ 7.1625 Ⓒ 30.6 Ⓓ 1.9125 [1]

3 $0.000\,008 \times 0.000\,05 =$

Ⓐ 0.000 000 04 Ⓑ 0.000 000 004 Ⓒ 0.000 000 0004 Ⓓ 0.000 000 000 04 [1]

4 What is $0.\dot{3}\dot{5}$ rounded to three decimal places?

Ⓐ 0.353 Ⓑ 0.354 Ⓒ 0.355 Ⓓ 0.356 [1]

5 $68.2805 \div 0.17 =$

Ⓐ 0.040 165 Ⓑ 0.401 65 Ⓒ 401.65 Ⓓ 4016.5 [1]

6 $5 \div 1.2 =$

Ⓐ $4.\dot{1}\dot{6}$ Ⓑ $4.1\dot{6}$ Ⓒ 4.166 666 667 Ⓓ none of these [1]

7 What is the average of 7.8, 2.94 and 3.21?

Ⓐ 11.81 Ⓑ 4.65 Ⓒ 8.75 Ⓓ 3.4875 [1]

8 0.01 divided by ten thousand is:

Ⓐ 0.000 000 01 Ⓑ 0.000 0001 Ⓒ 0.000 001 Ⓓ 0.000 01 [1]

9 What number can be multiplied by 0.094 to give 0.2444?

Ⓐ 2.6 Ⓑ 0.023 Ⓒ 0.385 Ⓓ 0.26 [1]

10 By how much does 34.27 exceed 15.49?

Ⓐ 49.76 Ⓑ 18.78 Ⓒ 19.22 Ⓓ 22.12 [1]

11 $12.168 \div \Delta = 156 \quad \Delta =$

Ⓐ 1898.208 Ⓑ 12.82 Ⓒ 0.078 Ⓓ 0.128 [1]

12 $74.25 + 18.63 \times 4.1 + 3.6 \div 0.9 =$

Ⓐ 154.633 Ⓑ 384.808 Ⓒ 171.37 Ⓓ 427.12 [1]

13 $\frac{15.8 - 2.42}{7.16 \times 0.03}$ correct to one decimal place is:

Ⓐ 62.3 Ⓑ 4.5 Ⓒ 15.8 Ⓓ 0.1 [1]

14 $0.004 \times 0.215 + 12.24 \div 1.6 =$

Ⓐ 0.031 1375 Ⓑ 7.650 5375 Ⓒ 0.031 46 Ⓓ 7.650 86 [1]

15 What is $0.02 \div 0.067$ correct to three decimal places?

Ⓐ 0.298 Ⓑ 0.299 Ⓒ 0.3 Ⓓ 0.300 [1]

PART B Write answers only in the space provided.

16 $28.47 \times 0.006 =$ ________________ 1

17 $0.009 \div 1.25 =$ ________________ 1

18 Write 17.236 84 correct to two decimal places. ________________ 1

19 $0.059 \times \Delta = 0.374\,65$ $\Delta =$ ________________ 1

20 $(241.6 + 13.234) \times 0.015 =$ ________________ 1

21 $\Delta \div 0.015 = 8.3$ $\Delta =$ ________________ 1

22 $15.96 + 2.4 \times 3.6 =$ ________________ 1

23 $82.1 \div 0.1 - 6.9 \div 0.3 =$ ________________ 1

24 What is 3.0862 to one decimal place? ________________ 1

25 $\dfrac{23.950\,35 \times 0.8}{15.7 \times 1.8} =$ ________________ 1

PART C Show all working.

26 Give the value of each of these and then round the answer to one decimal place:

a 0.08×16.982 2 marks

____

____

b $22.2 \div 371.4$ 2 marks

____

____

c $19.2 \times 5.03 \times 0.151$ 2 marks

____

____

27 a Neil has 18 fencing panels each 2.4 m long. What total length can they cover? 1 mark

____

b How many more panels does Neil need if he wants to cover a total length of 60 m? 1 mark

____

28 a What is the total weight of 240 boxes each weighing 1.125 kg? 1 mark

____

b Each box holds packets weighing 0.005 kg. How many packets are in each box? 1 mark

____

29 a Imogen multiplied 91.7016 by 13.38 and then divided the result by 0.48. What is Imogen's answer? 1 mark

____

b Imogen should have multiplied 91.7016 by 13.48 and then divided the result by 0.38. What is the difference between the answer Imogen got and the answer she should have got? 2 marks

____

____

30 A full bottle of medicine holds 0.36 L.

a How many doses of 0.008 L does the bottle hold? 1 mark

____

b Henry has taken 17 doses from a bottle. How much medicine (in litres) remains in the bottle? 1 mark

____

Total marks /40

LEVEL 2 TEST

PART A

Time allowed: 40 minutes

Marks

1 What is the product of $3\frac{7}{8}$ and $7\frac{2}{3}$?

Ⓐ $22\frac{13}{24}$ Ⓑ $29\frac{17}{24}$ Ⓒ $11\frac{13}{24}$ Ⓓ $21\frac{7}{12}$ 1

2 $0.000\,09 \times 0.000\,005 =$

Ⓐ 0.000 000 045 Ⓑ 0.000 000 0045 Ⓒ 0.000 000 000 45 Ⓓ 0.000 000 000 045 1

3 What is the reciprocal of $2\frac{3}{7}$?

Ⓐ $4\frac{1}{3}$ Ⓑ $\frac{7}{6}$ Ⓒ $\frac{3}{14}$ Ⓓ $\frac{7}{17}$ 1

4 What is the result when $8\frac{4}{5}$ is divided by 11?

Ⓐ $\frac{4}{5}$ Ⓑ $1\frac{1}{4}$ Ⓒ $2\frac{7}{40}$ Ⓓ $8\frac{4}{55}$ 1

5 $19.37 - 2.8 \times 3.45 =$

Ⓐ 9.71 Ⓑ 18.404 Ⓒ 57.1665 Ⓓ 64.0265 1

6 $4\frac{5}{6} - 2\frac{3}{5} =$

Ⓐ $2\frac{2}{11}$ Ⓑ $2\frac{7}{30}$ Ⓒ $2\frac{1}{15}$ Ⓓ $1\frac{23}{30}$ 1

7 $152.76 \div 0.038 =$

Ⓐ 4020 Ⓑ 2040 Ⓒ 0.0402 Ⓓ 0.0204 1

8 What number must be multiplied by $2\frac{1}{2}$ to give $3\frac{1}{4}$?

Ⓐ $\frac{10}{13}$ Ⓑ $8\frac{1}{8}$ Ⓒ $1\frac{3}{10}$ Ⓓ $\frac{3}{4}$ 1

9 The value of $\frac{19.6 \times 2.4}{6.5 \times 3.6}$ is closest to:

Ⓐ 2 Ⓑ 5 Ⓒ 26 Ⓓ 1080 1

10 $9\frac{3}{4} \div 2.75 =$

Ⓐ $2.\dot{4}\dot{5}$ Ⓑ $2.\dot{5}\dot{4}$ Ⓒ $3.\dot{4}\dot{5}$ Ⓓ $3.\dot{5}\dot{4}$ 1

11 $17\frac{4}{7} \times 23\frac{6}{11} =$

Ⓐ $391\frac{24}{77}$ Ⓑ $30\frac{53}{77}$ Ⓒ $413\frac{8}{11}$ Ⓓ $121\frac{67}{77}$ 1

12 How many pieces of cord 1.35 m long can be cut from a 25 m long cord?

Ⓐ 19 Ⓑ 18 Ⓒ 17 Ⓓ 16 1

13 $3.2 \times \Delta = 7.26$. What number does Δ represent?

Ⓐ 2.26 Ⓑ 2.268 75 Ⓒ 10.46 Ⓓ 23.232 1

14 A machine takes $5\frac{1}{2}$ hours to complete two cycles. How long does it take for each cycle?

Ⓐ $2\frac{11}{12}$ h Ⓑ $2\frac{1}{4}$ h Ⓒ $2\frac{3}{4}$ h Ⓓ $2\frac{4}{9}$ h 1

15 $6\frac{1}{5} \times 3\frac{2}{3} \div \frac{1}{4} =$

Ⓐ $5\frac{41}{60}$ Ⓑ $26\frac{14}{15}$ Ⓒ $72\frac{8}{15}$ Ⓓ $90\frac{14}{15}$ 1

PART B Write answers only in the space provided.

16 Find $3\frac{2}{5} \times 4\frac{1}{4}$. ____________ 1

17 What is $18.36 \div 0.09$? ____________ 1

18 $5\frac{3}{4} \div \frac{2}{3} =$ ____________ 1

19 $0.375 \times 0.025 =$ ____________ 1

20 What is $\frac{2}{5}$ of 16.42? ____________ 1

21 What is 64 million divided by 1.6? ____________ 1

22 Find $\frac{3.8 \times 0.09}{6.84 \div 0.02}$. ____________ 1

23 What is a quarter of three-quarters? ____________ 1

24 If an athlete ran a marathon, 42.195 km, in $3\frac{1}{4}$ hours what was the average speed to the nearest kilometre per hour? ____________ 1

25 What can $3\frac{5}{8}$ be multiplied by to give $2\frac{5}{12}$? ____________ 1

PART C Show all working.

26 a A 12.25 m piece of string is cut into 14 equal lengths. How long is each piece? [1 mark]

____

b If instead it was cut into 25 lengths, how much shorter would each length be? [2 marks]

____

____

27 a Arjun multiplied 406.98 by 7.65 and then divided by 2.8. What answer did he get? [1 mark]

____

b Arjun should have multiplied 406.98 by 2.8 and then divided by 7.65. What should his answer have been? [1 mark]

____

c About how many times larger is Arjun's answer than what it should have been? [1 mark]

____

28 Freya has $6\frac{3}{4}$ m of fabric.

a If she uses $4\frac{1}{2}$ m to make a dress, how much fabric will she have left? [1 mark]

____

b What fraction of the original amount of fabric would Freya use to make the dress? [1 mark]

____

c Freya needs $2\frac{2}{3}$ m to make a pair of pants and $4\frac{1}{4}$ m to make a jacket. Would she have enough fabric to make the pants and jacket instead of the dress? Justify your answer. [2 marks]

____

____

29 Three buckets of the same size contain different amounts of water. The red bucket is $\frac{1}{3}$ full, the blue bucket is $\frac{3}{10}$ full and the green one is $\frac{2}{5}$ full.

a Which bucket has the most water? [1 mark]

____

b How many buckets full of water do they hold altogether? [1 mark]

____

c What is the difference between the amount of water held by the red and green buckets? [1 mark]

____

30 Giselle bought $1\frac{3}{4}$ litres of cream and used $\frac{3}{5}$ of it. What fraction of a litre of cream remains unused? [2 marks]

____

____

Total marks /40

PRETEST

Time allowed: 15 minutes **Total marks: 15**

Marks

1 What is 10% of $4?

(A) 4c (B) 25c (C) 40c (D) $1 — 1

2 What is 25% as a simple fraction?

(A) $\frac{1}{8}$ (B) $\frac{1}{4}$ (C) $\frac{1}{5}$ (D) $\frac{1}{2}$ — 1

3 What is 50% of $4628?

(A) $2314 (B) $92.56 (C) $925.60 (D) $231.40 — 1

4 What is 10% of $800?

(A) $8 (B) $12.50 (C) $80 (D) $125 — 1

5 $\frac{1}{10}$ is:

(A) 5% (B) 10% (C) 20% (D) 1% — 1

6 If I get a $56 discount on a coat priced at $294, what price do I pay?

(A) $238 (B) $248 (C) $262 (D) $350 — 1

7 What is 50% of $11?

(A) $5.05 (B) $5.10 (C) $5.20 (D) $5.50 — 1

8 What is 25% of $25?

(A) $1 (B) $5 (C) $6.25 (D) $6.50 — 1

9 If there is a 50% discount on a suit priced at $350, what is the discounted price?

(A) $175 (B) $250 (C) $300 (D) $315 — 1

10 If I receive a $215 discount on an item priced at $2150, what percentage discount is that?

(A) 5% (B) 10% (C) 25% (D) 50% — 1

11 How much is a discount of 10% on an item priced at $7000?

(A) $70 (B) $140 (C) $1400 (D) $700 — 1

12 What is 25% of 500 g?

(A) 20 g (B) 125 g (C) 200 g (D) 250 g — 1

13 What price must be paid for a table if the original price is $900 but there is a 25% discount?

(A) $775 (B) $725 (C) $675 (D) $625 — 1

14 Tim receives a 10% staff discount. What must he pay for a shirt priced at $65?

(A) $6.50 (B) $60.50 (C) $59.50 (D) $58.50 — 1

15 Which is the greatest?

(A) 10% of 100 (B) 25% of 40 (C) 50% of 20 (D) They are all the same. — 1

Total marks — /15

LEVEL 2 TEST

PART A

Time allowed: 40 minutes

Marks

1 What is 80% as a fraction?

(A) $\frac{2}{25}$ (B) $\frac{4}{5}$ (C) $\frac{1}{80}$ (D) $\frac{1}{8}$ 1

2 How much is 30% of $600?

(A) $18 (B) $20 (C) $180 (D) $200 1

3 What percentage is 15 minutes of an hour?

(A) 15% (B) 20% (C) 25% (D) 30% 1

4 What is 2% of $100 000?

(A) $2000 (B) $20 000 (C) $5000 (D) $50 000 1

5 $320 out of $800 expressed as a percentage is:

(A) 25% (B) 30% (C) 36% (D) 40% 1

6 How much is a discount of 20% on $5500?

(A) $101 (B) $110 (C) $1010 (D) $1100 1

7 What percentage is 25 g of 1 kg?

(A) 2.5% (B) 25% (C) 4% (D) 40% 1

8 What percentage is 40 out of 200?

(A) 20% (B) 25% (C) 32% (D) 40% 1

9 70% is:

(A) $\frac{3}{4}$ (B) $\frac{7}{10}$ (C) $\frac{7}{100}$ (D) $\frac{3}{5}$ 1

10 What is 60% of 2 L?

(A) 30 mL (B) 120 mL (C) 300 mL (D) 1200 mL 1

11 What percentage is 13 out of 20?

(A) 65% (B) 70% (C) 77.5% (D) 93% 1

12 What is 9% of 5 m?

(A) 45 mm (B) 45 cm (C) 18 mm (D) 18 cm 1

13 What is 36% of $40 000?

(A) $9000 (B) $11 111 (C) $12 000 (D) $14 400 1

14 Nine months is about what percentage of a year?

(A) 65% (B) 75% (C) 80% (D) 90% 1

15 What would you pay for a wheelbarrow if the marked price is $180 and you receive a discount of 40% off the marked price?

(A) $45 (B) $72 (C) $108 (D) $135 1

Percentages Non-calculator (Level 2 Test)

PART B Write answers only in the space provided.

16 If 68% of cars are white, what percentage is **not** white? ______ 1

17 What is 35% of $2000? ______ 1

18 What percentage is 45 seconds of 1 minute? ______ 1

19 How much is a discount of 12% on $80? ______ 1

20 What is 7% of $5? ______ 1

21 Douggie scored 17 out of 25 in a test. What percentage mark is that? ______ 1

22 What is 60% of 3 kg? ______ 1

23 What percentage of $6 is 66 cents? ______ 1

24 What is 15% of 72? ______ 1

25 What price will you pay for a watch marked at $450 if you get $33\frac{1}{3}$% off the marked price? ______ 1

PART C Show all working.

26 a Pete cut 200 g from a 4 kg block of cheese. What percentage was that? (1 mark)

______

b Pete then cut 5% off the 200 g piece. How many grams was the smaller piece? (1 mark)

______

27 Jana is paid $1400 every week.

a Jana gives 6% of her weekly pay to charity. How much is that? (1 mark)

______

b Each week Jana pays $560 off her loan. What percentage of her pay is that? (1 mark)

______

28 The recommended retail price (RRP) of an outdoor setting is $600.

a A store offers a discount of 20% on the RRP. How much is that? (1 mark)

______

b What is the discounted price? (1 mark)

______

c A different store sells the setting for $450. What percentage discount is that on the RRP? (2 marks)

______

______

29 Amelia scored 68 out of 80 in her English test and 120 out of 150 in her History test.

a What was Amelia's percentage mark for English? (1 mark)

______

b Was Amelia's History mark better or worse than her English mark? Justify your answer with appropriate calculations. (2 marks)

______

______

______

30 a A house sold for 10% less than the asking price. If the asking price was $600 000, how much did the house sell for? (1 mark)

______

b The selling agent received 4% of the sale price. How much did the agent receive? (1 mark)

______

c What percentage of the asking price did the owner receive? (2 marks)

______

______

______

Total marks /40

LEVEL 2 TEST

PART A

Time allowed: 40 minutes

Marks

1 What is 28% of $840?

(A) $235.20 (B) $300.00 (C) $325.60 (D) $333.33 [1]

2 What percentage of 90 000 is 40 500?

(A) 50% (B) 45% (C) 39% (D) 22% [1]

3 What is 150% of 3.2 kg?

(A) 4.8 g (B) 48 g (C) 480 g (D) 4.8 kg [1]

4 What percentage is 10 minutes of $2\frac{1}{2}$ hours?

(A) 5% (B) $6\frac{2}{3}$% (C) $7\frac{1}{2}$% (D) $8\frac{3}{4}$% [1]

5 What is 14% of $125?

(A) $8.93 (B) $11.20 (C) $15.60 (D) $17.50 [1]

6 What price will you pay for a plant priced at $15 if you get a 15% discount?

(A) $10.00 (B) $12.25 (C) $12.75 (D) $13.25 [1]

7 What percentage of a hectare is 2500 m^2?

(A) 4% (B) 25% (C) 40% (D) 250% [1]

8 What is 20% as a fraction?

(A) $\frac{1}{20}$ (B) $\frac{1}{4}$ (C) $\frac{1}{50}$ (D) $\frac{1}{5}$ [1]

9 Last year Celia paid 9% of her total income in superannuation. If her income was $84 600 how much was the superannuation?

(A) $7614 (B) $9400 (C) $1064 (D) $10 638 [1]

10 $\frac{3}{20}$ is what percentage?

(A) 6% (B) 12% (C) 15% (D) $7\frac{1}{2}$% [1]

11 Last year George received 1825 mm of rain. In February, 412 mm fell. February's rainfall as a percentage of the whole year was closest to:

(A) 20% (B) 23% (C) 26% (D) 29% [1]

12 William received a pay rise of $2\frac{1}{2}$%. If his old salary was $80 400 per year, how much extra does he get now?

(A) $2010 (B) $2050 (C) $1809 (D) $1648 [1]

13 What is 62% of $19 000?

(A) $11 780 (B) $3065 (C) $3263 (D) $12 350 [1]

14 What percentage is 18 hours of a day?

(A) $66\frac{2}{3}$% (B) 70% (C) 75% (D) 82% [1]

15 Which is the largest amount?

(A) 32% of 5597 (B) 21% of 8210 (C) 4% of 47 300 (D) 87% of 2147 [1]

PART B Write answers only in the space provided.

16 What is 3% of $9560? ________________ [1]

17 What percentage is 8 months of a year? ________________ [1]

18 What is 85% of 2.5 t? ________________ [1]

19 Express $\frac{17}{20}$ as a percentage. ________________ [1]

20 What would you pay for a TV that was priced at $800 but is now discounted by 15%? ____________ [1]

21 Find 78% of $93. ________________ [1]

22 What percentage of 2400 is 2100? ________________ [1]

23 How much is a discount of 5% on $36 000? ________________ [1]

24 500 mL is what percentage of 8 L? ________________ [1]

25 Find $12\frac{1}{2}$% of 160. ________________ [1]

PART C Show all working.

26 a Fifty-five per cent of workers at a factory are male. If there are 320 workers, how many are male? [1 mark]

____

b Twenty-seven of the female workers have worked at the factory for more than 10 years. What percentage of female workers have worked at the factory for more than 10 years? [2 marks]

____

____

c One-quarter of the males and one-third of the females received a pay rise. What percentage of the workforce received a pay rise? [2 marks]

____

____

27 The population of Australia is about 24 million.

a Around 32% of Australians live in NSW. What is the approximate population of NSW? [1 mark]

____

b Around 20.5% of Australians live in Sydney. About how many people is that? [1 mark]

____

c About what percentage of the population of NSW live in Sydney? [1 mark]

____

28 A lounge suite is priced at $3840 and a matching dining suite at $1160.

a Ray gets a discount of 15% and buys the lounge suite. How much does he save? [1 mark]

____

b Ray also buys the dining suite, paying $1102. What percentage does Ray save on the dining suite? [2 marks]

____

____

c What percentage does Ray save altogether? [2 marks]

____

____

____

29 a A customer uses a supermarket docket to save 4c per litre on petrol. If petrol sells for $1.25 per litre, what is the percentage saving? [1 mark]

____

b The petrol station also has a loyalty card offering savings of 4% off the petrol price. How many cents per litre will a customer save using the loyalty card? [1 mark]

____

Total marks /40

LEVEL 2 TEST PART A

Time allowed: 40 minutes

Marks

1 $\frac{3}{4}$ as a percentage is:
(A) 34% (B) 66% (C) 70% (D) 75% [1]

2 As a decimal, 60% is:
(A) 0.6 (B) 0.06 (C) 0.66 (D) none of these [1]

3 $\frac{2}{5}$ as a decimal is:
(A) 0.25 (B) 0.04 (C) 0.4 (D) 0.52 [1]

4 15% =
(A) $\frac{3}{25}$ (B) $\frac{3}{20}$ (C) $\frac{5}{33}$ (D) $\frac{1}{6}$ [1]

5 0.8 =
(A) $\frac{1}{8}$ (B) $\frac{5}{6}$ (C) $\frac{4}{5}$ (D) $\frac{7}{8}$ [1]

6 As a percentage 0.03 =
(A) 3% (B) 30% (C) 0.3% (D) 0.03% [1]

7 $\frac{21}{10}$ =
(A) 0.21 (B) 0.021 (C) 2.1 (D) 2.01 [1]

8 Which of these is **not** equal to the others?
(A) 0.05 (B) 5% (C) $\frac{1}{5}$ (D) $\frac{1}{20}$ [1]

9 Which is the greatest?
(A) 86% (B) $\frac{17}{20}$ (C) 0.8 (D) $\frac{21}{25}$ [1]

10 $37\frac{3}{4}$% =
(A) 0.375 (B) $\frac{151}{4}$ (C) 0.3775 (D) $\frac{161}{400}$ [1]

11 Which is largest?
(A) 9% (B) 0.9 (C) $\frac{9}{100}$ (D) They are all the same. [1]

12 Which is smallest?
(A) $\frac{1}{8}$ (B) 12.5% (C) 0.125 (D) They are all the same. [1]

13 $66\frac{2}{3}$% =
(A) $\frac{2}{3}$ (B) $\frac{3}{5}$ (C) $\frac{6}{11}$ (D) $\frac{33}{50}$ [1]

14 $\frac{5}{6}$ as a decimal is:
(A) 0.56 (B) 0.65 (C) $0.7\dot{8}$ (D) $0.8\dot{3}$ [1]

15 Which are in order from smallest to largest?
(A) $\frac{1}{6}$, 16%, 0.17 (B) 16%, $\frac{1}{6}$, 0.17 (C) 16%, 0.17, $\frac{1}{6}$ (D) 0.17, $\frac{1}{6}$, 16% [1]

PART B Write answers only in the space provided.

16 What is $\frac{1}{3}$ as a decimal? ______________ [1]

17 What is 35% as a simple fraction? ______________ [1]

18 What is 0.075 as a percentage? ______________ [1]

19 What is $\frac{7}{25}$ as a percentage? ______________ [1]

20 What is 0.06 as a fraction in simplest form? ______________ [1]

21 Express 150% in decimal form. ______________ [1]

22 Find $\frac{5}{8}$ as a decimal. ______________ [1]

23 Express $1\frac{1}{4}$ as a percentage. ______________ [1]

24 Find 2.4 as an improper fraction in simplest form. ______________ [1]

25 Convert 44% to a simple fraction. ______________ [1]

PART C Show all working.

26 Convert 0.72 to a:

a percentage [1 mark]

____

b fraction in simplest form [1 mark]

____

27 What is $17\frac{1}{2}\%$ as a:

a decimal? [1 mark]

____

b simple fraction? [1 mark]

____

28 a Write $2\frac{1}{2}\%$ as a decimal. [1 mark]

____

b Write $\frac{1}{50}$ as a decimal. [1 mark]

____

c Write the numbers $2\frac{1}{2}\%$, $\frac{1}{50}$ and 0.28 in order from lowest to highest. [1 mark]

____

29 a Write $\frac{1}{12}$ as a decimal. [1 mark]

____

b What simple fraction must be added to $\frac{1}{12}$ to give $\frac{7}{12}$? [1 mark]

____

c Write $\frac{7}{12}$ as a decimal. [1 mark]

____

30 a Write $\frac{3}{5}$ as a percentage. [1 mark]

____

b Write $\frac{23}{25}$ as a percentage. [1 mark]

____

c What percentage is halfway between the percentages in parts **a** and **b**? [1 mark]

____

d What fraction, in simplest form, is halfway between $\frac{3}{5}$ and $\frac{23}{25}$? [2 marks]

____

____

Total marks /40

LEVEL 2 TEST

PART A

Time allowed: 40 minutes

Marks

1 7.5 as a percentage is:

(A) $7\frac{1}{2}\%$ (B) 75% (C) 750% (D) 0.075% — 1

2 What is $\frac{5}{24}$ as a decimal?

(A) $0.208\dot{3}$ (B) $0.20\dot{8}\dot{3}$ (C) $0.2\dot{0}\dot{8}\dot{3}$ (D) $0.\dot{2}\dot{0}\dot{8}\dot{3}$ — 1

3 Which is largest?

(A) $\frac{3}{10}$ (B) 35% (C) $0.31\dot{6}$ (D) $\frac{1}{3}$ — 1

4 $3\frac{1}{4}\% =$

(A) $\frac{13}{400}$ (B) $\frac{7}{150}$ (C) $\frac{7}{200}$ (D) $\frac{17}{500}$ — 1

5 Which is smallest?

(A) 83% (B) $\frac{6}{7}$ (C) $0.8\dot{3}$ (D) $\frac{17}{20}$ — 1

6 Which is in order from lowest to highest?

(A) 79%, $\frac{39}{50}$, 0.81, $\frac{4}{5}$ (B) 79%, $\frac{4}{5}$, $\frac{39}{50}$, 0.81 (C) $\frac{39}{50}$, 79%, $\frac{4}{5}$, 0.81 (D) $\frac{39}{50}$, $\frac{4}{5}$, 79%, 0.81 — 1

7 Which statement is correct? I $0.045 = \frac{9}{200}$ II $0.045 = 4\frac{1}{2}\%$

(A) I but not II (B) II but not I (C) both I and II (D) neither I nor II — 1

8 0.625 as a fraction is:

(A) $\frac{127}{200}$ (B) $\frac{5}{8}$ (C) $\frac{31}{50}$ (D) $\frac{16}{25}$ — 1

9 $5\frac{2}{3}\%$ as a decimal is:

(A) 0.0567 (B) $0.05\dot{6}$ (C) 0.567 (D) $0.5\dot{6}$ — 1

10 Which is largest?

(A) $\frac{1}{200}$ (B) 0.005 (C) $\frac{1}{2}\%$ (D) They are all the same. — 1

11 Which is smallest?

(A) $\frac{5}{7}$ (B) $71\frac{1}{2}\%$ (C) 0.715 (D) They are all the same. — 1

12 Which is closest in value to $\frac{107}{136}$?

(A) 0.6 (B) 0.7 (C) 0.8 (D) 0.9 — 1

13 Which is closest to 64%?

(A) $\frac{5}{8}$ (B) $\frac{7}{11}$ (C) $\frac{8}{13}$ (D) $\frac{11}{18}$ — 1

14 Which is equal to $0.\dot{4}\dot{5}$?

(A) $\frac{9}{20}$ (B) $\frac{41}{90}$ (C) $\frac{4}{9}$ (D) $\frac{5}{11}$ — 1

15 Which is closest in value to 0.525?

(A) $\frac{4}{7}$ (B) $\frac{5}{9}$ (C) $\frac{6}{11}$ (D) $\frac{7}{13}$ — 1

PART B Write answers only in the space provided.

16 What is 0.7% as a decimal? ________________ 1

17 Convert $\frac{5}{12}$ to a percentage. ________________ 1

18 Express 0.375 as a simple fraction. ________________ 1

19 When expressed as a decimal, is $\frac{49}{75}$ a terminating or repeating decimal? ________________ 1

20 Express 1.055 as a percentage. ________________ 1

21 Convert 0.2176 to a fraction in simplest form. ________________ 1

22 Express $\frac{120}{333}$ as a decimal. ________________ 1

23 What is $1\frac{3}{4}$% as a decimal? ________________ 1

24 Express $\frac{11}{32}$ as a percentage. ________________ 1

25 What is $\frac{1}{5}$% as a fraction in simplest form? ________________ 1

PART C Show all working.

26 Write as fractions in simplest form:

a 95% — 1 mark

____

b 225% — 1 mark

____

c $0.\dot{3}$ — 1 mark

____

27 Write as repeating decimals:

a $\frac{4}{7}$ — 1 mark

____

b $6\frac{2}{3}$% — 1 mark

____

28 Express $\frac{13}{48}$ as a:

a decimal — 1 mark

____

b percentage correct to one decimal place — 1 mark

____

29 A report stated that $93\frac{3}{4}$% of people surveyed preferred route A for a new highway. What fraction of people surveyed did not prefer route A? — 1 mark

____

30 a Express $\frac{8}{45}$ as a decimal. — 1 mark

____

b Express $\frac{35}{198}$ as a decimal. — 1 mark

____

c Express $17\frac{2}{3}$% as a decimal. — 1 mark

____

d Arrange $\frac{8}{45}$, $\frac{35}{198}$ and $17\frac{2}{3}$% in ascending (from lowest to highest) order. — 1 mark

____

31 a What is 0.1225 as a percentage? — 1 mark

____

b What is $\frac{3}{25}$ as a percentage? — 1 mark

____

c What is the difference, as a percentage, between 0.1225 and $\frac{3}{25}$? — 1 mark

____

Total marks /40

PRETEST

Time allowed: 15 minutes **Total marks: 14**

Marks

1 Which amount of money is the greatest?

(A)  (B)  (C)  (D)  1

2 If raffle tickets cost $1.20 each, what is the cost of 12 tickets?

(A) 10c (B) $10.00 (C) $14.40 (D) $13.20 1

3 If I buy eight cans of dog food for $18.80 how much is each can?

(A) $1.10 (B) $2.35 (C) $2.10 (D) $2.55 1

4 What is the total cost of two loaves of bread costing $3.50 each and six bread rolls costing 45c each?

(A) $9.70 (B) $6.20 (C) $10.60 (D) $27.70 1

5 What is the change from $100.00 if you spend $63.35?

(A) $36.75 (B) $36.65 (C) $46.75 (D) $46.65 1

6 Grace spent $42.35 and had $98.45 left in her purse. How much did she have before the purchase?

(A) $56.10 (B) $148 (C) $140.08 (D) $140.80 1

7 What change should you receive from $50.00 if you spend $23.87?

(A) $26.15 (B) $26.10 (C) $26.00 (D) $26.20 1

8 Shaved ham is selling for $13.40 per kilogram. How much will you be charged for 200 g?

(A) $2.68 (B) $3.35 (C) $1.49 (D) $6.70 1

9 Together, a shirt and tie cost the same as two dresses. If the dresses cost $49.45 each and the tie costs $29.95, how much is the shirt?

(A) $19.50 (B) $40.40 (C) $79.90 (D) $68.95 1

10 Sid bought 3.2 kg of pears. The pears were selling for $2.40 per kilogram. Which is closest to the amount Sid was charged?

(A) $5.60 (B) $6.80 (C) $7.50 (D) $7.70 1

11 Screenguards for a phone can be bought for $34.95 each or two for $55. Which is closest to the amount you save on each guard when you buy two?

(A) $7.50 (B) $10.00 (C) $15.00 (D) $20.00 1

12 Angie has $6.75 in her pocket. She needs another $1.65 to buy a book. How much is the book?

(A) $5.10 (B) $7.40 (C) $8.10 (D) $8.40 1

13 Jenna paid $2.75 for 600 mL of chocolate milk. About what price is this per litre?

(A) $1.65 (B) $4.60 (C) $4.40 (D) $16.50 1

14 Nathan is paid $180 for three hours work. How long would he have to work to earn $330?

(A) $4\frac{1}{2}$ hours (B) 5 hours (C) $5\frac{1}{2}$ hours (D) 5 hours 50 min 1

Total marks /14

PRETEST

Time allowed: 15 minutes **Total marks: 15**

Marks

1 9 m =
(A) 9000 cm (B) 900 mm (C) 900 cm (D) 90 000 mm [1]

2 How many grams are in a kilogram?
(A) 1000 (B) 100 (C) 0.01 (D) 0.001 [1]

3 $\frac{1}{2}$ of a litre is:
(A) 5 mL (B) 50 mL (C) 500 mL (D) 5000 mL [1]

4 $\frac{1}{4}$ of an hour is:
(A) 25 seconds (B) 15 seconds (C) 25 minutes (D) 15 minutes [1]

5 50 km =
(A) 500 m (B) 5000 m (C) 5000 cm (D) 50 000 m [1]

6 8 minutes =
(A) 800 seconds (B) 600 seconds (C) 540 seconds (D) 480 seconds [1]

7 0.6 L =
(A) 6000 mL (B) 600 mL (C) 60 mL (D) 6 mL [1]

8 300 g =
(A) 0.3 kg (B) 0.03 kg (C) 3 kg (D) 30 kg [1]

9 2 m and 8 mm is:
(A) 2.008 m (B) 2.08 m (C) 2.8 m (D) 20 008 mm [1]

10 25 g =
(A) 250 mg (B) 2500 mg (C) 25 000 mg (D) 250 000 mg [1]

11 70 cm =
(A) 7 mm (B) 7 m (C) 700 mm (D) 7000 mm [1]

12 30 000 mm =
(A) 300 cm (B) 3 m (C) 3 km (D) 30 m [1]

13 20 mL =
(A) 0.2 L (B) 0.02 L (C) 0.002 L (D) 0.0002 L [1]

14 4.6 kg =
(A) 4006 g (B) 4600 g (C) 4060 g (D) 460 g [1]

15 7.04 L =
(A) 7 L and 4 mL (B) 7 L and 40 mL (C) 7 L and 400 mL (D) 7 L and 4000 mL [1]

Total marks /15

GST, Discounts and Best Buys Non-calculator

LEVEL 2 TEST — PART A

Time allowed: 40 minutes

Marks

1 How much is a discount of 25% on an item priced at $40.00?
(A) $1 (B) $5 (C) $10 (D) $12 — 1

2 Which is the cheapest rate?
(A) 1 for $7.00 (B) 2 for $13.00 (C) 3 for $19.00 (D) 5 for $30.00 — 1

3 Petrol is selling for $1.20 per litre. What will you pay for 50 L?
(A) $52.00 (B) $60.00 (C) $75.00 (D) $80.00 — 1

4 Grapes are selling for $4.20 per kilogram. For what amount will you pay $2.10?
(A) 20 g (B) 50 g (C) 200 g (D) 500 g — 1

5 The price of a car is $25 000 before GST. What is the price after the GST (10%) has been added?
(A) $25 025 (B) $25 250 (C) $26 000 (D) $27 500 — 1

6 Which is the most expensive per litre?
(A) 2 L for $9.00 (B) 3 L for $12.00 (C) 4 L for $15.00 (D) 6 L for $23.00 — 1

7 Five bottles of juice cost $16.50. What is the price of each bottle?
(A) $3.30 (B) $3.50 C $3.70 (D) $3.90 — 1

8 Which is the best buy?
(A) 1 kg for $13.00 (B) 2 kg for $25.00 (C) 10 kg for $125.00 (D) 20 kg for $225.00 — 1

9 What will you pay for a book if it is originally priced at $35.00 but a discount of 10% is given?
(A) $3.50 (B) $31.50 (C) $33.50 (D) $38.50 — 1

10 What is the price per kilogram if you buy 25 kg for $80.00?
(A) $2.75 (B) $3.20 (C) $3.60 (D) $3.75 — 1

11 A shop offers: 'Buy two and get the second for half-price'. If the full price is $6.00 what will you pay for two items with this offer?
(A) $6.50 (B) $7.50 (C) $9.00 $12.00 — 1

12 How much is each item if they are selling for $15 per dozen?
(A) $1.25 (B) $1.40 (C) $1.50 (D) $1.75 — 1

13 Which price per litre is different from the others?
(A) 500 mL for $2.00 (B) 600 mL for $2.50 (C) 1 L for $4.00 (D) 1.5 L for $6.00 — 1

14 What is the most expensive rate?
(A) $3 for 40 minutes (B) $2 for $\frac{1}{2}$ hour (C) $5 for 1 hour (D) $7.20 for $1\frac{1}{2}$ hours — 1

15 $1 buys 50 g. At that price how many grams can be bought for $60.00?
(A) 20 (B) 300 (C) 1200 (D) 3000 — 1

GST, Discounts and Best Buys Non-calculator (Level 2 Test)

PART B Write answers only in the space provided.

16 If apples cost 60c each, how much will you pay for four? ________ [1]

17 If 5 kg costs \$8.00, what is the price per kilogram? ________ [1]

18 How much is a discount of 20% on a belt priced at \$70.00? ________ [1]

19 How much is the GST if the price including GST is \$22.00? ________ [1]

20 If oil costs \$3.50 per litre, what will 12 L cost? ________ [1]

21 What is the price per kilogram if 200 g costs 80 cents? ________ [1]

22 How many cakes costing 70 cents each can be bought with \$4.00? ________ [1]

23 What is the lowest price that can be paid for seven buns if they can be bought for 65c each or five for \$3.00? ________ [1]

24 How much will you save on 6 kg if you buy for \$1.25 per kilogram instead of \$1.30 per kilogram? ________ [1]

25 If you save 4 cents per litre on every litre of petrol, how much will you save when buying 60 L? ________ [1]

PART C Show all working.

26 Too-right toilet rolls can be bought in 'small' packs of six for \$5.25, 'medium' packs of eight for \$7 or 'large' packs of 12 for \$10.50.

a How much will you pay for four small packs? [1 mark]

____

b How much will you pay for three medium packs? [1 mark]

____

c Which is the cheapest way to buy 24 rolls of Too-right toilet paper? Justify your answer. [2 marks]

____

____

27 A toy is marked for sale for \$42.00 at a shop which is offering 25% off marked prices.

a How much will you pay for the toy from this shop? [1 mark]

____

b Another shop has the same toy marked at \$40.00 and is offering 30% off marked prices. How much will you save by buying the toy from the second shop? [2 marks]

____

____

28 a What is the price per kilogram if you buy a 5 kg pack for \$52.00? [1 mark]

____

b What is the price per kilogram if you buy a 7 kg pack for \$71.40? [1 mark]

____

c A 9 kg pack costs \$90.90. Which of the three packs offers the cheapest unit price and what is that price? [1 mark]

____

d How much would you save on the 5 kg pack if it could be bought for the unit price of the 7 kg pack? [1 mark]

____

e Give a reason why you might choose to buy the 5 kg pack. [1 mark]

____

29 Cans of cat food can be bought for \$1.20 each. A carton of 12 of the cans can be bought for \$12.00.

a How much do you save on 12 cans when you buy a carton? [1 mark]

____

b A special promotion on the single cans offers 'buy two and get a third one free'. When the promotion is on which is the cheapest way to buy 12 cans and by how much? [2 marks]

____

____

Total marks ___ / 40

LEVEL 2 TEST   PART A

Time allowed: 40 minutes

Marks

1 Some insect repellent costs $6.50 before GST. How much will it cost after the 10% GST is added?
(A) $6.95   (B) $7.05   (C) $7.15   (D) $7.25   1

2 Which is the cheapest rate?
(A) 2 for $3.50   (B) 3 for $5.20   (C) 5 for $8.90   (D) 7 for $12.50   1

3 DVDs are selling under a 'buy two get one free' offer. If three DVDs are bought the cheapest one is free. How much would be charged for three DVDs priced at $24.98, $15.98 and $19.98?
(A) $35.96   (B) $40.96   (C) $44.96   (D) $60.94   1

4 Which is the best buy?
(A) 10 kg for $6.50   (B) 20 kg for $12.50   (C) 25 kg for $15.50   (D) 50 kg for $29.95   1

5 A shop offers a discount of 20% off all marked prices. What will you pay for a jumper marked at $64?
(A) $44   (B) $51.20   (C) $48   (D) $56.80   1

6 Which is the most expensive price for each item?
(A) 6 for $12.90   (B) 8 for $16.80   (C) 9 for $18.90   (D) 11 for $23.10   1

7 What is the lowest price that can be paid for 15 buns if they sell for 45c each or six for $2.50?
(A) $6.25   (B) $7.50   (C) $6.75   (D) $6.35   1

8 Samara buys 450 g of grapes for $1.35. What is the price per kilogram?
(A) 60c   (B) $3.33   (C) $3.00   (D) $6.08   1

9 Which is the best buy?
(A) 700 g for $13.85   (B) 1 kg for $19.50   (C) 1.5 kg for $29.00   (D) 4 kg for $77.95   1

10 Which is closest to the amount you will save if given a 17% discount on a suit priced at $329?
(A) $56   (B) $19   (C) $49   (D) $66   1

11 Certain apples are selling for 68c each. What is the most number of apples that can be bought for $10.00?
(A) 6   (B) 7   (C) 14   (D) 15   1

12 A solar panel is for sale for $2552 including 10% GST. How much is the GST?
(A) $25.52   (B) $255.20   (C) $225.00   (D) $232.00   1

13 Ingrid bought 12 drinks for $10.20. At that price how much will seven drinks cost?
(A) $5.45   (B) $5.95   (C) $7.30   (D) $6.30   1

14 Which is the best value?
(A) 70 g for $0.55   (B) 110 g for $0.95   (C) 235 g for $2.10   (D) 620 g for $5   1

15 Which is the best buy?
(A) 500 mL for $2.75   (B) 600 mL for $3.10   (C) 750 mL for $4.00   (D) 800 mL for $4.40   1

GST, Discounts and Best Buys Calculator Allowed (Level 2 Test)

PART B Write answers only in the space provided.

16 If a bottle of soda water costs 75c, how much will you pay for 15 bottles? ______________ [1]

17 If a dozen eggs costs $6.60, how much is each egg? ______________ [1]

18 How much is a discount of 35% on an item for sale for $560? ______________ [1]

19 If mangoes are selling for $4.80 per kilogram, how much will you pay for 2.5 kg? ______________ [1]

20 If you buy 600 mL of juice for $3.90, what is the price per litre? ______________ [1]

21 How much will you pay for electrical work if the price before GST is $875 and 10% GST is then added? ______________ [1]

22 What will you pay for a mattress priced at $895 if you receive a discount of 40%? ______________ [1]

23 Selma paid $49.50 for petrol. If the price was $1.25 per litre, how much petrol did she buy? ________ [1]

24 If 0.4 kg of mince costs $4.70, how much would 2 kg cost? ______________ [1]

25 What was the price before GST if the total with GST is $550? ______________ [1]

PART C Show all working.

26 **a** A shop sells 24 cans of passionfruit drink for $10.08. What is the price per can? [1 mark]

____

b Each can holds 375 mL. What is the price per litre? [1 mark]

____

c The shop also sells 1.5 L bottles of the same drink for $1.70. How much more would you need to pay for the same quantity as 24 cans if you bought bottles instead? [3 marks]

____

____

27 Which is the better buy: 375 g for $3.15 or 1.6 kg for $13.44? Justify your answer with appropriate calculations. [2 marks]

____

____

28 A shirt is for sale for $79.97 including GST (10%).

a How much is the GST? [1 mark]

____

b The shop offers a discount of 15% for cash. What is the cash price? [1 mark]

____

c Another shop has the same shirts for sale but only in packs of three for $190. Give a reason why you might choose to buy the pack of three. [1 mark]

____

d Give a reason why you might choose to buy a shirt from the first shop. [1 mark]

____

29 Travis received two quotes for replacing some tiles. One quote was $860 including GST. The other was for $750 + GST.

a How much was the second quote with GST (10%) added? [1 mark]

____

b Which quote should Travis take? Justify your answer. [1 mark]

____

____

30 Joy got 20% off when she bought a boxset of DVDs and paid $50. What was the original price? [2 marks]

____

____

Total marks /40

LEVEL 2 TEST

PART A

Time allowed: 40 minutes

	Marks
1 In simplest form the ratio 12 : 6 is: (A) 4 : 3 (B) 2 : 1 (C) 1 : 2 (D) 6 : 1	1
2 In a class of 19 students there are 11 boys. The ratio of boys to girls is: (A) 19 : 11 (B) 11 : 19 (C) 8 : 11 (D) 11 : 8	1
3 The ratio of old to new books in a bookcase is 3 : 8. The fraction of books that are old is: (A) $\frac{3}{8}$ (B) $\frac{8}{3}$ (C) $\frac{3}{11}$ (D) $\frac{8}{11}$	1
4 If there are six boys for every five girls at a party then the ratio of girls to boys is: (A) 6 : 5 (B) 5 : 6 (C) 6 : 11 (D) 5 : 11	1
5 Which is **not** equal to 3 : 4? (A) 6 : 8 (B) 30 : 40 (C) 8 : 9 (D) 51 : 68	1
6 $\frac{5}{7}$ of students in a class are girls. The ratio of girls to boys is: (A) 5 : 7 (B) 2 : 7 (C) 2 : 5 (D) 5 : 2	1
7 In simplest form the ratio 15 : 18 is: (A) 5 : 8 (B) 1 : 3 (C) 5 : 6 (D) 5 : 9	1
8 The ratio 0.7 to 3 is: (A) 30 : 7 (B) 7 : 30 (C) 3 : 70 (D) 70 : 3	1
9 The ratio of hens to ducks is 5 to 2. If there are 20 hens, how many ducks are there? (A) 17 (B) 8 (C) 50 (D) 6	1
10 There are 20 children in kindergarten. The ratio of boys to girls is 3 : 2. How many girls are there? (A) 4 (B) 6 (C) 8 (D) 12	1
11 The ratio $4 : \frac{1}{2}$ is the same as: (A) 2 : 1 (B) 1 : 2 (C) 1 : 8 (D) 8 : 1	1
12 Meg and Barney share \$50 000 in the ratio 4 : 1. What is Barney's share? (A) \$10 000 (B) \$12 500 (C) \$15 000 (D) \$25 000	1
13 In simplest form the ratio 56 : 24 is: (A) 7 : 3 (B) 8 : 3 (C) 10 : 7 (D) 28 : 12	1
14 There are 18 puppies out of a total of 72 dogs at a shelter. The ratio of puppies to other dogs is: (A) 1 : 3 (B) 1 : 4 (C) 1 : 5 (D) 1 : 6	1
15 The ratio of trucks to cars on a road is 3 : 10. If there are 390 trucks, how many cars are there? (A) 117 (B) 397 (C) 900 (D) 1300	1

Ratio Non-calculator **(Level 2 Test)**

PART B Write answers only in the space provided. Give all ratios in simplest form.

16 The ratio of pink to blue is 3 : 4. What is the ratio of blue to pink? ________________ [1]

17 Simplify 9 : 15. ________________ [1]

18 There are 12 men and 8 women at a meeting. What is the ratio of men to women? ________________ [1]

19 Write 28 : 7 in simplest form. ________________ [1]

20 In a group of 30 children there are 18 girls. What is the ratio of boys to girls? ________________ [1]

21 Write the ratio 1.8 : 4.5 in simplest form. ________________ [1]

22 The ratio of red to green apples in a bowl is 7 : 2. What fraction of the apples is green? ________________ [1]

23 For every nine white cars in a yard there are two red cars. If there are 18 red cars, how many cars are white? ________________ [1]

24 Write $9 : \frac{2}{3}$ in simplest form. ________________ [1]

25 The ratio of red to blue marbles in a bag is 8 : 3. If there are 48 red marbles, how many marbles are blue? ________________ [1]

PART C Show all working.

26 A box holds 8 green, 6 blue and 16 yellow pegs.

a What is the ratio, in simplest form, of:

i green to yellow pegs? [1 mark]

____

ii yellow to blue pegs? [1 mark]

____

b Another box has green and blue pegs in the ratio 8 : 5. Which of the two boxes has the higher ratio of blue to green pegs? Justify your answer. [2 marks]

____

____

____

27 The ratio of black to white tiles in a flooring pattern is 2 : 3.

a If 60 black tiles are used, how many white should be used? [1 mark]

____

b If 48 white tiles are used, how many black tiles should be used? [1 mark]

____

c If 520 tiles are used altogether how many should be black and how many white? [2 marks]

____

____

28 There are twenty-four chocolates in a box. Ten are dark chocolate and the rest are milk chocolate.

a What is the ratio, in simplest form, of dark to milk chocolates? [1 mark]

____

b Nova ate two dark chocolates. What is the new ratio of dark to milk chocolates? [1 mark]

____

c Next Nova eats two milk chocolates from the box. Nova says that the ratio is now back to what it was at the beginning. Is she correct? Explain why or why not. [2 marks]

____

____

29 Glenn and Dave share a prize of $12 000. Glenn receives $8000 and Dave gets the rest.

a What is the ratio of Glenn's share to Dave's share? [1 mark]

____

b If, instead, they share the money in the ratio 5 : 3 how much more, or less, will Dave receive? [2 marks]

____

____

Total marks [/40]

LEVEL 2 TEST

PART A

Time allowed: 40 minutes

Marks

1 There are 84 women and 56 men at a conference. In simplest form the ratio of men to women is:
(A) 2 : 3 (B) 3 : 2 (C) 4 : 3 (D) 3 : 4 [1]

2 The ratio $3\frac{1}{2} : 5\frac{1}{2}$ is:
(A) 3 : 5 (B) 1 : 2 (C) 5 : 8 (D) 7 : 11 [1]

3 The ratio 40 minutes to 3 hours is:
(A) 40 : 3 (B) 2 : 15 (C) 2 : 9 (D) 15 : 2 [1]

4 The ratio of green to gold balloons is 5 : 3. If there are 15 gold balloons, how many are green?
(A) 25 (B) 9 (C) 17 (D) 12 [1]

5 What is 2.5 : 0.5 in simplest form?
(A) 1 : 5 (B) 5 : 1 (C) 2 : 1 (D) 1 : 2 [1]

6 Of the 18 babies born in a hospital one day, 10 were boys. What was the ratio of girls to boys?
(A) 5 : 9 (B) 4 : 9 (C) 4 : 5 (D) 5 : 4 [1]

7 $\frac{2}{3} : \frac{3}{4} =$
(A) 1 : 2 (B) 2 : 1 (C) 3 : 4 (D) 8 : 9 [1]

8 Cheapa pens cost 60 cents each while Bettera pens cost $2.40 each. The ratio of the cost of Bettera to Cheapa pens is:
(A) 4 : 1 (B) 2 : 5 (C) 5 : 2 (D) 25 : 1 [1]

9 The ratio of salt to sugar in a sauce is 3 : 50. If there is 270 mg of salt in an average serve, how much sugar is there?
(A) 1.8 g (B) 4.5 g (C) 16.2 g (D) 5.4 g [1]

10 The ratio 90 000 to 1.44 million is:
(A) 1 : 16 (B) 3 : 40 (C) 5 : 8 (D) 3 : 400 [1]

11 The area of Victoria is about 237 600 km^2 while that of NSW is 809 400 km^2. The ratio of the size of Victoria to the size of NSW is closest to:
(A) 3 : 17 (B) 2 : 9 (C) 8 : 27 (D) 1 : 5 [1]

12 If $\frac{7}{11}$ of pups in a litter are male, the ratio of male to female pups is:
(A) 7 : 11 (B) 11 : 7 (C) 7 : 4 (D) 4 : 7 [1]

13 A rectangle has length and width in the ratio 6 : 5. If it is 30 cm wide, what is the perimeter?
(A) 55 cm (B) 66 cm (C) 110 cm (D) 132 cm [1]

14 Bill and Ben share $60 000 in the ratio 5 : 3. What is Ben's share?
(A) $20 000 (B) $22 500 (C) $25 000 (D) $24 000 [1]

15 A sum of money is divided in the ratio 3 : 5. If the smaller share is $75 000, what is the sum?
(A) $200 000 (B) $225 000 (C) $240 000 (D) $250 000 [1]

Ratio Calculator Allowed **(Level 2 Test)**

PART B Write answers only in the space provided.

16 What is the ratio of 4 months to a year in simplest form? ______________ [1]

17 There are 18 men and 15 women at a conference. What is the ratio of men to women? ___________ [1]

18 Write in simplest form: 90 cm to 1.5 m. ______________ [1]

19 Simplify $2\frac{3}{4} : 1\frac{1}{2}$. ______________ [1]

20 The ratio of blue to red marbles is 3 to 7. What is the percentage of blue marbles? ______________ [1]

21 The ratio of ripe to unripe tomatoes is 3 to 8. If there are 24 ripe tomatoes, how many are unripe? ______________ [1]

22 Jon sat for an exam where there were 108 questions. The ratio of correct to incorrect responses given by Jon was 7 : 5. How many questions did Jon get correct? ______________ [1]

23 Three-quarters of teachers at a school are female. What is the ratio of male to female teachers? ______ [1]

24 Write the ratio 0.6 : 0.08 in simplest form. ______________ [1]

25 The ratio of adults to children is 12 : 5. If there are 60 children, how many adults are there? ________ [1]

PART C Show all working.

26 The ratio of red to white roses in a display is 2 : 9.

a If 198 white roses are used, how many red roses are used? [1 mark]

____

b If 36 red roses are used, how many white roses are used? [1 mark]

____

c Jerry uses a total of 297 roses. How many of each colour did he use? [2 marks]

____

____

27 Jill invested \$12 500 and Kate invested \$22 500 in their new business.

a What is the ratio of Jill's investment to Kate's investment? [1 mark]

____

b The business makes a first profit of \$7000. If Jill and Kate share the profit in the ratio of their investments how much will each get? [2 marks]

____

____

28 For the first six weeks of a holiday the ratio of wet days to fine days was 2 to 5.

a How many days were wet? [1 mark]

____

b For the next four weeks the ratio of wet to fine days was 3 to 11. What was the ratio of wet days to fine days for the whole 10 weeks of the holiday? [2 marks]

____

____

29 Scott has 120 blocks. The blocks are either blue or red. 72 blocks are cubes and the rest are cylinders.

a What is the ratio of cubes to cylinders? [1 mark]

____

b One-third of the cubes and one-quarter of the cylinders are red. What is the ratio of red to blue blocks? [2 marks]

____

____

c What is the ratio of red cubes to blue cylinders? [1 mark]

____

d Scott got 40 new blocks. The new ratio of cubes to cylinders is 9 : 7. How many of the new blocks were cubes? [1 mark]

____

Total marks ___ / 40

PRETEST

PART A

Time allowed: 15 minutes **Total marks: 15**

Marks

1 How long is it from 7:40 pm until 8:20 pm?
(A) 20 minutes (B) 40 minutes (C) 80 minutes (D) 100 minutes 1

2 What is the time 15 hours after 8:30 am?
(A) 10:30 pm (B) 11:30 pm (C) 12:30 am (D) 1:30 am 1

3 What time is shown on this clock?

(A) 7:10 (B) 10:34 (C) 7:50 (D) 6:50 1

4 How long is it from 9:18 am until 3:37 pm?
(A) 5 hours 19 minutes (B) 5 hours 41 minutes (C) 6 hours 19 minutes (D) 6 hours 41 minutes 1

5 A television program begins at 1945. What time is this?
(A) a quarter to seven (B) a quarter to eight (C) a quarter to nine (D) a quarter to ten 1

6 What time is it $2\frac{1}{4}$ hours after 3:55 pm?
(A) 5:10 pm (B) 5:20 pm (C) 6:10 pm (D) 6:20 pm 1

7 What is the date 15 days after 25 April?
(A) 8 May (B) 9 May (C) 10 May (D) 11 May 1

8 How many seconds is 7.25 minutes?
(A) 435 (B) 445 (C) 475 (D) 725 1

9 Eli worked $2\frac{1}{2}$ hours on Friday, $1\frac{3}{4}$ hours on Saturday and $7\frac{3}{4}$ hours on Sunday. How many hours altogether did Eli work?
(A) 11 hours 20 minutes (B) 11 hours 12 minutes (C) $11\frac{3}{4}$ hours (D) 12 hours 1

10 How long is it from a quarter past four until a quarter to nine on the same morning?
(A) $4\frac{1}{2}$ hours (B) $4\frac{3}{4}$ hours (C) $5\frac{1}{4}$ hours (D) $5\frac{1}{2}$ hours 1

11 How long is it from 9 pm Wednesday until 7 am Friday?
(A) 26 hours (B) 34 hours (C) 38 hours (D) 46 hours 1

12 This watch has lost one of its hands.
Which of these times could the watch be showing?

(A) 7:00 (B) 8:00 (C) 7:30 (D) 8:30 1

13 A movie starts at 7:45 pm and runs for 2 hours 40 minutes. What time does it finish?
(A) 9:05 pm (B) 9:25 pm (C) 10:15 pm (D) 10:25 pm 1

14 Which of these evening times is the latest?
(A) 8:15 (B) 18:50 (C) a quarter to eight (D) all the same 1

15 How long is it from 0925 until 1750?
(A) 8 hours 15 minutes (B) 8 hours 25 minutes (C) 10 hours 15 minutes (D) 10 hours 25 minutes 1

Total marks / 15

Graphs of Authentic Data Calculator Allowed

LEVEL 2 TEST PART A

Time allowed: 40 minutes

Marks

Questions 1 to 12 use the graph on the right.

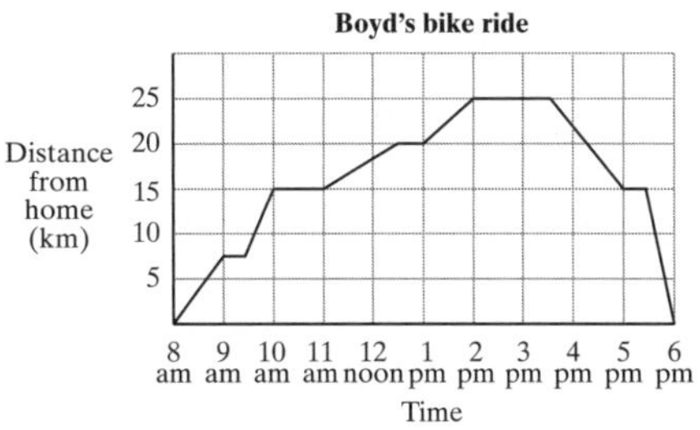

1 At what time did Boyd leave home?

(A) 8 am (B) 10 am (C) 2 pm (D) 6 pm 1

2 When did Boyd first stop?

(A) 9 am (B) 9:30 am (C) 2 pm (D) 3:30 pm 1

3 How long was Boyd away from home?

(A) 25 minutes (B) 8 hours (C) 9 hours (D) 10 hours 1

4 How far was Boyd from home at 10:30 am?

(A) 10 km (B) 15 km (C) 25 km (D) 35 km 1

5 Boyd is stopped whenever the graph is a:

(A) straight line (B) horizontal line (C) vertical line (D) perpendicular line 1

6 When did Boyd begin his journey home?

(A) 1 pm (B) 2 pm (C) 3:30 pm (D) 5:30 pm 1

7 What was Boyd's average speed in the first hour?

(A) 15 km/h (B) 10 km/h (C) 7.5 km/h (D) 5 km/h 1

8 How far did Boyd travel altogether?

(A) 25 km (B) 40 km (C) 50 km (D) 75 km 1

9 At which of these times was Boyd 15 km from home?

(A) 9:30 am (B) 11:30 am (C) 2:15 pm (D) 5:15 pm 1

10 Between which two times was Boyd travelling at the fastest average speed?

(A) 8 am and 9 am (B) 11 am and 12:30 pm (C) 2 pm and 3:15 pm (D) 5:30 pm and 6 pm 1

11 Between which two times was Boyd travelling at the slowest average speed?

(A) 8 am and 9 am (B) 11 am and 12:30 pm (C) 1 pm and 2 pm (D) 3:30 pm and 5 pm 1

12 What was Boyd's average speed between 9:30 am and 10 am?

(A) 7.5 km/h (B) 10 km/h (C) 15 km/h (D) 30 km/h 1

13 Which graph could **not** represent a real journey?

(A)
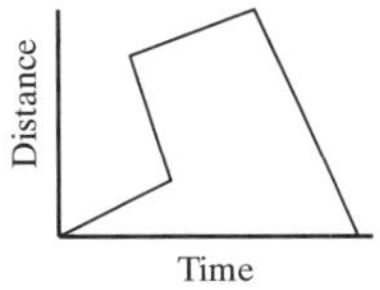

(B)
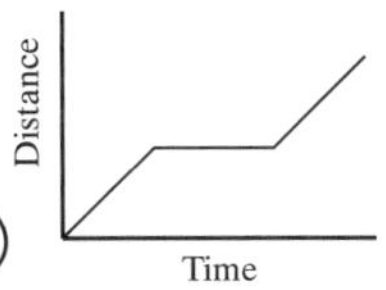

(C)
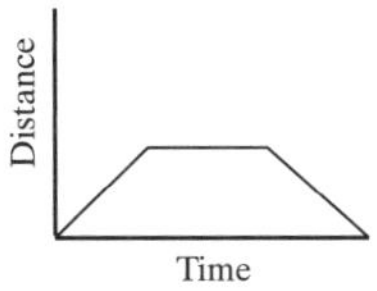

(D)
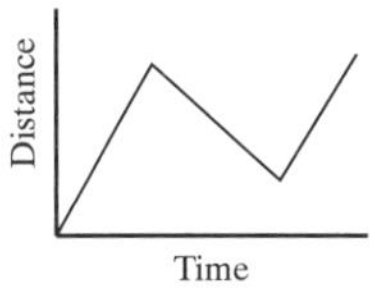

1

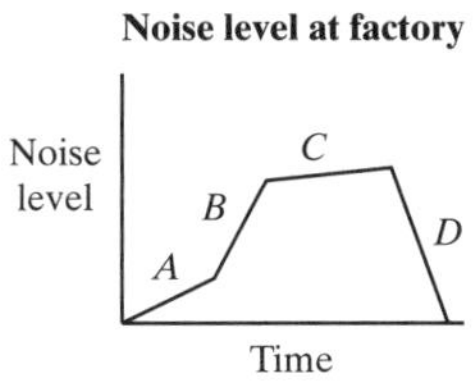

14 When is the noise level in this factory decreasing?

(A) A (B) B (C) C (D) D 1

15 When is the noise level in the factory increasing at the fastest rate?

(A) A (B) B (C) C (D) D 1

PART B Write answers only in the space provided.

All the questions in Part B refer to the graph on the right.

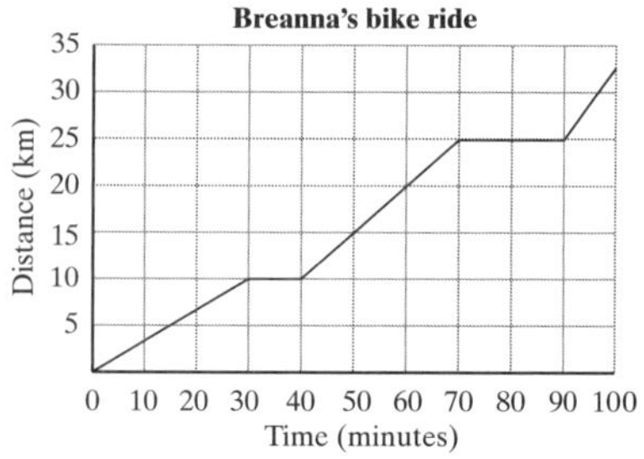

16 How far did Breanna ride in the first 10 minutes? ________________ [1]

17 How long was Breanna's first stop to rest? ________________ [1]

18 What was Breanna's average speed (in km/h) for the first half hour? ________________ [1]

19 When was Breanna travelling at the fastest average speed? ________________ [1]

20 How far had Breanna travelled after one hour? ________________ [1]

21 After how many minutes had she travelled 15 km? ________________ [1]

22 For how long was Breanna actually riding? ________________ [1]

23 How far did Breanna travel altogether? ________________ [1]

24 How far did Breanna travel in the last 10 minutes? ________________ [1]

25 Briefly explain why it is not possible to say how far Breanna is from her starting point at the finish.

____ [1]

PART C Show all working.

26 Vera left home at 9:30 am to travel to her sister's house. She travelled at an average speed of 60 km/h for two hours. She then stopped for half an hour before continuing, travelling 75 km in the next hour. She then arrived at her sister's house and stopped for two and a half hours. Finally Vera travelled straight home without stopping, arriving at 6 pm.

a Show this information on a travel graph. [4 marks]

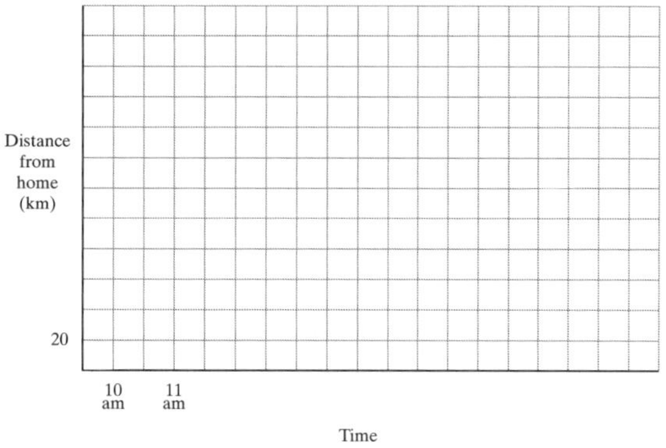

b How far did Vera travel altogether? [1 mark]

____

c What was Vera's average speed on the journey home? [2 marks]

____

d How much longer did the journey to her sister's house take than the return journey (not counting the time Vera was stopped)? [2 marks]

____

27

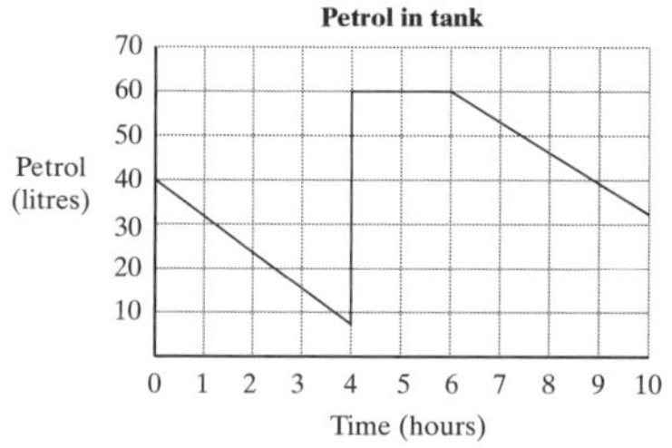

This graph shows the amount of petrol in a car over time.

a How much petrol was in the car at the start? [1 mark]

____

b What does the vertical line on the graph represent? [1 mark]

____

c What does the horizontal line on the graph represent? [1 mark]

____

d How much petrol was put in the car when it was refuelled? [1 mark]

____

e How much more petrol was used in the first hour than in the last hour? [2 marks]

____

Total marks /40

Algebra

PRETEST

Time allowed: 15 minutes **Total marks: 12**

Marks

1 What number comes next in this pattern? 5, 13, 21, 29, 37, ?

(A) 41 (B) 43 (C) 45 (D) 49 [1]

2 A pattern is formed by beginning with 2 and then adding 3 each time. What is the sixth number in this pattern?

(A) 15 (B) 17 (C) 18 (D) 20 [1]

3 Which number could replace ☺ to make this number sentence true? ☺ + 6 = 20 – ☺

(A) 4 (B) 5 (C) 6 (D) 7 [1]

4 What is the missing number in this pattern? 23, 37, ?, 65, 79, 93

(A) 49 (B) 50 (C) 51 (D) 53 [1]

This pattern is made with matchsticks. Questions 5 to 10 use this pattern.

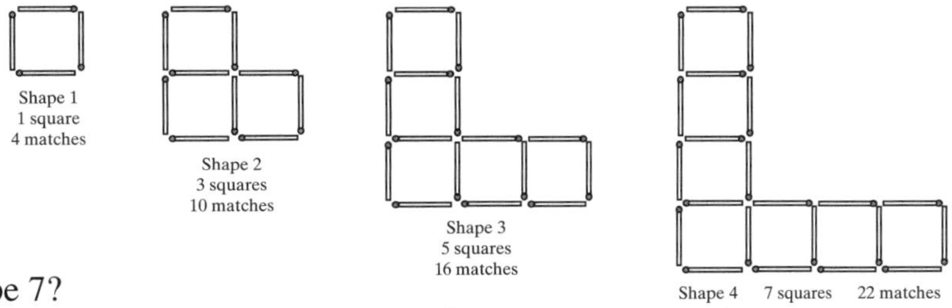

5 How many squares are in Shape 7?

(A) 9 (B) 11 (C) 13 (D) 15 [1]

6 What is the rule for the number of squares?

(A) 2 × shape number (B) 2 × shape number – 1

(C) 2 × shape number + 1 (D) 3 × shape number – 1 [1]

7 What number shape in the pattern will have 25 squares?

(A) 11 (B) 12 (C) 13 (D) 14 [1]

8 How many matches will be used in Shape 6?

(A) 36 (B) 34 (C) 28 (D) 26 [1]

9 What is the rule for the number of matches?

(A) 6 × shape number – 2 (B) 5 × shape number – 1

(C) 5 × shape number + 1 (D) 6 × shape number + 2 [1]

10 What number shape has 304 matches?

(A) 51 (B) 56 (C) 61 (D) 66 [1]

11 What number comes next in this pattern? 1, 1, 2, 3, 5, 8, 13, 21, ?

(A) 26 (B) 30 (C) 32 (D) 34 [1]

12 These are the first six numbers in a pattern: 3, 4, 6, 10, 18, 34.
Lily said the rule to get the next number is to double the previous number and then subtract 2.
Daisy said the rule is to take away 1 and then double. Who is correct?

(A) both Lily and Daisy (B) neither Lily nor Daisy

(C) Lily only (D) Daisy only [1]

Total marks /12

LEVEL 1 TEST PART A

Time allowed: 40 minutes

Marks

1 $3xy$ means:
(A) $3 + x + y$ (B) $3 + x \times y$ (C) $3 \times x + y$ (D) $3 \times x \times y$ 1

2 $2x + 5x =$
(A) $7x$ (B) $10x$ (C) $7x^2$ (D) $10x^2$ 1

3 $m + m + m + m + m =$
(A) $5 + m$ (B) $5m$ (C) m^5 (D) 5^m 1

4 The number 2 more than x is:
(A) $x + 2$ (B) $2x$ (C) $2 - x$ (D) z 1

5 $5 + a =$
(A) $5a$ (B) 6 (C) f (D) cannot be simplified 1

6 If $x = 4$ then $3x + 5 =$
(A) 17 (B) 39 (C) 27 (D) 32 1

7 $a + a + b + b + b + c =$
(A) $6abc$ (B) a^2b^3c (C) $2a + 3bc$ (D) $2a + 3b + c$ 1

8 Which is **not** correct?
(A) $x \times y = xy$ (B) $x \div y = \frac{x}{y}$ (C) $x \times x = 2x$ (D) $x + y = y + x$ 1

9 If $k = 2$ and $m = 5$, then $3km =$
(A) 325 (B) 90 (C) 30 (D) 17 1

10 $6m + 2n + 3m + 5n =$
(A) $16mn$ (B) $9m + 7n$ (C) $8m + 8n$ (D) $9n + 7m$ 1

11 $3a \times 5a =$
(A) $8a^2$ (B) $15a$ (C) $15a^2$ (D) $30a$ 1

12 If $p = 4$, then $3p^2 =$
(A) 3×4^2 (B) $(3 \times 4)^2$ (C) 34^2 (D) $3^2 \times 4$ 1

13 $8 - 3h + 1 =$
(A) $7 - 3h$ (B) $7 + 3h$ (C) $9 - 3h$ (D) $6h$ 1

14 $6q - q =$
(A) 6 (B) $5q$ (C) $6p$ (D) none of these 1

15 $\frac{24a}{4} =$
(A) $2a$ (B) $6a$ (C) $20a$ (D) $21a$ 1

PART B Write answers only in the space provided.

16 Simplify $3x + 2x + 4x$. ________________ 1

17 If $d = 3$, find the value of $2d - 5$. ________________ 1

18 $4a \times 3 =$ ________________ 1

19 $6m \times 2m =$ ________________ 1

20 $n + 5 + 3n + 4 =$ ________________ 1

21 Use symbols to write the sum of x and y. ________________ 1

22 $20z \div 5 =$ ________________ 1

23 Simplify $\frac{6x}{3}$. ________________ 1

24 If $x = 3$, what is the value of x^2? ________________ 1

25 Simplify $3ab \times 2a$. ________________ 1

PART C Show all working.

26 Fill in the missing values in the table. 3 marks

x	1	3		11	28
$x + 7$	8		13	18	

27 Simplify:

a $8p + 2p$ 1 mark

____

b $8p \times 2p$ 1 mark

____

c $8p \div 2p$ 1 mark

____

28 a Briefly explain why it is not necessary to know the value of y when evaluating the expression $3x + 8y + 5x - 2y + 2x - 6y$. 1 mark

____

b Find the value of $3x + 8y + 5x - 2y + 2x - 6y$ when $x = 57$. 1 mark

____

29 a Why cannot $2a + 3b$ be simplified? 1 mark

____

b Find the value of $2a + 3b$ when $a = 4$ and $b = 5$. 1 mark

____

30 Write expressions for:

a the number of cents in x dollars 1 mark

____

b the number of days in n weeks 1 mark

____

c the number 5 less than y 1 mark

____

31 Simplify:

a $a \times 5 + 3a$ 1 mark

____

b $9t + 7u - 4t + 2u$ 1 mark

____

Total marks /40

Algebra Calculator Allowed

LEVEL 2 TEST PART A

Time allowed: 40 minutes

Marks

1 If $t = 5$, then $2t^2 =$

(A) 625 (B) 225 (C) 100 (D) 50 — 1

2 $9x + 5y - 2x + 3y =$

(A) $7x + 8y$ (B) $7x + 2y$ (C) $5x + 8y$ (D) $5x + 2y$ — 1

3 $\frac{8m}{4m} =$

(A) $2m$ (B) 2 (C) $4m$ (D) $4m^2$ — 1

4 $a + b$ is the same as:

(A) c (B) $b + a$ (C) ab (D) $b - a$ — 1

5 $5x \times 3x =$

(A) $8x$ (B) $8x^2$ (C) $15x$ (D) $15x^2$ — 1

6 $9p \div p =$

(A) $8p$ (B) 8 (C) 9 (D) cannot be simplified — 1

7 $7h + 4h - h =$

(A) 10 (B) 11 (C) $10h$ (D) $11h$ — 1

8 If $m = 3$ and $n = 2$, then $4mn - 5n =$

(A) 9 (B) 10 (C) 14 (D) 380 — 1

9 Which expression is twice the product of a and b?

(A) $2a + b$ (B) $2ab$ (C) $2a + 2b$ (D) $(ab)^2$ — 1

10 $6k + 5 - 5k =$

(A) $k + 5$ (B) $5k$ (C) $6k$ (D) $11k - 5$ — 1

11 $8x + 11y =$

(A) $19xy$ (B) $19x + y$ (C) $19(x + y)$ (D) cannot be simplified — 1

12 $x \times y \div z =$

(A) $\frac{xy}{z}$ (B) $\frac{xz}{y}$ (C) $\frac{x}{yz}$ (D) $\frac{yz}{x}$ — 1

13 $w \times 3 - 2 =$

(A) w (B) $3w - 2$ (C) $w^3 - 2$ (D) none of these — 1

14 $\frac{6ab}{3b} =$

(A) $2a$ (B) $3a$ (C) $2ab$ (C) $3ab$ — 1

15 If $p = 4$, $q = 7$ and $r = 5$, then $pr - q =$

(A) 2 (B) 13 (C) 23 (D) 38 — 1

Algebra Calculator Allowed (Level 2 Test)

PART B Write answers only in the space provided.

16 Simplify $3x + 5x + 9y - 4y$. ______ [1]

17 $4p \times 3p =$ ______ [1]

18 $2 \times 6a - 3 \times 4a =$ ______ [1]

19 Simplify $\frac{6t}{9}$. ______ [1]

20 Write an expression for the number of minutes in x hours. ______ [1]

21 Simplify $5a + 6b - 3a + 4$. ______ [1]

22 If $a = 4$, what is the value of $2 \times (a + 3)$. ______ [1]

23 Simplify $6pq \times 2p$. ______ [1]

24 Write an expression for the number 8 less than x. ______ [1]

25 Simplify $x + x + x + y + y + y + y$. ______ [1]

PART C Show all working.

26 Simplify $3 \times 2x + 5x \times 4 + 6x$. [2 marks]

______

______

27 Fill in the missing values in the table. [2 marks]

x	0	1	3	7		12
$2x + 3$	3	5	9		23	27

28 If $x = 8$ and $y = 5$ find the value of:

a $9 - y$ [1 mark]

______

b $6x$ [1 mark]

______

c $3x - 4y$ [1 mark]

______

d xy^2 [1 mark]

______

29 a Simplify $3m + 4n + 5 - n + 7m$. [1 mark]

______

b Find the value of $3m + 4n + 5 - n + 7m$ when $m = 6$ and $n = 1$. [1 mark]

______

30 A pattern of triangles is made with matchsticks. The number of matchsticks at each stage is two more than three times the number of triangles.

a If m is the number of matchsticks and t the number of triangles, write an expression for m in terms of t. [1 mark]

______

b How many matchsticks are needed when there are eight triangles? [1 mark]

______

c Another pattern uses matchsticks to make squares. The number of matchsticks at each stage is 3 less than 4 times the number of squares. Complete the table to show the number of matchsticks, m, used for each of the number of squares, s, between 1 and 6. [1 mark]

s	1	2	3	4	5	6
m						

d For what number of matchsticks are both the number of squares and the number of triangles the same? [2 marks]

______

______

Total marks /40

Algebra Calculator Allowed

LEVEL 3 TEST — PART A

Time allowed: 40 minutes

Marks

1 If $p = -3$, what is the value of $2p^2$?

(A) -18 (B) 18 (C) -36 (D) 36 — 1

2 $3x^2 + 5x^2 =$

(A) $8x^2$ (B) $8x^3$ (C) $8x^4$ (D) cannot be simplified — 1

3 $7 + 6x - 8 + 4x =$

(A) $2x - 1$ (B) $2x + 1$ (C) $10x - 1$ (D) $10x + 1$ — 1

4 The number 6 less than the product of x and $2x$ is:

(A) $3x - 6$ (B) $6 - 3x$ (C) $6 - 2x^2$ (D) $2x^2 - 6$ — 1

5 If $a = 9$, $b = 7$ and $c = 6$, then $a(2b - c) =$

(A) 17 (B) 18 (C) 72 (D) 98 — 1

6 $5p - 3q + 7p - 4q =$

(A) $12p - 7q$ (B) $q - 2p$ (C) $12p - q$ (D) $12p + q$ — 1

7 $\dfrac{12a^2}{4ab} =$

(A) $\dfrac{3a}{b}$ (B) $\dfrac{a}{3b}$ (C) $\dfrac{6}{b}$ (D) $6b$ — 1

8 $6q - 3 \times 2q =$

(A) $12q^2 - 3$ (B) $12q^2 - 6q$ (C) q (D) 0 — 1

9 $-3 + 5m - 6 + 4m =$

(A) $9m - 9$ (B) $-9 + m$ (C) $3 - m$ (D) $3 + 9m$ — 1

10 $x \times (x + x + x + x) =$

(A) $4x^2$ (B) $5x^2$ (C) x^4 (D) $5x$ — 1

11 If $t = -2$ and $q = -5$ then $t - q =$

(A) -7 (B) 7 (C) -3 (D) 3 — 1

12 $3(2b + 4b) =$

(A) $9b$ (B) $18b$ (C) $9b^2$ (D) $18b^2$ — 1

13 What is the result when the product of 3 and y is added to the sum of 3 and $2y$?

(A) $8y$ (B) $y^3 + 2y + 3$ (C) $7y + 3$ (D) $5y + 3$ — 1

14 $8p \div 4p^2 =$

(A) $2p$ (B) $\dfrac{2}{p}$ (C) $\dfrac{p}{2}$ (D) $\dfrac{1}{2p}$ — 1

15 Which rule connects x and y in the table?

x	1	3	7	10
y	5	11	23	32

(A) $y = x + 4$ (B) $y = 2x + 3$ (C) $y = 3x + 2$ (D) $y = 4x + 1$ — 1

Algebra Calculator Allowed (Level 3 Test)

PART B Write answers only in the space provided.

16 Simplify $5a - 2b + 3a - 7b - 9a$. ________________ 1

17 Write an expression for the number of hours in x days. ________________ 1

18 If $p = 7$, find the value of $8p - 2p^2$. ________________ 1

19 $5xy \times 4xz =$ ________________ 1

20 Simplify $2xy \div 6x^2$. ________________ 1

21 $-2 + 6m - 3 - 10m =$ ________________ 1

22 What is the result when $3x$ is subtracted from x? ________________ 1

23 What is half of $8x^2$? ________________ 1

24 If $m = 3$ and $n = -4$, what is the value of $2(3m + n)$. ________________ 1

25 $3x^2 - 5x + 4x - 2x^2 =$ ________________ 1

PART C Show all working.

26 Simplify:

a $8x \times (2x + 3x)$ 1 mark

____

b $6k - 3k + 5 - 2k + 11$ 1 mark

____

27 Simplify:

a $5p \times 2q - 3 \times 4p + 7 \times pq$ 2 marks

____

____

b $12k \div 6 - 6k^2 \div 2k$ 2 marks

____

____

28 Simplify:

a $12n^2 \div (2n + 4n)$ 1 mark

____

b $12n^2 \div 2n + 4n$ 1 mark

____

29 Write a simple expression for the number nine more than the sum of x and seven. 1 mark

____

30 If $y = 8 - 3x$ find the value of:

a y when $x = 5$ 1 mark

____

b x when $y = 5$ 1 mark

____

31 **a** Complete the table for the values of y given that $y = 2x + 1$. 1 mark

x	0	1	2	3	4	5	6	7
y								
z								

b Fill in the values of z using the rule $z = 4x \times (x + 1) + 1$ 2 marks

c Write a rule for z in terms of y. 1 mark

____

Total marks /40

PRETEST

Time allowed: 15 minutes **Total marks: 16**

Marks

1 What number can be added to 7 to give 16?
(A) 7 (B) 9 (C) 11 (D) 23 [1]

2 What is the missing number? $4 \times ? = 8 \times 6$
(A) 3 (B) 9 (C) 10 (D) 12 [1]

3 What number can be multiplied by 4 to give 20?
(A) 5 (B) 6 (C) 16 (D) 20 [1]

4 What number can be subtracted from 24 to leave 8?
(A) 3 (B) 12 (C) 16 (D) 32 [1]

5 What is the missing number? $12 + 24 = 30 + ?$
(A) 6 (B) 8 (C) 18 (D) 42 [1]

6 What number can be divided by 3 to give 12?
(A) 4 (B) 9 (C) 15 (D) 36 [1]

7 Ed thought of a number. He doubled it and added 6 to get 20. What number did he think of?
(A) 5 (B) 6 (C) 7 (D) 8 [1]

8 What is the missing number? $3 \times ? = 7 + 8$
(A) 4 (B) 5 (C) 6 (D) 7 [1]

9 From which number can 9 be subtracted to leave 6?
(A) 3 (B) 9 (C) 12 (D) 15 [1]

10 What is the missing number? $42 - ? = 26$
(A) 14 (B) 16 (C) 24 (D) 26 [1]

11 In 5 years time, Max will be 21. He will then be half his father's age. How old is his father now?
(A) 32 (B) 37 (C) 42 (D) 47 [1]

12 What is the missing number? $246 \div 3 = 100 - ?$
(A) 12 (B) 18 (C) 19 (D) 23 [1]

13 Which is the same as $3 + 9$?
(A) $9 + 3$ (B) $9 - 3$ (C) 9×3 (D) $9 \div 3$ [1]

14 Tilly has 20 beads. She gives six to Holly and half of the rest to Kobie. How many beads does Tilly then have?
(A) 5 (B) 6 (C) 7 (D) 8 [1]

15 $5x + 3x =$
(A) $8x$ (B) $8x^2$ (C) $15x$ (D) $15x^2$ [1]

16 $6a + 9 - 2 =$
(A) $13a$ (B) $15a - 2$ (C) $6a + 7$ (D) $6a - 7$ [1]

Total marks /16

LEVEL 1 TEST PART A

Time allowed: 40 minutes

Marks

1 If $2x = 10$ then $x =$

(A) 5 (B) 8 (C) 12 (D) 20 [1]

2 If $p + 7 = 25$ then $p =$

(A) 18 (B) 19 (C) 12 (D) 32 [1]

3 If $16 - t = 7$ then $t =$

(A) 9 (B) 10 (C) 11 (D) 13 [1]

4 If $\frac{a}{6} = 12$ then $a =$

(A) 2 (B) 6 (C) 36 (D) 72 [1]

5 If $y - 8 = 13$ then $y =$

(A) 5 (B) 7 (C) 21 (D) 25 [1]

6 If $3k - 7 = 11$ then $k =$

(A) $1\frac{1}{3}$ (B) 4 (C) 5 (D) 6 [1]

7 If $2m + 9 = 17$ then $m =$

(A) 4 (B) 7 (C) 11 (D) 13 [1]

8 If $\frac{3n}{5} = 12$ then $n =$

(A) 7.2 (B) 15 (C) 20 (D) 57 [1]

9 What is the solution to the equation $6x + 5 = 29$?

(A) $x = 3$ (B) $x = 4$ (C) $x = 5\frac{2}{3}$ (D) $x = 144$ [1]

10 What is the solution to $\frac{m}{4} - 2 = 18$?

(A) $m = 4$ (B) $m = 5$ (C) $m = 64$ (D) $m = 80$ [1]

11 If $\frac{n}{7} + 3 = 10$ then $n =$

(A) 1 (B) 28 (C) 49 (D) 91 [1]

12 The solution to $4a - 9 = 17$ is:

(A) $a = 2$ (B) $a = 6\frac{1}{2}$ (C) $a = 32$ (D) $a = 104$ [1]

13 Seven more than three times x equals 10 can be written as:

(A) $7 - 3x = 10$ (B) $7 + 3x = 10$ (C) $4x = 10$ (D) none of these [1]

14 Fifi bought five buckets and received $5 change from $50. How much was each bucket?

(A) $5 (B) $6 (C) $8 (D) $9 [1]

15 What is the value of x if $7x - 2x + 3x + 4x = 60$?

(A) 720 (B) 72 (C) 48 (D) 5 [1]

PART B Write answers only in the space provided.

16 If $x + 17 = 39$ then $x =$ ________________ 1

17 If $8p = 168$ then $p =$ ________________ 1

18 If $a - 23 = 23$ then $a =$ ________________ 1

19 If $\frac{m}{7} = 14$ then $m =$ ________________ 1

20 If $52 - q = 38$ then $q =$ ________________ 1

21 Solve $y - 16 = 47$. ________________ 1

22 Solve $9n = 432$. ________________ 1

23 Solve $t + 35 = 60$. ________________ 1

24 What is the solution to the equation $\frac{k}{5} = 20$? ________________ 1

25 What is the solution to the equation $28 - z = 28$? ________________ 1

PART C Show all working.

26 Solve:

a $5x + 14 = 39$ (2 marks)

b $\frac{x}{3} - 2 = 9$ (2 marks)

c $45 + 3x = 99$ (2 marks)

d $12x - 17 = 19$ (2 marks)

e $\frac{x}{4} + 6 = 19$ (2 marks)

f $35 - 2x = 17$ (2 marks)

27 Three more than seven times a certain number is 87.

a Tayla said the number was 8. Briefly explain why she must be wrong. (1 mark)

b Let x be the number. Write an equation to show the information. (1 mark)

c Solve the equation and find the number. (1 mark)

Total marks /40

LEVEL 2 TEST PART A

Time allowed: 40 minutes

Marks

1 What is the solution to $x + 18 = 23$?

(A) $x = 4$ (B) $x = 5$ (C) $x = 7$ (D) $x = 41$ [1]

2 If $81 - n = 53$ then $n =$

(A) 28 (B) 34 (C) 38 (D) 134 [1]

3 What is the solution to $7x = 45$?

(A) $x = 6\frac{2}{7}$ (B) $x = 6\frac{3}{7}$ (C) $x = 6\frac{4}{7}$ (D) $x = 6\frac{5}{7}$ [1]

4 What is the solution to $\frac{a}{5} = 75$?

(A) $a = 15$ (B) $a = 80$ (C) $a = 375$ (D) $a = 575$ [1]

5 Solve $6c + 15 = 15$.

(A) $c = 0$ (B) $c = 1$ (C) $c = 5$ (D) $c = 6$ [1]

6 If $2\frac{1}{2} + m = 7\frac{1}{2}$ then $m =$

(A) $4\frac{1}{2}$ (B) 5 (C) $5\frac{1}{2}$ (D) 10 [1]

7 If $9p = 327$ then $p =$

(A) $35\frac{2}{9}$ (B) $36\frac{1}{3}$ (C) 63 (D) 2943 [1]

8 If $2t - 7 = 19$ then $t =$

(A) 6 (B) 12 (C) 13 (D) 52 [1]

9 If $\frac{3x}{4} = 27$ then $x =$

(A) $20\frac{1}{4}$ (B) $7\frac{2}{3}$ (C) $10\frac{1}{3}$ (D) 36 [1]

10 If $4x + 3x = 420$ then $x =$

(A) 35 (B) 60 (C) 136 (D) $104\frac{1}{4}$ [1]

11 What is the solution to $4z - 13 = 58$?

(A) $z = 11.25$ (B) $z = 11.75$ (C) $z = 17.25$ (D) $z = 17.75$ [1]

12 Peter is 5 years older than Greg. The sum of their ages is 67. How old is Peter?

(A) 31 (B) 36 (C) 41 (D) 46 [1]

13 Rose bought four packets of nails and received \$5 change from \$20. How much was each packet?

(A) \$3.25 (B) \$3.75 (C) \$4.25 (D) \$6.25 [1]

14 Six more than five times a number, n, is 41. Which is correct?

(A) $6n + 5 = 41$ (B) $6n - 5 = 41$ (C) $5n + 6 = 41$ (D) $5n - 6 = 41$ [1]

15 Which equation has $x = 2$ as a solution?

(A) $12x + 4 = 20$ (B) $9 + 7x = 25$ (C) $\frac{x}{6} + \frac{2}{3} = 1$ (D) $\frac{x}{8} - 5 = 11$ [1]

PART B Write answers only in the space provided.

16 What is the solution to $x + 2\frac{1}{4} = 7$? ______ [1]

17 Solve $59 + x = 72$. ______ [1]

18 Solve $9k = 0$. ______ [1]

19 If $m - 2.5 = 3.1$, what is the value of m? ______ [1]

20 Solve $\frac{x}{8} = 4$. ______ [1]

21 If $2q + 5 = 17$, what is the value of q? ______ [1]

22 Solve $3k + 8 = 20$. ______ [1]

23 Solve $\frac{x}{3} + 8 = 17$. ______ [1]

24 If $17 - 3n = 2$ what is the value of n? ______ [1]

25 Solve $\frac{4d}{5} = 20$. ______ [1]

PART C Show all working.

26 Solve:

a $5x + 3.2 = 7.45$ [2 marks]

______

______

b $6m - 728 = 2943$ [2 marks]

______

______

c $\frac{a}{5} + 19 = 24$ [2 marks]

______

______

d $46 - 3g = 20$ [2 marks]

______

______

e $\frac{n}{6} - \frac{1}{2} = 7$ [2 marks]

______

______

27 Ellen is 5 years older than Guy and 7 years younger than Stanley. Let Guy's age be x years.

a What is Ellen's age in terms of x? [1 mark]

______

b What is Stanley's age in terms of x? [1 mark]

______

c The sum of all the ages is 44. Write a simple equation that could be solved to find the value of x. [1 mark]

______

______

d How old is Ellen? [2 marks]

______

______

______

______

Total marks /40

Equations Calculator Allowed

LEVEL 3 TEST PART A

Time allowed: 40 minutes

Marks

1 What is the solution to the equation $x + 17 = 13$?

(A) $x = 4$ (B) $x = 30$ (C) $x = -4$ (D) $x = -30$ [1]

2 What is the solution to $25 - b = 31$?

(A) $b = -6$ (B) $b = 6$ (C) $b = 56$ (D) $b = -56$ [1]

3 What is the solution to $c - 13 = -8$?

(A) $c = -21$ (B) $c = -5$ (C) $c = 5$ (D) $c = 21$ [1]

4 What is the solution to $17x + 56 = 294$?

(A) $x = 14$ (B) $x = 16$ (C) $x = 20\frac{10}{17}$ (D) $x = 290\frac{12}{17}$ [1]

5 Solve $\frac{d}{3} + 6 = 18$.

(A) $d = 1$ (B) $d = 8$ (C) $d = 9$ (D) $d = 36$ [1]

6 What is the solution to $5x - 3.2 = 7.4$?

(A) $x = 0.84$ (B) $x = 2.12$ (C) $x = 8.04$ (D) $x = 6.76$ [1]

7 If $137 + x = 495$ then $x =$

(A) 358 (B) –358 (C) 632 (D) –632 [1]

8 The solution to $-2 + a = 6$ is $a =$

(A) 4 (B) 8 (C) –4 (D) –8 [1]

9 Solve $2x - 5 = -11$.

(A) $x = 8$ (B) $x = 3$ (C) $x = -3$ (D) $x = -8$ [1]

10 If $5p + 12 = 7$ then $p =$

(A) –1 (B) 1 (C) 3.8 (D) –3.8 [1]

11 For which of these equations is $x = 7$ **not** a solution?

(A) $5x - 40 = -5$ (B) $9 - 2x = -5$ (C) $-16 + 3x = -5$ (D) $4x - 33 = -5$ [1]

12 Zara is 9 years older than Kyle. The sum of their ages is 105. How old is Kyle?

(A) 47 (B) 48 (C) 57 (D) 58 [1]

13 The sum of three times a number and the amount by which the number exceeds 6 is 90. Let the number be x. Which is correct?

(A) $3x + 6 = 90$ (B) $2x - 6 = 90$ (C) $4x + 6 = 90$ (D) $4x - 6 = 90$ [1]

14 The change from \$$d$ when x tubs of yoghurt costing \$$y$ each are bought is \$$c$. Which is correct?

(A) $d - xy = c$ (B) $xy - d = c$ (C) $d + c = xy$ (D) $xy - c = d$ [1]

15 Ahmed earns \$$x$ per hour. James earns \$5 per hour less than Ahmed. Together they earn \$87 per hour. Which is correct?

(A) $x + 5 = 87$ (B) $x - 5 = 87$ (C) $2x + 5 = 87$ (D) $2x - 5 = 87$ [1]

Equations Calculator Allowed **(Level 3 Test)**

PART B Write answers only in the space provided.

16 Solve $x + 3.16 = 8.43$. ________ [1]

17 Solve $12 + x = 4$. ________ [1]

18 Solve $8g = 2$. ________ [1]

19 If $p - 9 = -2$ what is the value of p? ________ [1]

20 Solve $4y - 3 = 0$. ________ [1]

21 If $5b + 7 = 2$ what is the value of b? ________ [1]

22 If $20 - 3t = -4$ what is the value of t? ________ [1]

23 Solve $\frac{c}{12} = \frac{3}{4}$. ________ [1]

24 What is the solution to $12a - 15 = -3$? ________ [1]

25 If $\frac{5n}{7} = 2$, what is the value of n? ________ [1]

PART C Show all working.

26 Solve:

a $13h - 184 = 687$ [2 marks]

b $176 = 94 + 8x$ [2 marks]

c $6n - 15 = -42$ [2 marks]

d $9k + 154 = 46$ [2 marks]

e $\frac{x}{4} = \frac{5}{12}$ [2 marks]

27 A worker charges \$125 plus \$45 per hour. Sally was charged \$890.

a Let h be the number of hours for which Sally was charged. Write an equation that could be solved to find the number of hours. [1 mark]

b For how many hours was Sally charged? [1 mark]

c Kelly paid a different worker \$1145 for the same number of hours. That worker charged \$125 plus a different hourly rate. What was that hourly rate? [1 mark]

28 There are 39 people at a meeting. There are 15 more females than males. How many males are at the meeting? [2 marks]

Total marks /40

Coordinates, Position and Transformations

PRETEST

Time allowed: 15 minutes **Total marks: 15**

Marks

Questions 1 to 5 use the diagram on the right.

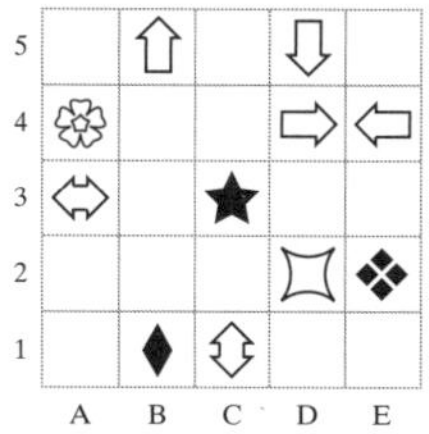

1 Which object is found at D5?

(A) ⇧ (B) ⇨ (C) ⇦ (D) ⇩

1

2 Where is ❖?

(A) E2 (B) E3 (C) D2 (D) D3

1

3 Which square is directly right of C3?

(A) C4 (B) B3 (C) C2 (D) D3

1

4 If ⌑ is moved one square left and two squares up, where will it be?

(A) B3 (B) C4 (C) E4 (D) E3

1

5 If ◆ has been moved three squares down and one square left, where did it move from?

(A) A4 (B) C4 (C) E2 (D) A5

1

6 If  is turned through a quarter-turn in a clockwise direction, what will it look like?

(A)  (B)  (C)  (D) 

1

7 Which shows a reflection over the dotted line?

(A)  (B)  (C)  (D) 

1

8 What will 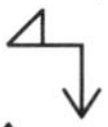 look like after a half-turn?

(A)  (B)  (C)  (D) 

1

9 If  is flipped over the vertical line and then over the horizontal line what will it look like?

(A)  (B)  (C)  (D) 

1

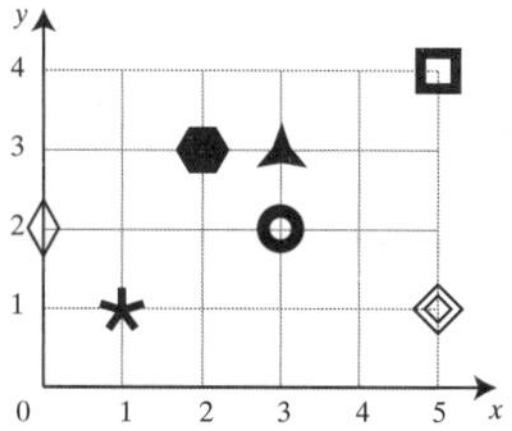

10 On the grid on the right, what is found at (2, 3)?

(A) ⬢ (B) ▲ (C) ● (D) ◈

1

11 On the grid on the right, where is ◇ found?

(A) (2, 0) (B) (0, 2) (C) (2, 2) (D) none of these

1

12 Which of these shapes will look the same when flipped over a horizontal line?

(A) ↓ (B) ◣ (C) ◗ (D) 

1

13 Which of these will look the same after a half-turn?

(A) ▼ (B)  (C)  (D) ✮

1

14 Which of these will look the same when flipped over a vertical line?

(A) ◣ (B) ← (C) ⬇ (D) ☽

1

15 Which of these will look the same after a quarter-turn (in either direction)?

(A) ✵ (B) ❄ (C) ✿ (D) ☆

1

Total marks /15

LEVEL 2 TEST PART A

Time allowed: 40 minutes

Marks

1 What special name is given to the point (0, 0)?

Ⓐ centre Ⓑ origin Ⓒ opening Ⓓ pivot 1

2 Which **must** be true about any point on the x -axis?

Ⓐ $x = 0$ Ⓑ $y = 0$ Ⓒ $x \neq 0$ Ⓓ $y \neq 0$ 1

Questions 3 to 8 refer to the grid on the right.

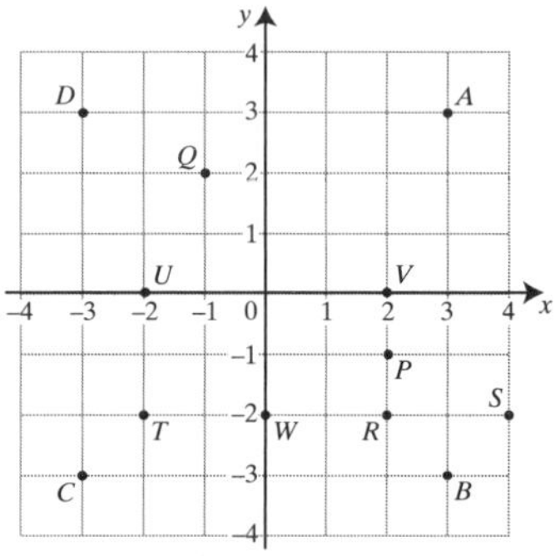

3 What are the coordinates of P?

Ⓐ (–1, 2) Ⓑ (1, –2) Ⓒ (2, –1) Ⓓ (–2, 1) 1

4 Which point is at (–3, 3)?

Ⓐ A Ⓑ B Ⓒ C Ⓓ D 1

5 How many units is it from A to B?

Ⓐ 3 Ⓑ 4 Ⓒ 5 Ⓓ 6 1

6 Which point lies at (0, –2)?

Ⓐ T Ⓑ U Ⓒ W Ⓓ none of these 1

7 If Q moves two units right and three down, where will it be?

Ⓐ (1, –1) Ⓑ (2, –1) Ⓒ (–3, –1) Ⓓ (2, –2) 1

8 Which point would be at (1, –1) if it moved three left and one up?

Ⓐ S Ⓑ T Ⓒ U Ⓓ V 1

Questions 9 to 15 use the grid on the right.

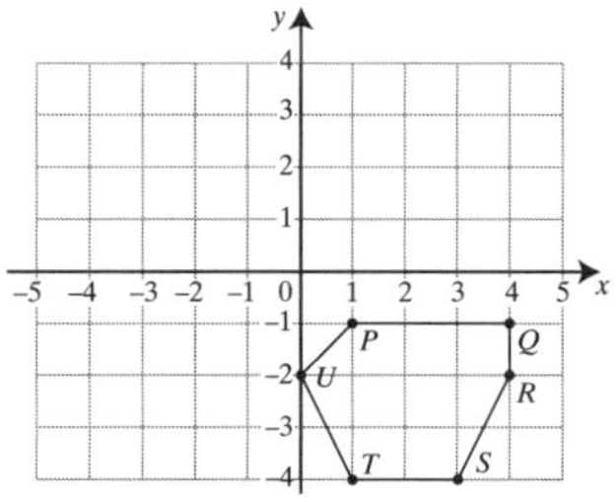

9 If $PQRSTU$ is translated five units up and one right, what will the coordinates of P' be?

Ⓐ (2, 4) Ⓑ (2, 5) Ⓒ (5, 2) Ⓓ (5, 4) 1

10 If $PQRSTU$ is reflected in the x-axis, what will the coordinates of Q' be?

Ⓐ (1, 4) Ⓑ (4, 1) Ⓒ (–4, –1) Ⓓ (–1, –4) 1

11 If $PQRSTU$ is rotated 180° about O, what will the coordinates of S' be?

Ⓐ (3, –4) Ⓑ (–4, 3) Ⓒ (–3, 4) Ⓓ (4, –3) 1

12 If $PQRSTU$ is reflected in the y-axis, what will the coordinates of R' be?

Ⓐ (2, 4) Ⓑ (4, 2) Ⓒ (–4, –2) Ⓓ (–2, –4) 1

13 If $PQRSTU$ is rotated 90° about O in an anticlockwise direction, what will the coordinates of T' be?

Ⓐ (–4, –1) Ⓑ (–1, –4) Ⓒ (1, 4) Ⓓ (4, 1) 1

14 If $PQRSTU$ is rotated 90° about O in a clockwise direction, what will the coordinates of U' be?

Ⓐ (–2, 0) Ⓑ (0, –2) Ⓒ (2, 0) Ⓓ (0, 2) 1

15 What translation could move S to (1, –2)?

Ⓐ two left, two up Ⓑ six left, three up Ⓒ five left, four up Ⓓ six left, two up 1

PART B Write answers only in the space provided.

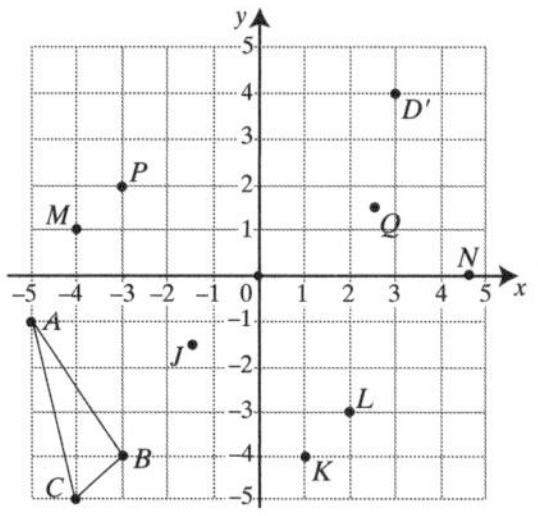

16 What are the coordinates of P? ________________ 1

17 Which point is found at $(1, -4)$? ________________ 1

18 Plot on the diagram and label the point $R(-2, -3)$. ________________ 1

19 What are the coordinates of Q? ________________ 1

20 Plot and label the point $S(0, -\frac{1}{2})$. ________________ 1

21 If ΔABC was rotated 180° about O, what would be the coordinates of A'? ________________ 1

22 What would be the result if ΔABC was translated three units left and two units down, followed by another translation two units up and three units right? ________________ 1

23 What single transformation could produce the same result as reflecting ΔABC first in the y-axis and then in the x-axis? ________________ 1

24 If ΔABC was reflected in the y-axis what would be the coordinates of C'? ________________ 1

25 If D' is the image of D after a translation two units right and five units down, what are the coordinates of D? ________________ 1

PART C Show all working.

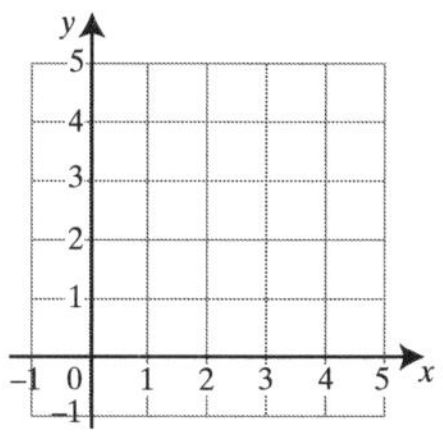

26 a Plot and label the points $P(1, 4)$, $Q(0, 1)$ and $R(3, 0)$ and join to form a triangle. 1 mark

b The triangle PQR is translated three units right and one unit up. Draw triangle $P'Q'R'$, labelling the vertices. 3 marks

c If instead ΔPQR was moved three down and one left, what would the coordinates of P' be? 1 mark

____

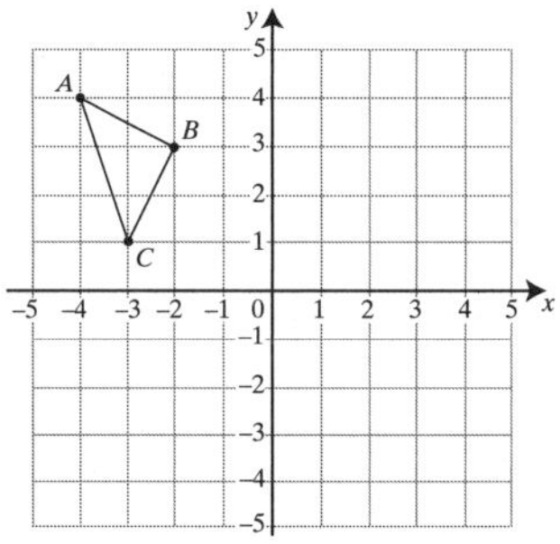

27 a Draw the image, labelling the vertices, when ΔABC is reflected in the x-axis. 3 marks

b Briefly describe the relationship between the coordinates of each point and its image. 1 mark

____

____

c If instead ΔABC was reflected in the y-axis, what would be the coordinates of B'? 1 mark

____

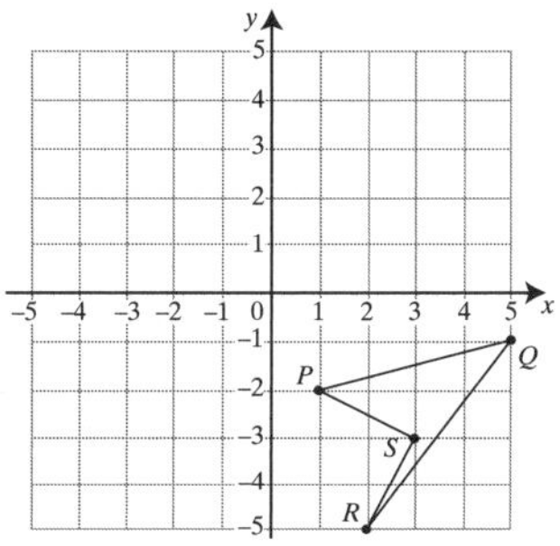

28 a Draw the image, labelling the vertices, when $PQRS$ is rotated 90° about O in a clockwise direction. 3 marks

b Describe the relationship between the coordinates of each point and its image under the above transformation. 1 mark

____

____

c If instead $PQRS$ had been rotated 90° about O in an anticlockwise direction, what would be the coordinates of S'? 1 mark

____

Total marks /40

LEVELS 1 AND 2 TEST PART A

Time allowed: 40 minutes

Marks

1 $3m$ means:
(A) $3 + m$ (B) $m + m + m$ (C) $m \times m \times m$ (D) none of these
1

2 If $p = 5$, $3p =$
(A) 125 (B) 35 (C) 15 (D) 8
1

3 Which of these points lies on the x-axis?
(A) (–1, –2) (B) (3, 3) (C) (0, 3) (D) (3, 0)
1

4 What is the solution to $x + 7 = 14$?
(A) $x = 2$ (B) $x = 7$ (C) $x = 9$ (D) $x = 21$
1

5 $2x + 3x =$
(A) $5x$ (B) $5x^2$ (C) $6x^2$ (D) $10x$
1

6 Which point lies at (2, –3)?
(A) P (B) Q (C) R (D) S
1

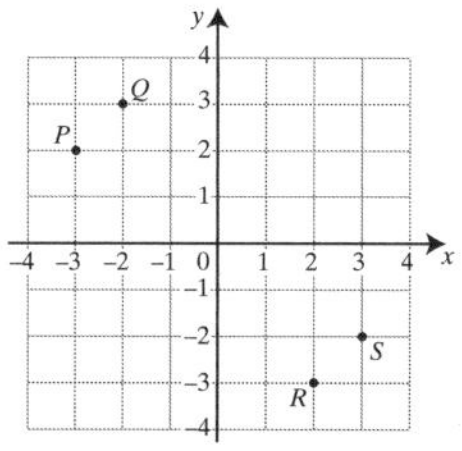

7 $\dfrac{8p}{2} =$
(A) 4 (B) 6 (C) $4p$ (D) $6p$
1

8 $2a \times 4a =$
(A) $6a$ (B) $6a^2$ (C) $8a$ (D) $8a^2$
1

9 If $9n = 36$ then $n =$
(A) 4 (B) 6 (C) 27 (D) 324
1

10 If $a = 6$ and $b = 2$ then $ab =$
(A) 62 (B) 12 (C) 8 (D) 3
1

11 $8y - 2y - 3 =$
(A) $6y - 3$ (B) $3y$ (C) $4y - 3$ (D) 3
1

12 If $n = 4$, $2n^2 =$
(A) 32 (B) 36 (C) 64 (D) 576
1

13 $5 + 7d =$
(A) $12d$ (B) $35d$ (C) $57d$ (D) $7d + 5$
1

14 What is the solution to $9 - x = 1$?
(A) $x = 7$ (B) $x = 8$ (C) $x = 9$ (D) $x = 10$
1

15 $12p \div 2p =$
(A) 10 (B) $10p$ (C) 6 (D) $6p$
1

PART B Write answers only in the space provided.

16 Simplify $3 \times a \times 4 \times b \times b$. ________________ 1

17 Write $5p^2q$ in expanded form. ________________ 1

18 Simplify $3n + 2n + 4n$. ________________ 1

19 If $t = 6$, then $t - 5 =$ ________________ 1

20 Simplify $2 \times 3x$. ________________ 1

21 If $7 - q = 2$ what is the value of q? ________________ 1

22 Simplify $\frac{6t}{2}$. ________________ 1

23 Simplify $4a + 2b - a$. ________________ 1

24 If $a = 3$, what is the value of $a^2 + a$? ________________ 1

25 Solve $2x = 842$. ________________ 1

PART C Show all working.

26 Simplify:

a $3 \times 2x + 5 \times 4x$ 1 mark

____

b $2a \times 3b + 5a \times b - 7ab$ 1 mark

____

c $9x \times x - 4x \times 2x + 3x \times 5$ 1 mark

____

27 a Simplify $5x + 4 + 2x + 3$. 1 mark

____

b If $x = 2$, what is the value of $5x + 4 + 2x + 3$? 1 mark

____

28 Solve:

a $8x - 13 = 19$ 2 marks

____

____

b $\frac{x}{2} + 47 = 53$ 2 marks

____

____

29 Refer to the diagram below.

a What are the coordinates of Q? 1 mark

____

b Which point is at $(-2, 4)$? 1 mark

____

c Mark and label the point $M(1.5, 2.5)$. 1 mark

d If $PQRS$ moves three units right and two units down, what are the coordinates of P'? 1 mark

____

e If ΔABC is reflected in the x-axis, what are the coordinates of B'? 1 mark

____

f If $PQRS$ was rotated 90° in a clockwise direction about O, what are the coordinates of S'? 1 mark

____

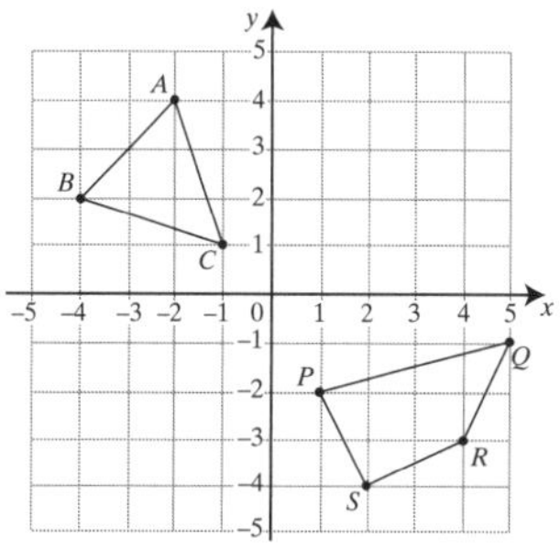

Total marks /40

LEVELS 2 AND 3 TEST — PART A

Time allowed: 40 minutes

Marks

1 $5x - 2y + 3x =$

Ⓐ $2x - 2y$ Ⓑ $2x + 2y$ Ⓒ $8x - 2y$ Ⓓ $8x + 2y$ 1

2 If $a = 2$ and $b = 3$ then $ab^2 =$

Ⓐ 12 Ⓑ 18 Ⓒ 36 Ⓓ 529 1

3 If $4x + 7 = 13$ then $x =$

Ⓐ 1.5 Ⓑ 2.5 Ⓒ 11.25 Ⓓ 20 1

4 $16x \div 4x \times 2x =$

Ⓐ $\frac{2}{x}$ Ⓑ $2x$ Ⓒ $8x$ Ⓓ $8x^2$ 1

5 Which could be the coordinates of P?

Ⓐ (3, 2) Ⓑ (–3, 2) Ⓒ (–3, –2) Ⓓ (3, –2) 1

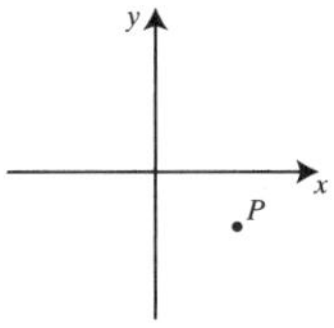

6 $8y \div 8y =$

Ⓐ 0 Ⓑ 1 Ⓒ y Ⓓ $8y$ 1

7 If $\frac{3n}{5} = 8$ then $n =$

Ⓐ $4\frac{1}{3}$ Ⓑ $4\frac{4}{5}$ Ⓒ $7\frac{2}{5}$ Ⓓ $13\frac{1}{3}$ 1

8 Which is **not** equal to $5x$?

Ⓐ $x + x + x + x + x$ Ⓑ $9x - 4x$ Ⓒ $x \times 5$ Ⓓ $x \times x \times x \times x \times x$ 1

9 $\frac{8x^2}{2xy} =$

Ⓐ $\frac{4x}{y}$ Ⓑ $4xy$ Ⓒ $\frac{8}{y}$ Ⓓ $8y$ 1

10 3 less than 5 times y is equal to 8 can be written as:

Ⓐ $3 - 5y = 8$ Ⓑ $2y = 8$ Ⓒ $5y - 3 = 8$ Ⓓ $5y = 8 - 3$ 1

11 Under which transformation will the arrow look exactly the same?

Ⓐ reflection in the x-axis Ⓑ reflection in the y-axis

Ⓒ rotation of 90° about O Ⓓ rotation of 180° about O 1

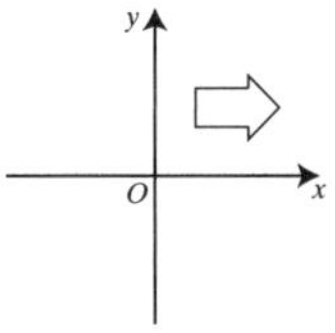

12 $9k + 4m - 3k + m =$

Ⓐ $6k + 5m$ Ⓑ $6k + 3m$ Ⓒ $12k + 3m$ Ⓓ $12k - 5m$ 1

13 The solution to the equation $5n - 7 = 11$ is:

Ⓐ $n = \frac{3}{5}$ Ⓑ $n = \frac{4}{5}$ Ⓒ $n = 3\frac{3}{5}$ Ⓓ $n = 3\frac{4}{5}$ 1

14 If $a = -5$, what is the value of $3 - a$?

Ⓐ –2 Ⓑ 2 Ⓒ 8 Ⓓ –8 1

15 $4xy \times 4x =$

Ⓐ $16xy$ Ⓑ $16x^2y$ Ⓒ $16xy^2$ Ⓓ $(4xy)^2$ 1

Algebra, Equations and Coordinates Calculator Allowed **(Levels 2 and 3 Test)**

PART B Write answers only in the space provided.

16 What is the solution to the equation $19 - 2y = 7$? ________________ [1]

17 Simplify $\frac{8x}{3} \div 2x$. ________________ [1]

18 If $2ab = 24$ and $b = 3$, what is the value of a? ________________ [1]

19 $3x^2 + 2x^2 =$ ________________ [1]

20 If $\frac{x}{3} + 1 = 5$ then $x =$ ________________ [1]

21 If $m = 4$ and $n = 6$, what is the value of $3m - 2n$? ________________ [1]

22 Simplify $7x - 2 + 3x - 4$. ________________ [1]

23 Write the rule that connects x and y. ________________ [1]

x	1	2	4	8	11
y	1	4	10	22	31

24 Solve $4x + 6x = 15$. ________________ [1]

25 If $P(-2, 3)$ is translated left two units and down five units what are the coordinates of P'? ________ [1]

PART C Show all working.

26 Simplify:

a $7p - 9 + 5q - p + 2q + 3$ [1 mark]

____

b $a^2 + 4a + 2a^2$ [1 mark]

____

c $3p \times 2q \times 4 + 5 \times 4p$ [1 mark]

____

27 Solve:

a $7x - 92 = 411$ [2 marks]

____

____

b $73 = \frac{x}{6} + 45$ [2 marks]

____

____

28 a Complete the table of values. [1 mark]

x	0	1	2	3	4
$3x + 1$					

b What value of x would produce a value of 55 in the table? [2 marks]

____

____

29

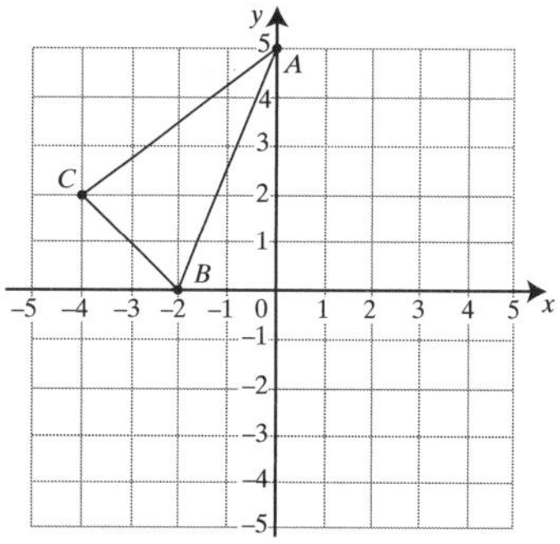

a What are the coordinates of A? [1 mark]

____

b Draw the image of ΔABC, labelling the vertices, after it has been rotated 180° about O. [2 marks]

c If instead ΔABC was reflected in the y-axis, what would be the coordinates of C'? [1 mark]

____

d What transformation of $\Delta A'B'C'$ would produce the same result as reflecting ΔABC in the y-axis? [1 mark]

____

Total marks /40

PRETEST

Time allowed: 15 minutes **Total marks: 14**

1 Which of these units is the smallest?

Ⓐ km^2 Ⓑ cm^2 Ⓒ mm^2 Ⓓ m^2 1

2 Which of these units is the largest?

Ⓐ km^2 Ⓑ cm^2 Ⓒ mm^2 Ⓓ m^2 1

3 Which unit would be best to measure the area of a page?

Ⓐ km^2 Ⓑ m^2 Ⓒ cm^2 Ⓓ ha 1

4 The area of which of these would most likely be measured in square kilometres?

Ⓐ football field Ⓑ housc block Ⓒ shopping centre Ⓓ town 1

5 One hectare is equal to how many square metres?

Ⓐ 100 Ⓑ 1000 Ⓒ 10 000 Ⓓ 100 000 1

6 The shaded area is closest to how many square units?

Ⓐ 11 Ⓑ 21

Ⓒ 26 Ⓓ 31 1

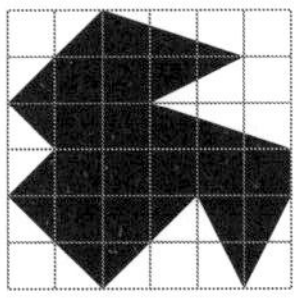

7 What is the area of a square of side length 5 m?

Ⓐ 10 m^2 Ⓑ 12.5 m^2 Ⓒ 20 m^2 Ⓓ 25 m^2 1

8 What is the area of this rectangle?

Ⓐ 7 m^2 Ⓑ 10 m^2

Ⓒ 14 m^2 Ⓓ 20 m^2 1

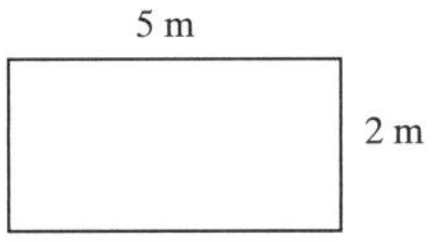

9 What is the perimeter of the rectangle in question 8?

Ⓐ 7 m Ⓑ 10 m Ⓒ 14 m Ⓓ 20 m 1

10 The shaded triangle has a base of length 42 mm. What is the perpendicular height?

Ⓐ 40 mm Ⓑ 140 mm

Ⓒ 175 mm Ⓓ 203 mm 1

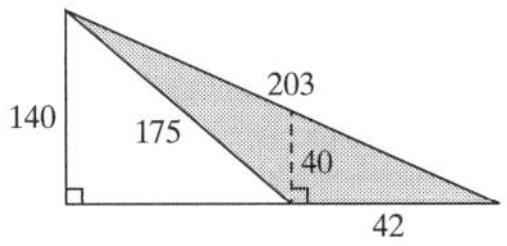

11 What is the perimeter of a square of side length 10 cm?

Ⓐ 40 cm Ⓑ 60 cm Ⓒ 80 cm Ⓓ 100 cm 1

12 How many more tiles will fit on this floor?

Ⓐ 42 Ⓑ 43

Ⓒ 44 Ⓓ 45 1

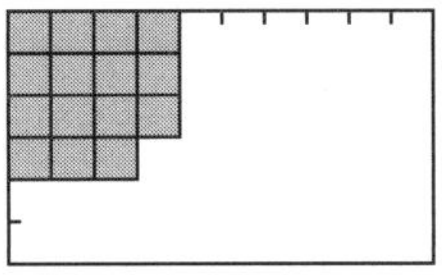

13 What is the area of a rectangle 4 m long and 2 m wide?

Ⓐ 4 m^2 Ⓑ 8 m^2 Ⓒ 12 m^2 Ⓓ 64 m^2 1

14 What is the area of this triangle?

Ⓐ 12 cm^2 Ⓑ 18 cm^2

Ⓒ 22 cm^2 Ⓓ 24 cm^2 1

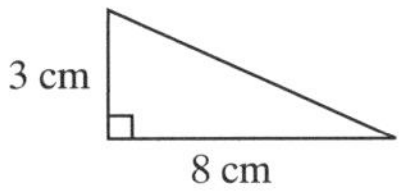

Total marks /14

Area Calculator Allowed

LEVEL 1 TEST PART A

Time allowed: 40 minutes

1 For which shape is the area **not** found by multiplying the base by the height?

(A) square (B) rectangle (C) triangle (D) parallelogram 1

2 What is the area of a square of side length 6 cm?

(A) 24 cm^2 (B) 18 cm^2 (C) 60 cm^2 (D) 36 cm^2 1

3 What is the area of a rectangle 7 cm long and 6 cm wide?

(A) 42 cm^2 (B) 26 cm^2 (C) 21 cm^2 (D) 52 cm^2 1

4 A square has an area of 64 m^2. How long is each side?

(A) 4 m (B) 8 m (C) 12 m (D) 16 m 1

5 How many square centimetres are in 1 m^2?

(A) 100 (B) 1000 (C) 10 000 (D) 100 000 1

6 A triangle has a base length of 12 m and perpendicular height of 8 m. What is its area?

(A) 96 m^2 (B) 24 m^2 (C) 56 m^2 (D) 48 m^2 1

7 Which rectangle has the greatest area?

(A)
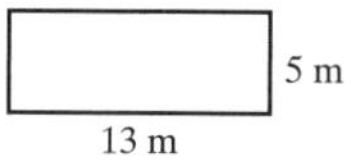

(B)
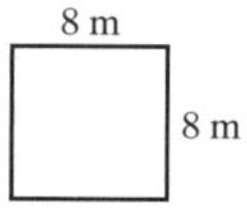

(C)
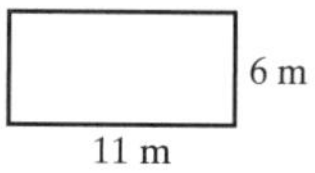

(D)
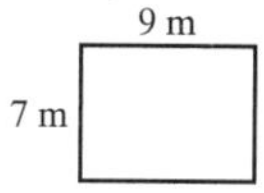

1

8 What is the area of this parallelogram?

(A) 46 cm^2 (B) 60 cm^2

(C) 92 cm^2 (D) 120 cm^2

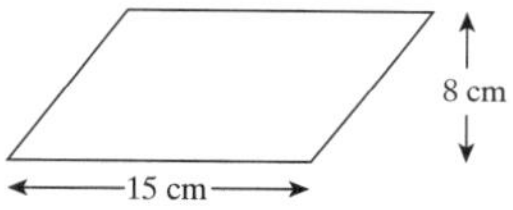

1

9 How many square millimetres are in 1 cm^2?

(A) 10 (B) 100 (C) 1000 (D) 10 000 1

10 What is the area of this triangle?

(A) 15 m^2 (B) 30 m^2

(C) 32 m^2 (D) 60 m^2

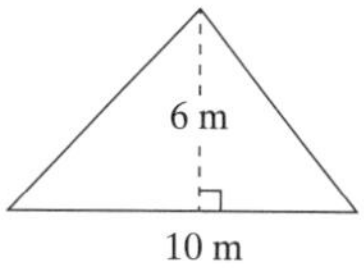

1

11 A rectangle is 14 cm long and has an area of 140 cm^2. How wide is it?

(A) 10 cm (B) 14 cm (C) 5 cm (D) 20 cm 1

12 What is the area of this triangle?

(A) 40 m^2 (B) 60 m^2

(C) 68 m^2 (D) 127.5 m^2

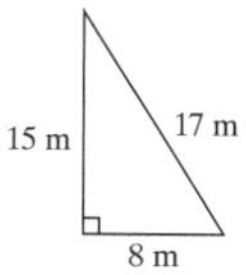

1

13 The area of a paddock is 24 000 m^2. How many hectares is this?

(A) 2.4 (B) 24 (C) 240 (D) 2400 1

14 The perimeter of a square is 16 m. What is its area?

(A) 16 m^2 (B) 24 m^2 (C) 36 m^2 (D) 64 m^2 1

15 A parallelogram has base 12 m, perpendicular height 8 m and sloping height 10 m. What is its area?

(A) 30 m^2 (B) 80 m^2 (C) 96 m^2 (D) 120 m^2 1

PART B Write answers only in the space provided.

16 Place in order from smallest to largest: mm^2, km^2, cm^2, m^2, ha. ____________ [1]

17 What is the area of a square of side length 11 cm? ____________ [1]

18 What is the area of a rectangle with length 19 cm and width 16 cm? ____________ [1]

19 What is the area of a triangle with base length 22 cm and perpendicular height 12 cm? ____________ [1]

20 What is the area of a parallelogram with base length 48 cm and perpendicular height 37 cm?

____________ [1]

21 What fraction of the rectangle is shaded? ____________ [1]

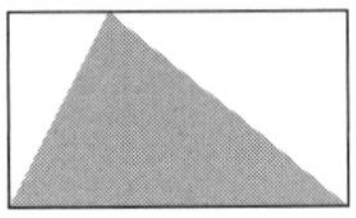

22 A field has an area of 180 000 m^2. How many hectares is that? ____________ [1]

23 What is the area of this triangle? ____________ [1]

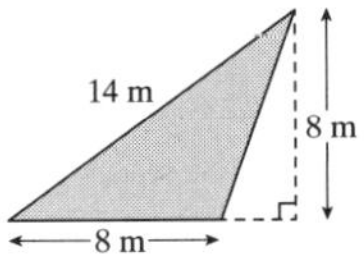

24 How many square kilometres is 9 000 000 m^2? ____________ [1]

25 What is the area of this rectangular block of land? ____________ [1]

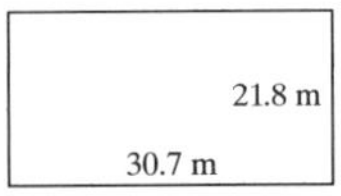

PART C Show all working.

26 a What is the area of this paddock in square metres? [1 mark]

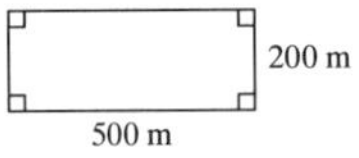

____

b What is that area in hectares? [1 mark]

____

c Another paddock is 600 m long and 300 m wide. How many more hectares is it? [1 mark]

____

27 The perimeter of this triangle is 90 m.

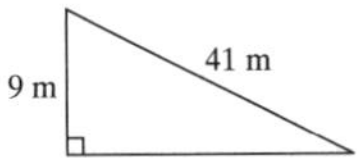

a What is the length of the missing side? [1 mark]

____

b What is the area of the triangle? [1 mark]

____

28 A swimming pool is to be surrounded by an area of paving.

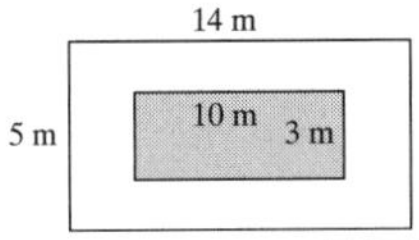

a What is the total area? [1 mark]

____

b What is the area of the pool? [1 mark]

____

c What is the total cost of the paving at \$54 per square metre? [2 marks]

____

____

29 a A rectangle has an area of 51 cm^2. If it is 3 cm wide, how long is it? [1 mark]

____

b If the rectangle was 1 cm wider, how many more square centimetres would the area be? [1 mark]

____

30 A yard is in the shape of a parallelogram. A 2 m wide pathway is to be built as shown.

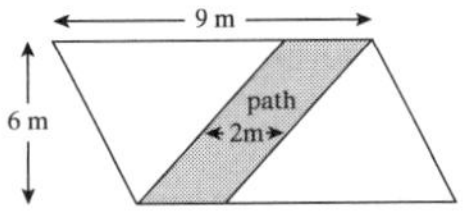

a What is the area of the yard? [1 mark]

____

b What is the area of the path? [1 mark]

____

c What fraction of the whole yard will be pathway? [1 mark]

____

d One side of the path is lawn and the other is garden. What is the area of lawn? [1 mark]

____

Total marks ___ / 40

Area Calculator Allowed

LEVEL 2 TEST

PART A

Time allowed: 40 minutes

1 Which unit would be used to measure the area of a garage floor?

(A) cm^2 (B) ha (C) m^2 (D) km^2 1

2 The perimeter of a square is 44 cm. What is its area?

(A) 44 cm^2 (B) 60.5 cm^2 (C) 88 cm^2 (D) 121 cm^2 1

3 A rectangle is twice as long as it is wide. The area of the rectangle is 288 cm^2. What is the length?

(A) 12 cm (B) 24 cm (C) 48 cm (D) 96 cm 1

4 How many square tiles of side length 30 cm will fit on a floor 3 m long and 2.4 m wide?

(A) 24 (B) 42 (C) 80 (D) 240 1

5 A parallelogram has an area of 70 m^2. If the base is 5 m what is the perpendicular height?

(A) 3.5 m (B) 7 m (C) 14 m (D) 28 m 1

6 What is the area of this triangle?

(A) 95 337.5 mm^2 (B) 114 114 mm^2

(C) 131 950 mm^2 (D) 227 287.5 mm^2 1

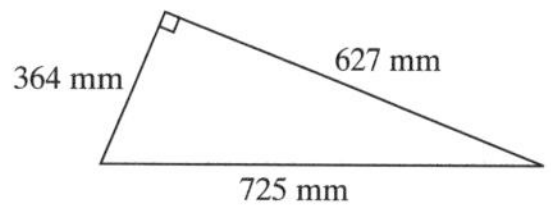

7 How many square metres are in 4 km^2?

(A) 2000 (B) 4000 (C) 2 000 000 (D) 4 000 000 1

8 A triangle has an area of 320 cm^2. What is the area of a parallelogram with the same length base and perpendicular height?

(A) 160 cm^2 (B) 320 cm^2 (C) 640 cm^2 (D) There is not enough information. 1

9 What is the area of this block of land in hectares?

(A) 1.7 ha (B) 17 ha (C) 170 ha (D) 1700 ha 1

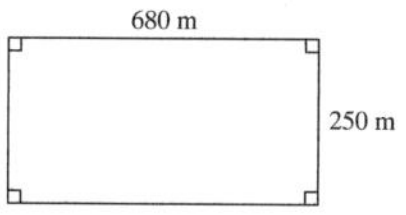

10 What is the area between the two rectangles?

(A) 102 m^2 (B) 58 m^2 (C) 24 m^2 (D) 82.5 m^2 1

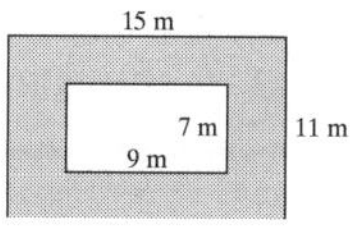

11 What is this area?

(A) 140 m^2 (B) 132 m^2 (C) 3672 m^2 (D) 176 m^2 1

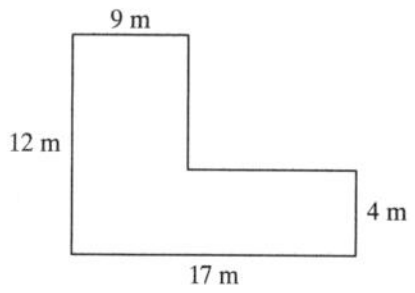

12 Which has the greatest area?

(A) 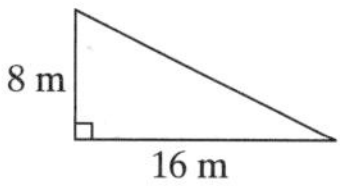

(B) 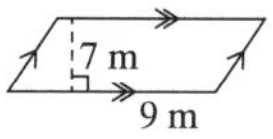

(C) 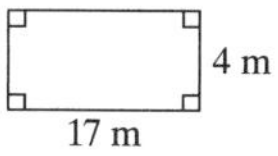

(D) 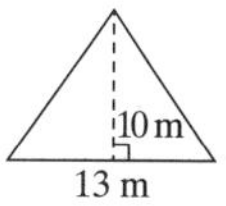

1

13 What is the area of this triangle?

(A) 210 m^2 (B) 184.5 m^2 (C) 129.15 m^2 (D) 126 m^2 1

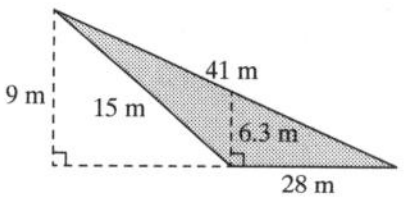

14 How many hectares are in a square kilometre?

(A) 100 (B) 1000 (C) 10 000 (D) 100 000 1

15 The shaded area is:

(A) 592 m^2 (B) 192 m^2 (C) 444 m^2 (D) 296 m^2 1

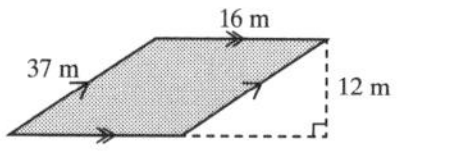

PART B Write answers only in the space provided.

16 What is the area of a rectangle with length 9 cm and width 65 mm? ______________ 1

17 What is the area, in square metres, of a square of side length 87 cm? ______________ 1

18 Convert 216 000 cm^2 to square metres. ______________ 1

19 Find the area, in hectares, of a triangle with base length 780 m and perpendicular height 235 m.

______________ 1

20 Find the difference between the area of squares of sides 8 cm and 9 cm. ______________ 1

21 A square has an area of 1225 cm^2. How long is each side? ______________ 1

22 What is the area of this triangle? ______________ 1

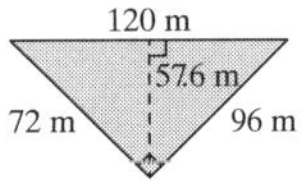

23 Find the area in hectares of a rectangular block of land 2.35 km long and 1.45 km wide. ______________ 1

24 A triangle has area 3901 cm^2. If the base length is 94 cm, what is the perpendicular height?

______________ 1

25 What is the area of this shape? ______________ 1

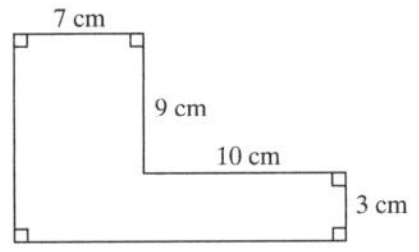

PART C Show all working.

26 The playing area for a game of rugby union is 100 m long and 70 m wide. Is this larger or smaller than a hectare? Justify your answer. 1 mark

____

27 A bedroom is 3.6 m long and 3.2 m wide. The four walls, which are all 2.4 m high, are to be painted. The room has one window, which is 1.6 m wide and 1.2 m high, and one door 82 cm wide and 2.05 m high, which will not be painted.

a Find the area of the window. 1 mark

____

b Find the area of the door in square metres. 1 mark

____

c Find the area to be painted. 2 marks

____

____

d Find the number of cans of paint needed if the walls are to have two coats and if one can of paint contains 4 L of paint and 1 L covers an area of 16 m^2. 2 marks

____

____

28 A rug is made from 12 parallelograms, each with base length 60 cm.

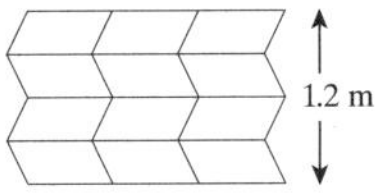

a What is the total area of the rug in square metres? 2 marks

____

____

b The rug is placed on a floor in a room 3.6 m long and 3 m wide. What fraction of the floor is covered by the rug? 2 marks

____

____

29 Find the shaded area. (All measurements are in metres.)

a 2 marks

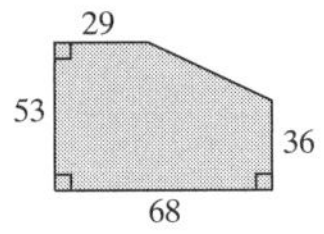

b 2 marks

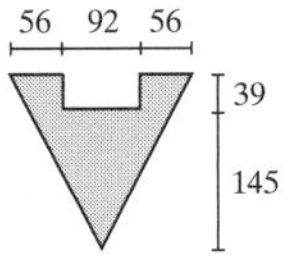

____

____

____

Total marks /40

LEVEL 3 TEST PART A

Time allowed: 40 minutes

1 What is the area of a square, if the perimeter is 4 m?

(A) 1 m^2 (B) 2 m^2 (C) 4 m^2 (D) 16 m^2 1

2 A rectangle is 2754 mm long and 836 mm wide. The area of the rectangle is closest to:

(A) 230 000 cm^2 (B) 2 300 000 cm^2 (C) 2.3 m^2 (D) 0.23 m^2 1

3 How many square centimetres are in 9 m^2?

(A) 300 (B) 900 (C) 30 000 (D) 90 000 1

4 Two triangles have the same area. The base of the first is twice the length of the second base. The height of the second triangle must be:

(A) a quarter of the first (B) equal to the first (C) twice that of the first (D) half the first 1

5 What is the shaded area?

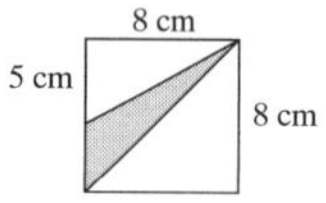

(A) 12 cm^2 (B) 20 cm^2 (C) 40 cm^2 (D) 32 cm^2 1

6 The area of NSW is about 800 000 km^2. How many hectares is that?

(A) 8 million (B) 80 million (C) 800 million (D) 8 billion 1

7 The area of the shaded parallelogram is:

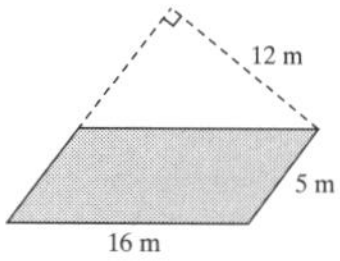

(A) 60 m^2 (B) 80 m^2

(C) 192 m^2 (D) not enough information 1

8 A square has a side length three times that of a smaller square. The area of the larger square will be how many times the area of the smaller square?

(A) 3 (B) 6 (C) 9 (D) 12 1

9 What is the area of the shaded triangle?

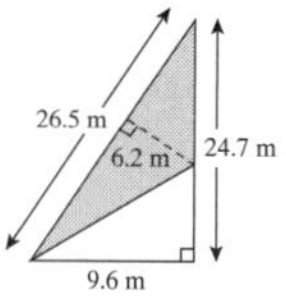

(A) 118.56 m^2 (B) 29.76 m^2 (C) 82.15 m^2 (D) 76.57 m^2 1

10 A 1 m wide path surrounds a garden bed as shown. What is the area of the garden bed?

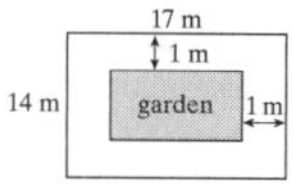

(A) 180 m^2 (B) 192 m^2 (C) 195 m^2 (D) 208 m^2 1

11 5 760 000 mm^2 is the same as:

(A) 576 cm^2 (B) 5.76 m^2 (C) 57.6 m^2 (D) 5760 cm^2 1

12 A floor has area 22.75 m^2. It is covered with square tiles 25 cm long. How many tiles are there?

(A) 91 (B) 455 (C) 364 (D) 8281 1

13 The area of this shape is:

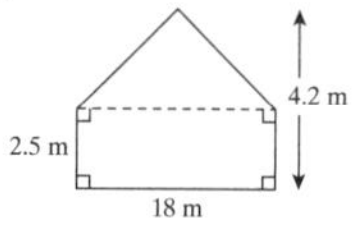

(A) 37.8 m^2 (B) 60.3 m^2 (C) 53.1 m^2 (D) 82.8 m^2 1

14 This shape is made from a parallelogram and its reflection and a triangle. The area of the triangle is 24 cm^2. What is the area of each parallelogram?

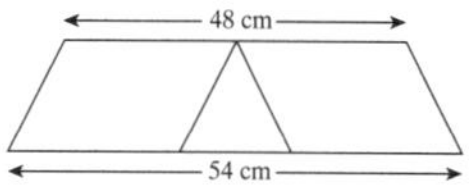

(A) 144 cm^2 (B) 96 cm^2 (C) 192 cm^2 (D) 156 cm^2 1

15 What is the area of this shape?

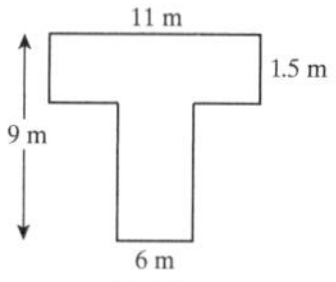

(A) 34.5 m^2 (B) 61.5 m^2 (C) 70.5 m^2 (D) 90 m^2 1

PART B Write answers only in the space provided.

16 How many square metres are in 2.35 km^2? ________________ 1

17 What is the perimeter of a rectangle with area 76 cm^2 and width 40 mm? ________________ 1

18 A rectangular paddock is 1.2 km long and 850 m wide. How many hectares is the paddock?

________________ 1

19 A square has an area of 5.29 cm^2. What is its perimeter? ________________ 1

20 If a rectangle has a perimeter of 28 cm, what is the largest area it could have? ________________ 1

21 A triangle has an area of 60 cm^2. Another triangle has a base length four times that of the first triangle, but it is half the height. What is the area of the second triangle? ________________ 1

22 Find the shaded area. (All measurements are in metres.) ________________ 1

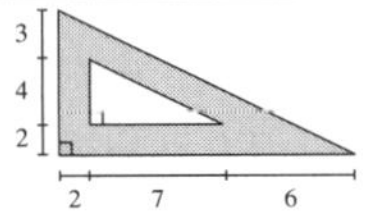

23 A rectangular paddock has an area of 2.6 ha.
If it is 208 m long, how wide is it? ________________ 1

24 Find the shaded area. ________________ 1

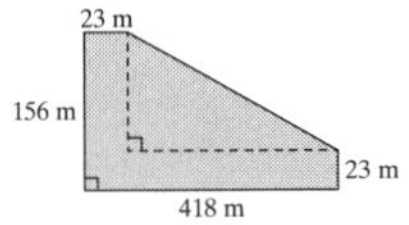

25 Find the approximate area of this land, giving the answer to the nearest 10 ha. ________________ 1

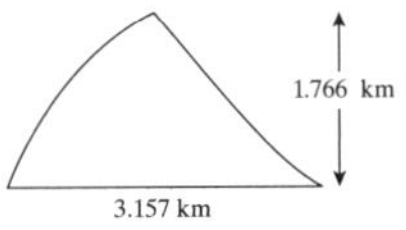

PART C Show all working.

26 A basketball court is 28 m long and 15 m wide while a netball court is 30.5 m long and 15.25 m wide. Nick said the difference in length is 2.5 m and the difference in width is 0.25 m so the difference in area is 2.5 m × 0.25 m or 0.625 m^2. Explain why Nick is wrong and find the actual difference in area. 3 marks

____

____

____

27 A rectangle has an area of 36 m^2 and a perimeter of 24 m. What is the difference between its length and width? 2 marks

____

____

28 a Find the area of the triangle. 1 mark

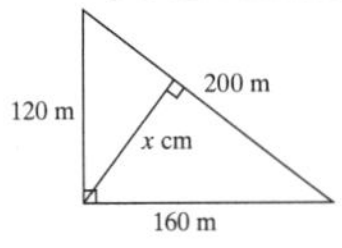

____

b Find the value of x. 2 marks

____

____

29 The diagram shows a floor that is to be paved.

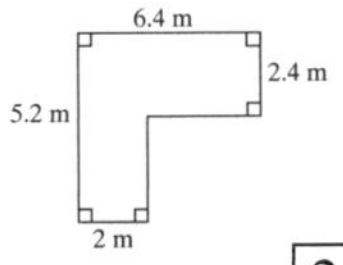

a Find the area of the floor. 2 marks

____

____

b The pavers are 400 mm by 400 mm and can be bought for $6.95 each. What is the cost of the required number of pavers? 2 marks

____

____

30 The unshaded part of this space is a parallelogram. What fraction of the space is shaded? 3 marks

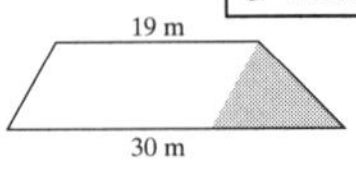

____

____

____

Total marks /40

Three-dimensional Space, Volume and Capacity

PRETEST

Time allowed: 15 minutes **Total marks: 14**

1 Which is **not** a prism?

(A) 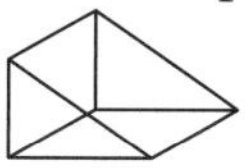 (B)  (C) 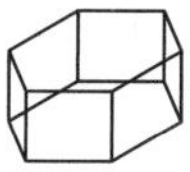 (D) 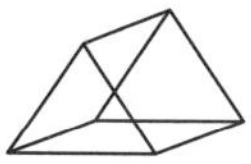 1

2 How many edges does a cube have?

(A) 12 (B) 10 (C) 8 (D) 6 1

3 What shape is the base of a pentagonal pyramid?

(A) triangle (B) square (C) rectangle (D) pentagon 1

4 What capacity might a carton of milk have?

(A) 1 L (B) 10 L (C) 1 mL (D) 10 mL 1

5 Which is the net of a triangular prism?

(A) 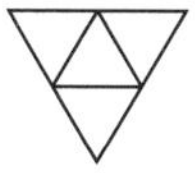 (B) 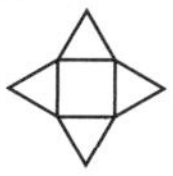 (C) 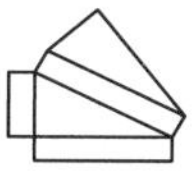 (D) 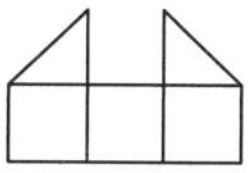 1

6 How many vertices does a rectangular prism have?

(A) 6 (B) 8 (C) 10 (D) 12 1

7 Which container has the most juice? (All measurements are in millilitres.)

(A) 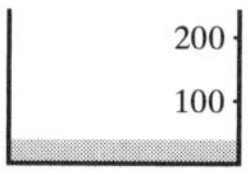

(B) 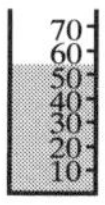

(C) 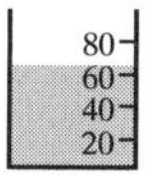

(D) 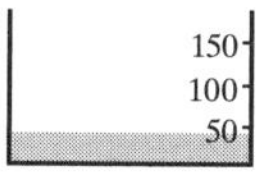

1

8 This prism is made from how many blocks?

(A) 17 (B) 18 (C) 20 (D) 24

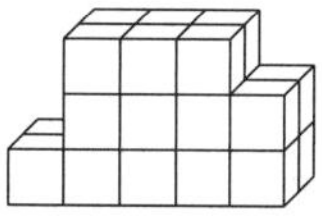 1

9 How many faces does a triangular pyramid have?

(A) 3 (B) 4 (C) 5 (D) 6 1

10 Which prism has the greatest number of blocks?

(A) 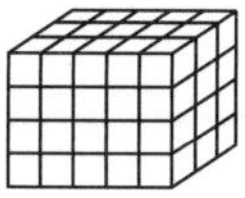 (B) 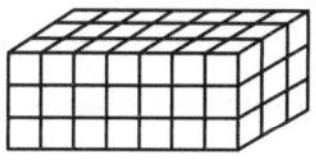 (C) 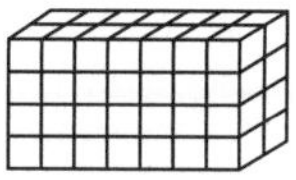 (D) 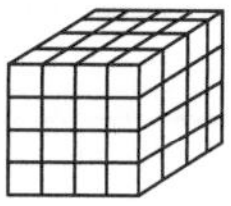 1

11 This is the net of a cube. When folded, which face is opposite face F?

(A) A (B) B (C) C (D) D

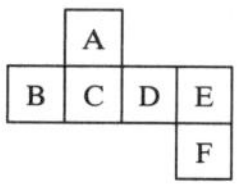

1

12 The volume of which of these would be measured in cubic centimetres?

(A) sitting room (B) shoe box (C) shipping container (D) silo 1

13 A corner has been cut off this cube. If all the corners are cut off in the same way how many faces will the object then have?

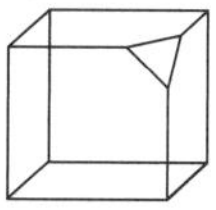

(A) 6 (B) 12 (C) 14 (D) 18 1

14 What shape is the base of this prism?

(A) triangle (B) rectangle (C) hexagon (D) octagon

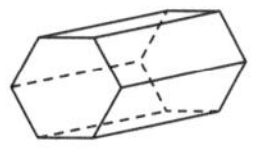 1

Total marks /14

LEVEL 1 TEST PART A

Time allowed: 40 minutes

1 What is the volume of a rectangular prism that is 5 m long, 4 m wide and 3 m high?

(A) 20 m³ (B) 24 m³ (C) 60 m³ (D) 94 m³ 1

2 What is the volume of a cube of side 2 cm?

(A) 6 cm³ (B) 8 cm³ (C) 12 cm³ (D) 24 cm³ 1

3 How many bricks are in this stack?

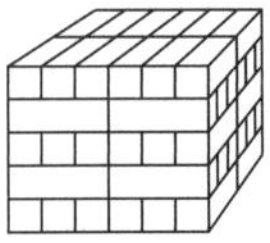

(A) 26 (B) 36 (C) 56 (D) 60 1

4 The capacity of a standard bucket would be closest to:

(A) 1 L (B) 10 L (C) 100 L (D) 1 kL 1

5 1 ML is:

(A) 1 millilitre (B) 1 macrolitre (C) 1 microlitre (D) 1 megalitre 1

6 Which prism has the greatest volume? 1

(A) 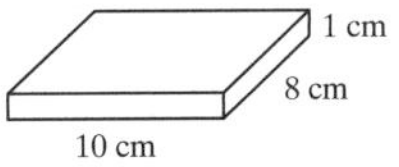

(B) 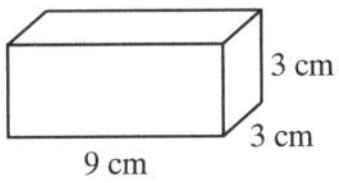

(C) 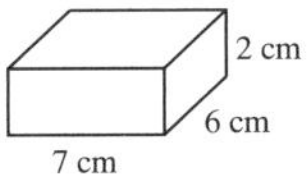

(D) 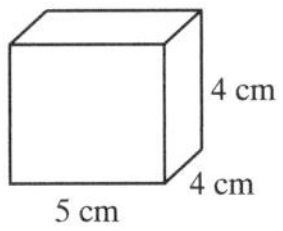

7 Which of these has a uniform cross-section?

(A) cylinder (B) sphere (C) cone (D) pyramid 1

8 A bottle has a capacity of 2 L. How many glasses that hold 250 mL can be filled from the bottle?

(A) 4 (B) 8 (C) 12 (D) 125 1

9 The object at right was made using six identical cubes. What is the top view?

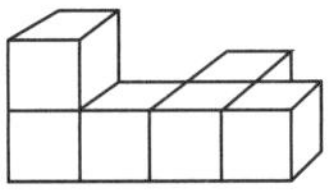

(A) 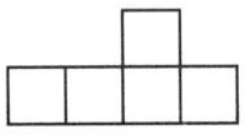 (B) 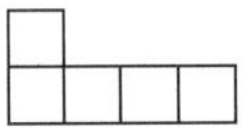 (C) 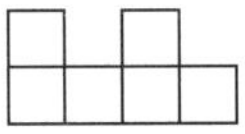 (D) 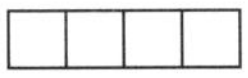 1

10 The volume of a container is 560 cm³. What is its capacity?

(A) 560 mL (B) 56 mL (C) 5.6 L (D) 56 L 1

11 3.15 kL is how many litres?

(A) 315 (B) 3150 (C) 31 500 (D) 315 000 1

12 What is the volume of this prism?

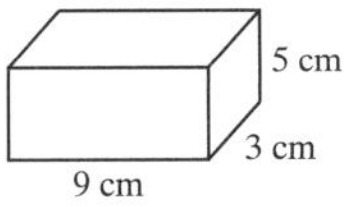

(A) 17 cm³ (B) 67.5 cm³ (C) 87 cm³ (D) 135 cm³ 1

13 A prism of height 4 cm has a square base of side length 6 cm. What is its volume?

(A) 64 cm³ (B) 96 cm³ (C) 144 cm³ (D) 216 cm³ 1

14 Which has the smallest volume? 1

(A) 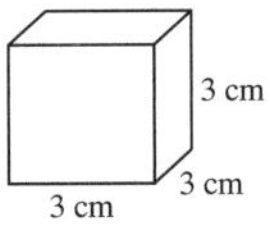

(B) 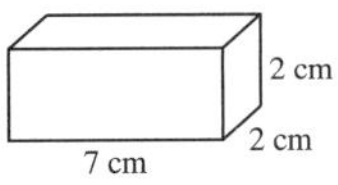

(C) 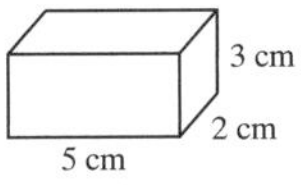

(D) 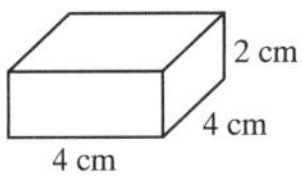

15 The base of a prism has an area of 20 cm² and the height is 5 cm. What is the volume?

(A) 50 cm³ (B) 100 cm³ (C) 200 cm³ (D) 2000 cm³ 1

PART B Write answers only in the space provided.

16 What is the volume of a rectangular prism 4 cm long, 3 cm wide and 2 cm high? ______________ 1

17 How many millilitres are in 6 L? ______________ 1

18 What shape is the constant cross-section of a triangular prism? ______________ 1

19 The volume of a jar is 620 cm³. What is its capacity in millilitres? ______________ 1

20 Complete: 72 000 L = ________ kL. 1

21 Draw the top view of the cylinder. 1

22 What is the volume of a prism if the base area is 9 m² and the height is 4 m? ______________ 1

23 What is the volume of this prism? ______________ 1

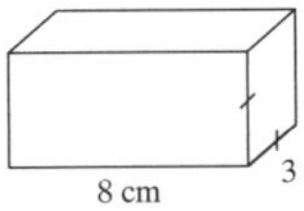

24 What is the volume of a cube of side 1 m? ______________ 1

25 What is the capacity in litres of the cube in Question 24? ______________ 1

PART C Show all working.

26 This prism was made by placing three cubes together.

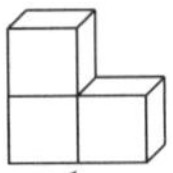

a What type of prism is it? 1 mark

____

b Draw the view from the:

i front 1 mark **ii** right side 1 mark

iii top 1 mark **iv** back 1 mark

c If each cube has a side length of 1 cm, what is the volume of the prism? 1 mark

____

d If the prism was hollow and watertight, how much liquid would it hold? 1 mark

____

27 A swimming pool is 25 m long and 8 m wide. How many litres of water would be needed to fill the pool to a constant depth of 1.5 m? 2 marks

____

____

____

28 The diagram shows the top view of a base for a statue. The base consists of three square-based prisms of decreasing size placed on top of each other. The bottom prism has a side length of 90 cm, the middle one has a side length of 60 cm and the top one has a side length of 30 cm. Each prism has a height of 20 cm.

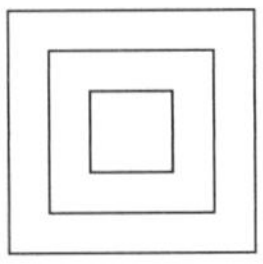

a What will the fact that the prisms have a square cross-section mean about the views from the front, back, left and right sides? 1 mark

____

____

b What is the volume of the top prism? 1 mark

____

c What is the total volume, in cubic centimetres, of all three prisms? 3 marks

____

____

____

d What is the total volume in cubic metres? 1 mark

____

Total marks /40

LEVEL 2 TEST — PART A

Time allowed: 40 minutes

1 A prism has a volume of 875 cm^3. What is its capacity?
(A) 87.5 mL (B) 875 mL (C) 8.75 L (D) 875 L — 1

2 What is the volume of a rectangular prism 30 cm long, 20 cm wide and 85 mm high?
(A) 51 000 cm^3 (B) 51 000 mm^3 (C) 510 cm^3 (D) 5100 cm^3 — 1

3 800 kL =
(A) 0.8 ML (B) 0.08 ML (C) 8 ML (D) 0.008 ML — 1

4 Ten cubes are stuck together to make this object, which is then painted all over. How many of the 10 cubes will have paint on exactly three faces?

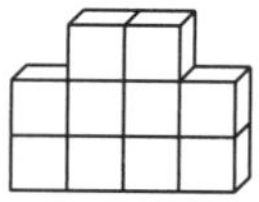

(A) 0 (B) 2 (C) 4 (D) 6 — 1

5 A rectangular pyramid has been glued to a rectangular prism, with faces matching exactly. How many edges does the new object have?
(A) 8 (B) 16 (C) 20 (D) 24 — 1

6 Which of these has a uniform cross-section that is triangular?
(A) square pyramid (B) triangular pyramid (C) triangular prism (D) cone — 1

7 A container that holds 1000 L has a volume of:
(A) 1 m^3 (B) 1000 m^3 (C) 1000 cm^3 (D) 100 000 cm^3 — 1

8 The object at right was formed by placing three rectangular prisms beside each other. What is the view from the right side?

(A) 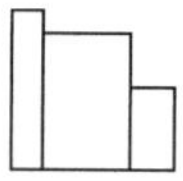 (B)  (C) 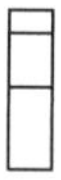 (D) 

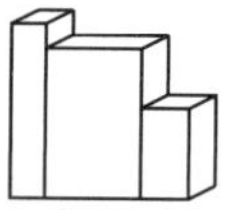
front

— 1

9 How many bottles that hold 375 mL can be filled from a 4 L container?
(A) 8 (B) 9 (C) 10 (D) 11 — 1

10 1 cm^3 is how many cubic millimetres?
(A) 10 (B) 100 (C) 1000 (D) 10 000 — 1

11 Which has the greatest capacity?

(A) 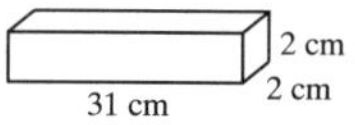

(B) 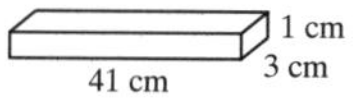

(C) 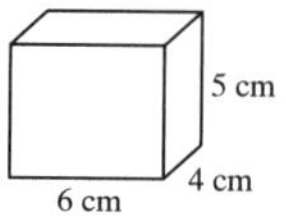

(D) 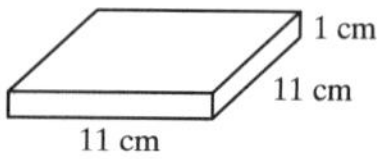

— 1

12 Which is closest to the capacity of a rectangular prism 9 cm long, 8 cm wide and 7 cm high?
(A) 50 L (B) 50 mL (C) 500 mL (D) 5 L — 1

13 7.02 L is the same as:
(A) 7 L 2 mL (B) 7 L 20 mL (C) 7 L 200 mL (D) 70 002 mL — 1

14 This is the base of a prism of height 8 cm. What is the volume of the prism?

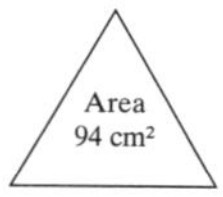

(A) 102 cm^3 (B) 188 cm^3 (C) 376 cm^3 (D) 752 cm^3 — 1

15 For which prism is the volume found by multiplying the area of the shaded face, A, by h?

(A) 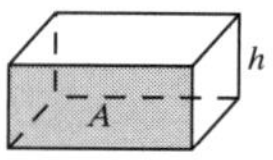

(B) 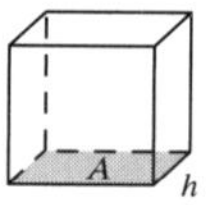

(C) 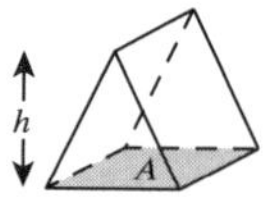

(D) 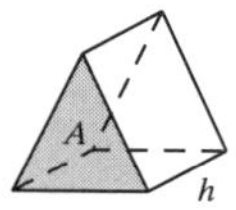

— 1

PART B Write answers only in the space provided.

16 How many millilitres are in $3\frac{1}{2}$ L? ________ 1

17 What is the volume of a rectangular prism 23 cm long, 15 cm wide and 9 cm high? ________ 1

18 A tank has a volume of 2.85 m^3. How many litres of water will it hold? ________ 1

19 The bases of two identical square pyramids are stuck together.
How many faces will the new object have? ________ 1

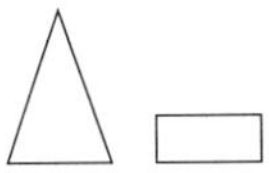

20 These are two of the faces of a prism. What type of prism is it? ________ 1

21 If the two faces are instead faces of a pyramid, what type of pyramid must it be? ________ 1

22 6.25 kL is how many litres? ________ 1

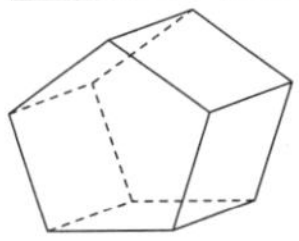

23 What shape is the constant cross-section of this prism? ________ 1

24 What is the volume of a cube of side length 4 cm? ________ 1

25 25 600 kL is how many megalitres? ________ 1

PART C Show all working.

26 This object is created from cubes of side length 1 cm.

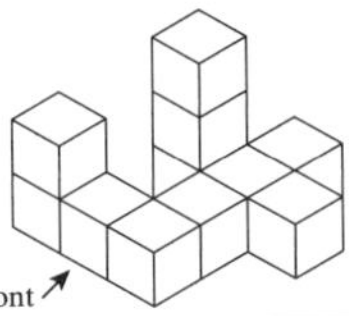

front

a What is the volume of the object? 1 mark

____

b Draw the view from the:
i front 1 mark **ii** top 1 mark

iii right side 1 mark **iv** back 1 mark

27 A garden pond is in the form of a rectangular prism 2.4 m long and 1.25 m wide. It can be filled to a depth of 30 cm.

a What is its volume in cubic metres? 2 marks

____

____

b What is its capacity in litres? 1 mark

____

c If water flows into the pond at the rate of 5 L every minute, how many hours will it take to fill? 1 mark

____

28 a The outside dimensions, in millimetres, of a tank in the shape of a rectangular prism are given as 1725 × 700 × 730. Find the volume in cubic metres to two decimal places. 2 marks

____

____

b The inside dimensions are each 25 mm less than the outside dimensions. Find the volume inside the tank. Give the answer to two decimal places. 2 marks

____

____

____

c About how many fewer litres does the tank actually hold than what is calculated using the outside dimensions? 2 marks

____

____

Total marks /40

LEVEL 3 TEST

PART A

Time allowed: 40 minutes

1 0.25 ML =

(A) 250 000 L (B) 2 500 000 L (C) 25 000 L (D) 2500 L 1

2 A farm dam has a capacity of 18 ML. What is its volume?

(A) 18 000 m^3 (B) 180 000 m^3 (C) 1 800 000 m^3 (D) 18 000 000 m^3 1

3 What is the volume of a rectangular prism 3.6 m long, 1.25 m wide and 50 cm high?

(A) 225 m^3 (B) 2.25 m^3 (C) 225 cm^3 (D) 225 000 cm^3 1

4 Of which solid could this **not** be a face?

(A) triangular prism (B) triangular pyramid

(C) pentagonal prism (D) pentagonal pyramid

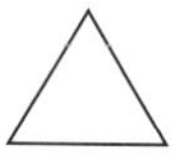

1

5 1 m^3 is how many cubic centimetres?

(A) 100 (B) 1000 (C) 100 000 (D) 1 000 000 1

6 A prism has volume 250 mm^3. What is its capacity?

(A) 0.25 mL (B) 2.5 mL (C) 25 mL (D) 250 mL 1

7 A rectangular prism of height 9 cm has volume 216 cm^3. What could its other dimensions be?

(A) 5 cm by 5 cm (B) 12 cm by 2 cm (C) 7 cm by 4 cm (D) 5 cm by 3.5 cm 1

8 How many wooden blocks that are each 4 cm long, 2 cm wide and 3 cm high can be stacked in a box that is 80 cm long, 60 cm wide and 20 cm high?

(A) 2000 (B) 3600 (C) 3900 (D) 4000 1

9 A rectangular prism has volume 4896 cm^3. If the prism is 18 cm long and 16 cm wide, how high is it?

(A) 1.7 m (B) 17 cm (C) 17 mm (D) 1.7 mm 1

10 If each of the dimensions of a rectangular prism doubles, the new volume will be how many times the original volume?

(A) 2 (B) 4 (C) 6 (D) 8 1

11 The square bases of two identical pyramids are stuck together, matching exactly. How many more edges than vertices does the new object have?

(A) 2 (B) 4 (C) 6 (D) 8 1

12 5.15 L – 87 mL =

(A) 4.28 L (B) 4.72 L (C) 5.063 L (D) 5.1413 L 1

13 The front view and side view of an object are shown. Which could be the top view?

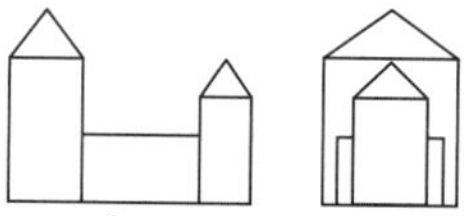

(A) 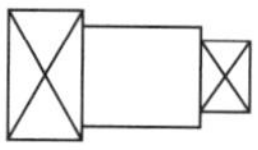 (B) 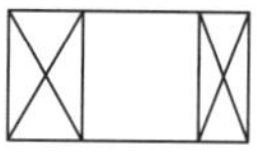 (C) 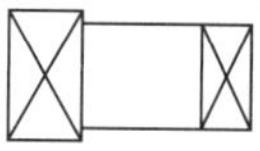 (D) 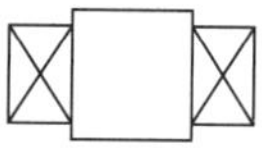

1

14 5 kL and 700 mL = ?

(A) 5.7 kL (B) 5.07 kL (C) 5.007 kL (D) 5.0007 kL 1

15 Which dimensions will be for a rectangular prism with a volume different to the others?

(A) 35 m × 9 m × 4 m (B) 21 m × 10 m × 6 m

(C) 18 m × 14 m × 5 m (D) 16 m × 15 m × 7 m 1

PART B Write answers only in the space provided.

16 A cube has volume 1331 cm^3. What is the length of each side? ______________ 1

17 12.05 L = 12 L and how many millilitres? ______________ 1

18 A prism is made up of 12 layers. Each layer has 12 cubes of side length 1 cm. What is the volume of the prism? ______________ 1

19 A carton contains 24 cans of soft drink. Each can holds 375 mL. How many litres of soft drink does the carton contain? ______________ 1

20 The area of the shaded face is 312 cm^2. What is the volume? ______________ 1

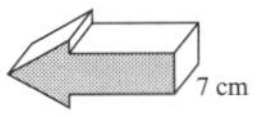

21 What is the object in Question 20? ______________ 1

22 What is the capacity, in millilitres, of a cube of side 7 cm? ______________ 1

23 How many litres is 7240 L + 5.3 kL + 1900 mL? ______________ 1

24 What is the volume, in cubic metres, of a rectangular prism with sides 80 cm by 80 cm by 1.2 m?

______________ 1

25 A hole has been cut through this prism.
What is the volume of the remaining solid? ______________ 1

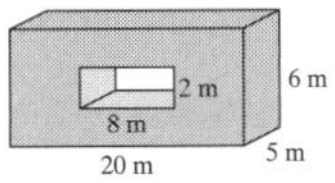

PART C Show all working.

26 Toby said: 'A square-based prism is a cube'. Is Toby correct? Explain why or why not. 2 marks

____

____

27 These are the five faces of a prism.

a What type of prism is it? 1 mark

____

b The prism is stuck to the top of a cube. The faces that are stuck together match exactly. What is the new solid? 1 mark

____

c Draw for the new solid the:

i top view 1 mark **ii** side view 1 mark

28 A floor for a shed is to be a rectangular slab of concrete. It will be 5.5 m long, 3.8 m wide and 30 cm thick.

a How many cubic metres of concrete will be needed? 2 marks

____

____

b How much more concrete will be needed if the slab is to be 10 cm longer? 2 marks

____

____

c If concrete costs $250 per cubic metre, how much extra does each extra centimetre in length cost, if the width and depth remain the same? 2 marks

____

____

29

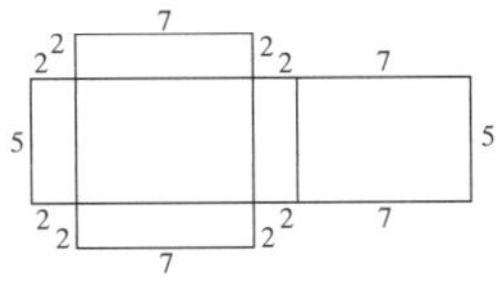

a This is the net of what type of prism? 1 mark

____

b What is the volume of the prism? (All dimensions are in centimetres.) 1 mark

____

c What would be the volume if each of the dimensions tripled? 1 mark

____

Total marks /40

LEVELS 1 AND 2 TEST

PART A

Time allowed: 40 minutes

1 What is the perimeter of a rectangle 7 cm long and 3 cm wide?

(A) 10 cm (B) 20 cm (C) 21 cm (D) 42 cm 1

2 What is the area of a rectangle 5.5 m long and 3.5 m wide?

(A) 9 m^2 (B) 18 m^2 (C) 15.25 m^2 (D) 19.25 m^2 1

3 Which is closest to the volume of a rectangular prism 6.2 m long, 3.6 m wide and 2.4 m high?

(A) 54 m^3 (B) 24 m^3 (C) 46 m^3 (D) 107 m^3 1

4 What is the area of this triangle?

(A) 390 cm^2 (B) 450 cm^2 (C) 116 cm^2 (D) 780 cm^2 1

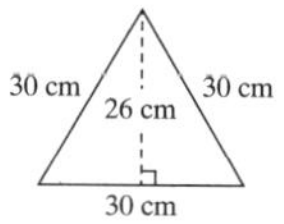

5 6.07 km is 6 km and how many metres?

(A) 0.0007 (B) 7 (C) 70 (D) 700 1

6 What is the area, in hectares, of a rectangular paddock 400 m long and 250 m wide?

(A) 0.1 ha (B) 1 ha (C) 1.3 ha (D) 10 ha 1

7 Which expression will give the area of the shaded triangle?

(A) $\frac{1}{2} \times 9 \times 8$ (B) $\frac{1}{2} \times 9 \times 10$ (C) $\frac{1}{2} \times 10 \times 17$ (D) $\frac{1}{2} \times 17 \times 4.8$ 1

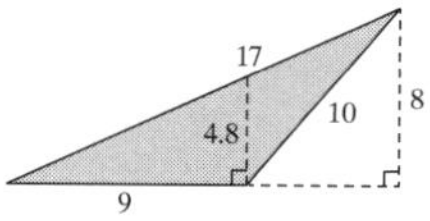

8 A carton has a capacity of 600 mL. What is its volume?

(A) 0.6 m^3 (B) 600 cm^3 (C) 60 cm^3 (D) 6 cm^3 1

9 Which unit would be best to measure the length of a basketball court?

(A) centimetres (B) kilometres (C) millimetres (D) metres 1

10 Sid said the area of this triangle is 30 cm^2 and the perimeter is 30 cm. Which is correct?

(A) area but not perimeter (B) perimeter but not area

(C) both perimeter and area (D) neither 1

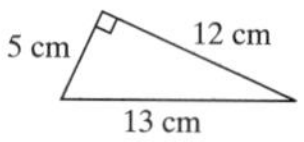

11 What is the volume of a cube of side 5 cm?

(A) 20 cm^3 (B) 25 cm^3 (C) 125 cm^3 (D) 150 cm^3 1

12 Using the ruler provided, what is the length of the pencil?

(A) 68 mm (B) 73 mm (C) 78 mm (D) 8 cm 1

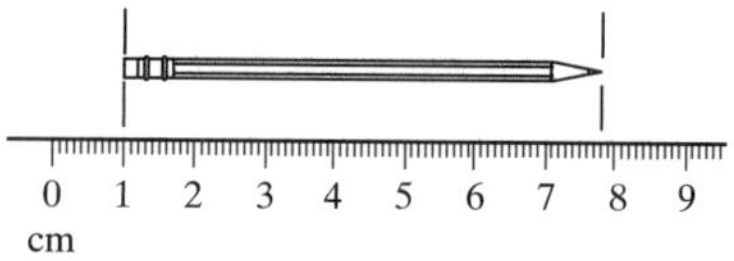

13 Which has the greatest area? (All measurements are in centimetres.)

(A) 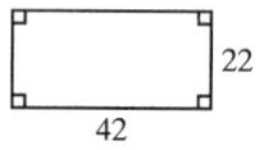

(B) 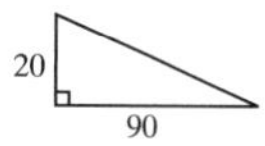

(C) 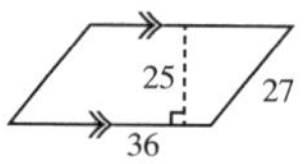

(D) 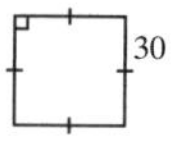

1

14 From a 3 m length of elastic two pieces are cut off. One of those pieces is 45 cm long and the other is 225 mm. What length of elastic remains?

(A) 2.325 m (B) 23.25 cm (C) 300 mm (D) 3 cm 1

15 A square has perimeter 36 cm. What is its area?

(A) 24 cm^2 (B) 81 cm^2 (C) 96 cm^2 (D) 324 cm^2 1

Length, Area and Volume Calculator Allowed **(Levels 1 and 2 Test)**

PART B Write answers only in the space provided.

16 What is the area of this parallelogram? ______________ 1

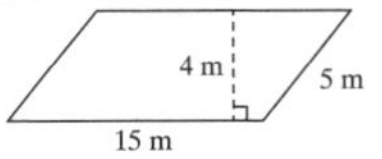

17 A square paddock has an area of 4 ha. How long is each side? ______________ 1

18 What is the volume of a rectangular prism 9 cm long, 8 cm wide and 3.5 cm high? ______________ 1

19 What is the perimeter of a regular octagon of side length 5 cm? ______________ 1

20 How many litres are in 2.04 ML? ______________ 1

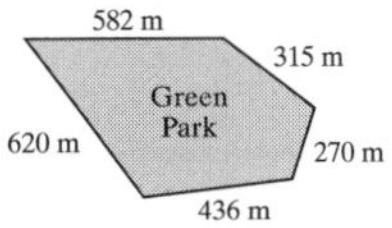

21 What is the perimeter of the park in kilometres? ______________ 1

22 What is the area, in square metres, of a rectangle that is 1.68 m long and 825 mm wide? ______________ 1

23 How many metres are in 0.04 km? ______________ 1

24 Arrange in order from smallest to largest: 1 cm^2, 1 km^2, 1 mm^2, 1 m^2, 1 ha. ______________ 1

25 If 1 L of water weighs 1 kg, what is the weight of 1 m^3 of water? ______________ 1

PART C Show all working.

26 a What is the perimeter, in metres, of this rectangle? 1 mark

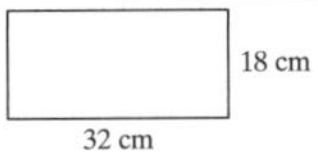

____

b What is the area in square centimetres? 1 mark

____

c If this is the base of a rectangular prism 12 cm high, what is the volume in cubic centimetres? 1 mark

____

d What is the capacity of the prism in litres? 1 mark

____

27 The perimeter of a rectangle is 1.8 m. If the rectangle is twice as long as it is wide, find its area. 2 marks

____

____

____

28 This is a plan of a yard.

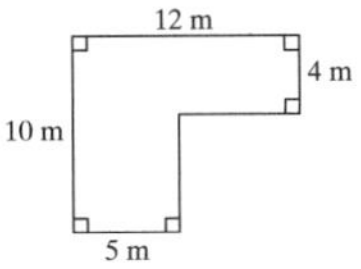

a Find the cost of fencing the whole yard at $24.50 per metre. 2 marks

____

____

b Find the cost of paving the yard at $79 per square metre. 2 marks

____

____

c Find the amount of sand required to put under the pavers if the sand is to be 30 mm thick. 1 mark

____

____

29 a Find the distance, in kilometres, around this block of land. 2 marks

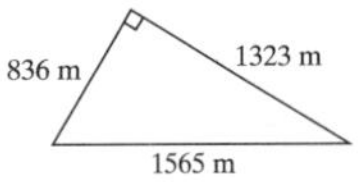

____

____

b Find the area in hectares to one decimal place. 2 marks

____

____

____

Total marks /40

Length, Area and Volume Calculator Allowed

LEVELS 2 AND 3 TEST PART A

Time allowed: 40 minutes

1 A tank has a volume of 19.5 m^3. What is its capacity?

(A) 19.5 L (B) 195 L (C) 1950 L (D) 19 500 L

2 In which diagram can the area be found by multiplying b by h?

(A) 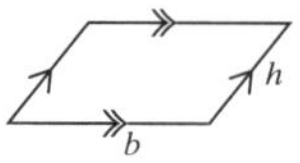

(B) 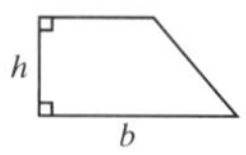

(C) 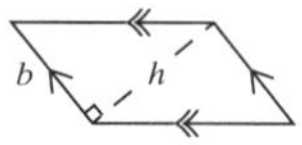

(D) 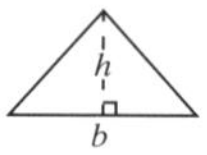

3 A rectangle 8 cm long has an area of 48 cm^2. What is its perimeter?

(A) 14 cm (B) 24 cm (C) 28 cm (D) 48 cm

4 Which of these rectangles has the greatest perimeter?

(A) 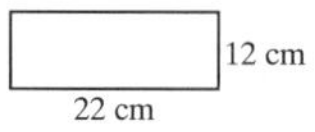

(B) 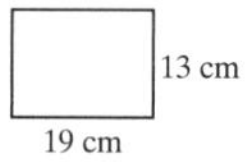

(C) 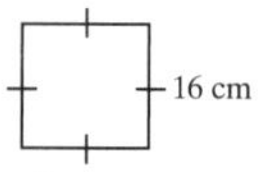

(D) 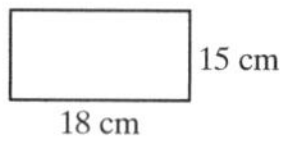

5 Which of the rectangles in Question 4 has the greatest area?

(A) A (B) B (C) C (D) D

6 A square has an area of 144 m^2. What is its perimeter?

(A) 24 m (B) 36 m (C) 48 m D 60 m

7 How many kilolitres are in 0.9 ML?

(A) 900 (B) 0.0009 (C) 9000 (D) 900 000

8 What is the area of the shaded triangle? (All measurements are in metres.)

(A) 726 m^2 (B) 1056 m^2 (C) 1144 m^2 (D) 1320 m^2

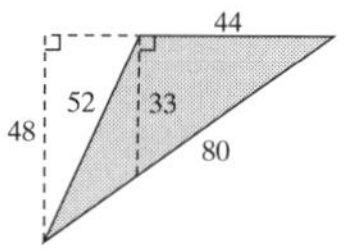

9 How many square pavers, side length 40 cm, would be needed to cover an area 4 m by 2.4 m?

(A) 60 (B) 166 (C) 600 (D) 960

10 What is the volume of a rectangular prism 2 m long, 37 cm wide and 58 mm high?

(A) 4292 cm^3 (B) 4292 mm^3 (C) 4 292 000 mm^3 (D) 0.042 92 m^3

11 What is the shaded area?

(A) 97 m^2 (B) 113 m^2 (C) 118 m^2 (D) 142 m^2

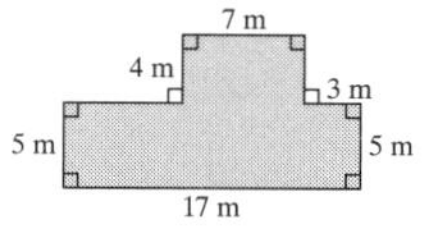

12 What is the perimeter of the shape in Question 11?

(A) 41 m (B) 45 m (C) 50 m (D) 52 m

13 What is the area of this parallelogram?

(A) 28.8 cm^2 (B) 44.8 cm^2 (C) 288 cm^2 (D) 448 cm^2

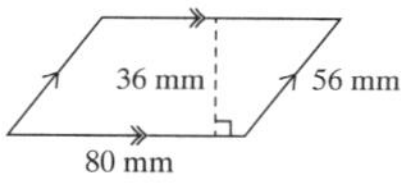

14 0.203 m is:

(A) 20 cm and 3 mm (B) 2 cm and 3 mm (C) 203 cm (D) 20.3 mm

15 A rectangle is divided into three triangles. What is the area of the rectangle?

(A) 108 cm^2 (B) 120 cm^2 (C) 144 cm^2 (D) 168 cm^2

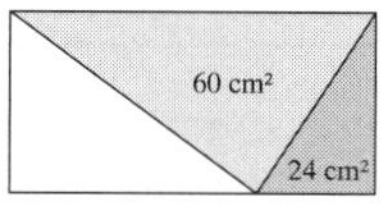

Marks: 1 1 1 1 1 1 1 1 1 1 1 1 1 1 1

Length, Area and Volume Calculator Allowed (Levels 2 and 3 Test)

PART B Write answers only in the space provided.

16 What is the volume of a cube of side 3 m? ______________ 1

17 How many millilitres are in 0.35 L? ______________ 1

18 What is the area of this triangle? ______________ 1

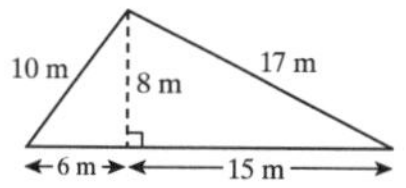

19 Find the sum of 19.25 m, 674 cm and 328 mm. Give the answer in metres. ______________ 1

20 A square has perimeter 64 cm. What is its area? ______________ 1

21 What is the capacity, in litres, of a rectangular prism 20 cm by 10 cm by 5 cm? ______________ 1

22 What is the area of this parallelogram? ______________ 1

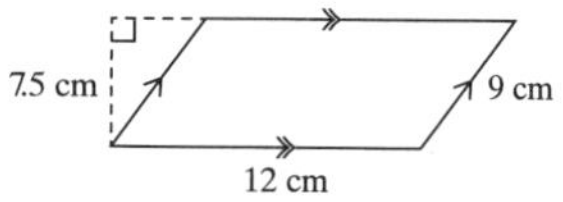

23 How many square metres are in a square kilometre? ______________ 1

24 How many 2450 mm fence panels would be needed to cover a length of 19.6 m? ______________ 1

25 What fraction of a cubic metre is a cubic centimetre? ______________ 1

PART C Show all working.

26 A pool is 12 m by 5 m. A fence is to be built around the pool, at a distance of 1.5 m from the pool on all sides.

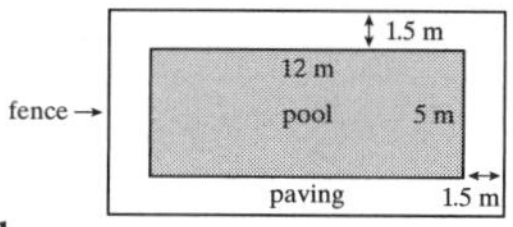

a Find the total cost of fencing the pool, if fencing costs $32 per metre and there is one 1 m gate costing $82. 2 marks

____

____

b The area between the pool and the fence will be paved. Find the cost of the paving at $34 per square metre. 2 marks

____

____

c The pool is 1.5 m deep. Find its volume. 1 mark

____

d How many litres of water will the pool hold? 1 mark

____

27 This shape is made up of an isosceles right-angled triangle, a rectangle and a parallelogram.

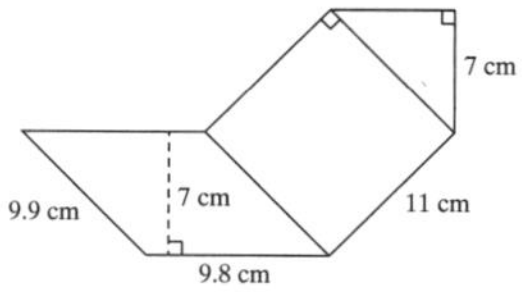

a Find the perimeter of the shape. 1 mark

____

b Find the area of the shape. 3 marks

____

____

____

28 A triangular block of land has measurements as shown.

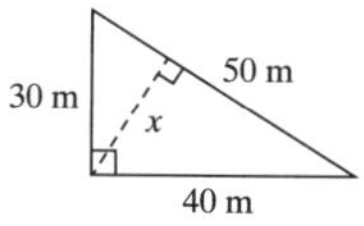

a Find the length of wire required to fence the land if there are to be five strands. 1 mark

____

b Find the area of the land in square metres. 1 mark

____

c Find the distance marked *x* on the diagram. 1 mark

____

29 A 3 L drink container is a rectangular prism with a square base of side 12.5 cm and it is 20 cm high. What percentage of the container will be empty? 2 marks

____

____

Total marks /40

Angles

PRETEST

Time allowed: 15 minutes **Total marks: 15**

1 A right angle measures:
(A) 80° (B) 90° (C) 100° (D) 180° 1

2 A straight angle measures:
(A) 90° (B) 100° (C) 180° (D) 360° 1

3 An acute angle measures:
(A) less than 90° (B) between 90° and 180°
(C) between 180° and 360° (D) more than 360° 1

4 Which angle would measure about 135°?
(A) 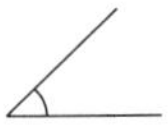 (B)  (C)  (D)  1

5 Which is a reflex angle?
(A) 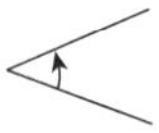 (B) 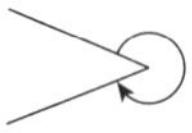 (C) 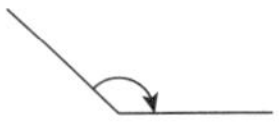 (D) 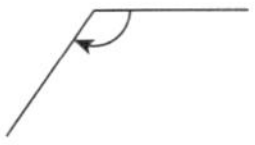 1

6 What is the size of the shaded angle?
(A) 24° (B) 56° (C) 66° (D) 76°
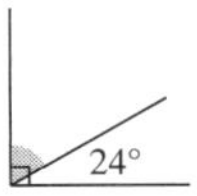

1

7 Angles in a revolution add to:
(A) 90° (B) 180° (C) 270° (D) 360° 1

8 What is the size of the shaded angle?
(A) 40° (B) 50° (C) 110° (D) 130°
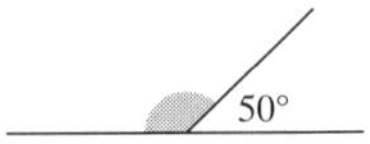

1

9 What type of angle measures 108°?
(A) acute (B) reflex (C) obtuse (D) straight 1

10 Which correctly completes this sentence? Vertically opposite angles are:
(A) horizontal (B) equal (C) complementary (D) supplementary 1

11 What is the size of the shaded angle?
(A) 90° (B) 180° (C) 210° (D) 270°
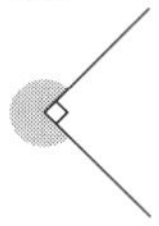
1

12 An angle measuring which of these sizes would be a reflex angle?
(A) 80° (B) 140° (C) 180° (D) 240° 1

13 An angle measuring which of these sizes would be an obtuse angle?
(A) 80° (B) 140° (C) 240° (D) 280° 1

14 What is the size of the shaded angle?
(A) 68° (B) 108° (C) 116° (D) 136°
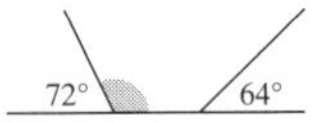

1

15 What is the size of the shaded angle?
(A) 102° (B) 112° (C) 132° (D) 192°
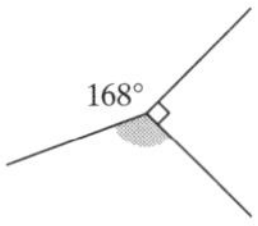

1

Total marks /15

Angle Relationships Calculator Allowed

LEVEL 1 TEST PART A

Time allowed: 40 minutes

Questions 1 to 3 refer to the angle on the right.

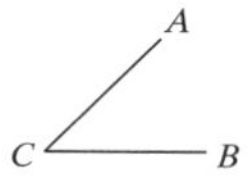

1 What is the vertex of the angle shown?

(A) *A* (B) *B* (C) *C* (D) *AB* 1

2 What could the angle be called?

(A) $\angle ACB$ (B) $\angle BCA$ (C) $\angle C$ (D) all of these 1

3 Which is an arm of the angle?

(A) *AB* only (B) *BC* only (C) *AC* only (D) both *AC* and *BC* 1

Questions 4 and 5 refer to the diagram on the right.

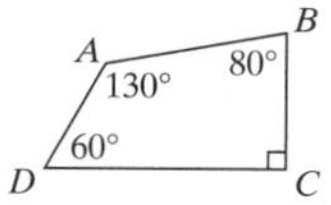

4 What is the size of $\angle DAB$?

(A) 60° (B) 80° (C) 90° (D) 130° 1

5 What is the size of $\angle BCD$?

(A) 60° (B) 80° (C) 90° (D) 130° 1

6 Which symbol means 'is parallel to'?

(A) ≡ (B) ⊥ (C) || (D) ||| 1

7 What is the complement of 70°?

(A) 20° (B) 30° (C) 110° (D) 290° 1

8 The angles marked • and × are:

(A) co-interior (B) corresponding (C) alternate (D) adjacent 1

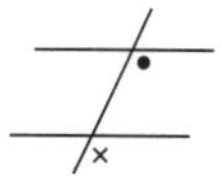

9 The angles marked • and × are:

(A) co-interior (B) corresponding (C) alternate (D) adjacent 1

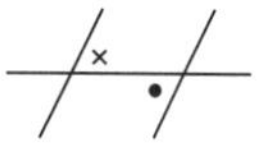

10 The angles marked • and × are:

(A) co-interior (B) corresponding (C) alternate (D) adjacent 1

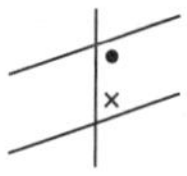

11 The angles marked • and × are:

(A) co-interior (B) corresponding (C) alternate (D) adjacent 1

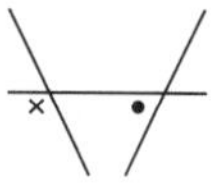

12 What is the supplement of 38°?

(A) 52° (B) 62° (C) 122° (D) 142° 1

13 If two parallel lines are cut by a transversal the corresponding angles are:

(A) equal (B) complementary (C) supplementary (D) adjacent 1

14 If two parallel lines are cut by a transversal the co-interior angles are:

(A) equal (B) complementary (C) supplementary (D) adjacent 1

15 If two parallel lines are cut by a transversal the alternate angles are:

(A) equal (B) complementary (C) supplementary (D) adjacent 1

PART B Write answers only in the space provided.

16 What is the size of the shaded angle? ____________ [1]

16
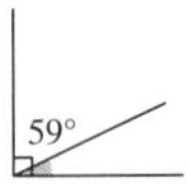

17 What is the size of the shaded angle? ____________ [1]

17
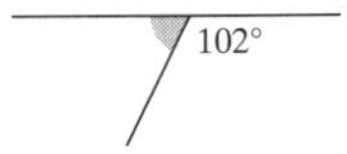

18 What is the size of the shaded angle? ____________ [1]

18
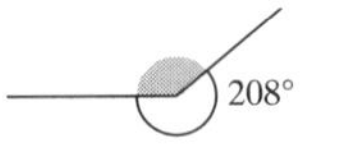

19 Complete: A pair of lines is parallel if the alternate angles are ____________. [1]

20 Complete: A pair of lines is parallel if the co-interior angles are ____________. [1]

21 Complete: A pair of lines is parallel if the corresponding angles are ____________. [1]

22 What is the size of the shaded angle? ____________ [1]

22
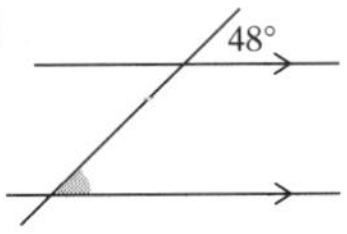

23 What is the size of the shaded angle? ____________ [1]

23
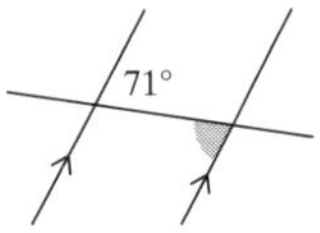

24 What is the size of the shaded angle? ____________ [1]

24
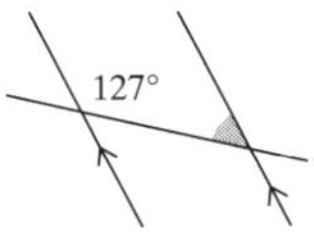

25 What is the size of the shaded angle? ____________ [1]

25
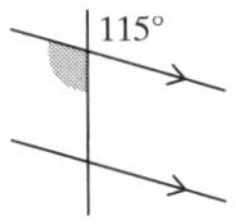

PART C Show all working.

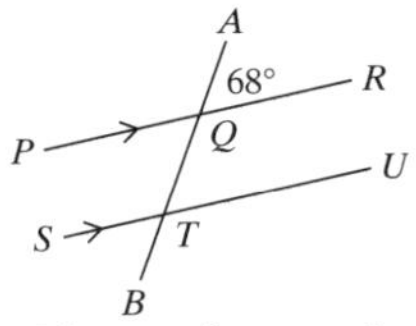

26 a Name the angle that is marked 68°. [1 mark]

____

b Briefly explain why $\angle PQT$ must also be 68°. [1 mark]

____

c How do we know from the diagram that PR is parallel to SU? [1 mark]

____

d What is the size of $\angle QTU$? Give a reason for your answer. [1 mark]

____

e Name an angle that corresponds to $\angle PQT$. [1 mark]

____

f Name an angle alternate to $\angle PQT$. [1 mark]

____

g What is the size of $\angle QTS$? [1 mark]

____

27 Determine whether AB is parallel to CD in these diagrams. Justify your answer.

a [2 marks]

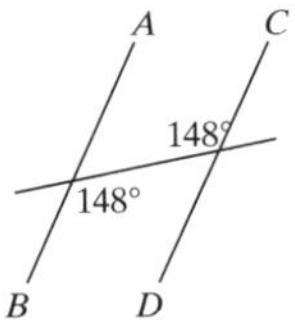

____

____

b [2 marks]

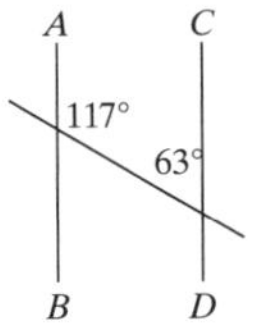

____

____

c [2 marks]

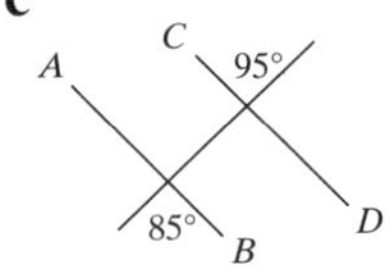

____

____

28 AB and CD are straight lines intersecting at E. $\angle DEF$ is a right angle. $\angle AEC = 126°$.

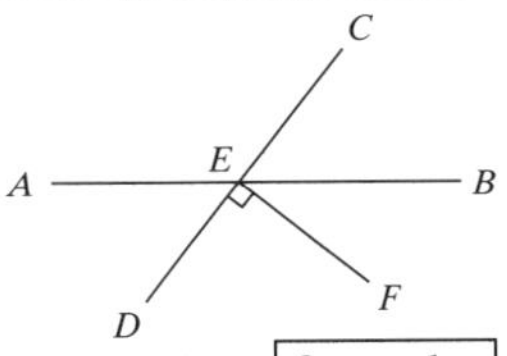

Find the size of $\angle BEF$, giving reasons. [2 marks]

____

____

Total marks /40

Angle Relationships Calculator Allowed

LEVEL 2 TEST PART A

Time allowed: 40 minutes

1 What is the vertex of the angle shown?

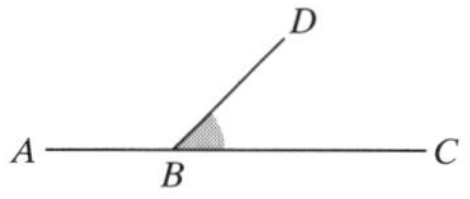

(A) *A* (B) *B* (C) *C* (D) *D* 1

2 What is the common arm of the two marked angles?

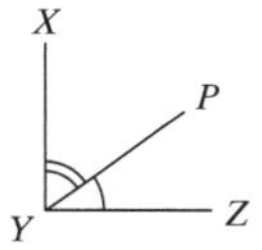

(A) *Y* (B) *XY* (C) *YZ* (D) *PY* 1

3 The two marked angles in the diagram above are:

(A) adjacent (B) alternate (C) equal (D) obtuse 1

4 Which of these angles must measure 90°?

(A)  (B)  (C) 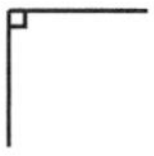 (D)  1

5 What type of angles can be formed when a pair of straight lines intersect?

(A) alternate (B) corresponding (C) co-interior (D) vertically opposite 1

6 Which symbol means 'is perpendicular to'?

(A) ≡ (B) ⊥ (C) || (D) ||| 1

7 What is the size of the shaded angle?

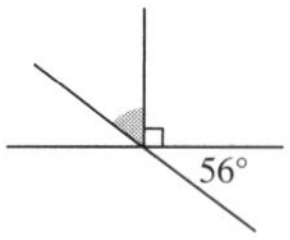

(A) 68° (B) 56° (C) 34° (D) 22° 1

8 Complementary angles:

(A) add to 90° (B) add to 180° (C) add to 360° (D) are equal 1

9 Which angle is **not** equal to 84°?

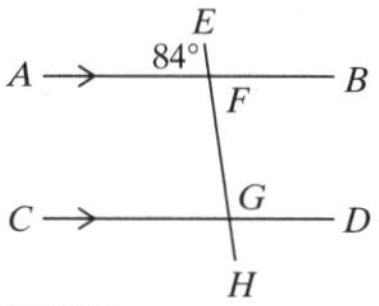

(A) ∠*EGC* (B) ∠*DGH* (C) ∠*BFG* (D) ∠*FGD* 1

10 Referring to the diagram in Question 9, what type of angles are ∠*CGH* and ∠*FGD*?

(A) alternate (B) co-interior (C) corresponding (D) vertically opposite 1

11 Referring to the diagram in Question 9, what type of angles are ∠*BFH* and ∠*EGD*?

(A) alternate (B) co-interior (C) corresponding (D) vertically opposite 1

12 What type of angles are supplementary when a pair of parallel lines is cut by a transversal?

(A) co-interior (B) corresponding (C) alternate (D) adjacent 1

13 What is the size of the shaded angle?

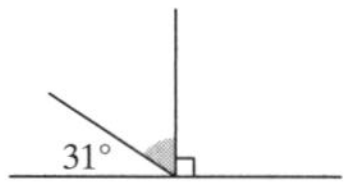

(A) 31° (B) 51° (C) 59° (D) 69° 1

14 Which is correct?

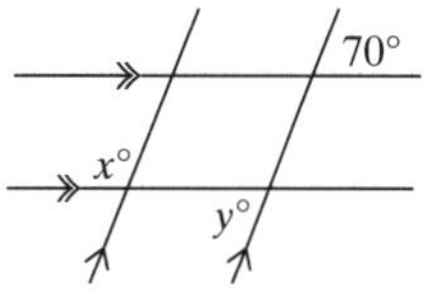

(A) $x = 70$ and $y = 70$ (B) $x = 70$ and $y = 110$

(C) $x = 110$ and $y = 70$ (D) $x = 110$ and $y = 110$ 1

15 In which diagram is *AB* parallel to *CD*?

(A) 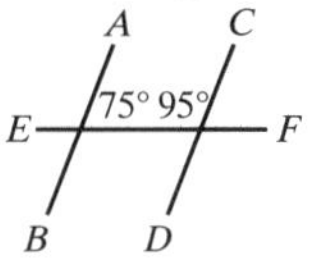

(B) 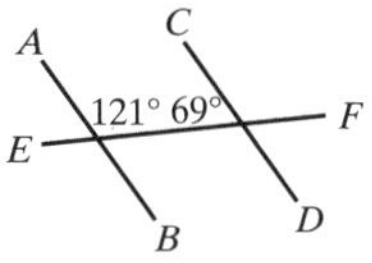

(C) 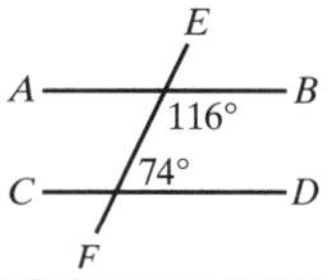

(D) 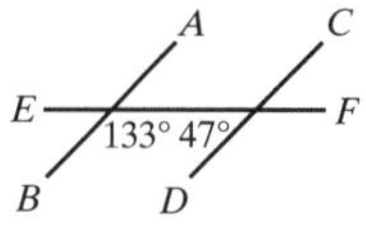

1

PART B Write answers only in the space provided.

The diagram on the right is used in Questions 16 to 21.

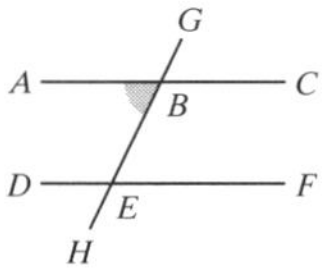

16 Name the shaded angle. ________________ 1

17 Name an angle that corresponds to the shaded angle. ________________ 1

18 Name an angle that is adjacent to the shaded angle. ________________ 1

19 Name an angle that is alternate to the shaded angle. ________________ 1

20 Name an angle that is vertically opposite the shaded angle. ________________ 1

21 Name an angle that, with the shaded angle, forms a pair of co-interior angles. ________________ 1

22 What is the supplement of 55°? ________________ 1

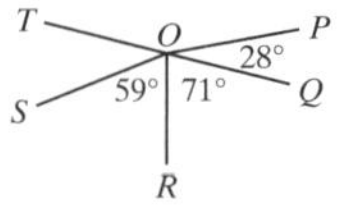

23 If *TOQ* is a straight line, what is the size of $\angle TOP$? ________________ 1

24 What size are each of the two angles formed when a right angle is divided in half? ________________ 1

25 What type of angle is $\angle ADB$? ________________ 1

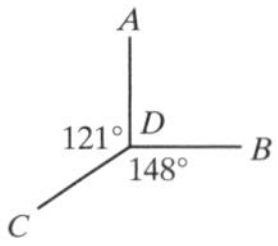

PART C Show all working.

26 Referring to the diagram:

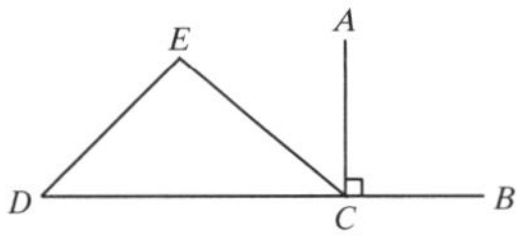

a name a pair of complementary angles 1 mark

____

b name a pair of adjacent angles 1 mark

____

c name a pair of supplementary angles 1 mark

____

d briefly explain why it is okay to refer to $\angle E$ but not $\angle C$ 1 mark

____

27 $\angle PTB = 75°$

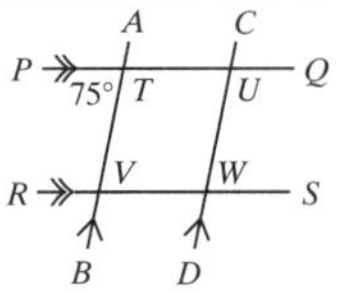

a Name three other angles that measure 75°. 1 mark

____

b What is the size of $\angle PTA$? 1 mark

____

c Name three other angles that are the same size as $\angle PTA$. 1 mark

____

28 a Is *EF* parallel to *GH*? Give a reason for your answer. 2 marks

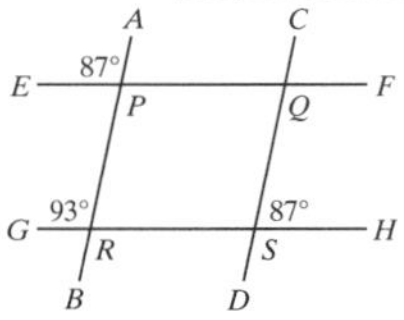

____

____

b Is *AB* parallel to *CD*? Justify your answer. 2 marks

____

____

29 a Explain why *AD* must be parallel to *BC*. 1 mark

____

____

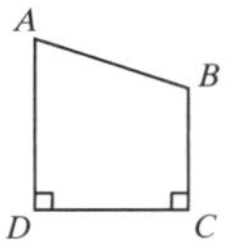

b If $\angle DAB = 63°$, what is the size of $\angle ABC$? 1 mark

____

30 *AB* is parallel to *CD*. *TR* is perpendicular to *CD*. $\angle PQA = 50°$. Find the size of $\angle TRS$, giving reasons. 2 marks

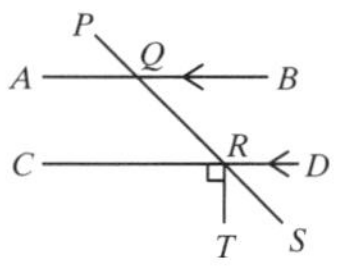

____

____

____

Total marks /40

Angle Relationships Calculator Allowed

LEVEL 3 TEST PART A

Time allowed: 40 minutes

1 What is the name of the shaded angle?

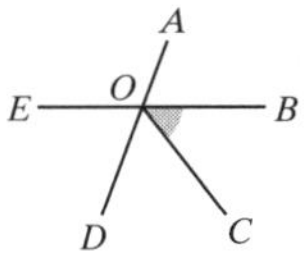

(A) $\angle OBC$ (B) $\angle BCO$ (C) $\angle COB$ (D) $\angle OCB$ 1

2 Referring to the diagram in Question 1, which angle is adjacent to the shaded angle?

(A) $\angle ABO$ (B) $\angle BAO$ (C) $\angle COD$ (D) $\angle DOE$ 1

3 In this diagram, which is the transversal?

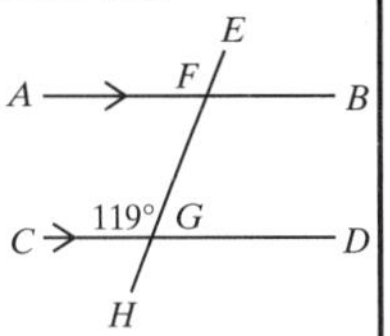

(A) AF (B) FB (C) CD (D) EH 1

4 Referring to the diagram in Question 3, which is correct?

(A) $\angle AFH = 61°$ and $\angle BFG = 61°$

(B) $\angle AFH = 61°$ and $\angle BFG = 119°$

(C) $\angle AFH = 119°$ and $\angle BFG = 61°$

(D) $\angle AFH = 119°$ and $\angle BFG = 119°$ 1

5 Referring to the diagram in Question 3, which angle corresponds to the one marked 119°?

(A) $\angle EFA$ (B) $\angle AFG$ (C) $\angle DGH$ (D) $\angle BFG$ 1

6 A pair of lines cut by a transversal will be parallel when:

(A) alternate angles are equal

(B) co-interior angles are equal

(C) corresponding angles are supplementary

(D) all of these 1

7 Angles measuring 41° and 49° must be:

(A) adjacent (B) complementary (C) supplementary (D) none of these 1

8 Angles measuring 127° and 73° must be:

(A) vertically opposite (B) complementary (C) supplementary (D) none of these 1

9 If two lines are perpendicular, they:

(A) never meet (B) meet at right angles (C) are complementary (D) are supplementary 1

10 What is the value of x?

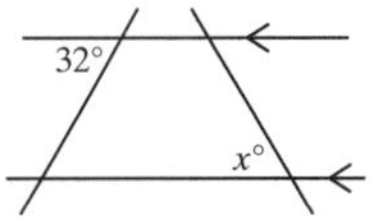

(A) 37° (B) 53° (C) 143° (D) not enough information 1

11 What is the value of x?

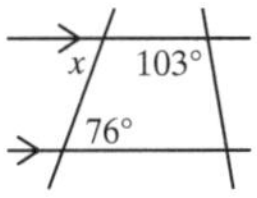

(A) 76° (B) 87° (C) 103° (D) 114° 1

12 What is the value of y?

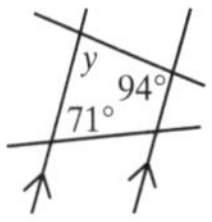

(A) 71° (B) 86° (C) 94° (D) 109° 1

13 If an angle measuring $x°$ and one measuring $y°$ are complementary then:

(A) $x = y$ (B) $x = 90 - y$ (C) $y = 180 - x$ (D) none of these 1

14 With a pair of co-interior angles, formed by parallel lines, which could be correct?

(A) One is acute and one is obtuse.

(B) Both are acute.

(C) Both are obtuse.

(D) One is acute and one is reflex. 1

15 What is the supplement of $x°$?

(A) $90° - x°$ (B) $180° - x°$ (C) $x° - 90°$ (D) $x° - 180°$ 1

PART B Write answers only in the space provided.

16 What is the symbol for 'is perpendicular to'? ______ [1]

17 The angles marked • and × are what type of angles? ______ [1]

18 What is the vertex of $\angle PRQ$? ______ [1]

19 What is the common arm of $\angle JKL$ and $\angle LKM$? ______ [1]

20 Find the value of x. ______ [1]

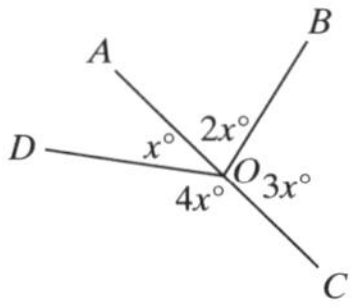

21 In the diagram above, what is the size of $\angle BOC$? ______ [1]

22 Referring to the diagram at right, $x =$ ______ [1]

23 Referring to the diagram at right, $y =$ ______ [1]

24 Referring to the diagram at right, $z =$ ______ [1]

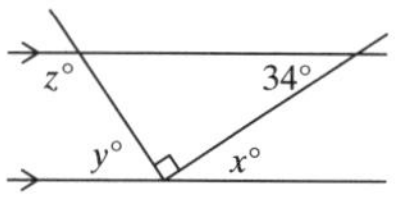

25 What is the supplement of the complement of 59°? ______ [1]

PART C Show all working.

26 Find the value of x in each diagram, giving reasons.

a [2 marks]

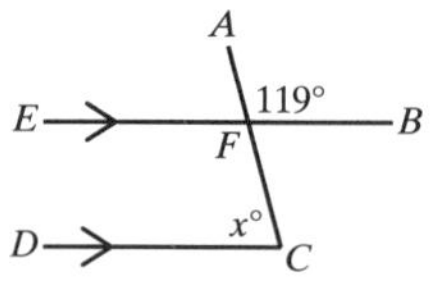

b [2 marks]

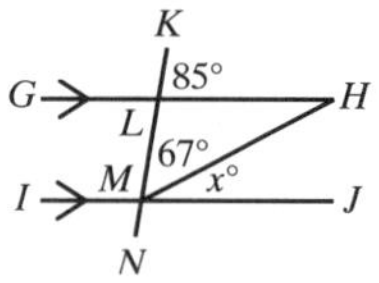

c [2 marks]

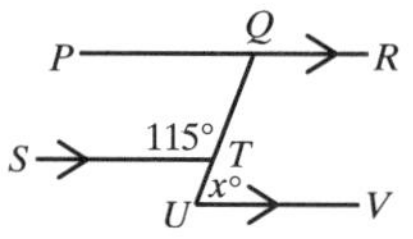

d [2 marks]

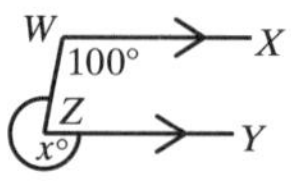

27 a If $\angle KCD = 74°$, is IJ parallel to KL? Justify your answer. [2 marks]

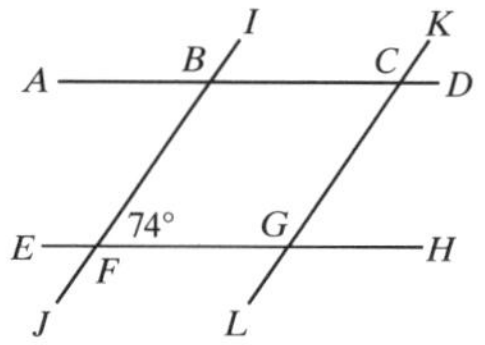

b If $\angle ABI = 106°$, is AD parallel to EH? Justify your answer. [2 marks]

28 $\angle EFD = 141°$ and $\angle BDF = 101°$. Find the size of $\angle ABD$, giving reasons. [3 marks]

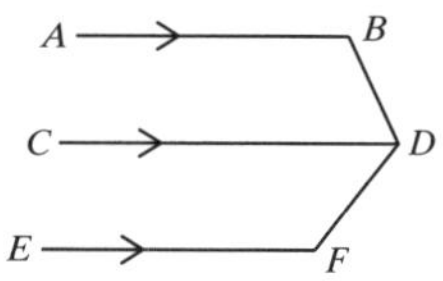

Total marks /40

Properties of Geometrical Figures

PRETEST

Time allowed: 15 minutes **Total marks: 12**

1 Which of these is a parallelogram?

(A) 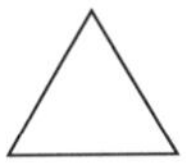 (B) 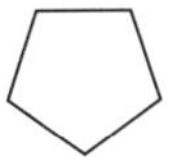 (C) 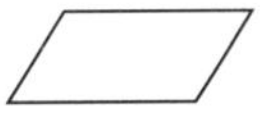 (D) 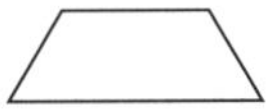

1

2 Which has exactly six sides?

(A) octagon (B) trapezium (C) heptagon (D) hexagon

1

3 Which has exactly two lines of symmetry?

(A) 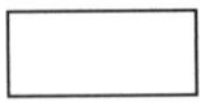 (B)  (C) 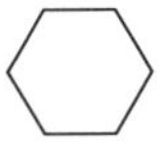 (D) 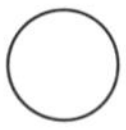

1

4 What type of triangle has all its sides equal?

(A) right-angled (B) equilateral (C) isosceles (D) scalene

1

5 Which is a regular pentagon?

(A) 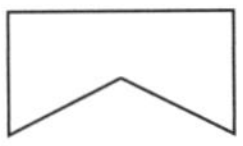 (B) 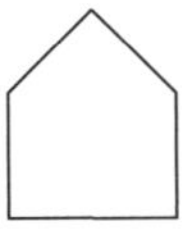 (C)  (D) 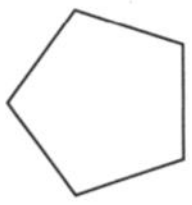

1

6 Which shape has **no** parallel sides?

(A) trapezium (B) rectangle (C) square (D) triangle

1

7 What will this shape L look like after a quarter-turn in a clockwise direction?

(A) L (B) Γ (C)  (D) 

1

8 What name is given to the line that passes through the centre of a circle from one side to the other?

(A) diameter (B) radius (C) circumference (D) sector

1

9 One square is missing from this symmetrical design. Which is it?

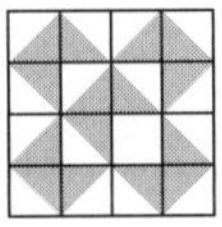

(A)  (B)  (C)  (D) 

1

10 How many diagonals does a rectangle have?

(A) 4 (B) 2 (C) 1 (D) 0

1

11 Which of these shapes is a decagon?

(A) 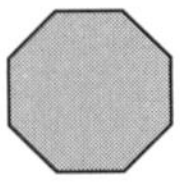 (B) 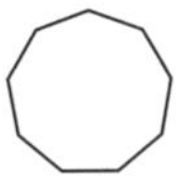 (C) 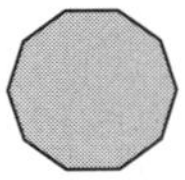 (D) 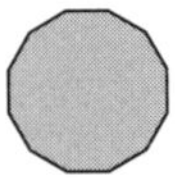

1

12 Nigel folds a piece of paper in half and cuts out a shape.
What does it look like when unfolded?

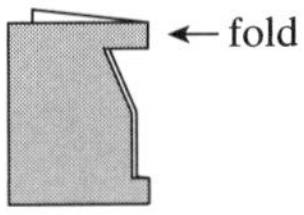

(A)  (B)  (C)  (D) 

1

Total marks /12

LEVEL 1 TEST

PART A

Time allowed: 40 minutes

1 Which is a quadrilateral?

(A) pentagon (B) pyramid (C) prism (D) parallelogram 1

2 What type of triangle has all its angles equal?

(A) equilateral (B) isosceles (C) scalene (D) right-angled 1

3 What do the angles of a triangle add up to?

(A) 100° (B) 160° (C) 180° (D) 360° 1

4 Which has exactly one line of symmetry?

(A) 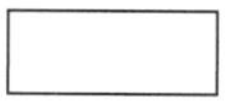 (B) 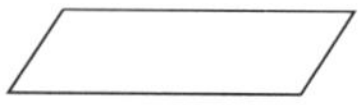 (C) 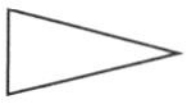 (D)  1

5 Which is an obtuse-angled triangle?

(A)  (B)  (C) 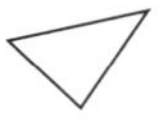 (D) 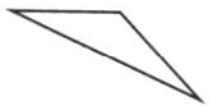 1

6 What size is each angle of a square?

(A) 45° (B) 60° (C) 90° (D) 100° 1

7 An isosceles triangle must have:

(A) all angles different (B) two equal angles (C) three equal angles (D) one right angle 1

8 What is the size of the shaded angle?

(A) 60° (B) 70° (C) 80° (D) 110° 1

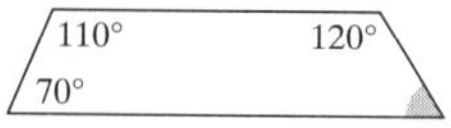

9 What type of quadrilateral is the one in Question 8?

(A) parallelogram (B) rhombus (C) trapezium (D) kite 1

10 In the triangle at right $AB = AC$. $\angle ABC = 70°$. What is the size of $\angle ACB$?

(A) 40° (B) 50° (C) 60° (D) 70° 1

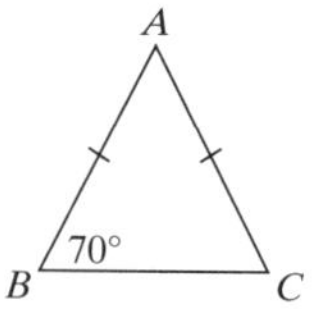

11 In the triangle at right what is the size of $\angle BAC$?

(A) 40° (B) 50° (C) 60° (D) 70° 1

12 What type of triangle is ΔABC (above right)?

(A) equilateral (B) isosceles (C) scalene (D) right-angled 1

13 In the triangle at right what is the size of $\angle QRS$?

(A) 150° (B) 100° (C) 80° (D) 70° 1

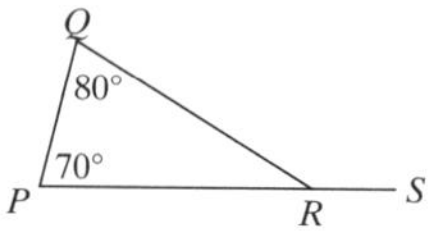

14 What type of triangle is ΔPQR (above right)?

(A) equilateral (B) isosceles (C) scalene (D) right-angled 1

15 Which of these quadrilaterals must have all its sides equal?

(A) rectangle (B) rhombus (C) kite (D) trapezium 1

Properties of Geometrical Figures Calculator Allowed **(Level 1 Test)**

PART B Write answers only in the space provided.

16 What size is each angle of an equilateral triangle? ________________ 1

17 How many lines of symmetry does a square have? ________________ 1

18 Draw an acute-angled scalene triangle. 1

19 What name is given to any parallelogram with adjacent sides equal? ________________ 1

20 'All squares are rectangles.' True or false? ________________ 1

21 'All rectangles are squares.' True or false? ________________ 1

22 What do the angles of a quadrilateral add up to? ________________ 1

23 'The diagonals of a parallelogram are always equal.' True or false? ________________ 1

24 A triangle has a right angle and another angle of 40°. What is the size of the third angle of the triangle? ________________ 1

25 One angle of a parallelogram measures 65°. What is the size of the opposite angle? ________________ 1

PART C Show all working.

26 *JKLM* is a rectangle.

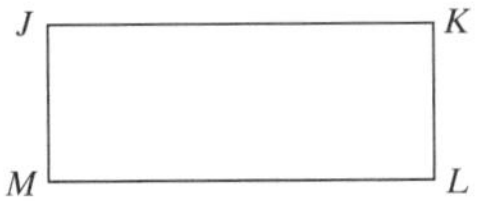

a What is the size of $\angle KLM$? 1 mark

____

b Draw the diagonals on the diagram. 1 mark

c Are the diagonals equal in length? 1 mark

____

d Do the diagonals bisect each other? 1 mark

____

e Do the diagonals meet at right angles? 1 mark

____

f Do the diagonals bisect the angles of the rectangle? 1 mark

____

27 In ΔPQR, $PR = QR$ and $\angle PQR = 40°$.

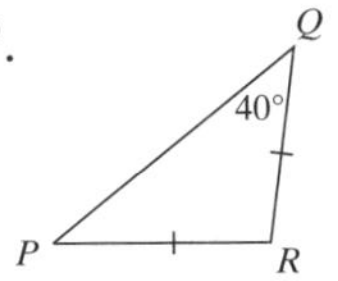

a Briefly explain why $\angle QPR$ must also be 40°. 1 mark

____

____

b Find the size of $\angle PRQ$. 1 mark

____

c What type of triangle is ΔPQR? 1 mark

____

28 In ΔABC, $BC = 7$ cm, $\angle ABC = 45°$ and $\angle CAB = 71°$.

a Sketch the triangle (not to scale) and mark on it all the information. 1 mark

b What is the size of $\angle BCA$? 1 mark

____

c What type of triangle is ΔABC? 1 mark

____

29

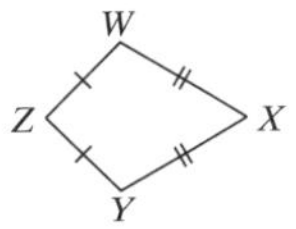

a What type of quadrilateral is this? 1 mark

____

b If $\angle ZWX = 104°$, what is the size of $\angle ZYX$? 1 mark

____

c If also $\angle WZY = 84°$, what is the size of $\angle WXY$? 1 mark

____

Total marks /40

LEVEL 2 TEST — PART A

Time allowed: 40 minutes

1 Which is **not** a quadrilateral?

(A) rhombus (B) rectangle (C) trapezium (D) pentagon [1]

2 Which shows an acute-angled isosceles triangle?

(A) 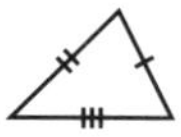 (B) 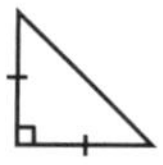 (C)  (D)  [1]

3 What single transformation will make ☜ look like ☝?

(A) anticlockwise rotation through 90° (B) clockwise rotation through 90°

(C) rotation through 180° (D) reflection in left side [1]

4 The angles of a parallelogram add up to:

(A) 180° (B) 260° (C) 280° (D) 360° [1]

5 For which of these are both pairs of opposite sides **not** necessarily parallel?

(A) square (B) rhombus (C) rectangle (D) trapezium [1]

6 Which has more than one axis of symmetry?

(A) 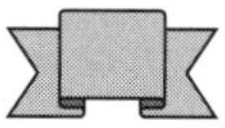 (B)  (C)  (D)  [1]

7 What is the size of the remaining angle?

(A) 105° (B) 115° (C) 135° (D) 255°

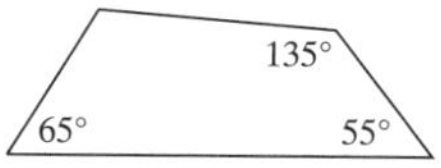

[1]

8 For which of these are the diagonals always equal?

(A) rhombus (B) rectangle (C) trapezium (D) kite [1]

9 What is the order of rotational symmetry for a square?

(A) 1 (B) 2 (C) 4 (D) 8 [1]

10 A scalene triangle has:

(A) three sides equal (B) two sides equal (C) no sides equal (D) all angles equal [1]

11 What is the size of the remaining angle in the triangle?

(A) 54° (B) 58° (C) 64° (D) 68°

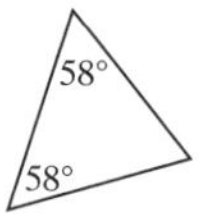

[1]

12 What is the length of the third side of this triangle?

(A) 7.3 cm (B) 6.15 cm (C) 5.7 cm (D) 5 cm

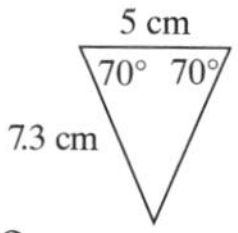

[1]

13 Which quadrilateral has diagonals that always bisect each other at right angles?

(A) a rectangle but not a rhombus (B) a rhombus but not a rectangle

(C) neither a rectangle nor rhombus (D) both a rectangle and a rhombus [1]

14 What is the size of $\angle BCD$?

(A) 75° (B) 83° (C) 115° (D) 135°

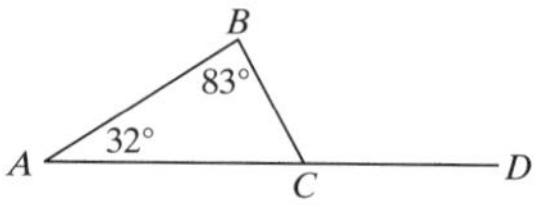

[1]

15 Which is **not** a convex quadrilateral?

(A)  (B)  (C)  (D) 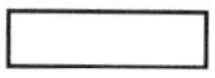 [1]

PART B Write answers only in the space provided.

16 What special name is given to a rhombus with one angle 90°? ______________ [1]

17 How many axes of symmetry does an ordinary parallelogram (one that is not also one of the other special quadrilaterals) have? ______________ [1]

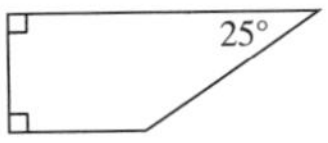

18 What type of quadrilateral is this? ______________ [1]

19 What is the size of the unmarked angle in the above quadrilateral? ______________ [1]

20 A quadrilateral has three right angles. What type of quadrilateral must it be? ______________ [1]

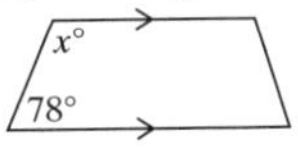

21 What is the value of x? ______________ [1]

22 A triangle has one angle of 37° and another of 102°. What is the size of the third angle? ______________ [1]

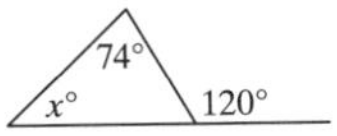

23 What is the value of x? ______________ [1]

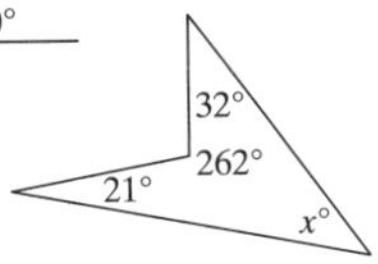

24 What is the value of x? ______________ [1]

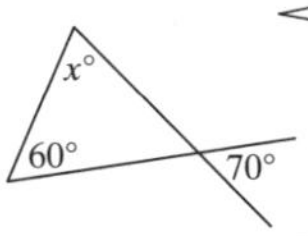

25 What is the value of x? ______________ [1]

PART C Show all working.

26 State whether these properties are true or false for every parallelogram:

a the opposite sides are equal [1 mark]

____

b the diagonals are equal [1 mark]

____

c the diagonals bisect each other [1 mark]

____

27 *PQRS* is a rectangle. $\angle PSQ = 60°$. *T* is a point on *SR* such that $TR = QR$.

a Show all the given information on a diagram. [1 mark]

b What type of triangle is ΔTQR? [1 mark]

____

c What is the size of $\angle TQR$? [1 mark]

____

d What is the size of $\angle SQT$? [1 mark]

____

28 *ABCD* is a rhombus. $\angle BAC = 60°$.

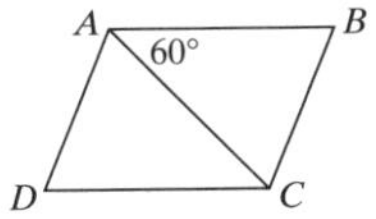

a What type of triangle is ΔABC? Justify your answer. [2 marks]

____

____

b What is the size of $\angle ABD$? Give reasons. [2 marks]

____

____

29 ΔDAB is right-angled at *A*. $\angle ADB = 64°$. *C* is a point on side *DB*. $AD = AC$.

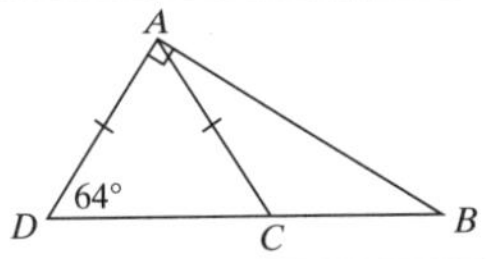

a What is the size of $\angle ABD$? [1 mark]

____

b What is the size of $\angle DAC$? [1 mark]

____

c What is the size of $\angle ACB$? [1 mark]

____

d What type of triangle is ΔACB? [1 mark]

____

Total marks / 40

LEVEL 3 TEST PART A

Time allowed: 40 minutes

1 Which could **not** be the lengths of the sides of a triangle?

(A) 1 cm, 2 cm, 3 cm (B) 5 cm, 16 cm, 17 cm
(C) 7 cm, 7 cm, 7cm (D) 32 cm, 94 cm, 1.1 m 1

2 What type of triangle has one angle of 50° and one of 70°?

(A) isosceles (B) scalene (C) equilateral (D) not enough information 1

3 How many lines of symmetry does a rhombus have?

(A) 0 (B) 2 (C) 4 (D) more than 4 1

4 Which property is **not** true for a rectangle?

(A) The adjacent sides are perpendicular. (B) The opposite angles are equal.
(C) The diagonals are equal. (D) The diagonals bisect the angles of the rectangle. 1

5 A quadrilateral has exactly one pair of opposite angles equal. What could it be?

(A) trapezium (B) rhombus (C) kite (D) rectangle 1

6 A parallelogram has rotational symmetry of what order?

(A) 0 (B) 1 (C) 2 (D) 4 1

7 *ABCE* is a parallelogram. What is *ABDE*?

(A) parallelogram (B) kite (C) trapezium (D) pentagon 1

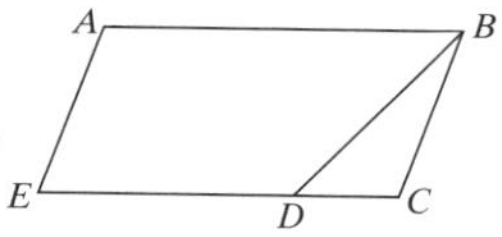

8 Which is correct?

(A) All parallelograms are rhombuses. (B) All rhombuses are kites.
(C) All kites are trapeziums. (D) All trapeziums are parallelograms. 1

9 What is the size of ∠*RPQ*?

(A) 48° (B) 58° (C) 66° (D) 68° 1

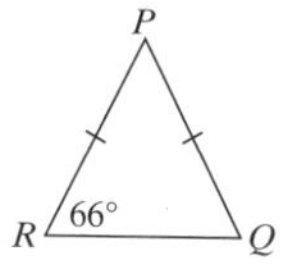

10 How many lines of symmetry does a scalene triangle have?

(A) 3 (B) 2 (C) 1 (D) 0 1

11 This triangle is:

(A) acute-angled (B) right-angled (C) obtuse-angled (D) not enough information 1

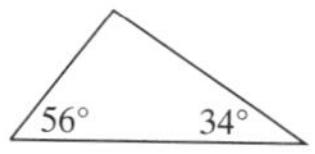

12 *ABCD* is a parallelogram. ∠*ABC* = 111°. What is the size of ∠*BCD*?

(A) 69° (B) 83° (C) 89° (D) 111° 1

13 A quadrilateral has diagonals that are not equal but which bisect each other at right angles. What could it be?

(A) rhombus (B) parallelogram (C) square (D) kite 1

14 If an equilateral triangle is cut along one of its lines of symmetry the two resulting triangles will be:

(A) equilateral (B) right-angled and isosceles
(C) isosceles but not right-angled (D) right-angled and scalene 1

15 ∠*BCD* =

(A) ∠*BAC* + ∠*ABC* (B) ∠*ABC* + ∠*BCA*
(C) 180° − ∠*ABC* (D) 180° − ∠*BAC* 1

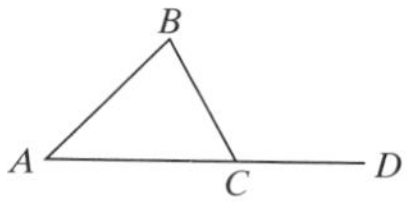

Properties of Geometrical Figures Calculator Allowed **(Level 3 Test)**

PART B Write answers only in the space provided.

16 What type of special quadrilateral is both a rhombus and a rectangle? ______________ 1

17 How many lines of symmetry does a kite have? ______________ 1

18 One angle of an isosceles triangle is 102°. What are the sizes of the two remaining angles? ______________ 1

19 Name a quadrilateral that has one pair of opposite sides both equal and parallel. ______________ 1

20 What is the value of x? ______________ 1

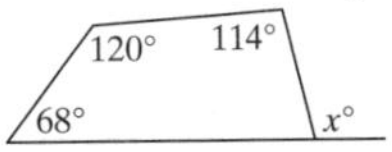

21 The largest angle of a triangle is three times the size of the smallest angle and the other angle is twice the size of the smallest angle. What is the size of the smallest angle? ______________ 1

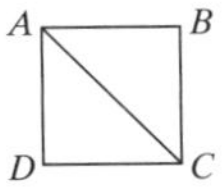

22 *ABCD* is a square. What is the size of ∠*BAC*? ______________ 1

23 'One diagonal of a rhombus must divide it into two equilateral triangles.' True or false? ______________ 1

24 What type of triangle has one angle of 55° and another of 70°? ______________ 1

25 Briefly explain why a triangle cannot be reflex-angled. ______________ 1

PART C Show all working.

26 In Δ*PQR*, *PQ* = 7 cm, *PR* = 9 cm, ∠*PQR* = 80° and ∠*PRQ* = 50°.

a Sketch the triangle (not to scale) showing all the information. 1 mark

b What is the length of *RQ*? Justify your answer. 2 marks

____

____

27 Ken said: 'If a quadrilateral has diagonals that meet at right angles it must be a kite.'

a Sketch a quadrilateral that proves Ken wrong. 1 mark

b What further requirement for the diagonals is necessary to ensure that the quadrilateral is a kite? 1 mark

____

c What further requirement for the diagonals will mean that the quadrilateral must be a rhombus? 1 mark

____

28 *ABCD* is a parallelogram. ∠*ABC* = 114°. *E* is a point on *AD* such that *ED* = *CD*. Find the size of ∠*AEC*, giving reasons. 3 marks

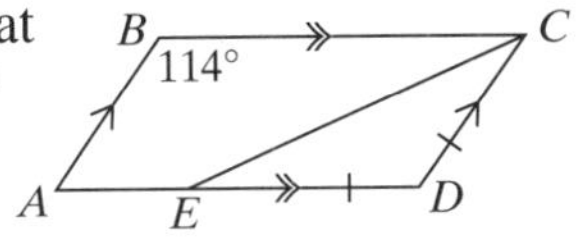

____

____

____

29 *JKLM* is a square. Triangle *JKN* is equilateral.

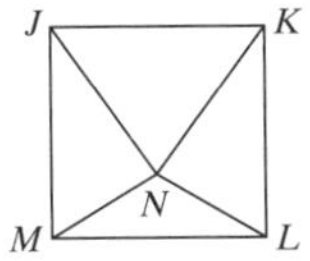

a What is the size of ∠*NKL*? Give reasons. 2 marks

____

____

b Explain why *KN* = *KL*. 1 mark

____

c What is the size of ∠*KLN*? 1 mark

____

d What is the size of ∠*MNL*? 1 mark

____

e What type of triangle is Δ*MNL*? 1 mark

____

Total marks /40

Geometrical Reasoning Calculator Allowed

LEVEL 1 TEST PART A

Time allowed: 40 minutes

1 Which of these is a quadrilateral?

(A) cylinder (B) heptagon (C) parallelogram (D) sphere 1

2 What type of angle measures 160°?

(A) acute (B) reflex (C) straight (D) obtuse 1

3 What do the angles of a trapezium add up to?

(A) 160° (B) 180° (C) 280° (D) 360° 1

4 What is the size of $\angle BCD$?

(A) 57° (B) 68° (C) 116° (D) 119° 1

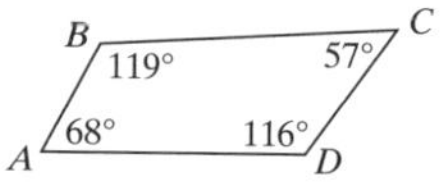

5 What type of quadrilateral is the one in Question 4?

(A) kite (B) rhombus (C) trapezium (D) none of these 1

6 What is the complement of 75°?

(A) 15° (B) 25° (C) 105° (D) 125° 1

7 What type of triangle has exactly two equal sides?

(A) equilateral (B) isosceles (C) scalene (D) obtuse-angled 1

8 The angles marked ● and ♦ are:

(A) alternate (B) co-interior
(C) corresponding (D) vertically opposite 1

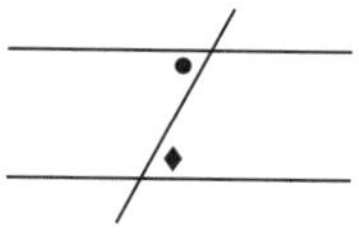

9 If a pair of parallel lines is cut by a transversal, the corresponding angles are:

(A) adjacent (B) equal (C) complementary (D) supplementary 1

10 Which shape has exactly two lines of symmetry?

(A) 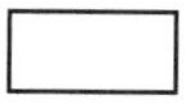 (B)  (C)  (D)  1

11 Which is **not** necessarily a parallelogram?

(A) square (B) rectangle (C) rhombus (D) trapezium 1

12 What is the size of $\angle RPQ$?

(A) 20° (B) 70° (C) 80° (D) 90° 1

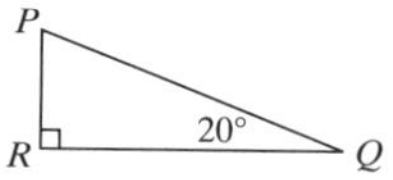

13 What type of triangle is the one in Question 12?

(A) equilateral (B) isosceles (C) scalene (D) obtuse-angled 1

14 Which is correct?

(A) $x = 85$ and $y = 85$ (B) $x = 85$ and $y = 95$
(C) $x = 95$ and $y = 85$ (D) $x = 95$ and $y = 95$ 1

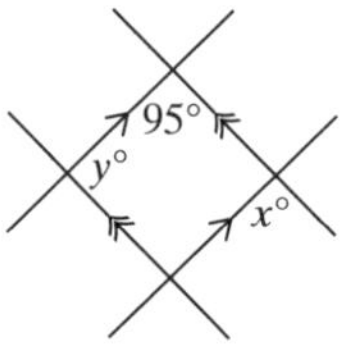

15 Which quadrilateral must have one pair of opposite sides both equal and parallel?

(A) kite (B) rhombus (C) trapezium (D) none of these 1

Geometrical Reasoning Calculator Allowed **(Level 1 Test)**

PART B Write answers only in the space provided.

16 What is the supplement of 80°? ______ [1]

17 What name is given to any four-sided figure? ______ [1]

18 What do the angles of a triangle add up to? ______ [1]

19 Name the angle that is shaded in the diagram. ______ [1]

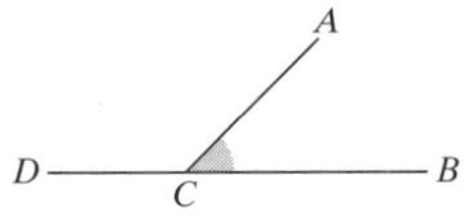

20 What size is the largest angle of a right-angled triangle? ______ [1]

21 What is the value of x? ______ [1]

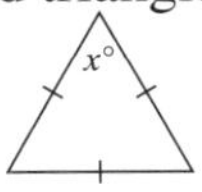

22 How many lines of symmetry does the triangle in Question 21 have? ______ [1]

23 'AB is parallel to CD.' True or false? ______ [1]

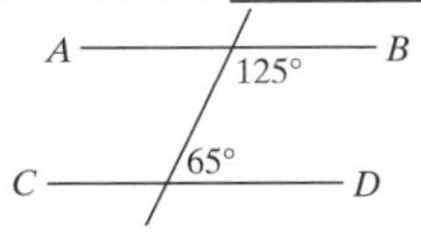

24 What is the value of x? ______ [1]

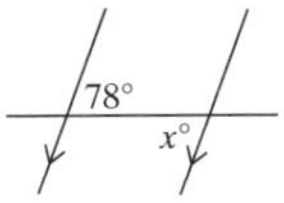

25 If a quadrilateral has all its angles equal, what special quadrilateral must it be? ______ [1]

PART C Show all working.

26 $TQRS$ is a parallelogram.
$PQ = TQ$.
$\angle TSR = 68°$.

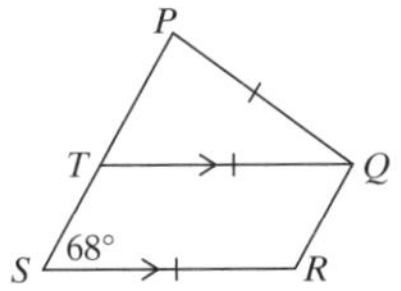

a Give a reason why $\angle PTQ = 68°$. [1 mark]

______

b Give a reason why $\angle TQR = 68°$. [1 mark]

______

c Find the size of $\angle PQR$, giving reasons. [2 marks]

______

______

d What type of special quadrilateral is $PQRS$? [1 mark]

______

27 $BD = CD$. $\angle ABC = 115°$.

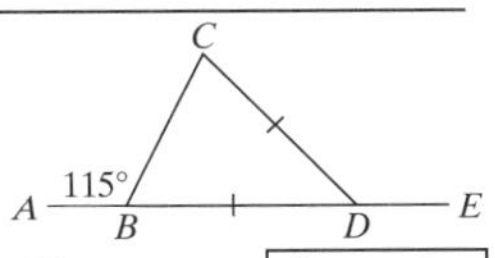

a What is the size of $\angle CBD$? Give a reason for your answer. [2 marks]

______

______

b What is the size of $\angle BCD$? Give a reason for your answer. [2 marks]

______

______

c What is the size of $\angle CDE$? Give a reason for your answer. [2 marks]

______

______

28 AD is parallel to EH.
$\angle RCD = 72°$ and
$\angle BFE = 128°$.

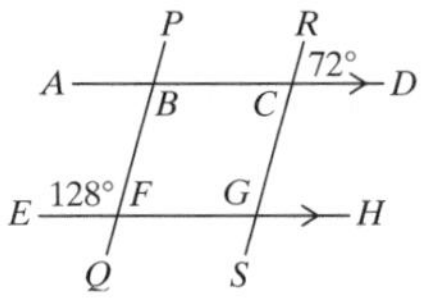

a Why does $\angle BCG = 72°$? [1 mark]

______

b Find the size of $\angle CGF$. [1 mark]

______

c Is PQ parallel to RS? Justify your answer. [2 marks]

______

______

Total marks /40

LEVEL 2 TEST

PART A

Time allowed: 40 minutes

1 In which diagram are *x* and *y* not necessarily equal? [1]

(A) 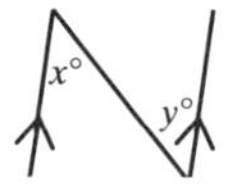

(B) 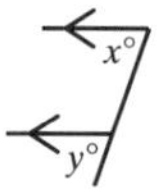

(C) 

(D) 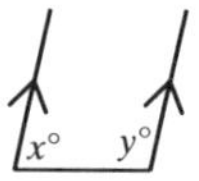

2 Which has the most lines of symmetry? [1]

(A) 
(B) 
(C) 
(D) 

3 Which is **not** necessarily a parallelogram? [1]

(A) square (B) rectangle (C) kite (D) rhombus

4 What is the size of $\angle RSP$? [1]

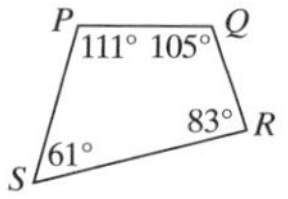

(A) 61° (B) 83° (C) 105° (D) 111°

5 What type of special quadrilateral is pictured? [1]

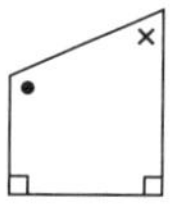

(A) kite (B) rhombus (C) trapezium (D) pentagon

6 What type of angle is the one marked • in the quadrilateral in Question 5? [1]

(A) straight (B) reflex (C) acute (D) obtuse

7 The angles marked × and • in the quadrilateral in Question 5 are: [1]

(A) co-interior (B) complementary (C) corresponding (D) none of these

8 Which quadrilateral has diagonals that do not necessarily meet at right angles? [1]

(A) rhombus (B) rectangle (C) square (D) kite

9 What is the value of *x*? [1]

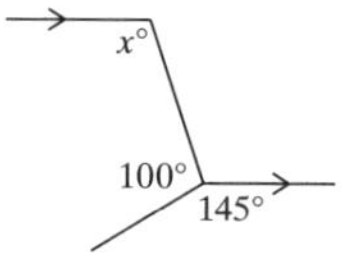

(A) 80 (B) 100 (C) 115 (D) 145

10 What is the value of *a*? [1]

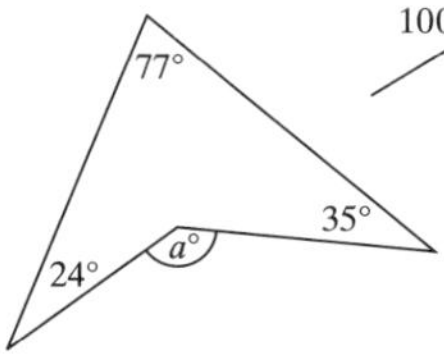

(A) 44 (B) 59 (C) 136 (D) 224

11 Which pair of lines must be parallel? [1]

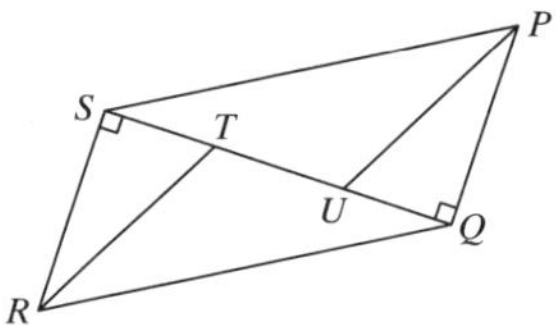

(A) *SP* and *RQ* (B) *SR* and *PQ*
(C) *RT* and *UP* (D) none of them

12 The angles marked × and • are: [1]

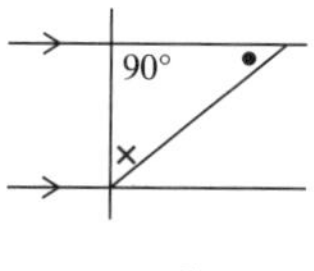

(A) complementary (B) co-interior (C) corresponding (D) alternate

13 A pair of lines will be parallel if: [1]

(A) the alternate angles are supplementary (B) the corresponding angles are equal
(C) vertically opposite angles are complementary (D) the co-interior angles are equal

14 What is the value of *x*? [1]

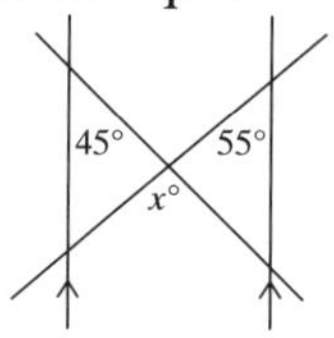

(A) 80 (B) 90 (C) 100 (D) 110

15 What is the symbol for 'is perpendicular to'? [1]

(A) $\equiv$ (B) $\perp$ (C) $\leftrightarrow$ (D) ∇

Geometrical Reasoning Calculator Allowed **(Level 2 Test)**

PART B Write answers only in the space provided.

16 What special name is given to a rhombus that has a right angle? ______________ 1

17 What special name is given to a parallelogram with adjacent sides equal? ______________ 1

18 A regular hexagon can be divided into six equilateral triangles as shown.

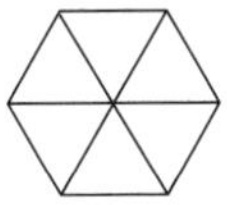

What size is each angle of the hexagon? ______________ 1

19 What is the supplement of 60°? ______________ 1

20 Three of the angles of a quadrilateral measure 48°, 82° and 109°.

What is the size of the other angle? ______________ 1

21 What is the order of rotational symmetry of an equilateral triangle? ______________ 1

22 What is the size of the shaded angle? ______________ 1

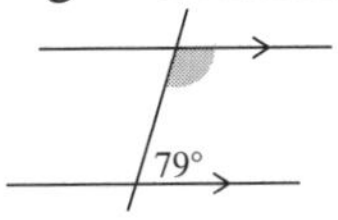

23 An isosceles triangle has one angle of 120°. What is the size of each of the other angles? ______________ 1

24 $\angle AEB = 29°$, $\angle AEC = 76°$ and $\angle BED = 84°$.

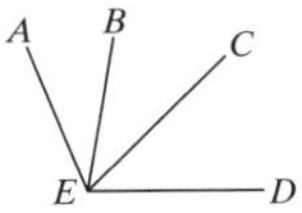

What is the size of $\angle CED$? ______________ 1

25 The diagram shows a square and four equilateral triangles.

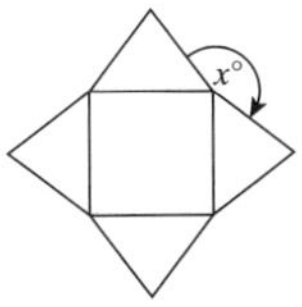

What is the value of x? ______________ 1

PART C Show all working.

26 a What order of rotational symmetry does this shape have? 1 mark

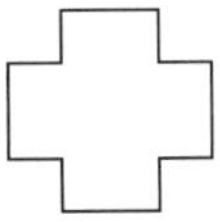

____

b Draw in all the lines of symmetry. 1 mark

c The lines of symmetry divide the shape into identical quadrilaterals. What type of special quadrilateral are they? 1 mark

____

27 a What is the value of x? 1 mark

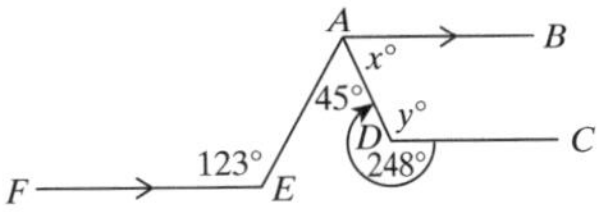

____

b What is the value of y? 1 mark

____

c Is AB parallel to DC? Give a reason for your answer. 1 mark

____

28 a Find the value of x. 1 mark

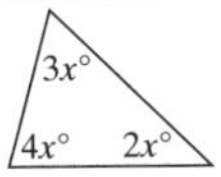

____

b What is the size of the largest angle? 1 mark

____

c What type of triangle is it? 1 mark

____

29 $ABCD$ is a parallelogram. FBC is a straight line.

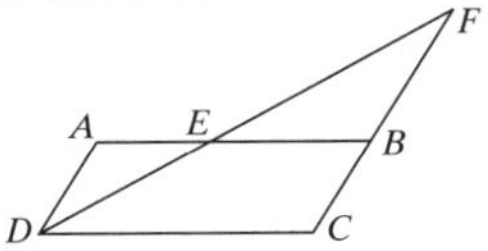

a Why does $\angle FBE = \angle BCD$? 1 mark

____

b Why does $\angle EFB = \angle ADE$? 1 mark

____

c $\angle FCD = 118°$. What is the size of $\angle ADC$? 1 mark

____

d FD bisects $\angle ADC$. What is the size of $\angle EDC$? 1 mark

____

e What type of triangle is ΔFCD? 2 marks

____

____

Total marks /40

LEVEL 3 TEST PART A

Time allowed: 40 minutes

1 A triangle has one angle of 55° and one angle of 70°. What type of triangle is it?

(A) scalene (B) isosceles (C) equilateral (D) right-angled 1

2 Which quadrilateral must have diagonals that bisect the angles of the quadrilateral?

(A) kite (B) rectangle (C) rhombus (D) trapezium 1

3 What is the value of x?

(A) 68 (B) 82 (C) 88 (D) 92 1

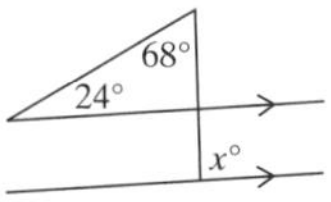

4 What is the complement of 83°?

(A) 7° (B) 17° (C) 97° (D) 277° 1

5 What is the value of x?

(A) 70 (B) 110 (C) 120 (D) 140 1

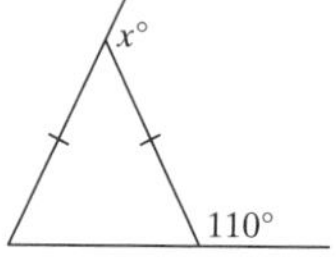

6 $\angle ABD = \angle DBC$. What is the size of $\angle ADB$?

(A) 27° (B) 54° (C) 63° (D) 72° 1

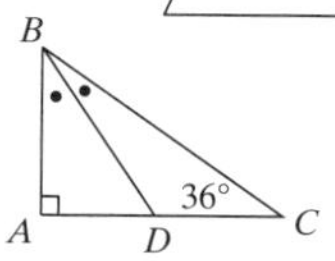

7 What is the value of x?

(A) 36 (B) 57 (C) 78 (D) 102 1

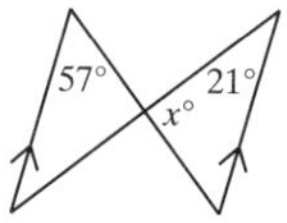

8 Which is **not** correct?

(A) Every parallelogram is a trapezium.
(B) Every rhombus is a parallelogram.
(C) Every square is a rhombus.
(D) Every rectangle is a square. 1

9 What is the value of x?

(A) 88 (B) 98 (C) 118 (D) 154 1

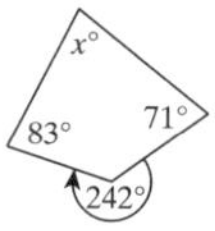

10 The shaded angle would be:

(A) right (B) acute (C) reflex (D) obtuse 1

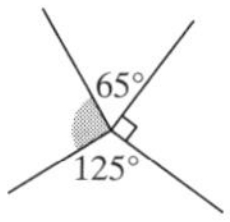

11 Which is **not** a property of a rhombus?

(A) Adjacent sides are equal.
(B) Opposite sides are parallel.
(C) Diagonals are equal.
(D) Diagonals are perpendicular. 1

12 What is the value of x?

(A) 54 (B) 58 (C) 61 (D) 64 1

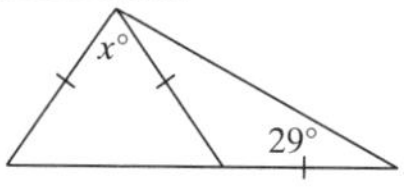

13 Which is correct?

(A) $x = 84$ and $y = 84$ (B) $x = 84$ and $y = 96$
(C) $x = 96$ and $y = 84$ (D) $x = 96$ and $y = 96$ 1

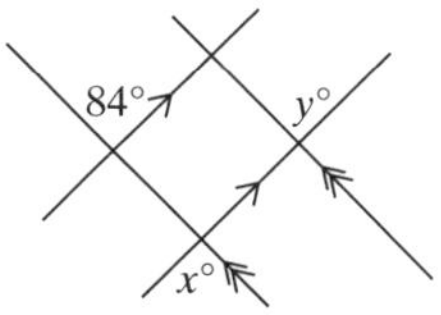

14 Which has rotational symmetry?

(A) kite (B) equilateral triangle (C) right-angled triangle (D) trapezium 1

15 What is the value of x?

(A) 20 (B) 29 (C) 38 (D) 61 1

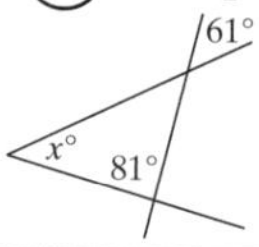

Geometrical Reasoning Calculator Allowed **(Level 3 Test)**

PART B Write answers only in the space provided.

16 Mark all the axes of symmetry on this figure.  **1**

17 What special quadrilateral has adjacent sides equal and perpendicular? ______________ **1**

18 This heptagon is divided into five triangles.
What must its angles add up to? ______________ **1**

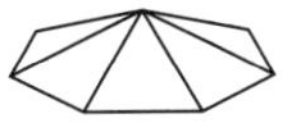

19 A quadrilateral has four equal sides and an angle of 90°.
What is the size of each of the remaining angles? ______________ **1**

20 What is the value of x? ______________ **1**

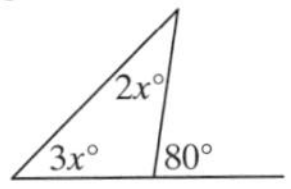

21 What type of special quadrilateral is this? ______________ **1**

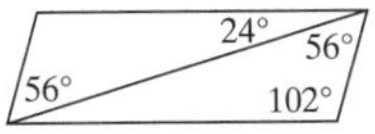

22 What is the value of x? ______________ **1**

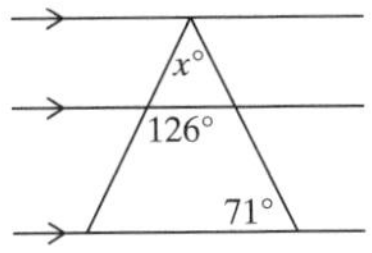

23 Why is AB parallel to CD? ______________ **1**

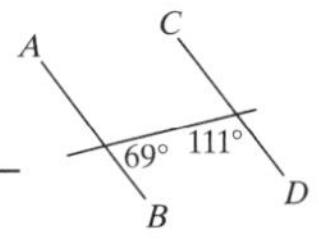

24 What is the value of x? ______________ **1**

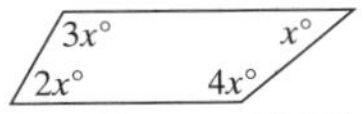

25 Is the quadrilateral in Question 24 a special quadrilateral? If so, what is it? ______________ **1**

PART C Show all working.

26 AC is parallel to DF. $BE = DE$.
$\angle ABG = 110°$.

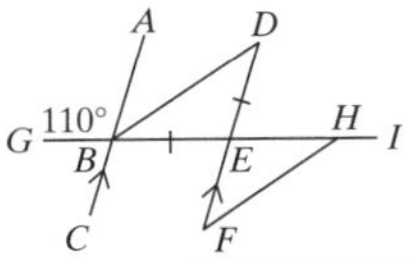

a Find the size of $\angle BDE$.
Give reasons. **2 marks**

____

____

____

b Explain why DB must bisect $\angle ABE$. **1 mark**

____

____

c If ΔEHF is isosceles, is BD parallel to FH? Justify your answer. **2 marks**

____

____

27 $ABCD$ is a parallelogram. P is a point on AB such that $PC = BC$.
Q is a point on DC such that $AD = AQ$.
Explain why $\angle PCB = \angle DAQ$. **2 marks**

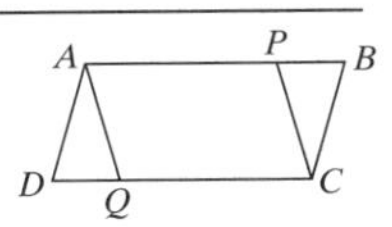

____

____

28 $PQRS$ is a square. T is a point on diagonal QS such that $\angle QTR = 109°$.

a Show the information on a diagram. **1 mark**

b Explain why $\angle RQT = 45°$. **1 mark**

____

c What type of triangle is $\angle QTR$? **1 mark**

____

d Find the size of $\angle TRS$, giving reasons. **2 marks**

____

____

29 $AB = AC$. $CD = CE$. $\angle CAB = 72°$.
Find $\angle DEB$, giving reasons. **3 marks**

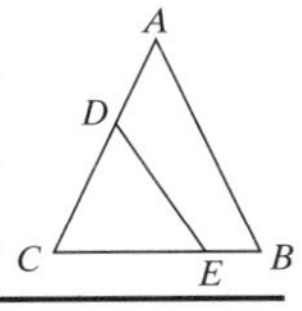

____

____

____

Total marks / 40

PRETEST

Time allowed: 15 minutes **Total marks: 13**

Marks

This table shows the number of goals scored in a netball game. It is used in Questions 1 to 5.

Goals scored in game			
Scorer	**Team**	**Position**	**Number of goals**
Matilda	Pearls	Goal shooter	29
Lily	Rubies	Goal shooter	38
Zena	Pearls	Goal attack	35
Josie	Rubies	Goal attack	27

1 Who scored the most goals?

(A) Matilda (B) Lily (C) Zena (D) Josie 1

2 Who is the goal attack for the Rubies?

(A) Matilda (B) Lily (C) Zena (D) Josie 1

3 Which team won and by how many goals?

(A) Pearls by 1 (B) Pearls by 5 (C) Rubies by 1 (D) Rubies by 5 1

4 What is the total number of goals scored in the game?

(A) 65 (B) 119 (C) 129 (D) 131 1

5 How many more goals were scored in total by the two goal shooters than the two goal attacks?

(A) 1 (B) 5 (C) 7 (D) 17 1

The picture graph below right shows the number of trees planted one week. It is used in Questions 6 to 9.

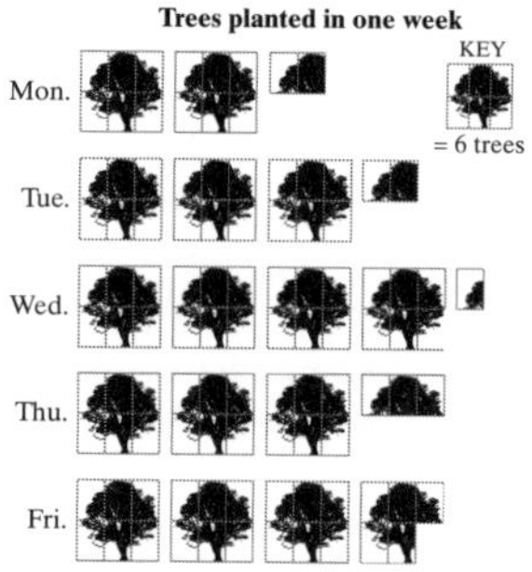

6 How many trees were planted on Tuesday?

(A) 17 (B) 18 (C) 19 (D) 20 1

7 On what day were 21 trees planted?

(A) Monday (B) Wednesday (C) Thursday (D) Friday 1

8 How many trees were planted altogether?

(A) 100 (B) 101 (C) 102 (D) 103 1

9 How many more trees were planted on Friday than on Monday?

(A) 9 (B) 8 (C) 7 (D) 6 1

This graph shows the number of students in each year who are in the school orchestra. It is used for Questions 10 to 13.

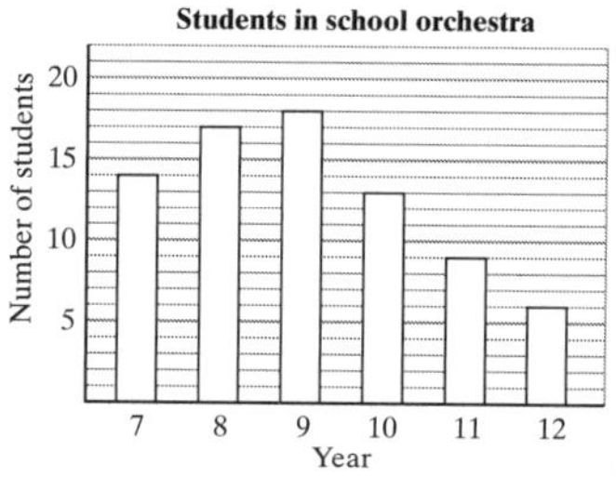

10 How many Year 8 students are in the orchestra?

(A) 15 (B) 16 (C) 17 (D) 18 1

11 What year has exactly 13 students in the orchestra?

(A) 7 (B) 8 (C) 10 (D) 11 1

12 How many students altogether are in the orchestra?

(A) 65 (B) 67 (C) 75 (D) 77 1

13 How many more Year 8 and 9 students are in the orchestra than Year 11 and 12 students?

(A) 17 (B) 18 (C) 19 (D) 20 1

Total marks /13

LEVELS 1 AND 2 TEST PART A

Time allowed: 40 minutes

Marks

This dot plot shows the number of times each score occurred when a dice was rolled. It is used in Questions 1 to 5.

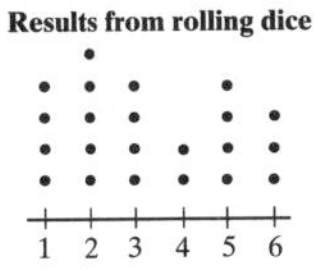

1 Which score occurred the most often?

Ⓐ 2 Ⓑ 3 Ⓒ 5 Ⓓ 6 1

2 Which of these scores did **not** occur four times?

Ⓐ 1 Ⓑ 3 Ⓒ 4 Ⓓ 5 1

3 How many times was the dice rolled?

Ⓐ 20 Ⓑ 21 Ⓒ 22 Ⓓ 23 1

4 How many times did a score more than 4 occur?

Ⓐ 2 Ⓑ 5 Ⓒ 7 Ⓓ 9 1

5 How many more times did 1, 2 or 3 occur than 4, 5 or 6?

Ⓐ 3 Ⓑ 4 Ⓒ 5 Ⓓ 6 1

This graph shows the height of a river during a flood. It is used in Questions 6 to 10.

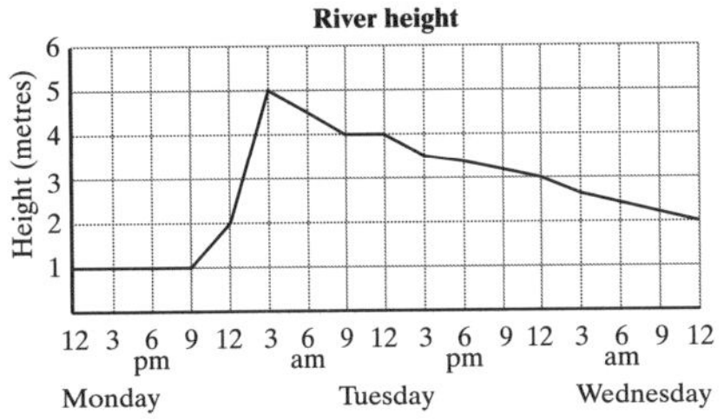

6 What was the river height at 12 noon on Tuesday?

Ⓐ 1 m Ⓑ 2.3 m Ⓒ 3.3 m Ⓓ 4 m 1

7 The normal height of the river is 1 m. How far above the normal height did the river rise?

Ⓐ 1 m Ⓑ 4 m Ⓒ 5 m Ⓓ 6 m 1

8 At what time on Monday did the river begin to rise above the normal height?

Ⓐ 9 am Ⓑ 9 pm Ⓒ noon Ⓓ midnight 1

9 How many hours was it from when the river began to rise until it reached the maximum height?

Ⓐ 2 Ⓑ 3 Ⓒ 6 Ⓓ 9 1

10 At which of these times was the height of the river closest to 2.5 m?

Ⓐ 10:30 pm Mon. Ⓑ 1:30 am Tue. Ⓒ 6 am Tue. Ⓓ 6 am Wed. 1

This frequency distribution table was drawn for a set of scores. It is used in Questions 11 to 15.

Score	Tally	Frequency
6	卌 II	7
7		9
8	卌 卌 III	13
9	卌 III	8
10	IIII	4

11 The tally for the score of 7 was left out. What should it be?

Ⓐ IIIII IIII Ⓑ 卌 卌 I Ⓒ 卌 II Ⓓ 卌 IIII 1

12 What is the total frequency?

Ⓐ 38 Ⓑ 39 Ⓒ 40 Ⓓ 41 1

13 What is the most common score?

Ⓐ 8 Ⓑ 10 Ⓒ 13 Ⓓ 16 1

14 How many times was the score more than 8?

Ⓐ 2 Ⓑ 8 Ⓒ 12 Ⓓ 25 1

15 How many times was the score **between** 6 and 10?

Ⓐ 3 Ⓑ 30 Ⓒ 34 Ⓓ 37 1

PART B Write answers only in the space provided.

This stem-and-leaf plot shows the height (in cm) of all the students in a class. It is used for Questions 16 to 20.

12	6
13	4 8 9
14	0 1 2 3 5 5 5 7 8
15	1 2 4 4 6 7 9
16	0 3 7

16 How many students are in the class? __________ 1

17 How tall is the tallest student? __________ 1

18 What is the difference in height between the tallest and shortest students? __________ 1

19 How many students are less than 140 cm tall? __________ 1

20 How many students are more than 155 cm tall? __________ 1

Forty students voted for the best artwork in a display. The graph shows the votes received by each artist and is used in Questions 21 to 25.

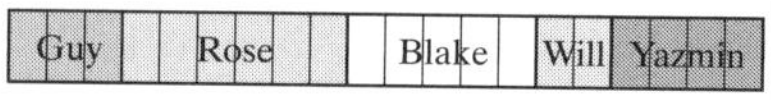

21 Who got the most votes? __________ 1

22 How many voted for Will? __________ 1

23 Which artist did 10 students vote for? __________ 1

24 How many more students voted for Yazmin than for Guy? __________ 1

25 What fraction of the students voted for Rose? __________ 1

PART C Show all working.

26 A dice was rolled a number of times and the results were: 3, 2, 3, 6, 4, 5, 6, 6, 1, 1, 4, 6, 2, 1, 6, 4, 1, 5, 1, 6, 2, 3, 3, 2, 1, 4, 1, 6, 2, 6.

a Complete the frequency distribution table for this data. 3 marks

Score	Tally	Frequency
1		
2		
3		
4		
5		
6		
Total		

b Draw a frequency histogram. 3 marks

27 a In one class seven students have blue eyes, nine have brown, five have green and three have hazel eyes. Complete a sector graph for this data (using the divisions marked). 3 marks

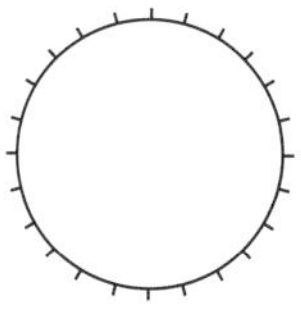

b What size is the angle for green eyes? 1 mark

28

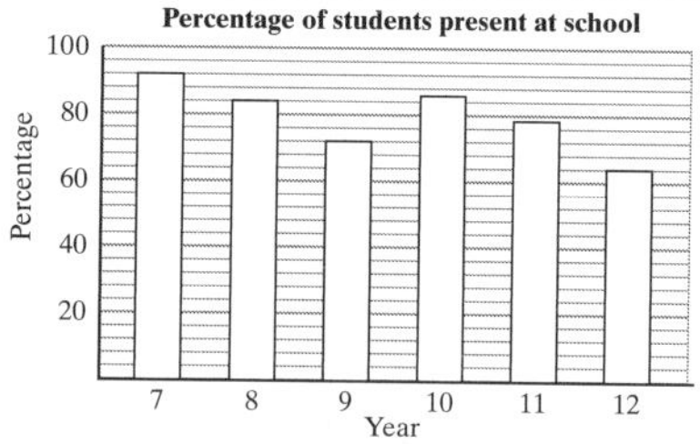

This graph shows the percentage of students present at school one day.

a In what year were the highest percentage of students present? 1 mark

b What percentage of students were absent in Year 10? 1 mark

c Is it possible to tell how many more students were present in Year 8 than Year 9? Explain why or why not. 2 marks

d Give an advantage of using percentages rather than actual numbers in the graph. 1 mark

Total marks /40

LEVELS 2 AND 3 TEST PART A

Time allowed: 40 minutes

Marks

The dot plot below right was used to show the results of a test marked out of 10.
It is used in Questions 1 to 4.

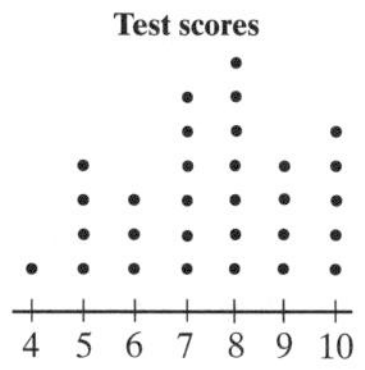

1 How many students took part in the test?

(A) 7 (B) 30 (C) 50 (D) 226 — 1

2 What was the most common score?

(A) 7 (B) 8 (C) 9 (D) 10 — 1

3 How many students scored more than 8?

(A) 2 (B) 9 (C) 16 (D) 86 — 1

4 What fraction of those doing the test scored full marks?

(A) $\frac{1}{4}$ (B) $\frac{1}{5}$ (C) $\frac{1}{6}$ (D) $\frac{1}{7}$ — 1

A group of people at a resort were asked what their favourite activity was. The results are shown in the divided bar graph which is used in Questions 5 to 8.

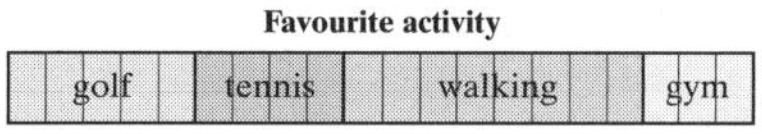

5 Which activity was the most popular?

(A) golf (B) tennis (C) walking (D) gym — 1

6 What percentage chose walking?

(A) 12.5% (B) 36% (C) 40% (D) 44% — 1

7 If 24 people chose tennis, how many chose golf?

(A) 25 (B) 27 (C) 28 (D) 30 — 1

8 If a sector graph had been drawn instead, what size would the angle for gym need to be?

(A) 15° (B) 18° (C) 20° (D) 54° — 1

A number of people were asked which colour they preferred for a banner.
The results are shown in this graph which is used in Questions 9 to 12.

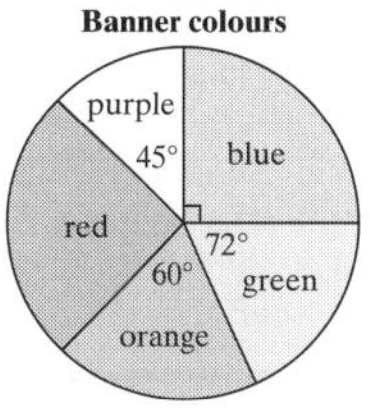

9 Which colour was the least popular?

(A) blue (B) green (C) orange (D) purple — 1

10 What is the angle size for red?

(A) 88° (B) 90° (C) 93° (D) 96° — 1

11 Which colour was chosen by exactly $\frac{1}{5}$ of those surveyed?

(A) blue (B) green (C) orange (D) purple — 1

12 If 24 of those surveyed chose green, how many chose purple?

(A) 15 (B) 16 (C) 18 (D) 20 — 1

13 Which shows the correct tally marks for a frequency of 12?

(A) ||||| ||||| || (B) 卌 卌 卌 (C) 卌 卌 || (D) 卌 卌 ⊤ — 1

14 What is the correct name for a graph commonly referred to as a pie chart?

(A) histogram (B) divided bar graph (C) sector graph (D) dot plot — 1

15 To display which information would a line graph be appropriate?

(A) the way students come to school (B) the number of pets students have

(C) the colour of cars (D) the temperature during the day — 1

PART B Write answers only in the space provided. All questions refer to the graph shown.

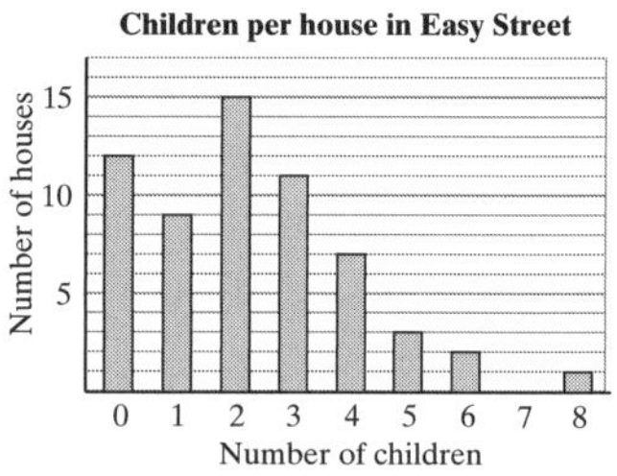

16 How many houses have exactly four children? ________________ 1

17 How many houses have exactly seven children? ________________ 1

18 What is the greatest number of children per house? ________________ 1

19 What is the most common number of children per house? ____________ 1

20 How many houses have five or more children? ________________ 1

21 How many houses are in the street? ________________ 1

22 How many children live in the street? ________________ 1

23 What percentage of houses have no children? ________________ 1

24 What fraction of the houses have more than five children? ________________ 1

25 Why would it not be a good idea to survey those houses with six or more children? ______________ 1

PART C Show all working.

26

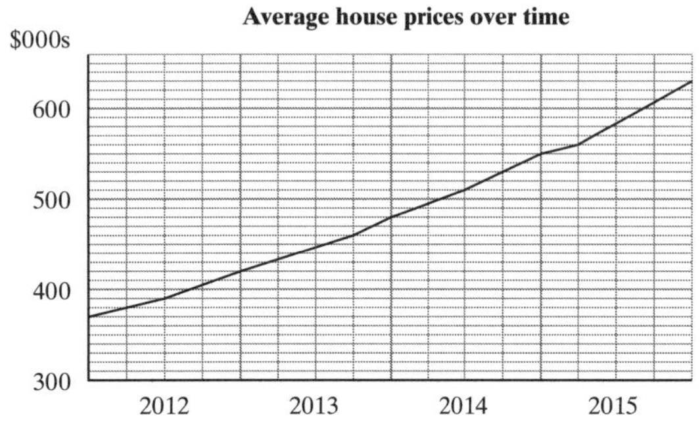

This graph appeared in a newspaper.

a What was the average house price at the beginning of 2014? 1 mark

____

b When was the average house price $550 000? 1 mark

____

c How much did average house prices increase during 2013? 1 mark

____

d What year had the biggest increase in average house prices? 1 mark

____

e Explain why the graph is misleading and the effect caused by this. 2 marks

____

____

27 These are marks in an examination: 76, 84, 60, 64, 86, 71, 77, 68, 82, 59, 73, 95, 78, 62, 56, 82, 89, 65, 91, 73, 82, 77, 57, 85, 64.

a Construct an ordered stem-and-leaf plot for these marks. 3 marks

b What percentage of marks are above 80%? 1 mark

____

c Give a reason why a stem-and-leaf plot is preferable to the raw scores. 1 mark

____

d Give a reason why a dot plot would not be appropriate for these scores. 1 mark

____

28 A bowler kept a record of the number of wickets he took in each innings of the cricket games he played. The results are shown in the frequency table.

Wickets	Frequency
0	4
1	7
2	13
3	12
4	5
5	3
6	1

Construct a frequency histogram. 3 marks

Total marks /40

Mean, Mode, Median and Range Calculator Allowed

LEVELS 1 AND 2 TEST PART A

Time allowed: 40 minutes

Marks

1 For the scores 5, 6, 7, 10, 11, 12, 12 what is the mean?
(A) 7 (B) 9 (C) 10 (D) 12 [1]

2 For the scores 5, 6, 7, 10, 11, 12, 12 what is the median?
(A) 7 (B) 9 (C) 10 (D) 12 [1]

3 For the scores 5, 6, 7, 10, 11, 12, 12 what is the mode?
(A) 7 (B) 9 (C) 10 (D) 12 [1]

4 For the scores 5, 6, 7, 10, 11, 12, 12 what is the range?
(A) 7 (B) 9 (C) 10 (D) 12 [1]

5 What is the mean of the scores 78, 78, 94 and 98?
(A) 20 (B) 78 (C) 86 (D) 87 [1]

6 What is the median of the scores 78, 78, 94 and 98?
(A) 20 (B) 78 (C) 86 (D) 87 [1]

7 What is the mode of the scores 78, 78, 94 and 98?
(A) 20 (B) 78 (C) 86 (D) 87 [1]

8 What is the range of the scores 78, 78, 94 and 98?
(A) 20 (B) 78 (C) 86 (D) 87 [1]

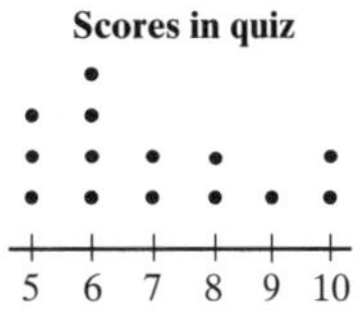

9 For the scores in the dot plot, what is the mean?
(A) 5 (B) 6 (C) 6.5 (D) 7 [1]

10 For the scores in the dot plot, what is the median?
(A) 5 (B) 6 (C) 6.5 (D) 7 [1]

11 For the scores in the dot plot, what is the mode?
(A) 5 (B) 6 (C) 6.5 (D) 7 [1]

12 For the scores in the dot plot, what is the range?
(A) 5 (B) 6 (C) 6.5 (D) 7 [1]

Test marks

6	5 8
7	0 3 7 7 7
8	1 1 2 5 6 8
9	2 4

13 For the scores in the stem-and-leaf plot, what is the range?
(A) 24 (B) 26 (C) 27 (D) 29 [1]

14 For the scores in the stem-and-leaf plot, what is the mode?
(A) 1 (B) 7 (C) 77 (D) 81 [1]

15 For the scores in the stem-and-leaf plot, what is the median?
(A) 18 (B) 77 (C) 79 (D) 81 [1]

PART B Write answers only in the space provided.

16 What is the average of 6, 7 and 11? ________________ 1

17 What is the mean of 17 and 23? ________________ 1

18 What is the median of 8, 9, 9, 12, 15, 16 and 18? ________________ 1

19 What is the range of 11, 9, 3, 7, 21 and 15? ________________ 1

20 What is the mode of 8, 4, 8, 2, 1, 7, 8, 5, 1, 4, 2 and 8? ________________ 1

21 What is the median of 6, 6, 14 and 20? ________________ 1

22 What is the mean of 9, 17 and 42? (Give the answer correct to one decimal place.) ________________ 1

23 What is the range of 158, 624, 971 and 1007? ________________ 1

24 What is the mode of 5, 5, 5, 7, 7, 7, 7, 8, 8, 8, 8, 8, 9, 9 and 10? ________________ 1

25 What is the median of 18, 23, 13, 19, 24 and 20? ________________ 1

PART C Show all working.

26 Twelve students did a test and these are the marks: 78, 83, 69, 75, 82, 79, 80, 67, 73, 77, 75 and 71.

a What was the mean mark? 1 mark

____

b What was the median? 1 mark

____

c What was the range? 1 mark

____

d Kitty was one of the students. She scored 75. What conclusions can be made about how Kitty performed in the test? Justify your answer. 1 mark

____

27

Score	14	15	16	17	18	19	20
Frequency	13	19	21	28	24	25	29

a What is the range? 1 mark

____

b What is the mode? 1 mark

____

c What is the total frequency? 1 mark

____

d What is the mean? Give the answer to one decimal place. 1 mark

____

e What is the median? 1 mark

____

28 The heights of the seven players in a team, in centimetres, are 165, 171, 158, 152, 166, 169 and 160.

a What is the median height? 1 mark

____

b What is the mean height? 1 mark

____

c What is the range? 1 mark

____

d The player who is 171 cm tall is injured and replaced by a player who is 150 cm tall. Explain what difference this will make to the median, mean and range. 3 marks

____

____

____

Total marks /40

Mean, Mode, Median and Range Calculator Allowed

LEVELS 2 AND 3 TEST PART A

Time allowed: 40 minutes

Marks

1 What is the mean of the scores 8, 18, 21, 8, 15?

(A) 8 (B) 13 (C) 14 (D) 15 — 1

2 What is the mode of the scores 8, 18, 21, 8, 15?

(A) 8 (B) 13 (C) 14 (D) 15 — 1

3 What is the median of the scores 8, 18, 21, 8, 15?

(A) 8 (B) 14 (C) 15 (D) 21 — 1

4 What is the range of the scores 8, 18, 21, 8, 15?

(A) 8 (B) 13 (C) 14 (D) 21 — 1

5 Which of these is a measure of spread?

(A) mean (B) mode (C) median (D) range — 1

6 What is the median of the scores 18, 16, 12, 13, 19, 14, 18 and 20?

(A) 16 (B) 17 (C) 18 (D) 19 — 1

7 What is the mean of 39, 22, 52, 70 and 47?

(A) 46 (B) 47 (C) 48 (D) 52 — 1

8 This dot plot was used to show the results of a quiz marked out of 10. Which of these is not equal to 7?

(A) mean (B) mode (C) median (D) range — 1

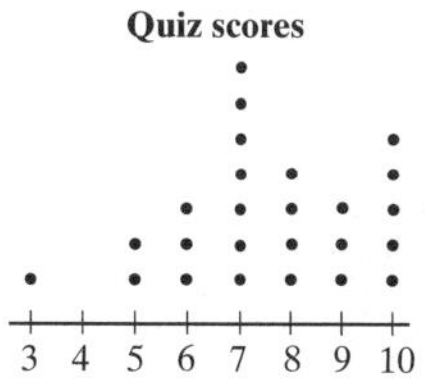

9 In everyday language, the 'average' usually refers to which of these?

(A) mean (B) median (C) mode (D) range — 1

10 The scores achieved by students in a test have been placed in this stem-and-leaf plot. What is the range?

(A) 28 (B) 72 (C) 49 (D) 55 — 1

4	7
5	0 3 8
6	1 1 4 5 7 9 9
7	0 1 2 2 5 5 5 6 8
8	2 3 3 6 7
9	1 4 6

11 Referring to the stem-and-leaf plot in Question 10, what is the mode?

(A) 61 (B) 69 (C) 72 (D) 75 — 1

12 Referring to the stem-and-leaf plot in Question 10, what is the median?

(A) 72 (B) 75 (C) 73.5 (D) 69 — 1

13 If a score of 68 was added to the stem-and-leaf plot in Question 10, which would change?

(A) mode (B) median (C) range (D) none of these — 1

14 For the scores 9, 15, 38 and 38 which of these measures is equal to 26.5?

(A) mean (B) median (C) mode (D) range — 1

15 For the scores 19, 28, 42, 34, 28 and 14 which is **not** equal to 28?

(A) range (B) mode (C) median (D) mean — 1

PART B Write answers only in the space provided.

16 What is the mean of 3, 7 and 29? __________ 1

17 What is the median of the scores 5, 7, 11 and 19? __________ 1

18 What is the range of the scores 17, 42, 13, 31, 28, 20 and 36? __________ 1

19 What is the mode of the scores 1, 1, 1, 2, 2, 2, 2, 3, 3, 3, 3 and 3? __________ 1

20 If the mean of six scores is 5, what is the sum of the scores? __________ 1

21 The sum of eight scores is 118. What is the mean? __________ 1

22 What is the median of the scores 31, 34, 29, 32, 28, 54, 34, 25, 34 and 28? __________ 1

23 The sum of some scores is 1563.7 and the mean is 82.3. How many scores are there? __________ 1

24 The range of some scores is 26. If the lowest score is 37 what is the highest score? __________ 1

25 There are three scores in a data set. The highest score is 42 and the mode is 24.
What is the mean? __________ 1

PART C Show all working.

26 These are the marks Darby scored in his class tests this year: 88, 59, 64, 57, 66, 78, 72, 87, 74, 90, 81, 73, 62, 69 and 78.

a Find the mean mark. 1 mark

____

b Find the range. 1 mark

____

c Find the median. 1 mark

____

d Find the mode. 1 mark

____

e Darby believed he had done better than Xavier in the tests. These are the marks Xavier scored: 75, 68, 72, 76, 66, 74, 75, 73, 77, 70, 78, 79, 72, 75 and 71. Find the mean of Xavier's scores and explain whether Darby was correct or not. 2 marks

____

____

f Find the range of Xavier's scores and explain how it is different to Darby's and what this means about their results. 2 marks

____

____

27 After five tests, Ella has a mean mark of 72%. If she scores 87% in her next test what will her new mean be? 2 marks

____

____

28 The seven players in a netball team have a mean height of 168 cm. A player who is 163 cm tall is replaced with one who is 170 cm tall. What is the new mean? 2 marks

____

____

29 **a** Find the mean of 2, 6, 8, 9 and 20. 1 mark

____

b Si said: 'If a score of 0 is added to those scores the mean will not change.' Explain why Si is wrong. 1 mark

____

c What number could be added to the scores so that the mean does not change? 1 mark

____

Total marks /40

LEVELS 1 AND 2 TEST — PART A

Time allowed: 40 minutes

Marks

1 What is the average of 5, 8 and 14?

Ⓐ 8   Ⓑ $8\frac{1}{3}$ Ⓒ $8\frac{2}{3}$ Ⓓ 9   [1]

2 What is the mean of 2, 5, 6, 11 and 11?

Ⓐ 6   Ⓑ 7   Ⓒ 8   Ⓓ 9   [1]

3 What is the range of 17, 18, 19, 27 and 35?

Ⓐ 17   Ⓑ 18   Ⓒ 19   Ⓓ 27   [1]

The dot plot on the right was drawn to show the marks in a test. It is used in Questions 4 to 7.

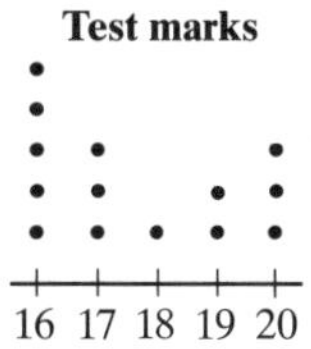

4 How many scored 20?

Ⓐ 2   Ⓑ 3   Ⓒ 4   Ⓓ 5   [1]

5 How many scored less than 18?

Ⓐ 7   Ⓑ 8   Ⓒ 9   Ⓓ 10   [1]

6 What is the mode?

Ⓐ 16   Ⓑ 17   Ⓒ 18   Ⓓ 20   [1]

7 What is the median?

Ⓐ 16   Ⓑ 16.5   Ⓒ 17   Ⓓ 17.5   [1]

This stem-and-leaf plot shows some marks out of 50. It is used in Questions 8 to 12.

1	8 9
2	1 3 6 9
3	0 2 4 7 7
4	3 4 6 8
5	0

8 How many marks are there?

Ⓐ 15   Ⓑ 16   Ⓒ 20   Ⓓ 21   [1]

9 How many marks are less than 30?

Ⓐ 5   Ⓑ 6   Ⓒ 7   Ⓓ 8   [1]

10 What is the range?

Ⓐ 13   Ⓑ 18   Ⓒ 32   Ⓓ 33   [1]

11 What is the mode?

Ⓐ 3   Ⓑ 7   Ⓒ 37   Ⓓ 73   [1]

12 What is the median?

Ⓐ 3   Ⓑ 32   Ⓒ 33   Ⓓ 34   [1]

This graph shows the result when some people were asked which of three countries they would prefer to visit. It is used in Questions 13 to 15.

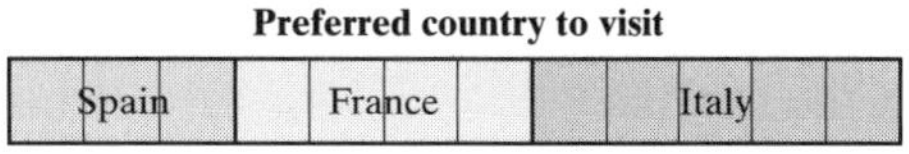

13 Which of the countries did most people prefer?

Ⓐ Spain   Ⓑ France   Ⓒ Italy   Ⓓ All three were the same.   [1]

14 What fraction chose France?

Ⓐ $\frac{1}{3}$ Ⓑ $\frac{1}{4}$ Ⓒ $\frac{1}{5}$ Ⓓ $\frac{5}{12}$ [1]

15 If 36 chose Spain, how many chose Italy?

Ⓐ 38   Ⓑ 48   Ⓒ 56   Ⓓ 60   [1]

PART B Write answers only in the space provided.

16 What is the range of the scores 7, 11, 19, 23 and 24? ________________ 1

17 What is the mode of the scores 8, 8, 9, 9, 9, 9, 9, 10, 11, 11 and 12? ________________ 1

18 What is the median of 13, 20 and 17? ________________ 1

19 What is the mean of 10, 20 and 60? ________________ 1

20 What is the median of the scores 5, 6, 10 and 11? ________________ 1

21 Write the tally marks for a frequency of 8. ________________ 1

A group of people were asked what their favourite milkshake flavour was and the results are shown in the sector graph which is used in Questions 22 to 25.

Favourite milkshake flavour

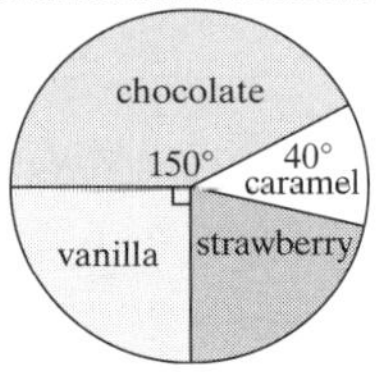

22 Which flavour is the most popular? ________________ 1

23 What is the angle size for strawberry? ________________ 1

24 What percentage chose vanilla as their favourite? ________________ 1

25 What fraction of those surveyed chose caramel? ________________ 1

PART C Show all working.

26 A frequency histogram was drawn showing the number of correct responses to a test made up of 15 multiple-choice questions.

Correct responses in test

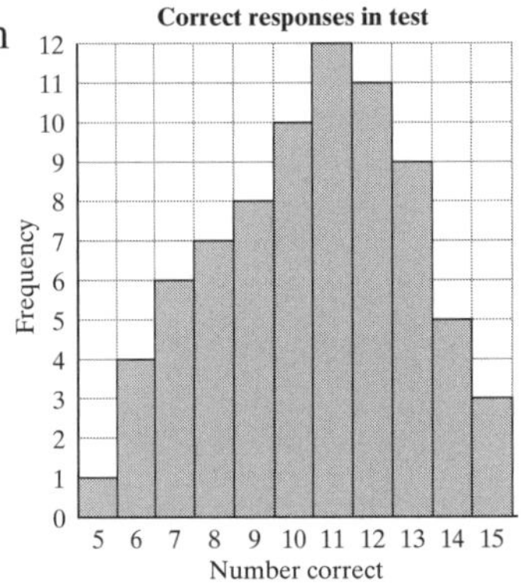

a How many students got all the questions correct? 1 mark

____

b What is the mode? 1 mark

____

c How many students did the test? 1 mark

____

d How many students scored more than 10? 1 mark

____

e What is the median? 1 mark

____

f How many students got fewer than half the questions correct? 1 mark

____

g Find the mean. Give the answer correct to one decimal place. 1 mark

____

27 These are the number of runs scored by the home teams in a twenty-twenty cricket competition:
148, 167, 189, 155, 141, 196, 137, 174, 182, 171, 159, 167, 175, 180, 183, 186, 144, 160, 172, 187.

a Place the scores into an ordered stem-and-leaf plot. 3 marks

b What is the range? 1 mark

____

c What is the median? 1 mark

____

d What is the mode? 1 mark

____

28 a The mean of eight numbers is 11.5. What is the sum of the numbers? 1 mark

____

b One of the numbers, 8, is subtracted. What is the new mean? 1 mark

____

Total marks /40

LEVELS 2 AND 3 TEST — PART A

Time allowed: 40 minutes

Marks

1 What is the median of the scores 29, 40, 36, 44, 17, 23, 39, 3, 32, 49, 22 and 44?
(A) 31 (B) 31.5 (C) 34 (D) 34.5 [1]

2 What is the mean of the scores 29, 40, 36, 44, 17, 23, 39, 3, 32, 49, 22 and 44?
(A) 31 (B) 31.5 (C) 34 (D) 34.5 [1]

3 By how much does the range of 29, 40, 36, 44, 17, 23, 39, 3, 32, 49, 22 and 44 exceed the mode?
(A) 2 (B) 4 (C) 5 (D) 6 [1]

4 Some swimmers represented their club at a meet. The mean age of the four male reps was 25 and the mean age of the five female reps was 16. What was the mean age of the reps?
(A) 18 (B) 18.5 (C) 20 (D) 20.5 [1]

The dot plot below shows the number of mistakes made by students in a test. It is used in Questions 5 to 8.

Mistakes in test

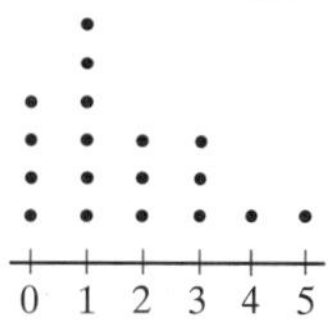

5 How many students made fewer than two mistakes?
(A) 6 (B) 10 (C) 13 (D) 16 [1]

6 How many mistakes were made altogether?
(A) 14 (B) 18 (C) 30 (D) 34 [1]

7 For this data, which two measures are equal?
(A) mode and range (B) range and mean (C) mean and median (D) median and mode [1]

8 The scores will be placed in a sector graph. What is the size of the angle for no mistakes?
(A) 22° (B) 40° (C) 80° (D) 102° [1]

9 The people at a weight-watching club were asked how many kilograms they had lost the previous week. The results are shown in the table. How many kilograms were lost altogether?

Number of kg	0	1	2	3	4
Number of people	5	4	6	1	2

(A) 10 (B) 18 (C) 27 (D) 32 [1]

10 Referring to the table in Question 9, what was the most common weight loss?
(A) 1 kg (B) 2 kg (C) 4 kg (D) 6 kg [1]

The sector graph below right shows the distribution of rainfall throughout the year. It is used in Questions 11 to 14.

Annual rainfall

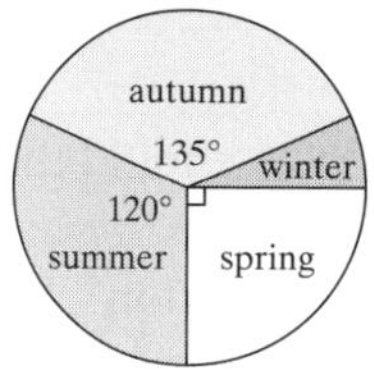

11 What size is the angle for winter?
(A) 5° (B) 15° (C) 25° (D) not enough information [1]

12 What percentage of the annual rainfall is in autumn?
(A) 13.5% (B) $33\frac{1}{3}$% (C) 37.5% (D) not enough information [1]

13 If the total annual rainfall was 1500 mm, how much rain fell in summer?
(A) 120 mm (B) 375 mm (C) 450 mm (D) 500 mm [1]

14 Which of these can be found for the information in the sector graph?
(A) mean (B) mode (C) median (D) range [1]

15 Which of these data sets has a mean of 20 and a median of 25?
(A) 20, 10, 25, 25, 20, 20
(B) 12, 14, 15, 25, 37, 47
(C) 5, 12, 20, 30, 38, 45
(D) 1, 1, 18, 32, 33, 35 [1]

PART B Write answers only in the space provided.

The mass, in kilograms, of 12 dogs were recorded in the ordered stem-and-leaf plot below, which is used in Questions 16 to 20.

1	2 6 9 9
2	1 3 5 ● 5 8
3	0 2

16 The mass of Billy's dog is circled because it cannot be read. What is the mass of Billy's dog? ________________ 1

17 What is the range? ________________ 1

18 What is the median? ________________ 1

19 What is the mode? ________________ 1

20 What is the mean? Give the answer correct to one decimal place. ________________ 1

One day Sam recorded the temperature every two hours and recorded the result in the graph on the right, which is used in Questions 21 to 23.

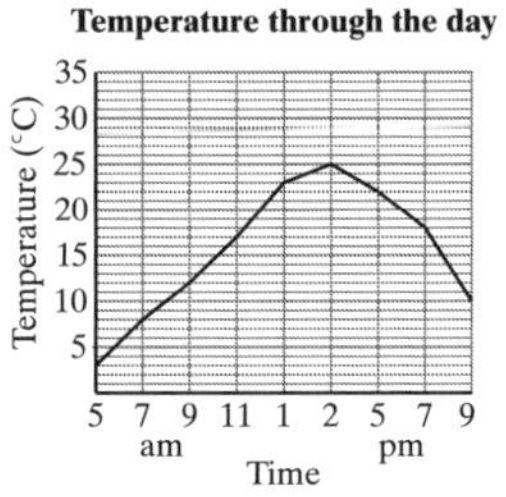

21 What was the temperature at 9 am? ________________ 1

22 What was the difference between the maximum and minimum temperature recorded? ____________ 1

23 When was the temperature 18°? ________________ 1

24 What is the mean of the scores 5, 5, 5, 6, 6, 6, 6, 6, 6, 7, 7, 7, 7, 8, 8 and 9? ________________ 1

25 The mean distance covered by eight participants in a charity event was 2.35 km. Another participant covered a distance of 6.4 km. What is the new mean? ________________ 1

PART C Show all working.

26 There are three scores in a data set. The mode is 32. Briefly explain why the median must also be 32. 2 marks

____

____

27 This graph appeared in a magazine.

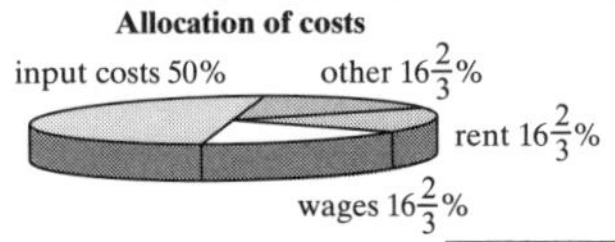

a Explain why the graph is misleading and the effect this has. 2 marks

____

____

b What size should the angle for wages in a sector graph be to correctly show this information? 1 mark

____

c Draw a sector graph and show the information correctly. 3 marks

28 The table shows the results of a survey conducted by a shampoo company. After issuing free samples of a new shampoo they asked: 'Would you buy this product?'

Response	Number
definitely	1
probably	3
maybe	11
probably not	2
definitely not	3

a What percentage of people replied 'probably'? 1 mark

____

b If a sector graph was drawn showing these results what would be the angle for 'maybe'? 1 mark

____

c Complete the divided bar graph to show the results. 3 marks

d Give two reasons why the results of this survey might not be very reliable. 2 marks

____

____

Total marks /40

Probability

PRETEST

Time allowed: 15 minutes **Total marks: 15**

Marks

1 The probability that a baby will be born somewhere in Australia today could be described as:

(A) likely (B) unlikely (C) impossible (D) certain 1

2 The chance of winning first prize in a lottery if you have just one ticket could be described as:

(A) likely (B) unlikely (C) impossible (D) certain 1

3 A bag holds eight red, one green and five blue marbles. The chance of choosing a green marble is:

(A) $\frac{1}{8}$ (B) $\frac{1}{5}$ (C) $\frac{1}{13}$ (D) $\frac{1}{14}$ 1

4 The chance of getting a head when a coin is tossed could be described as:

(A) unlikely (B) fifty-fifty (C) certain (D) impossible 1

5 A box holds 25 balls; eight are white, seven are orange, six are green and the rest are yellow. How many of the balls are yellow?

(A) 4 (B) 5 (C) 6 (D) 7 1

6 This spinner is spun once. Which symbol is most likely to occur?

(A) ☺ (B) ♥ (C) ♫ (D) ☆ 1

7 For the spinner in Question 6, which symbol is least likely to occur?

(A) ☺ (B) ♥ (C) ♫ (D) ☆ 1

8 For the spinner in Question 6, which symbol has a fifty-fifty chance of occurring?

(A) ☺ (B) ♥ (C) ♫ (D) ☆ 1

9 For the spinner in Question 6, how could you describe the chance that ☆ will occur?

(A) likely (B) unlikely (C) impossible (D) certain 1

10 For the spinner in Question 6, how could you describe the chance that ✈ will occur?

(A) likely (B) unlikely (C) impossible (D) certain 1

11 There is an 80% chance of an event occurring. How could you describe the chance that the event will occur?

(A) likely (B) unlikely (C) impossible (D) certain 1

12 What is the chance of rolling a 5 on a standard dice?

(A) fifty-fifty (B) 1 in 5 (C) 1 in 6 (D) 5 in 6 1

13 How many times would you expect to get a tail if you toss a coin 40 times?

(A) 10 (B) 20 (C) 30 (D) 40 1

14 Which has the best chance of occurring?

(A) a head when a coin is tossed (B) a 3 when a dice is rolled

(C) Tuesday when a day of the week is chosen (D) a red peg from a bag with three red and six blue pegs 1

15 Which outcome is most likely when a dice is rolled?

(A) an even number (B) 6 (C) number less than 6 (D) 3 or higher 1

Total marks /15

LEVEL 1 TEST

PART A

Time allowed: 40 minutes

	Marks

1 What is the probability of getting a head when tossing a coin?

(A) $\frac{1}{4}$ (B) $\frac{1}{3}$ (C) $\frac{1}{2}$ (D) $\frac{3}{4}$ — 1

2 How many different outcomes are possible when a standard dice is rolled?

(A) 1 (B) 3 (C) 4 (D) 6 — 1

3 What is the most likely outcome when a standard dice is rolled?

(A) 1 (B) 5 (C) 6 (D) All outcomes are equally likely. — 1

4 There are 10 balls in a bag; one is red, two are blue, three are green and four are white. A ball is taken from the bag without looking. What is the probability that the ball is green?

(A) $\frac{1}{10}$ (B) $\frac{1}{3}$ (C) $\frac{3}{10}$ (D) $\frac{1}{4}$ — 1

5 From the bag in Question 4, what is the probability that the ball is red?

(A) $\frac{1}{4}$ (B) $\frac{1}{3}$ (C) $\frac{1}{2}$ (D) $\frac{1}{10}$ — 1

6 From the bag in Question 4, what is the probability that the ball is blue or white?

(A) $\frac{1}{2}$ (B) $\frac{1}{6}$ (C) $\frac{2}{5}$ (D) $\frac{3}{5}$ — 1

7 From the bag in Question 4, what is the probability of getting a white ball?

(A) 0.2 (B) 0.4 (C) 0.6 (D) 0.8 — 1

8 From the bag in Question 4, what is the probability of getting a blue ball?

(A) 10% (B) 20% (C) 40% (D) 50% — 1

9 This is the sample space when a number is chosen from a particular set. {1, 2, 3, 4}
What is the probability of choosing 5?

(A) 0 (B) $\frac{1}{4}$ (C) $\frac{1}{5}$ (D) 1 — 1

10 This spinner is spun once. On what number is it most likely to stop?

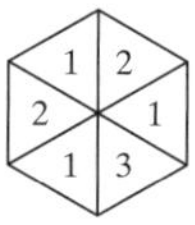

(A) 1 (B) 2
(C) 3 (D) All outcomes are equally likely. — 1

11 For the spinner in Question 10, what is the probability that it stops on 2?

(A) $\frac{1}{6}$ (B) $\frac{1}{3}$ (C) $\frac{1}{2}$ (D) $\frac{2}{3}$ — 1

12 For the spinner in Question 10 what outcome has a fifty-fifty chance of occurring?

(A) 1 (B) 2 (C) 3 (D) none of them — 1

13 From a normal pack of playing cards a card is chosen and its suit noted. What is the sample space?

(A) {1, 2, 3, 4, 5, 6} (B) {black, red}
(C) {jack, queen, king} (D) {hearts, diamonds, spades, clubs} — 1

14 An event with a probability of 1 would be:

(A) impossible (B) unlikely (C) likely (D) certain — 1

15 An event with a probability of 0 would be:

(A) impossible (B) unlikely (C) likely (D) certain — 1

Probability Calculator Allowed **(Level 1 Test)**

PART B Write answers only in the space provided.

16 What is the probability of rolling a 4 on a standard dice? ______________ 1

17 The names of the days of the week are placed in a hat and one is drawn without looking. What is the probability that it is Thursday? ______________ 1

18 There are five blue and seven red pegs in a basket. What is the probability that a peg chosen without looking is red? ______________ 1

19 Write the sample space if a whole number is chosen from the numbers greater than 3 and less than 8. ______________ 1

20 A card is chosen from a standard pack of 52 playing cards. What is the probability that it is red? ______________ 1

21 A bag holds 15 balls. Eleven of the balls are red and the rest are blue. What is the probability of a blue ball being chosen? ______________ 1

22 The probability of choosing a yellow ticket from a hat is $\frac{1}{2}$. If there are 120 tickets, how many are yellow? ______________ 1

23 What is the probability that you will sleep on the moon tonight? ______________ 1

24 What is the probability that you will win a raffle if you buy every ticket? ______________ 1

25 What is the probability of spinning ♥ on this spinner? ______________ 1

PART C Show all working.

26 A bag holds five blue, three green and four red marbles. One marble is taken from the bag without looking. What is the probability, as a fraction in simplest form, that the marble is:

a blue? **b** green? **c** red? 3 marks

______ ______ ______

27 A basket holds 24 pegs. Eight of the pegs are yellow, seven are green, three are black and the rest are white. What is the probability, as a fraction in simplest form, that the marble is:

a yellow? **b** green or black? **c** white? 3 marks

______ ______ ______

28 This spinner is spun once.

a List the sample space. 1 mark

____

b Which two outcomes have the same chance of occurring? 1 mark

____

c What is the probability, as a percentage, that it lands on ∇? 1 mark

____

d What is the probability, as a decimal, of either • or ∗? 1 mark

____

29 An unusual dice has six faces showing the numbers 1, 2, 2, 3, 3, 3.

a What is the sample space? 1 mark

____

b What is the probability of rolling 3? 1 mark

____

c How could you describe the chance of rolling a number less than 3? 1 mark

____

30 'The world can either end tomorrow or not end tomorrow. So the probability that the world will end tomorrow is $\frac{1}{2}$.' Is this true or false? Justify your answer. 2 marks

____

____

Total marks /40

LEVEL 2 TEST PART A

Time allowed: 40 minutes

Marks

1 An event is correctly described as unlikely to occur. Which could be its probability?

(A) 0.1 (B) 0.5 (C) 0.75 (D) 1.1 — 1

2 A bag holds five green, four blue and two white marbles. If one marble is taken from the bag without looking, what is the probability that it is white?

(A) $\frac{2}{9}$ (B) $\frac{2}{11}$ (C) $\frac{2}{5}$ (D) $\frac{1}{2}$ — 1

3 What is the probability of rolling an even number on a standard dice?

(A) $\frac{1}{6}$ (B) $\frac{1}{3}$ (C) $\frac{1}{2}$ (D) $\frac{1}{4}$ — 1

4 What is the probability of selecting a heart when choosing a card, without looking, from a standard pack of 52 playing cards?

(A) $\frac{1}{52}$ (B) $\frac{1}{26}$ (C) $\frac{1}{13}$ (D) $\frac{1}{4}$ — 1

5 From which box is the best chance of choosing a white ball?

(A) 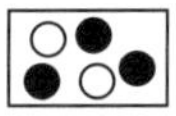 (B) 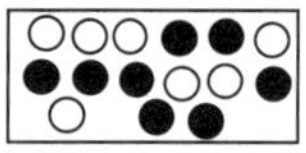 (C) 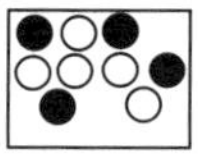 (D) 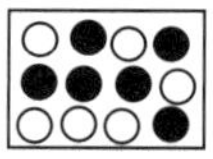 — 1

6 A letter is chosen from a box holding two E's, four A's and six I's. Which letter has a 50% chance of being chosen?

(A) A (B) E (C) I (D) none of them — 1

7 A peg is chosen from a bag holding eight white, six black and ten red pegs. What is the probability that it is black?

(A) $\frac{1}{6}$ (B) $\frac{1}{3}$ (C) $\frac{1}{5}$ (D) $\frac{1}{4}$ — 1

8 A standard dice is rolled once. What is the probability that it shows a number greater than 4?

(A) $\frac{1}{6}$ (B) $\frac{1}{3}$ (C) $\frac{1}{2}$ (D) $\frac{1}{4}$ — 1

9 The probability of an event is $\frac{3}{4}$. Which best describes the chance that the event will happen?

(A) fifty-fifty (B) likely (C) unlikely (D) certain — 1

10 A positive whole number less than 10 is chosen at random. What is the probability that it is 7?

(A) $\frac{1}{10}$ (B) $\frac{1}{9}$ (C) $\frac{1}{8}$ (D) $\frac{1}{7}$ — 1

11 Which could **not** be the probability of an event?

(A) 0.2 (B) $\frac{1}{10\,000}$ (C) 12% (D) $\frac{6}{5}$ — 1

12 A bag holds 18 counters; seven are pink, four are yellow, five are orange and the rest are purple. Which colour is most likely to be chosen?

(A) pink (B) yellow (C) orange (D) purple — 1

13 This spinner has sections in four colours. What is the probability that it lands on red (R)?

(A) 30% (B) 40% (C) $\frac{1}{3}$ (D) $\frac{1}{4}$ — 1

14 Which colour is the spinner in Question 13 least likely to land on?

(A) red (R) (B) blue (B) (C) green (G) (D) yellow (Y) — 1

15 What is the probability that the spinner in Question 13 lands on green (G) or blue (B)?

(A) 0.4 (B) 0.5 (C) 0.6 (D) 0.7 — 1

Probability Calculator Allowed **(Level 2 Test)**

PART B Write answers only in the space provided.

16 When a coin is tossed, what is the probability, as a percentage, of getting a tail? ________ [1]

17 What is the probability of choosing a queen from a standard pack of 52 playing cards? ________ [1]

18 What is the probability of an event that is certain to occur? ________ [1]

19 What is the probability of an event that is impossible? ________ [1]

20 What is the probability, as a percentage, of rolling a 3 on an unusual dice that has eight faces, two of which show 3? ________ [1]

21 List the sample space if the odd numbers between 0 and 10 are written on cards. ________ [1]

22 The probability of choosing a green marble from a bag is $\frac{1}{2}$. If there are 12 green marbles, how many marbles are in the bag? ________ [1]

23 What is the probability, as a decimal, of rolling a 5 or a 6 on a standard dice? ________ [1]

24 How many times would you expect to get a 4 if a dice is rolled 48 times? ________ [1]

25 A box holds pegs in three different colours: red, green and black. If the probability of getting a red peg is $\frac{2}{11}$ and of getting a green peg is $\frac{5}{11}$, what is the probability of getting a black peg? ________ [1]

PART C Show all working.

26 A bowl holds twelve black, eight green and five yellow jelly beans.

a One jelly bean is taken from the bowl. What is the probability (as a fraction in simplest form) that it is:

i yellow? **ii** red? **iii** not black? [3 marks]

________ ________ ________

b What is the probability, as a percentage, that the jelly bean is green? [1 mark]

____

c Joey ate all the yellow jelly beans. Now what is the probability as a percentage that the next one is green? [1 mark]

____

27 This spinner is spun once.

a What is the probability, as a fraction in simplest form, that it lands on a space marked •? [1 mark]

____

b Toby said the chance that it will land on a space marked ★ is 1 in 4 because ★ is one of the four shapes in the sample space. [2 marks]

Explain why Toby is wrong and give the correct probability that it will land on ★.

____

____

28 a The names of three girls (including Sally) and two boys are placed in a hat. One name is drawn from the hat. What is the probability that it is a girl? [1 mark]

____

b What is the probability that it is Sally? [1 mark]

____

c A girl's name is drawn from the hat. What is the probability that it is Sally? [1 mark]

____

29 The integers from 1 to 20 are written on 20 cards (one number on each card). One card is chosen. What is the probability that the number is:

a divisible by 5? [1 mark]

____

b both odd and divisible by 5? [1 mark]

____

c either odd or divisible by 5 but not both? [1 mark]

____

d either odd or divisible by 5 or both? [1 mark]

____

Total marks /40

Probability Calculator Allowed

LEVEL 3 TEST PART A

Time allowed: 40 minutes

Marks

1 A card is selected from a standard pack of 52 playing cards. What is the probability that it is a black queen?

(A) $\frac{1}{52}$ (B) $\frac{1}{26}$ (C) $\frac{1}{13}$ (D) $\frac{1}{4}$ 1

2 What is the probability of rolling a 5 on a standard dice?

(A) 0.2 (B) 0.6 (C) $0.1\dot{6}$ (D) 0.4 1

3 An event that has which of these probabilities is most likely to occur?

(A) 1 in 3 (B) $\frac{2}{5}$ (C) 25% (D) 0.31 1

4 The numbers from 1 to 100 are written on 100 cards, one number on each card. If one card is chosen at random, what is the probability that the number is a multiple of both 2 and 3?

(A) 0.16 (B) 0.17 (C) 0.67 (D) 0.76 1

5 What is the probability of selecting a red card from a pack of 50 cards if 15 are blue, 17 are green and the rest are red?

(A) 30% (B) 34% (C) 36% (D) 38% 1

6 Which spinner has the largest sample space?

(A) 

(B) 
(C) 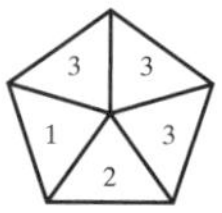

(D) 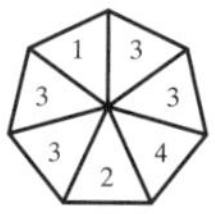

1

7 Which spinner in Question 6 has the best chance of landing on 3?

(A) A (B) B (C) C (D) D 1

8 Which spinner in Question 6 has the best chance of landing on 1?

(A) A (B) B (C) C (D) D 1

9 Which is least likely to occur?

(A) choosing a vowel from the alphabet (B) tossing a coin and getting a head

(C) choosing a club from a standard pack of cards (D) rolling a 6 on a standard dice 1

10 This spinner has a 1 in 3 chance of stopping on red. How many sections are red?

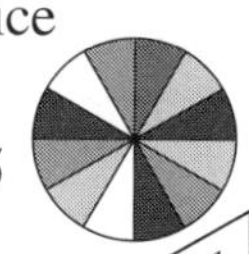

(A) 2 (B) 3 (C) 4 (D) 5 1

11 What is the probability that this spinner will stop on 2?

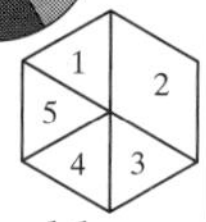

(A) $\frac{1}{5}$ (B) $\frac{1}{3}$ (C) $\frac{1}{6}$ (D) $\frac{2}{5}$ 1

12 There are eight red, 12 blue and five green marbles in a bag. Simon takes out all the green marbles and then takes another marble, without looking. What is the probability that the last marble is red?

(A) $\frac{8}{25}$ (B) $\frac{1}{2}$ (C) $\frac{2}{3}$ (D) $\frac{2}{5}$ 1

13 A spinner has a 1 in 3 chance of stopping on 4, 1 in 6 chance of stopping on 7 and a fifty-fifty chance of stopping on 2. Which could it be?

(A) 
(B) 
(C) 
(D) 
1

14 The integers from 1 to 24 are written on 24 cards, one number on each card. If one is taken without looking what is the probability that it shows a prime number?

(A) $\frac{1}{3}$ (B) $\frac{3}{8}$ (C) $\frac{5}{12}$ (D) $\frac{1}{4}$ 1

15 A packet holds pink and white marshmallows. There are twice as many white marshmallows as pink ones. If a marshmallow is taken without looking, what is the probability that it is pink?

(A) $\frac{1}{2}$ (B) $\frac{1}{3}$ (C) $\frac{1}{4}$ (D) $\frac{2}{3}$ 1

PART B Write answers only in the space provided.

16 What is the probability of choosing a black counter from a bag holding nine white and six black counters? (Give the answer as a fraction in simplest form.) ______________ 1

17 A card is chosen, without looking, from a standard pack of 52 playing cards. What is the probability that the card is a red spade? ______________ 1

18 The number when a standard dice is rolled is doubled and 5 added to it. What is the probability that the result is then greater than 7? ______________ 1

19 The names of eight people, including Usman, are placed in a hat and drawn out one at a time and placed in order on a table. What is the probability that Usman is the last name drawn out? ______________ 1

20 A box holds 70 white, 50 green and some blue tickets. The probability of selecting a green ticket from the box is $\frac{1}{3}$. How many blue tickets are in the box? ______________ 1

21 A dice was rolled 30 times. The number 6 occurred twice as many times as expected and 5 occurred four fewer times than 6. How many times did a number less than 5 occur?

______________ 1

22 The sample space for an experiment is {blue, red, green}. The probability of blue is $\frac{2}{3}$ and the probability of red is $\frac{1}{4}$. What is the probability of green? ______________ 1

23 Aaron said: 'The probability of seeing the comet as it passes is 150%.' Briefly explain why Aaron must be wrong. ______________________________

______________________________ 1

24 The chance of choosing a blue counter from a bag is 1 in 7. If there are 19 blue marbles in the bag, how many marbles are there altogether? ______________ 1

25 'If a book is open to a random page the probability that the first letter on that page is the letter "a" is $\frac{1}{26}$.' Briefly explain why this statement is wrong. ______________________________

______________________________ 1

PART C Show all working.

26 A jar holds jelly beans that are either red, green, yellow or black. The probability of taking, without looking, a red jelly bean is $\frac{1}{3}$, a green jelly bean is $\frac{2}{5}$, and a black jelly bean is $\frac{3}{20}$.

a What is the probability of taking a yellow jelly bean? [1 mark]

____

b If there are 24 green jelly beans in the jar, how many black ones are there? [2 marks]

____

____

c If all the green jelly beans are taken from the jar, what is the new probability of getting a red one? [2 marks]

____

____

27 The sample space when a card is drawn from a set of cards is {6, 7, 8, 9, 10}. Priscilla said the probability of getting a 7 must be $\frac{1}{5}$. Is she correct? Justify your answer. [2 marks]

____

____

28 A set of 20 cards includes one each of these winning cards:

win $10 | **win $5** | **win $2**

and the remaining cards are like this: **lose $1**

a If one of the cards is chosen without looking, what is the probability that you will: [1 mark]

i win $10?

____

ii win some money? (Give the answer as a decimal.) [1 mark]

____

iii win at least $5? (Give the answer as a percentage.) [1 mark]

____

b What word could be used to describe the chance of winning some money when a card is chosen? [1 mark]

____

29 A group of students was asked to shade each section on a spinner like that shown, using either red, green or blue pencils.

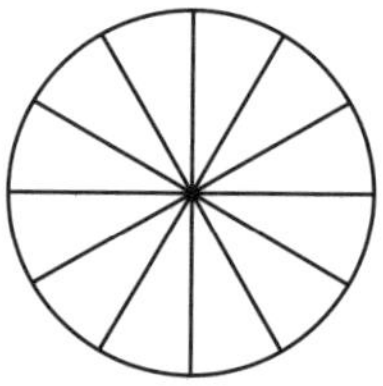

a Tia shaded her spinner so that each of the three colours was equally likely to occur. How many sections did Tia shade blue? [1 mark]

____

b Jake shaded five sections blue and seven sections red. How could you describe the chance that Jake's spinner will land on green? [1 mark]

____

c Hugo's spinner has a probability of landing on blue equal to $\frac{2}{3}$. How many sections did Hugo shade blue? [1 mark]

____

d Sasha's spinner has a fifty-fifty chance of landing on blue and is twice as likely to land on red as green. How many sections did Sasha shade red? [1 mark]

____

Total marks /40

Introduction to Exams

There are five exams, all testing material from Year 7 Australian Curriculum Mathematics.

There is an exam at each of three levels designed to be attempted without the use of a calculator. There are another two exams, at two different levels, for which the use of a calculator is allowed.

Each exam is worth 100 marks and the time allowed is 100 minutes (1 hour and 40 minutes).

Each exam is divided into three parts:

- Part A consists of 25 multiple-choice questions. There is one correct response for each question. The correct answer should be circled. You should allow about 25 minutes for this section.
- Part B consists of 30 short-answer questions. Write the answer only in the space provided. You should allow about 30 minutes for this section.
- Part C consists of questions that are more involved. They may have several parts and require you to demonstrate mathematical reasoning. You should allow about 45 minutes for this section.

Exam Paper 1: Level 1 Non-calculator

Instructions for all parts • Attempt all questions.
Time allowed: 1 hour 40 minutes • Calculators are not allowed.

Part A: Allow about 25 minutes for this part.
Part B: Allow about 30 minutes for this part.
Part C: Allow about 45 minutes for this part. Show all working for this part. **Total marks: 100**

EXAM PAPER 1: LEVEL 1 PART A

Fill in only one circle for each question.

Marks

1 $5x + x =$
(A) $5x$ (B) $5x^2$ (C) $6x$ (D) $6x^2$ [1]

2 $0.3 \times 0.2 =$
(A) 0.5 (B) 0.05 (C) 0.6 (D) 0.06 [1]

3 If $p = 5$, what is the value of $2p - 4$?
(A) 2 (B) 6 (C) 14 (D) 21 [1]

4 What is the area of a square of side length 3 cm?
(A) 9 cm^2 (B) 12 cm^2 (C) 6 cm^2 (D) 18 cm^2 [1]

5 $\frac{1}{5} + \frac{1}{4} =$
(A) $\frac{1}{9}$ (B) $\frac{2}{9}$ (C) $\frac{1}{10}$ (D) $\frac{9}{20}$ [1]

6 What is the median of the scores 5, 10 and 9?
(A) 5 (B) 8 (C) 9 (D) 10 [1]

7 $-3 - 7 =$
(A) -10 (B) -4 (C) 4 (D) 10 [1]

8 60% of \$200 =
(A) \$12 (B) \$30 (C) \$120 (D) \$130 [1]

9 $2a \times 3b =$
(A) $23ab$ (B) $5ab$ (C) $6ab$ (D) cannot be simplified [1]

10 $\frac{1}{10} \times \frac{1}{6} =$
(A) $\frac{1}{60}$ (B) $\frac{1}{30}$ (C) $\frac{4}{15}$ (D) $\frac{3}{5}$ [1]

11 What is the probability of rolling a 4 on a standard dice?
(A) $\frac{1}{2}$ (B) $\frac{1}{4}$ (C) $\frac{1}{5}$ (D) $\frac{1}{6}$ [1]

12 What is the volume of this rectangular prism?
(A) 32 cm^3 (B) 48 cm^3 (C) 60 cm^3 (D) 80 cm^3 [1]

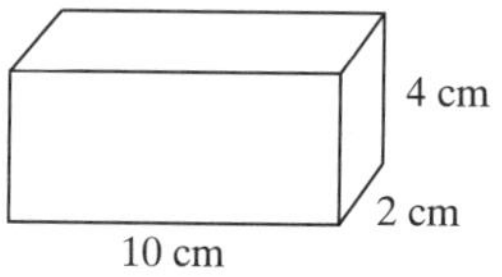

13 What is 7.2486 rounded to two decimal places?
(A) 7.24 (B) 7.25 (C) 724.86 (D) 7.86 [1]

EXAM PAPER 1 : LEVEL 1 — PART A

Marks

14 Which arrow is pointing to $1\frac{3}{4}$?

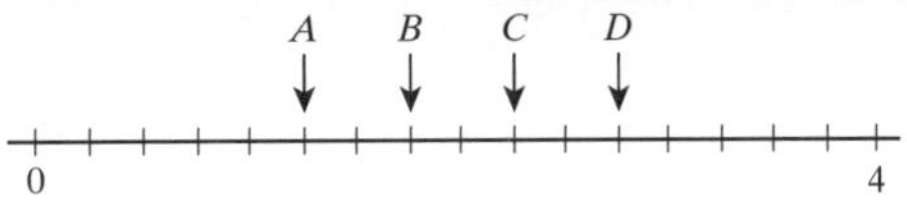

Ⓐ A　Ⓑ B　Ⓒ C　Ⓓ D　[1]

15 $2m + 5m + 7n =$

Ⓐ $7m + 7n$　Ⓑ $14mn$　Ⓒ $14m^2n$　Ⓓ $14mn^2$　[1]

16 What is the area of the triangle?

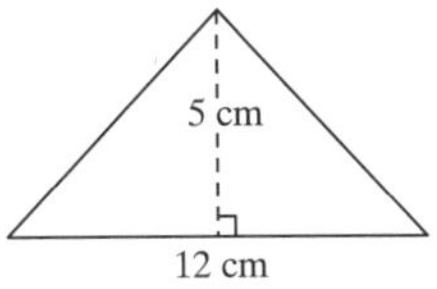

Ⓐ 60 cm²　Ⓑ 30 cm²　Ⓒ 17 cm²　Ⓓ 15 cm²　[1]

17 There are 12 men and 6 women at a meeting. What is the ratio of men to women in simplest form?

Ⓐ 6 : 1　Ⓑ 1 : 6　Ⓒ 2 : 1　Ⓓ 1 : 2　[1]

18 Which does **not** have the same value as 98×17?

Ⓐ $90 \times 17 + 8 \times 17$　Ⓑ $100 \times 17 - 2 \times 17$　Ⓒ $98 \times 10 + 98 \times 7$　Ⓓ $10 \times 90 + 7 \times 8$　[1]

19 The two marked angles are:

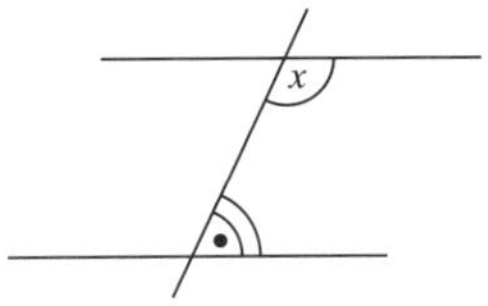

Ⓐ adjacent　Ⓑ alternate　Ⓒ co-interior　Ⓓ corresponding　[1]

20 Which is the best buy?

Ⓐ 2 for \$8.00　Ⓑ 3 for \$9.00　Ⓒ 5 for \$20.00　Ⓓ 7 for \$28　[1]

21 $5 - (-8) =$

Ⓐ 13　Ⓑ 3　Ⓒ –3　Ⓓ –13　[1]

22 $5^4 =$

Ⓐ $4 + 4 + 4 + 4 + 4$　Ⓑ $4 \times 4 \times 4 \times 4 \times 4$　Ⓒ $5 + 5 + 5 + 5$　Ⓓ $5 \times 5 \times 5 \times 5$　[1]

23 $1.2 \div 0.2 =$

Ⓐ 6　Ⓑ 0.6　Ⓒ 0.06　Ⓓ 0.006　[1]

24 What is 30% as a simple fraction?

Ⓐ $\frac{1}{3}$　Ⓑ $\frac{3}{10}$　Ⓒ $\frac{2}{5}$　Ⓓ $\frac{1}{30}$　[1]

25 What size is the angle for brown eyes?

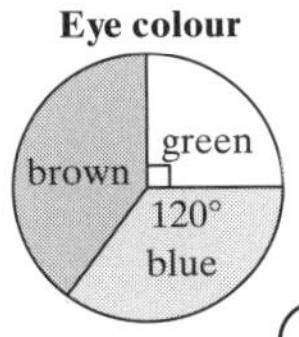

Ⓐ 90°　Ⓑ 120°　Ⓒ 140°　Ⓓ 150°　[1]

Total marks ⁄25

EXAM PAPER 1 : LEVEL 1 — PART B

Marks

1 What is $\frac{7}{8} - \frac{3}{8}$ in simplest form? ________________ 1

2 $0.06 \times 1000 =$ ________________ 1

3 3% of \$5000 = ________________ 1

4 Write 30 as the product of its prime factors. ________________ 1

5

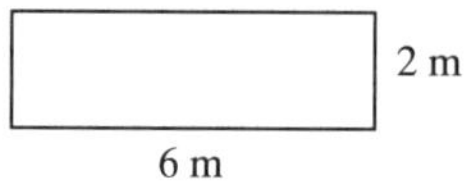

What is the area of this rectangle? ________________ 1

6 Write the ratio 8 : 12 in simplest form. ________________ 1

7 $4x + 3y + 2x + 5y =$ ________________ 1

8 What is $\frac{1}{3}$ as a decimal? ________________ 1

9 $6 + (-8) =$ ________________ 1

10 How much is 1 kg if 10 kg costs \$37.00? ________________ 1

11 If $x + 7 = 13$, what is the value of x? ________________ 1

12 What do the angles of a triangle add up to? ________________ 1

13

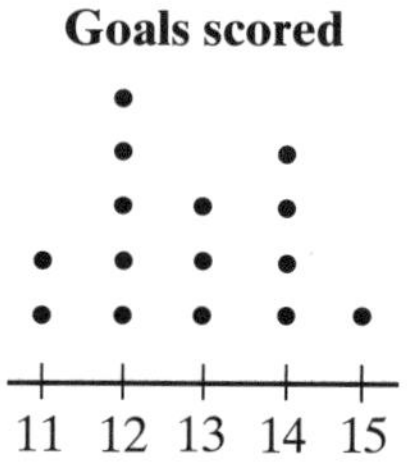

Referring to the dot plot, what is the mode? ________________ 1

14 Referring to the dot plot, what is the range? ________________ 1

15 What is the reciprocal of 4? ________________ 1

16 If $x = 3$ and $y = 2$, what is the value of xy? ________________ 1

17

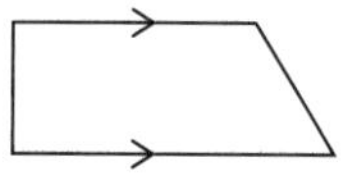

What type of quadrilateral is this? ________________ 1

18 If the volume of a container is 35 cm^3, what is its capacity in millilitres? ________________ 1

EXAM PAPER 1 : LEVEL 1 — PART B

Marks

19 What is $3\frac{7}{10}$ as an improper fraction? ______ 1

20

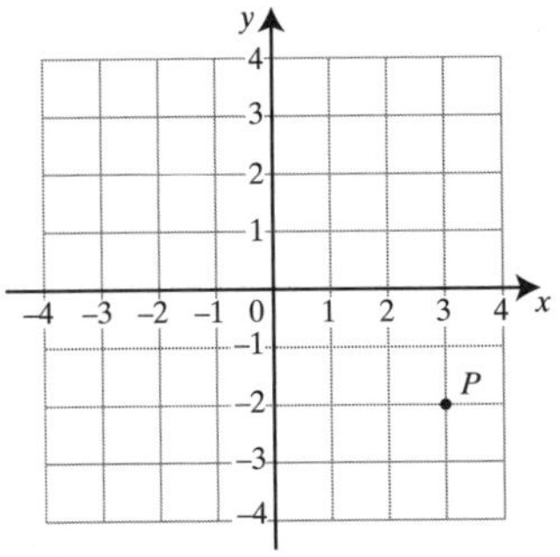

What are the coordinates of P? ______ 1

21 $10 \div \frac{1}{2} =$ ______ 1

22 What is the mean of 8 and 32? ______ 1

23 What fraction of a minute is 15 seconds? ______ 1

24

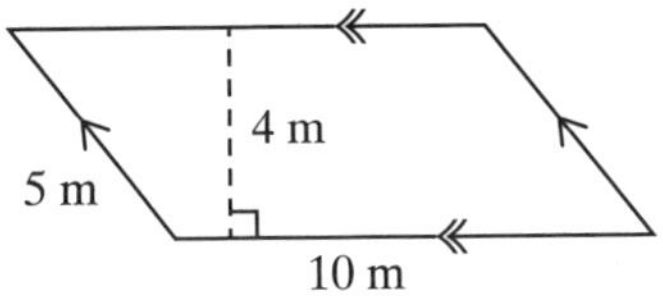

What is the area of this quadrilateral? ______ 1

25 What is $\frac{3}{4}$ as a percentage? ______ 1

26

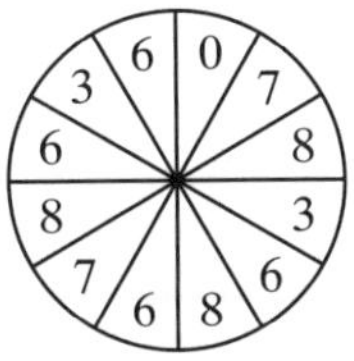

On what number is this spinner most likely to stop? ______ 1

27 What type of triangle has all its sides equal? ______ 1

28 $15m \div 5 =$ ______ 1

29 $-7 + 9 =$ ______ 1

30 What is half of a quarter? ______ 1

Total marks /30

EXAM PAPER 1 : LEVEL 1 PART C

1 If $a = 2$ and $b = 5$, find the value of:

a $b - a$ [1 mark]

b $5a + 4b$ [1 mark]

2 Solve:

a $2x + 3 = 11$ [2 marks]

b $\frac{x}{4} - 5 = 11$ [2 marks]

3 The heights of some trees were measured and the results are shown in the stem-and-leaf plot.

Heights of trees (metres)

1	3 4
2	0 2 5 5 8
3	2 5 6
4	0 3 7
5	2 3
6	8

a How tall was the tallest tree? [1 mark]

b What was the difference in height between the tallest and shortest tree? [1 mark]

c What was the most common height? [1 mark]

4 Find, giving answers in simplest form:

a $1\frac{2}{3} + 2\frac{1}{5}$ [2 marks]

b $\frac{7}{8} \div 1\frac{3}{4}$ [2 marks]

c $2\frac{1}{2} - \frac{5}{6}$ [2 marks]

5 The diagram shows the plan of a block of land.

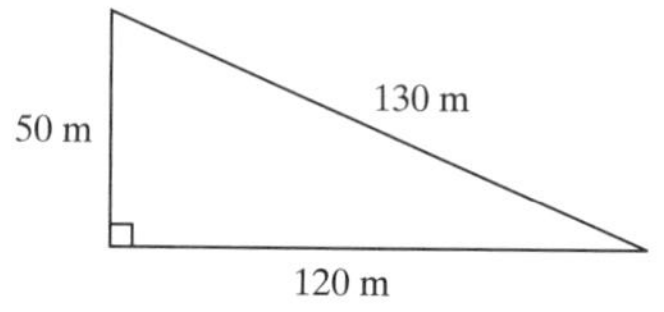

a Terry wants to build a fence around the land. How long will the fence be? [1 mark]

b How much wire will Terry need for the fence if it is to have five strands? [1 mark]

c Terry adds 10% to the amount of wire to allow for tying off and wastage. How much extra wire is that? [1 mark]

d What is the area of the land in square metres? [1 mark]

e What is the area in hectares? [1 mark]

6 **a** By drawing a factor tree for 196 write it as the product of its prime factors in index form. [2 marks]

b Find $\sqrt{196}$. [1 mark]

7 $ABCD$ is a rhombus.
The diagonals meet at E.
$\angle BAE = 50°$.

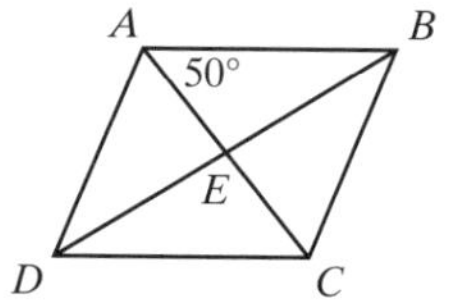

a What type of triangle is ΔABC? Give a reason for your answer. [2 marks]

b What is the size of $\angle AEB$? 1 mark

c What is the size of $\angle ACD$? Give a reason for your answer. 2 marks

8 a A shop is having a sale. How much is its discount of 30% on a chair priced at \$250? 1 mark

b The same chair can be bought for \$180 at another shop. Which is cheaper and by how much? 2 marks

9 The ratio of blue pegs to red pegs in a basket is 3:2.

a What fraction of the pegs are blue? 1 mark

b There are 24 blue pegs. How many pegs are there altogether? 1 mark

c If you choose a peg without looking, what is the probability that it is red? 1 mark

10 a Plot the point $S(-4, 0)$ on the diagram. 1 mark

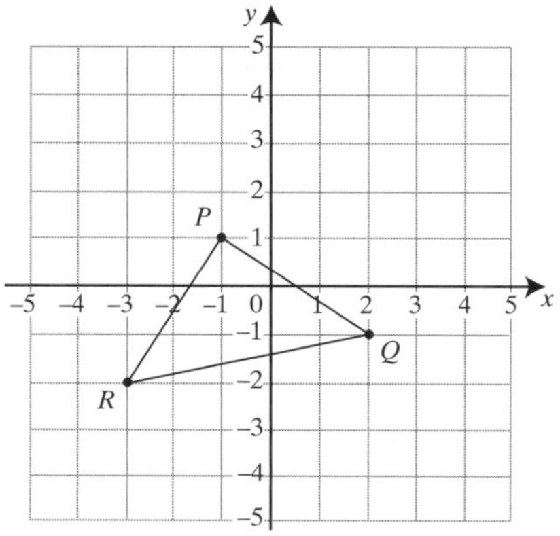

b Draw the result, labelling the vertices correctly, when ΔPQR is translated two units to the right and up four units. 3 marks

11 a What is the value of x? 1 mark

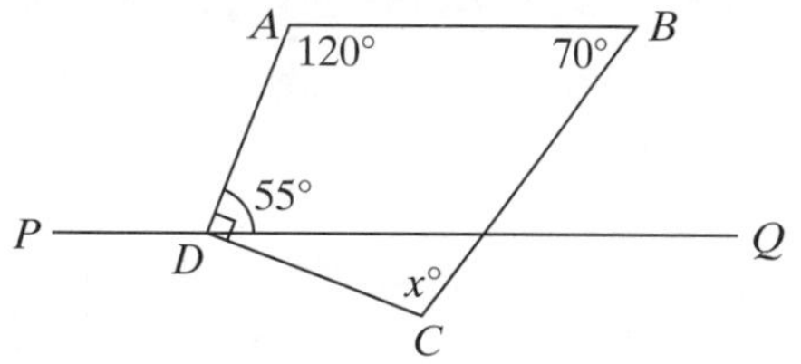

b Is PQ parallel to AB? Give a reason for your answer. 2 marks

12 a What is the volume of a cube of side length 10 cm? 1 mark

b Rhiann has two cubes of side length 10 cm. She cuts one in half and glues it on top of the other as shown in the diagram. What type of prism has Rhiann formed? 1 mark

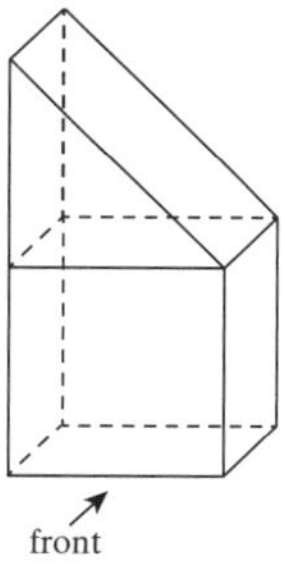

c Draw the view of Rhiann's prism from the left side. 1 mark

d What is the capacity of Rhiann's prism in litres? 1 mark

Total marks for PART C /45 **Total marks** /100

Exam Paper 2: Level 2 Non-calculator

Instructions for all parts • Attempt all questions.
Time allowed: 1 hour 40 minutes • Calculators are not allowed.

Part A: Allow about 25 minutes for this part.
Part B: Allow about 30 minutes for this part.
Part C: Allow about 45 minutes for this part. Show all working for this part. **Total marks: 100**

EXAM PAPER 2 : LEVEL 2 — PART A

Fill in only one circle for each question.

Marks

1 $-2 - 8 =$
(A) -10 (B) -6 (C) 6 (D) 10 — 1

2 $3^4 =$
(A) 3×4 (B) $3 + 3 + 3 + 3$ (C) $4 \times 4 \times 4$ (D) $3 \times 3 \times 3 \times 3$ — 1

3 Which has exactly four lines of symmetry?
(A)  (B)  (C)  (D) 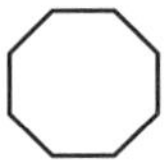 — 1

4 $0.02 \times 0.3 =$
(A) 0.6 (B) 0.06 (C) 0.006 (D) 0.0006 — 1

5 $\frac{1}{2} + \frac{1}{3} =$
(A) $\frac{1}{5}$ (B) $\frac{2}{5}$ (C) $\frac{1}{6}$ (D) $\frac{5}{6}$ — 1

6 If $a = 5$ and $b = 2$ then $3a + 4b =$
(A) 14 (B) 23 (C) 70 (D) 77 — 1

7 The area of this parallelogram is:
(A) 25 cm² (B) 30 cm² (C) 50 cm² (D) 60 cm² — 1

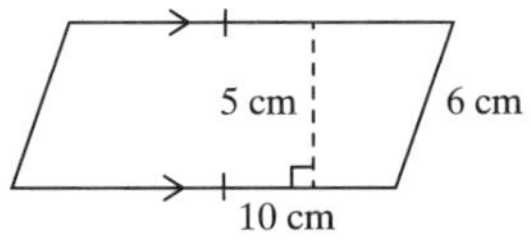

8 Which is **not** equal to 98×57?
(A) $100 \times 57 - 2 \times 98$ (B) $50 \times 98 + 7 \times 98$ (C) $90 \times 57 + 8 \times 57$ (D) $57 \times 100 - 2 \times 57$ — 1

9 Which fraction is largest?
(A) $\frac{2}{3}$ (B) $\frac{3}{4}$ (C) $\frac{5}{6}$ (D) $\frac{7}{12}$ — 1

10 Which is the best buy?
(A) 2 kg for $8.80 (B) 3 kg for $13 (C) 5 kg for $19 (D) 7 kg for $28 — 1

11 For the scores 3, 3, 5, 9 and 10, which of the following is equal to 7?
(A) mean (B) median (C) mode (D) range — 1

12 $9a + 3b - 7a + 2b =$
(A) $2a + b$ (B) $2a + 5b$ (C) $16a + 5b$ (D) $16a + b$ — 1

13 This object was made using nine blocks. What is the view from the right side?

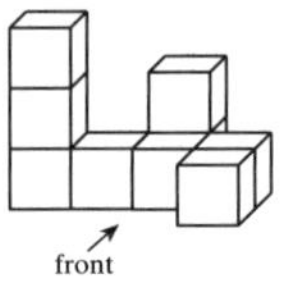

(A) 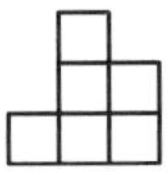 (B) 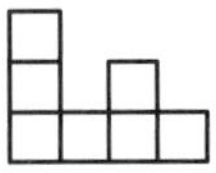 (C) 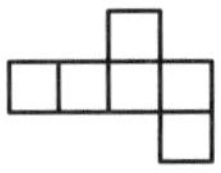 (D) 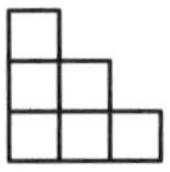 — 1

Marks

14 A box holds five red, three blue and two green marbles. If a marble is taken without looking, the probability that it is green is:

(A) $\frac{1}{2}$ (B) $\frac{1}{3}$ (C) $\frac{1}{4}$ (D) $\frac{1}{5}$

1

15 If the decimals 0.319, 0.303, 0.34 and 0.3078 are placed in order from lowest to highest, which one will be second?

(A) 0.319 (B) 0.303 (C) 0.34 (D) 0.3078

1

16 $-5 + (-9) =$

(A) 14 (B) -14 (C) 4 (D) -4

1

17 $2x \times 3x =$

(A) $6x$ (B) $6x^2$ (C) $5x$ (D) $5x^2$

1

18 Referring to the scores in the dot plot, what is the mode?

(A) 2 (B) 3 (C) 5 (D) 6

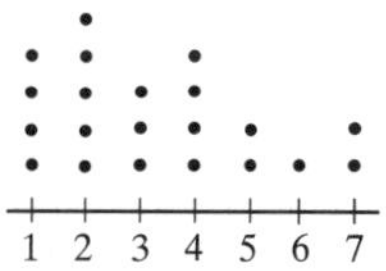

1

19 60% as a fraction in simplest form is:

(A) $\frac{1}{3}$ (B) $\frac{1}{6}$ (C) $\frac{3}{5}$ (D) $\frac{60}{100}$

1

20 What is the value of x?

(A) 30 (B) 40 (C) 70 (D) 110

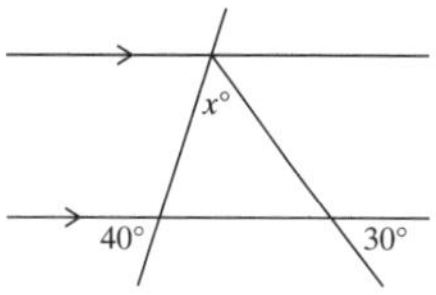

1

21 The solution to the equation $\frac{x}{5} - 2 = 8$ is:

(A) $x = 1.2$ (B) $x = 2$ (C) $x = 30$ (D) $x = 50$

1

22 The ratio 1 : 0.25 is the same as:

(A) 4 : 1 (B) 1 : 4 (C) 5 : 2 (D) 2 : 5

1

23 The diagram shows the distance Keith is from home at different times during a journey. Between which times was Keith travelling at the fastest average speed?

(A) 8 am to 10 am (B) 10 am to 11 am

(C) 11 am to 12.30 pm (D) 12.30 pm to 4 pm

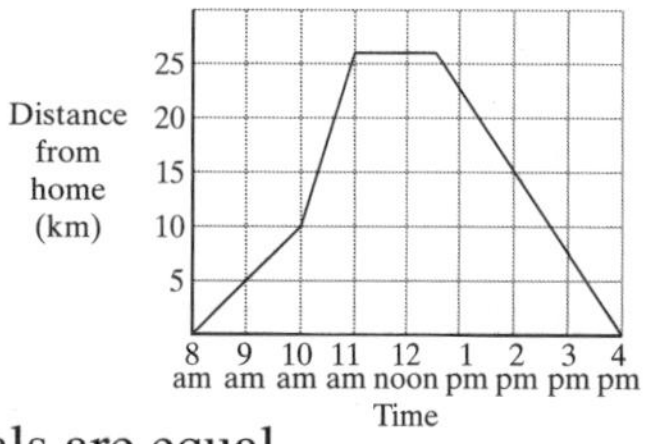

1

24 Which is **not** a property of a rhombus?

(A) The adjacent sides are equal. (B) The diagonals are equal.

(C) The opposite angles are equal. (D) The diagonals bisect each other.

1

25 $PQRS$ will be rotated clockwise about O through 90°. What will be the coordinates of P'?

(A) $(-1, -2)$ (B) $(-2, -1)$

(C) $(1, 2)$ (D) $(2, 1)$

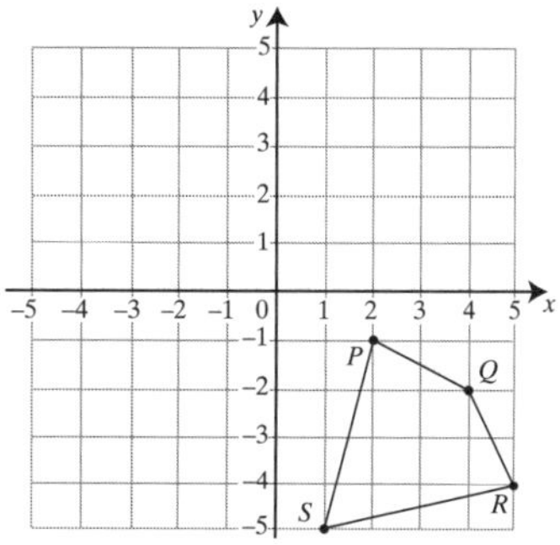

1

Total marks /25

Marks

1 $\sqrt{9} + \sqrt{16} =$ ____________ [1]

2 Simplify $3x + 2x + 5y$. ____________ [1]

3 $\frac{2}{3} \times \frac{4}{5} =$ ____________ [1]

4 Of the 20 children in a class, 11 are boys. What is the ratio of girls to boys? ____________ [1]

5 What is the area of a square of side length 5 cm? ____________ [1]

6 What is the probability of getting a 5 when a standard dice is rolled? ____________ [1]

7 Write 23.798 correct to one decimal place. ____________ [1]

8 $73 \times 99 + 73 =$ ____________ [1]

9 Place –38, 19, 7, –23, 0 and –6 in ascending (from lowest to highest) order. ____________ [1]

10

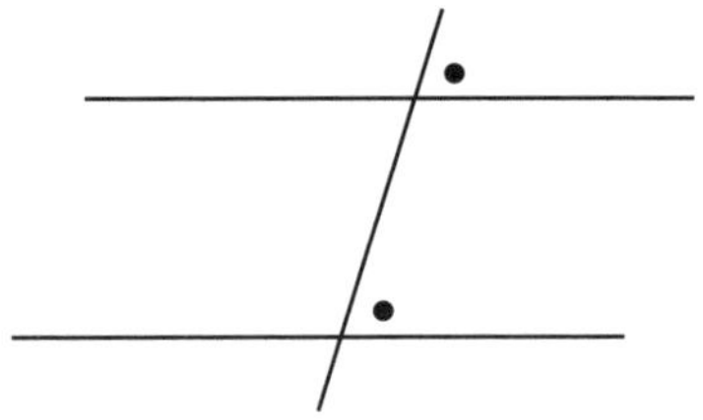

What type of angles are the pair marked in the diagram? ____________ [1]

11 What is the lowest common multiple of 24 and 36? ____________ [1]

12 What is three-quarters of a million? ____________ [1]

13 $-7 - -4 =$ ____________ [1]

14 If $x = 5$ and $y = 2$, what is the value of $4xy$? ____________ [1]

15 What percentage is 13 of 50? ____________ [1]

16 What is the mean of 5, 7 and 18? ____________ [1]

17 $9x \div x =$ ____________ [1]

18 What fraction of an hour is 40 minutes? ____________ [1]

Marks

19 What is $5\frac{7}{8}$ as an improper fraction? __________ [1]

20 $0.08 \div 0.002 =$ __________ [1]

21

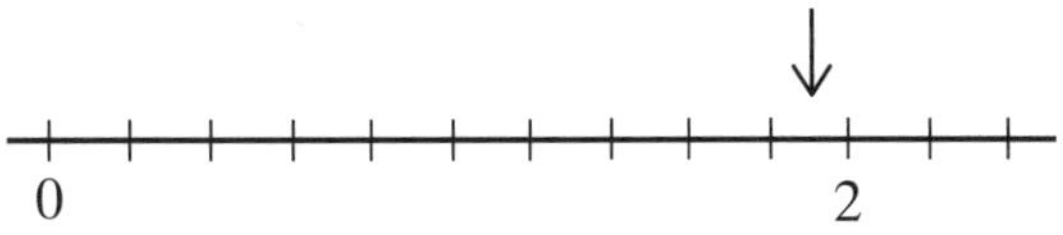

What fraction is found at the position shown on the number line? __________ [1]

22 What is the number 7 less than m? __________ [1]

23 What is the volume of a cube of side 20 cm? __________ [1]

24 What is $\frac{2}{3}$ as a decimal? __________ [1]

25

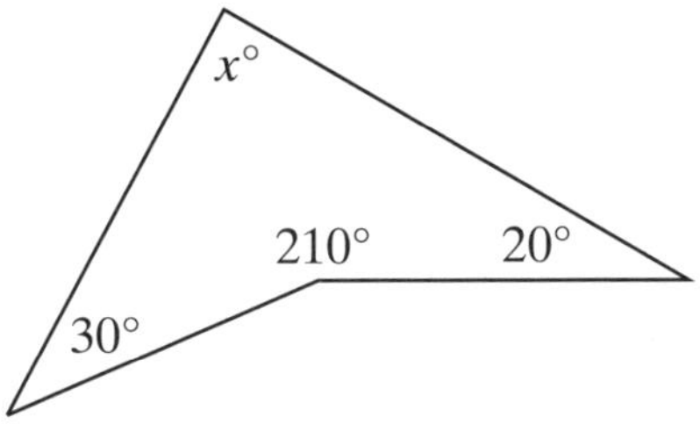

What is the value of x? __________ [1]

26 $4 - 1\frac{3}{5} =$ __________ [1]

27 What number is 9 more than –3? __________ [1]

28 $2^3 \times 5^4 =$ __________ [1]

29 A container has capacity 600 mL. What is its volume in cubic centimetres? __________ [1]

30 A rectangular paddock has an area of 1 ha. If it is 200 m long, how wide is it? __________ [1]

Total marks /30

1

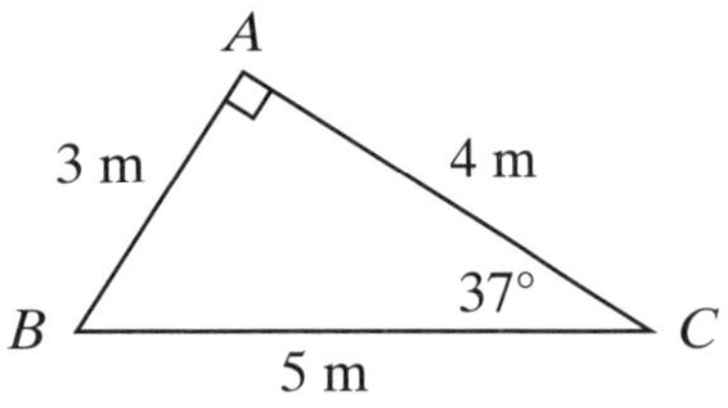

a What type of triangle is ΔABC? 1 mark

b What is the size of $\angle ABC$? 1 mark

c What is the area of the triangle? 1 mark

2 A group of students voted in an election. The sector graph shows who they voted for.

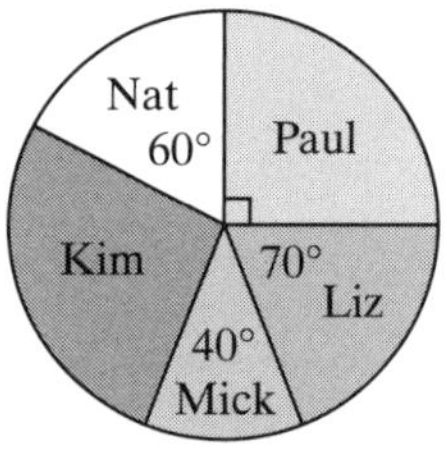

a Who got the most votes? 1 mark

b What percentage voted for Paul? 1 mark

c What is the angle for the sector for Kim? 1 mark

d What fraction voted for Mick? (Give the answer in simplest form.) 1 mark

e What is the probability that a person chosen from the group voted for Nat? 1 mark

f If 18 voted for Paul, how many voted for Liz? 2 marks

3 Find:

a $3\frac{3}{4} \div \frac{3}{5}$ 2 marks

b $5\frac{1}{4} - 2\frac{3}{5}$ 2 marks

4 **a** Complete a factor tree for 180. 1 mark

b Write 180 as the product of its prime factors in index form. 1 mark

5 **a** What type of quadrilateral is *ABCD*? 1 mark

b What is the size of $\angle ADE$? Give a reason for your answer. 2 marks

c Is *PS* parallel to *EC*? Justify your answer. 2 marks

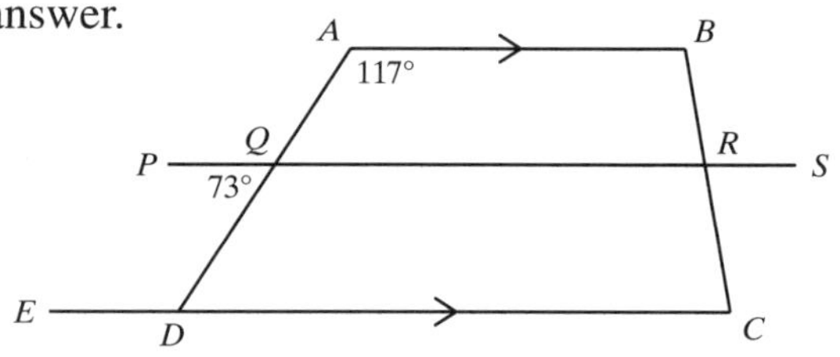

6 The maximum temperature in Buffalo one day was –2 °C and the minimum was –8 °C.

a What was the difference between the maximum and minimum temperatures? 1 mark

b The next day the maximum temperature was 7° higher. What was the maximum temperature that next day? 1 mark

7 **a** Show the point $P(-1, 2)$ on the diagram. 1 mark

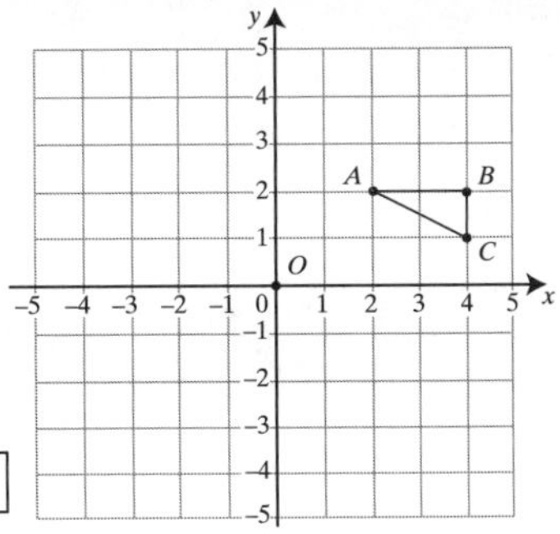

b What are the coordinates of *B*? 1 mark

c ΔABC is rotated through 180° about the origin. Draw the result on the diagram, labelling the vertices appropriately. 2 marks

d If, instead, ΔABC was reflected in the *x*-axis, what would be the coordinates of C'? 1 mark

8 Solve $5x - 3 = 17$. 1 mark

9 Two rectangular prisms are stacked as shown to make this solid.

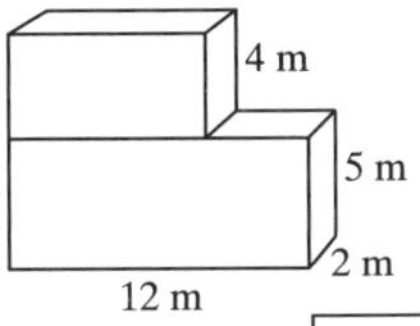

a What type of solid is it? 1 mark

b What is the volume of the bottom rectangular prism? 1 mark

c If the total volume of the solid is 184 m^3, what is the length of the top prism? 2 marks

d What is the capacity of the solid in litres? 1 mark

e Draw the top view of the solid. 1 mark

10 An electrician offers a 4% discount on a bill of $1200.

a How much is the discount? 1 mark

b What amount is left to pay after the discount has been allowed? 1 mark

c GST (10%) is then added to the bill. How much must be paid, including GST? 1 mark

11 The heights, in centimetres, of some children were recorded in this stem-and-leaf plot.

11	7
12	1 3 4 6 9
13	1 2 2 4 5 7 8
14	0 3 6 7 9
15	2 6 8

a How many children had their heights recorded? 1 mark

b How tall is the tallest child? 1 mark

c What is the range? 1 mark

d What is the median? 1 mark

e What is the modal height? 1 mark

12 Dan has 70 pieces of timber each 1.2 m long.

a What is the total length of all the pieces? 1 mark

b What is the area of each piece, in square metres, if they are all 0.09 m wide? 1 mark

Total marks for PART C /45 **Total marks** /100

Exam Paper 3: Level 3 Non-calculator

Instructions for all parts • Attempt all questions.
Time allowed: 1 hour 40 minutes • Calculators are not allowed.

Part A: Allow about 25 minutes for this part.
Part B: Allow about 30 minutes for this part.
Part C: Allow about 45 minutes for this part. Show all working for this part. **Total marks: 100**

EXAM PAPER: LEVEL 3 PART A

Fill in only one circle for each question.

	Marks
1 $0.5 \times 0.8 =$ (A) 0.4 (B) 0.04 (C) 0.004 (D) 0.0004	1
2 $\frac{2}{5} + \frac{5}{6} =$ (A) $\frac{7}{11}$ (B) $\frac{7}{30}$ (C) $1\frac{7}{30}$ (D) $1\frac{1}{3}$	1
3 $9x + 8 - 2x + 4 =$ (A) $19x$ (B) $7x + 12$ (C) $11x + 4$ (D) $11x - 4$	1
4 Which is largest? (A) $\frac{1}{4}$ (B) $\frac{1}{5}$ (C) $\frac{7}{30}$ (D) $\frac{4}{15}$	1
5 A container has a volume of 21 000 mm^3. What is its capacity? (A) 21 mL (B) 210 mL (C) 2.1 L (D) 21 L	1
6 What type of triangle could have angles of 76°, 52° and 62°? (A) equilateral (B) isosceles (C) scalene (D) none of these	1
7 What is $\frac{5}{12}$ as a decimal? (A) 0.512 (B) $0.\dot{4}\dot{1}\dot{6}$ (C) $0.4\dot{1}\dot{6}$ (D) $0.41\dot{6}$	1
8 What is the area? (A) 56 m^2 (B) 64 m^2 (C) 72 m^2 (D) 80 m^2 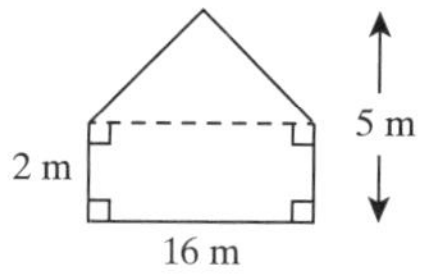 	1
9 If $a = 6$ and $b = 5$, then $ab^2 =$ (A) 65^2 (B) 6×5^2 $(6 \times 5)^2$ (D) none of these	1
10 $\frac{1}{6} \div \frac{1}{2} =$ (A) $\frac{1}{3}$ (B) $\frac{1}{12}$ (C) 3 (D) 12	1
11 The point P is at (3, 3). Which point is at (2, –4)? (A) A (B) B (C) C (D) D 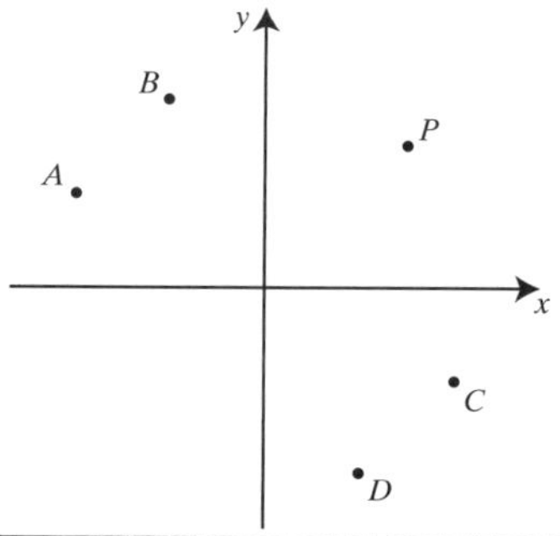 	1

Marks

12 Which is **not** necessarily a parallelogram?

(A) rectangle (B) rhombus (C) square (D) trapezium 1

13 What is the median of the scores 12, 7, 9, 12, 8, 4, 9, 12, 7?

(A) 7 (B) 8 (C) 9 (D) 12 1

14 Which arrow shows the position of $-\frac{3}{4}$ on the number line?

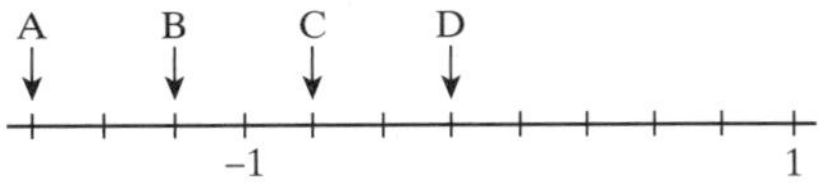

(A) A (B) B (C) C (D) D 1

15 $0.8 \div 0.0005 =$

(A) 1600 (B) 16 000 (C) 0.016 (D) 0.000 16 1

16 $4\frac{1}{3} - 2\frac{3}{4} =$

(A) $1\frac{5}{12}$ (B) $1\frac{7}{12}$ (C) $2\frac{5}{12}$ (D) $2\frac{7}{12}$ 1

17 If $12 - x = -17$ then $x =$

(A) 5 (B) −5 (C) 29 (D) −29 1

18 Which is the smallest?

(A) $\frac{1}{2}\%$ (B) 0.002 (C) $\frac{1}{200}$ (D) They are all the same. 1

19 The probability of choosing a black tile from a bag holding two black, one red and seven white tiles is:

(A) $\frac{1}{2}$ (B) $\frac{1}{3}$ (C) $\frac{1}{4}$ (D) $\frac{1}{5}$ 1

20 $2\frac{3}{5} \times 3\frac{3}{4} =$

(A) $6\frac{9}{20}$ (B) $7\frac{3}{20}$ (C) $7\frac{7}{20}$ (D) $9\frac{3}{4}$ 1

21 Which is **not** the same as 4×2^5?

(A) 2^7 (B) 4^4 (C) 2×4^3 (D) $4^2 \times 2^3$ 1

22 The mean of five scores is 16. A new score of 10 is included in the data set. What is the new mean?

(A) 13 (B) 14 (C) 15 (D) 16 1

23 What is $7\frac{1}{2}\%$ as a fraction in simplest form?

(A) $\frac{1}{15}$ (B) $\frac{3}{40}$ (C) $\frac{3}{20}$ (D) $\frac{9}{125}$ 1

24 The results of a survey about which of three pets was preferable are shown in the sector graph. What percentage of the people surveyed preferred a dog?

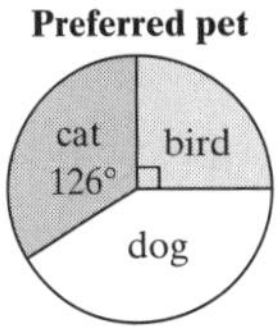

(A) 30% (B) 35% (C) 40% (D) 45% 1

25 What is the ratio $\frac{2}{5} : \frac{3}{4}$ in simplest form?

(A) 8 : 15 (B) 15 : 8 (C) 5 : 6 (D) 6 : 5 1

Total marks /25

EXAM PAPER 3 : LEVEL 3 — PART B

Marks

1 What is 5.0978 rounded to two decimal places? ______ 1

2 $\sqrt{5^2 - 3^2} =$ ______ 1

3 If $p = 2$ and $q = 5$, what is the value of $3p - 4q$? ______ 1

4 $0.6 \div \frac{1}{3} =$ ______ 1

5 What is 70% of $120? ______ 1

6 What is the solution to the equation $3x + 1 = 19$? ______ 1

7 $5 - (-6) =$ ______ 1

8 $4k \div k =$ ______ 1

9 Arrange 0.03, 0.3, 0.215 and 0.0251 in ascending order. ______ 1

10 $5 - 3p + 8 =$ ______ 1

11 If Ben and Cassie share $1200 in the ratio 3 : 2, what is Cassie's share? ______ 1

12 $9\frac{1}{4} - 6\frac{1}{2} =$ ______ 1

13 A quote from a builder is $2180 plus GST. What will be the total with GST (10%) added? ______ 1

14 What is 64% as a fraction in simplest form? ______ 1

15 $-8 + (-7) =$ ______ 1

16 A square paddock has all its sides $\frac{1}{2}$ km in length. What is the area of the paddock in hectares? ______ 1

17 What fraction of 5 L is 600 mL? ______ 1

18 $-2m - 7m =$ ______ 1

19 What is the probability of getting a prime number when a dice is rolled? ______ 1

Marks

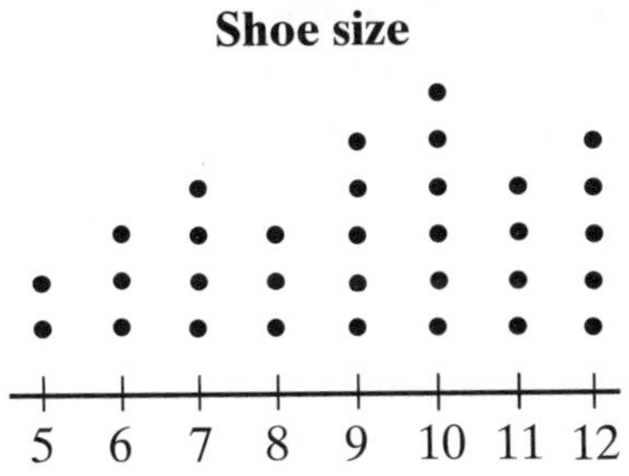

20 Referring to the dot plot, what is the range? ____________ 1

21 Referring to the dot plot, what is the mode? ____________ 1

22 Referring to the dot plot, what is the median? ____________ 1

23 What is 0.45 as a simple fraction? ____________ 1

24 What is $\frac{2}{3}$ of $1\frac{1}{2}$? ____________ 1

25

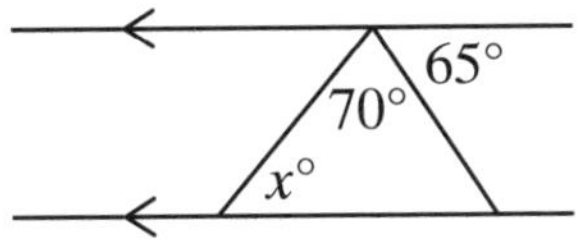

What is the value of x? ____________ 1

26 What fraction of a cubic metre is 100 cm^3? ____________ 1

27 $3x^2 + 4x - 2x^2 + 5x =$ ____________ 1

28 $8 \div 2\frac{2}{3} =$ ____________ 1

29 What is $6\frac{1}{4}$% as a decimal? ____________ 1

30

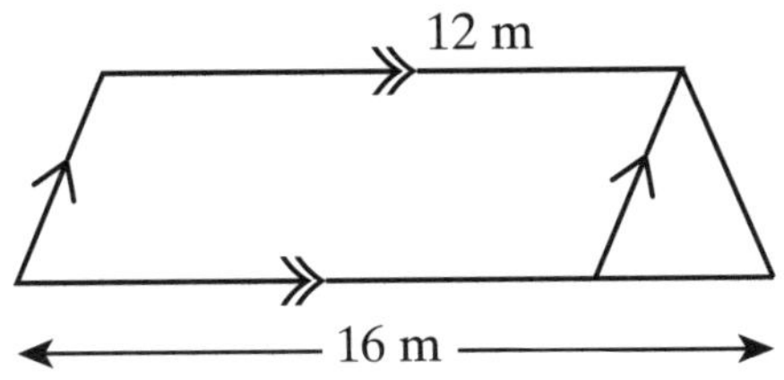

What fraction of the whole area is the area of the triangle? ____________ 1

Total marks /30

EXAM PAPER 3 : LEVEL 3 PART C

1 a Use a factor tree to express 1764 as the product of its prime factors in index form. 2 marks

b Find $\sqrt{1764}$. 1 mark

2 Solve:

a $9x - 37 = 215$ 2 marks

b $\frac{x}{5} + 48 = 101$ 2 marks

3 Find:

a $7\frac{3}{8} + 6\frac{4}{5}$ 2 marks

b $4\frac{5}{8} \times 3\frac{1}{5}$ 2 marks

c $\frac{1}{4} - \frac{1}{2} \times \frac{2}{5}$ 2 marks

d $2\frac{1}{2} \div 3\frac{2}{3}$ 2 marks

4 A group of 300 people were surveyed and asked which of five countries they would prefer to visit. The results are shown in the divided bar chart.

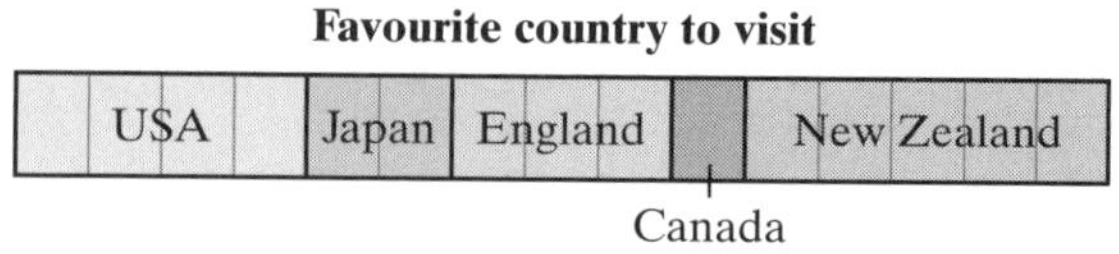

a How many people chose USA? 1 mark

b What percentage of those surveyed chose New Zealand? 1 mark

c How many more chose England than Canada? 1 mark

d What is the probability that a person from the group chose Japan? 1 mark

5 If $a = 3$, $b = -12$ and $c = -5$, find the value of:

a $b + c$ 1 mark

b $4a - b$ 1 mark

c $c - 7a$ 1 mark

6 The diagram shows a pool surrounded by paving.

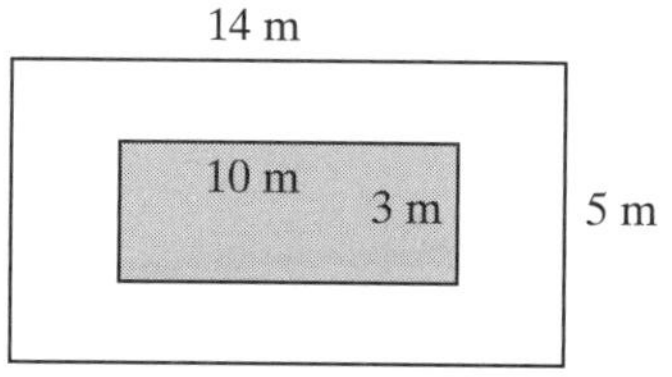

a Find the total cost of the paving at \$32 per square metre. 2 marks

b The pool holds 45 000 L of water when full. To what depth can it be filled? 2 marks

EXAM PAPER 3 : LEVEL 3 PART C

7 The graph shows the distance Peter is from home at different times on a journey.

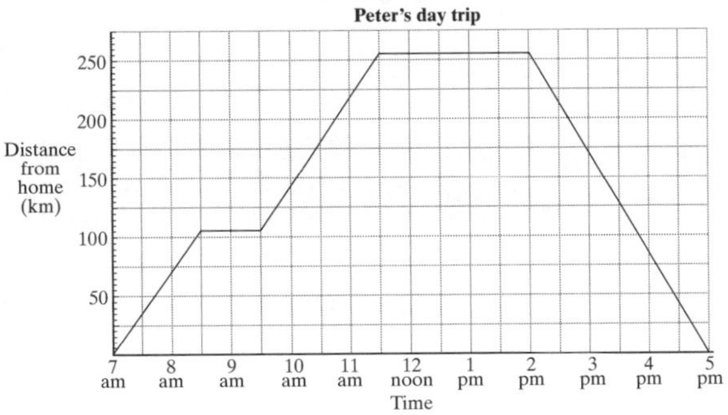

a How far did Peter travel altogether? 1 mark

b How long was he actually travelling? 1 mark

c What was his average speed for the part of the journey after he left home before his first stop? 1 mark

8 The results of an exam, marked out of 150, are shown in the stem-and-leaf plot.

Exam results

11	6 8
12	1 3 7 9
13	2 2 6 7 9
14	0 3 3 3 5 7 8
15	0 0

a What was the range? 1 mark

b What was the modal score? 1 mark

c What was the median? 1 mark

d What percentage of students scored full marks? 1 mark

9 **a** A store was offering 15% off all marked prices. The store was selling five CDs marked \$12.00 each that Natalie wanted. How much would Natalie pay for the five CDs? 2 marks

b Another store had the same CDs at \$12.50 each, but was offering 'Buy three, get one free'. How much would Natalie have to pay at this store for the five CDs? 1 mark

10 *AC* is parallel to *DF*. *BE* is perpendicular to *CE*. $\angle BED = 33°$.

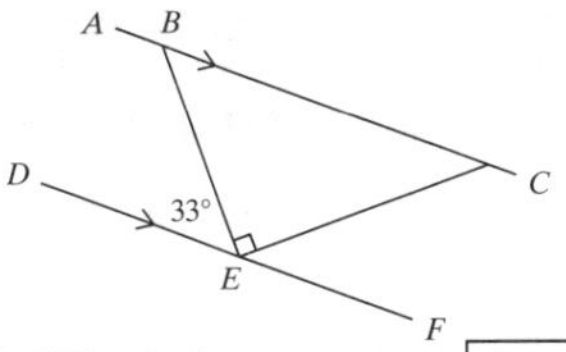

a Find the size of $\angle BCE$, giving reasons. 2 marks

b If $EC = 20$ cm and $BE = 30.8$ cm, find the area of ΔBCE. 1 mark

11 **a** Show the point $S(1.5, -2.5)$ on the diagram. 1 mark

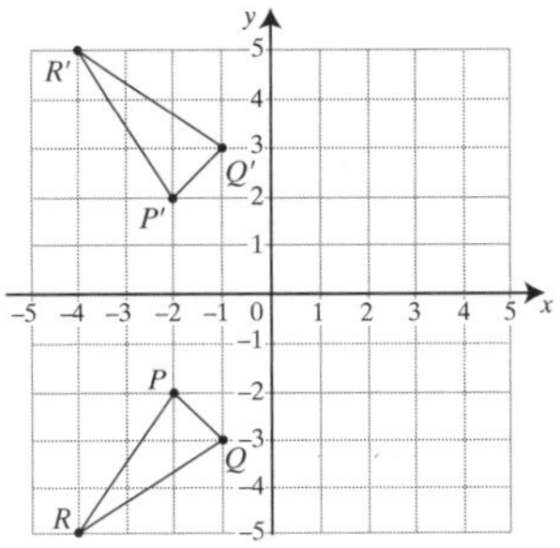

b If the point *S* is translated two units up and four units left, what will the coordinates of *S'* be? 1 mark

c Describe a single transformation that moves ΔPQR to $\Delta P'Q'R'$. 1 mark

d Describe a different combination of transformations that produce the same result. 1 mark

12 A rectangular deck 5.36 m wide and 2 m long is to be built using decking boards that are 2 m long and 0.08 m wide.

a What is the area of the deck in square metres? 1 mark

b How many decking boards would be needed? 1 mark

Total marks for PART C /45 **Total marks** /100

Exam Paper 4: Levels 1 and 2 Calculator Allowed

Instructions for all parts • Attempt all questions.
Time allowed: 1 hour 40 minutes • Calculators are allowed.

Part A: Allow about 25 minutes for this part.
Part B: Allow about 30 minutes for this part.
Part C: Allow about 45 minutes for this part. Show all working for this part. **Total marks: 100**

EXAM PAPER 4: LEVELS 1 AND 2 PART A

Fill in only one circle for each question.

Marks

1 What is the reciprocal of $1\frac{3}{5}$?

(A) $1\frac{5}{3}$ (B) $\frac{5}{8}$ (C) $2\frac{2}{3}$ (D) $\frac{5}{9}$ — 1

2 $5x + 8y - 2x + 3y =$

(A) $3x + 11y$ (B) $3x + 5y$ (C) $7x + 11y$ (D) $7x + 5y$ — 1

3 What number is the arrow pointing to?

(A) –2 (B) –4 (C) –7 (D) –8

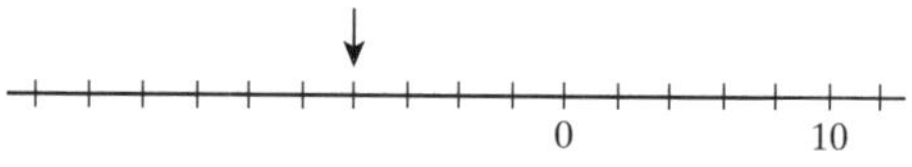

1

4 $0.000\,0125 \times 0.000\,008 =$

(A) 0.000 0001 (B) 0.000 000 01 (C) 0.000 000 001 (D) 0.000 000 0001 — 1

5 What is the mean of 38, 69, 87 and 101?

(A) 73.75 (B) 63 (C) 78 (D) 59 — 1

6 Which has the greatest volume?

(A) 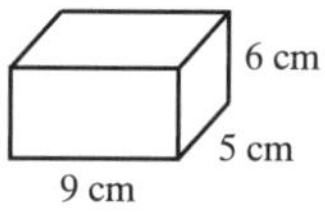

(B) 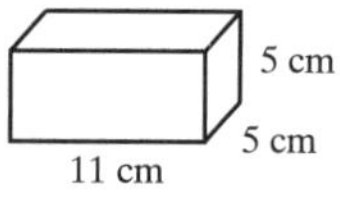

(C) 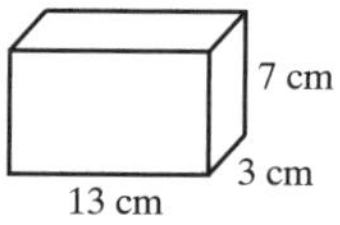

(D) 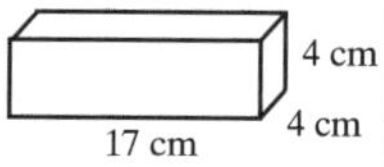

1

7 $xy^2 =$

(A) $x \times y \times x \times y$ (B) $x \times x \times y$ (C) $x \times y \times y$ (D) $x \times y \times 2$ — 1

8 Which fractions are in ascending (from lowest to highest) order?

(A) $\frac{2}{3}, \frac{3}{4}, \frac{5}{7}, \frac{7}{9}$ (B) $\frac{7}{9}, \frac{5}{7}, \frac{3}{4}, \frac{2}{3}$ (C) $\frac{2}{3}, \frac{3}{4}, \frac{7}{9}, \frac{5}{7}$ (D) $\frac{2}{3}, \frac{5}{7}, \frac{3}{4}, \frac{7}{9}$ — 1

9 Which is the best buy?

(A) 600 mL for \$2.40 (B) 1 L for \$3.60 (C) 2 L for \$7.40 (D) 3 L for \$10.60 — 1

10 What is the area of the triangle?

(A) 540 cm² (B) 900 cm² (C) 1125 cm² (D) 1812.5 cm² — 1

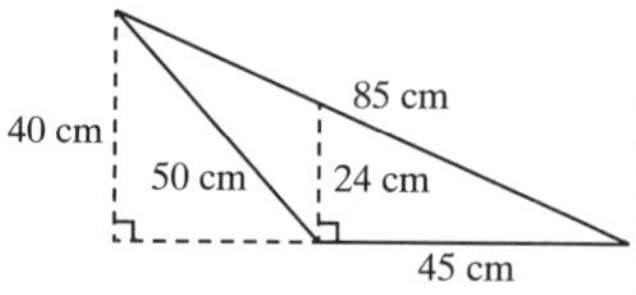

11 If $m = 9$ and $n = 8$ then $7mn =$

(A) 798 (B) 686 (C) 119 (D) 504 — 1

12 The ratio of men to women at a conference was 4 : 7. If there were 308 women, how many men were there?

(A) 112 (B) 176 (C) 196 (D) 539 — 1

EXAM PAPER 4: LEVELS 1 AND 2 — PART A

Marks

13 When rounded to two decimal places 13.299 63 becomes:

(A) 13.29 (B) 13.30 (C) 13.31 (D) 13.63 — 1

14 The marked angles are:

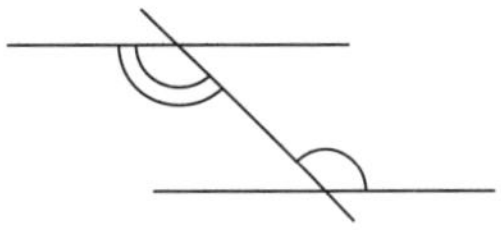

(A) alternate (B) corresponding (C) co-interior

(D) none of these because there are no parallel lines — 1

15 A regular hexagon has rotational symmetry of what order?

(A) 1 (B) 6 (C) 8 (D) 12 — 1

16 $\frac{5}{6}$ as a decimal is:

(A) 0.56 (B) $0.5\dot{6}$ (C) $0.8\dot{3}$ (D) $0.\dot{8}\dot{3}$ — 1

17 The sum of –7, –9 and –15 is:

(A) –31 (B) 17 (C) –17 (D) –13 — 1

18 What are the coordinates of P and Q?

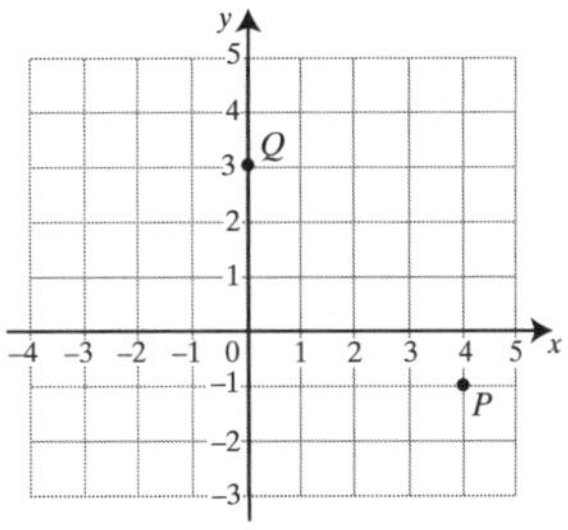

(A) $P(4, –1)$, $Q(0, 3)$ (B) $P(–1, 4)$, $Q(0, 3)$

(C) $P(4, –1)$, $Q(3, 0)$ (D) $P(–1, 4)$, $Q(3, 0)$ — 1

19 $9\frac{2}{3} \times 5\frac{6}{7} =$

(A) $45\frac{4}{7}$ (B) $46\frac{11}{21}$ (C) $56\frac{13}{21}$ (D) 57 — 1

20 $x =$

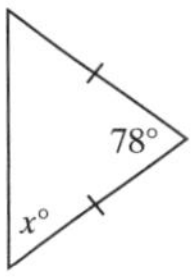

(A) 51 (B) 60 (C) 78 (D) 102 — 1

21 From which box is there the best chance of drawing a black ball?

(A) 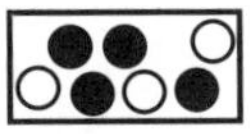 (B) 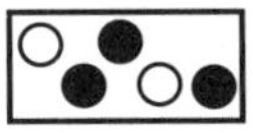 (C) 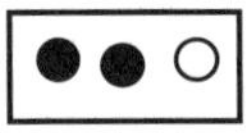 (D) 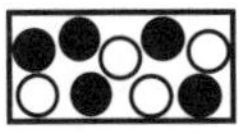 — 1

22 The solution to the equation $5k - 9 = 17$ is:

(A) $k = 1.6$ (B) $k = 1.8$ (C) $k = 5.2$ (D) $k = 5.4$ — 1

23 The front view and side view of a prism are shown. What is the top view?

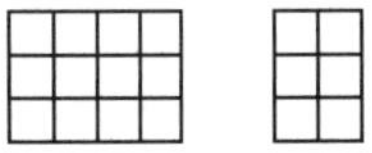

(A) 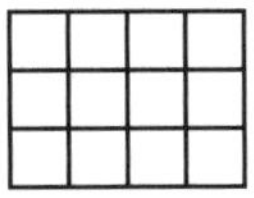 (B) 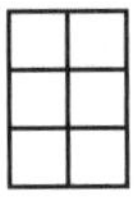 (C) 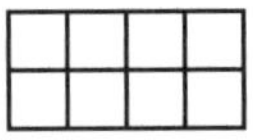 (D) 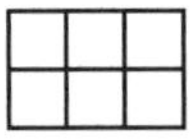 — 1

24 $\frac{2x}{6} =$

(A) $3x$ (B) $\frac{3}{x}$ (C) $\frac{1}{3x}$ (D) $\frac{x}{3}$ — 1

25 What is $3\frac{1}{2}\%$ as a decimal?

(A) 0.35 (B) 0.305 (C) 0.035 (D) 0.0305 — 1

Total marks /25

EXAM PAPER 4 : LEVELS 1 AND 2 — PART B

Marks

1 $\sqrt{6^2 + 8^2} =$ ____________ 1

2 $6x + 3x + 5 - 4 =$ ____________ 1

3 What is 65% of twenty thousand? ____________ 1

4

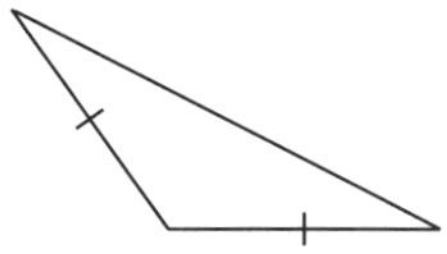

What type of triangle is this? ____________ 1

5 What is the median of 8, 15, 9, 2 and 5? ____________ 1

6 Write –5, –11, 0, –2, 8 and –17 in descending order. ____________ 1

7 What fraction (in simplest form) is 800 g of 1 kg? ____________ 1

8

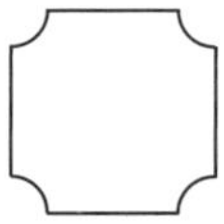

Draw in all the axes of symmetry for this shape. ____________ 1

9 If adding $\frac{5}{21}$ and $\frac{7}{9}$, what is the lowest common denominator? ____________ 1

10 What is the probability of choosing a blue marble from a bag holding nine blue, 12 red, one green and five yellow marbles? ____________ 1

11 $2a \times 3b \times 5 =$ ____________ 1

12

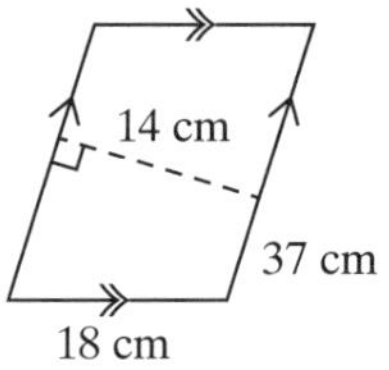

What is the area of this parallelogram? ____________ 1

13 What is $\frac{5}{9}$ as a decimal? ____________ 1

14 Write the ratio of 40 minutes to an hour and a half in simplest form. ____________ 1

15 $32 \div \frac{1}{2} =$ ____________ 1

16 What is the volume of a rectangular prism 7 m long, 6 m wide and 5 m high? ____________ 1

17 $217.6 - 3.8 \div 0.19 =$ ____________ 1

Marks

18 $8y \div 8 =$ ______ 1

19 What is the solution to the equation $\frac{x}{6} = 42$? ______ 1

20

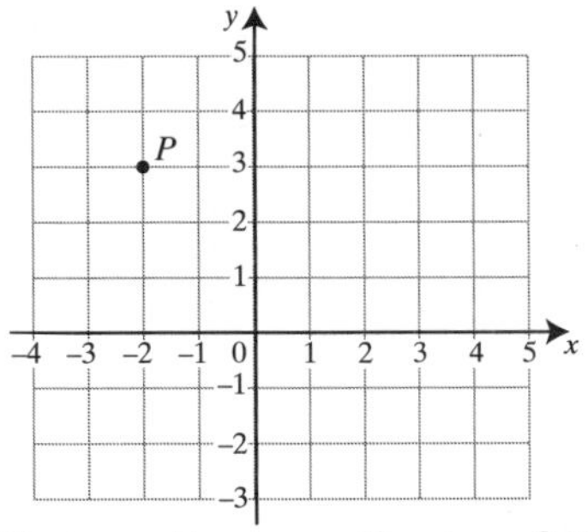

What are the co-ordinates of P? ______ 1

21 Referring to the diagram in Question 20, if point P is translated five units down and two units left, what will be the coordinates of P'? ______ 1

22 $2\frac{3}{4} + 5\frac{1}{3} \times 1\frac{3}{5} =$ ______ 1

23

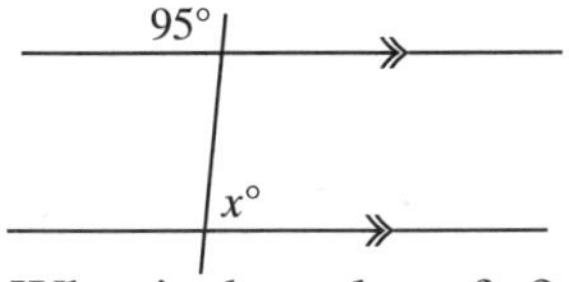

What is the value of x? ______ 1

24 What is the area, in square metres, of a rectangle 2 m long and 80 cm wide? ______ 1

25 What is the value of $\frac{7.8 - 3 \times 2.6}{6.35 + 2.9}$? ______ 1

26 Write 40 as the product of its prime factors in index form. ______ 1

27 If $p = 7$ and $q = 9$, what is the value of $6p - q$? ______ 1

28 What percentage is 45 minutes of an hour? ______ 1

29

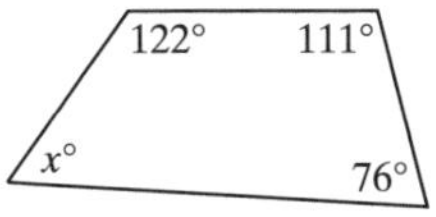

What is the value of x? ______ 1

30

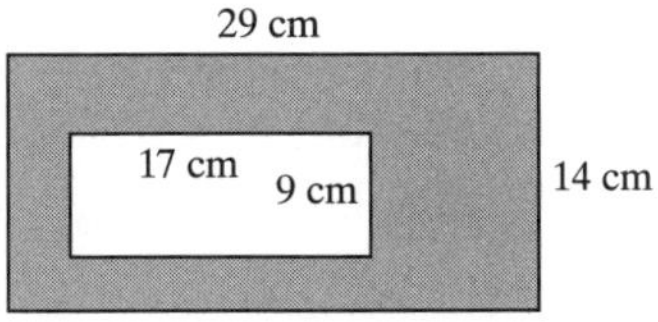

What is the shaded area? ______ 1

Total marks /30

1 The test marks of some students (out of 10) were recorded in the frequency distribution table.

Score	Tally	Frequency
6	IIII	
7	~~IIII~~ IIII	
8	~~IIII~~ I	
9	~~IIII~~	
10	III	
Total		

a Fill in the frequency column of the table. 1 mark

b How many students scored more than 8? 1 mark

c What is the range? 1 mark

d What is the mode? 1 mark

e What is the median? 1 mark

f Calculate the mean. 1 mark

g What percentage of the students scored 7? 1 mark

h If a student was chosen at random, what is the probability that he or she scored full marks? 1 mark

2 The ratio of red to white balls in a bag is 3 : 2.

a White balls make up what fraction of the balls in the bag? 1 mark

b If there are 60 red balls, how many white balls are there? 1 mark

3 a Frank paid \$4675 for a lounge suite. The original price was \$5000. What percentage discount was this? 2 marks

b Frank also bought a coffee table, originally priced at \$825. If he received a 12% discount on the coffee table, how much did Frank pay in total for the lounge suite, coffee table and \$125 for delivery? 2 marks

4 The diagram shows a spinner.

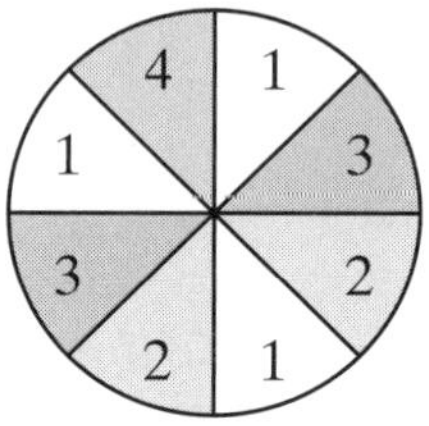

a List the sample space. 1 mark

b On what number is the spinner most likely to stop? 1 mark

c What is the probability, as a percentage, that the spinner will stop on 3? 1 mark

5 Solve:

a $96 - 11x = 19$ 2 marks

b $\frac{x}{7} - 19 = 46$ 2 marks

6 A bank balance showed an amount of –\$723.

a Briefly explain what the negative means. 1 mark

b If \$917 was put into the account, what would the new balance be? 1 mark

c If \$493 was then taken out of the account, what would be the balance? 1 mark

EXAM PAPER 4: LEVELS 1 AND 2 — PART C

7 **a** Express $\frac{18}{25}$ as a decimal. [1 mark]

b Write $\frac{18}{25}$, $72\frac{1}{2}\%$ and 0.7225 in ascending order. [1 mark]

8 An underground water tank is in the shape of a rectangular prism 2.8 m long, 1.1 m wide and 1.8 m deep.

a How many litres of water will it hold when full? [2 marks]

b If it is currently filled to a depth of 75 cm, how many more litres can it hold? [2 marks]

c If 6 L of water flows into the tank every minute, about how many hours will it take to fill the rest of the tank? [2 marks]

9

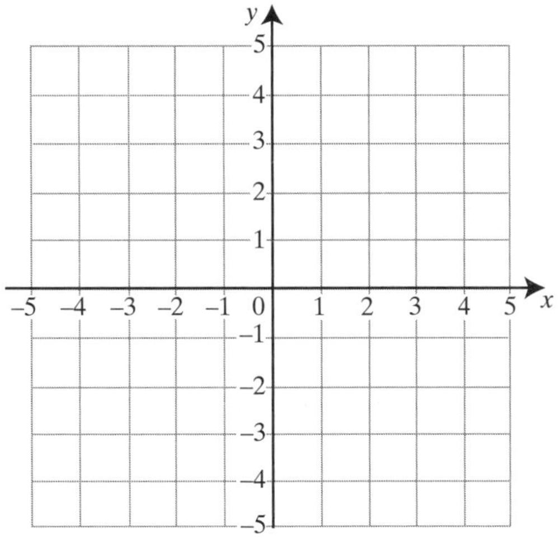

a Plot the points $P(3, 1)$, $Q(4, –3)$ and $R(1, –1)$ on the diagram, labelling the vertices. [1 mark]

b Show the result when ΔPQR is reflected in the y-axis, labelling the vertices appropriately. [1 mark]

10 **a** Megan has $4\frac{2}{3}$ cans of cat food and wants to share that amount equally among her seven cats. How much would each cat get? [1 mark]

b How many cans would Megan need to be able to give each cat $\frac{3}{4}$ can each? [1 mark]

11

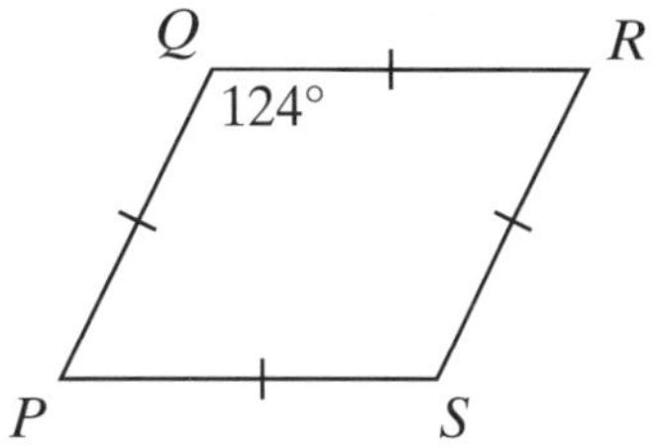

a What special type of quadrilateral is *PQRS*? [1 mark]

b What is the size of $\angle QPS$? Give a reason for your answer. [2 marks]

12 **a** Fill in the table using the rule $y = 2x – 3$. [2 marks]

x	2	3	5	8	12
y					

b For what value of x will $y = 99$? [1 mark]

13 The perimeter of this triangle is 2.38 km. What is the area in hectares, correct to one decimal place? [3 marks]

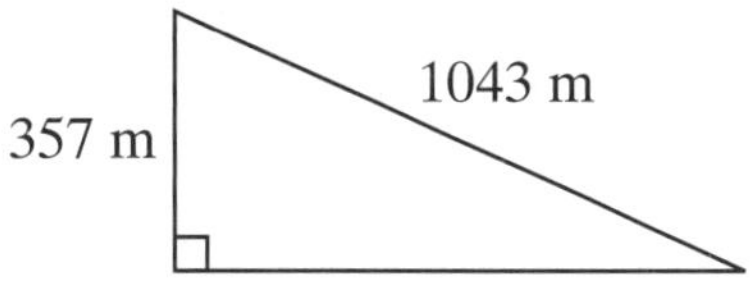

Total marks for PART C /45 **Total marks** /100

Exam Paper 5: Levels 2 and 3 Calculator Allowed

Instructions for all parts • Attempt all questions.
Time allowed: 1 hour 40 minutes • Calculators are allowed.

Part A: Allow about 25 minutes for this part.
Part B: Allow about 30 minutes for this part.
Part C: Allow about 45 minutes for this part. Show all working for this part. **Total marks: 100**

EXAM PAPER 5: LEVELS 2 AND 3 PART A

Fill in only one circle for each question.

Marks

1 What is the remainder when 3285 is divided by 36?

Ⓐ 1 Ⓑ 4 Ⓒ 6 Ⓓ 9 — 1

2 $2\frac{3}{5} \times 4\frac{1}{2} =$

Ⓐ $8\frac{3}{10}$ Ⓑ $8\frac{2}{5}$ Ⓒ $10\frac{1}{5}$ Ⓓ $11\frac{7}{10}$ — 1

3 The area of the triangle in square centimetres would be:

Ⓐ 1470 Ⓑ 1890 Ⓒ 2142 Ⓓ 4914 — 1

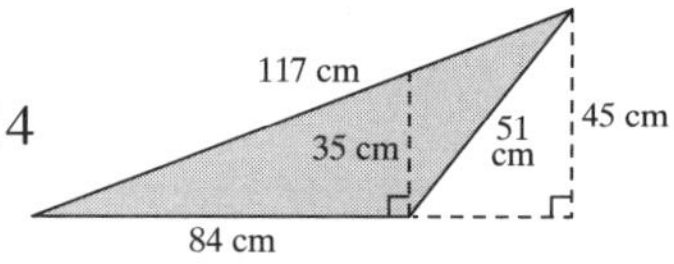

4 $\frac{109}{450}$ as a decimal is:

Ⓐ $0.\dot{2}$ Ⓑ $0.\dot{2}4$ Ⓒ $0.24\dot{2}$ Ⓓ $0.\dot{2}\dot{4}$ — 1

5 What is the capacity of a rectangular prism 3.2 m long, 1.6 m wide and 80 cm high?

Ⓐ 4096 kL Ⓑ 4096 L Ⓒ 4096 ML Ⓓ 4096 mL — 1

6 Which is the best buy?

Ⓐ 3 kg for \$7.05 Ⓑ 5 kg for \$11.25 Ⓒ 7 kg for \$16.10 Ⓓ 8 kg for \$18.30 — 1

7 What is the mean of the scores 19, 25, 17, 23, 21, 19, 16 and 22?

Ⓐ 19 Ⓑ 22 Ⓒ 20.5 Ⓓ 20.25 — 1

8 What is the value of x?

Ⓐ 70 Ⓑ 75 Ⓒ 80 Ⓓ 110 — 1

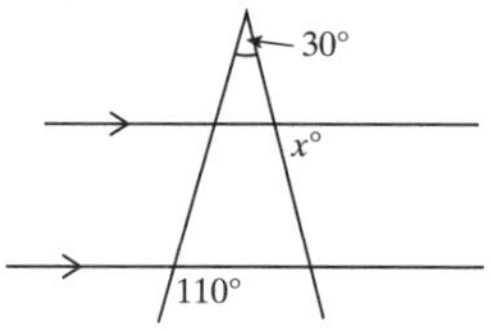

9 What would you pay for a suit priced at \$960 if given a 12.5% discount?

Ⓐ \$825 Ⓑ \$835 Ⓒ \$840 Ⓓ \$860 — 1

10 The probability of choosing a red ball from a box is $\frac{1}{4}$. The box holds nine blue, five white and four yellow balls, and the rest are red. How many red balls are in the box?

Ⓐ 2 Ⓑ 4 Ⓒ 6 Ⓓ 8 — 1

11 What size angle in a sector graph would represent $17\frac{1}{2}$%?

Ⓐ 21° Ⓑ 63° Ⓒ 5° Ⓓ 75° — 1

12 What is the value of x?

Ⓐ 68 Ⓑ 66 Ⓒ 58 Ⓓ 56 — 1

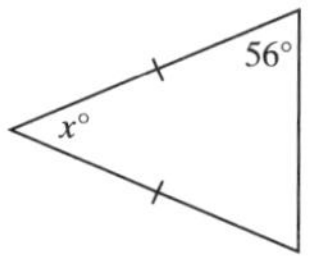

13 $-3 - 8 + (-4) - -6 =$

Ⓐ −1 Ⓑ −21 Ⓒ −13 Ⓓ −9 — 1

EXAM PAPER 5 : LEVELS 2 AND 3 — PART A

Marks

14 What number does ☆ represent if $8\frac{2}{3} \div ☆ = 3\frac{1}{4}$?

(A) $2\frac{2}{3}$ (B) $2\frac{3}{8}$ (C) $\frac{3}{8}$ (D) $28\frac{1}{6}$ [1]

15 $\sqrt{2890^2 - 2886^2} =$

(A) 2 (B) 4 (C) 152 (D) 23 104 [1]

16 If $p = 5$ and $q = 2$ then $pq^2 =$

(A) 20 (B) 40 (C) 50 (D) 100 [1]

17 What are the coordinates of P' if $\Delta P'Q'R'$ is the result after ΔPQR is reflected in the y-axis and then rotated through 90° in an anticlockwise direction?

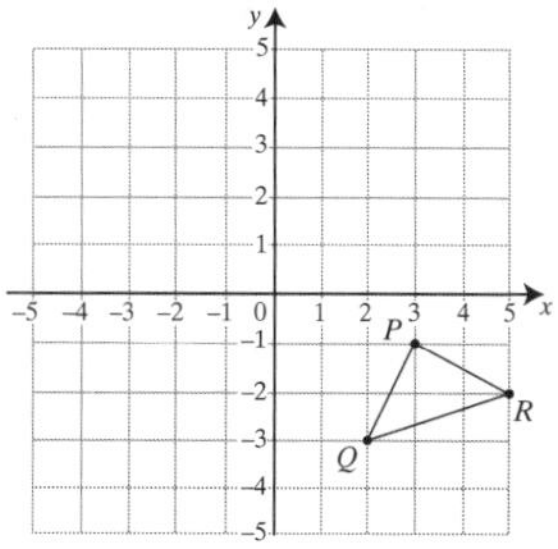

(A) (3, –1) (B) (1, –3) (C) (–1, 3) (D) (–3, 1) [1]

18 The solution to the equation $7x + 92 = 165$ is:

(A) $x = 10\frac{3}{7}$ (B) $x = 15\frac{6}{7}$ (C) $x = 18\frac{1}{7}$ (D) $x = 36\frac{5}{7}$ [1]

19 Which is **not** a property of a rectangle?

(A) The diagonals meet at right angles. (B) The diagonals are equal.
(C) The adjacent sides are perpendicular. (D) The diagonals bisect each other. [1]

20 Carole took 1 minute to complete a quiz and Liz took 45 seconds to complete the same quiz. The ratio of Liz's time to Carole's time is:

(A) 3 : 4 (B) 4 : 3 (C) 45 : 1 (D) 1 : 45 [1]

21 This object is made with 16 cubes. What is the view from the back?

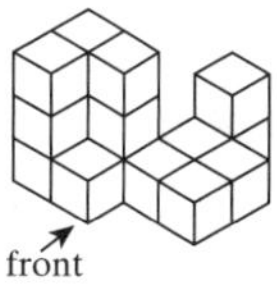

(A) 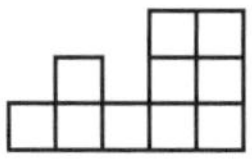 (B) 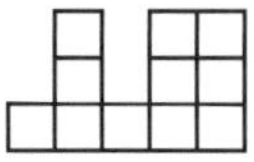 (C) 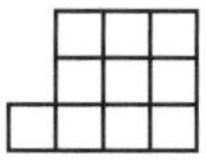 (D) 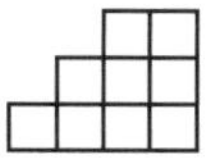 [1]

22 0.000 006 × 0.000 05 =

(A) 0.000 000 003 (B) 0.000 000 0003 (C) 0.000 000 000 03 (D) 0.000 000 000 003 [1]

23 What is the median of the scores in this stem-and-leaf plot?

1	5 7
2	0 2 2 3 4 6 8 9
3	1 4 8

(A) 22 (B) 23 (C) 24 (D) 25 [1]

24 What is the area of a square with perimeter 25 m?

(A) 25 m^2 (B) 20 m^2 (C) 36.0625 m^2 (D) 39.0625 m^2 [1]

25 Between which times was Sue travelling fastest?

(A) 8 am and 10 am (B) 11:30 am and 1 pm
(C) 3 pm and 4 pm (D) 4 pm and 6 pm [1]

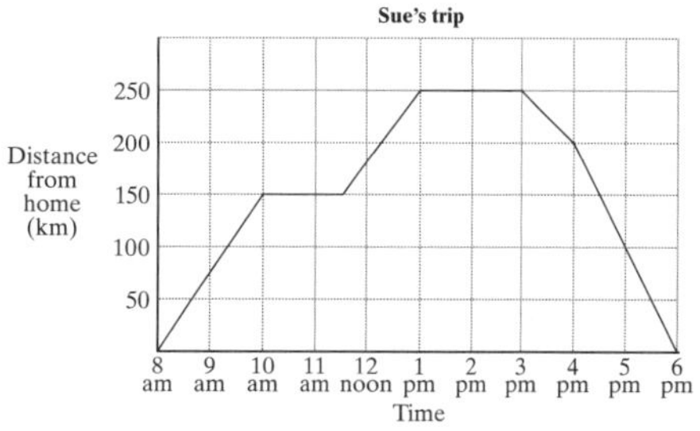

Total marks /25

EXAM PAPER 5 : LEVELS 2 AND 3 PART B

Marks

1 $7 - -13 =$ _______ 1

2 What is the highest common factor of 56 and 98? _______ 1

3 What is 3.895 786 rounded to two decimal places? _______ 1

4 What is the mode of the scores 9, 2, 5, 4, 2, 5, 9, 6, 2, 11, 4, 8? _______ 1

5 $\frac{1}{2}x \times 6y =$ _______ 1

6 What quadrilateral is both a rectangle and a rhombus? _______ 1

7 Simplify $8x - 7 + 3x - 2$. _______ 1

8 A contractor charges $90 per hour plus GST (10%). How much would have to be paid for 14 hours work? _______ 1

9 What is the value of 3^7? _______ 1

10 If $a = -3$, what is the value of $11 - a$? _______ 1

11 What is 87% of fifty thousand? _______ 1

12 What is $\frac{5}{12}$ as a decimal? _______ 1

13 $12xy \div 4y =$ _______ 1

14 What is $\frac{3.78 - 2.5}{0.9 \times 1.45}$ to one decimal place? _______ 1

15 Simplify the ratio $\frac{2}{3} : \frac{3}{4}$. _______ 1

16 What is the solution to the equation $\frac{3x}{4} = 24$? _______ 1

17 What fraction is 25 minutes of $2\frac{1}{2}$ hours? _______ 1

18 What is the reciprocal of $2\frac{4}{5}$? _______ 1

19 A cube has volume 17 576 cm^3. What is the length of each side? _______ 1

Marks

20 What is the price per litre if 600 mL costs \$3.45? ____________ 1

21 What is $\frac{5}{8}$ of 7.24? ____________ 1

22 Arrange $\frac{1}{3}$, $\frac{2}{5}$, $\frac{3}{8}$ and $\frac{7}{20}$ in ascending order. ____________ 1

23 What is the probability of choosing, without looking, a red marble from a box holding 12 red and 18 other marbles? ____________ 1

24

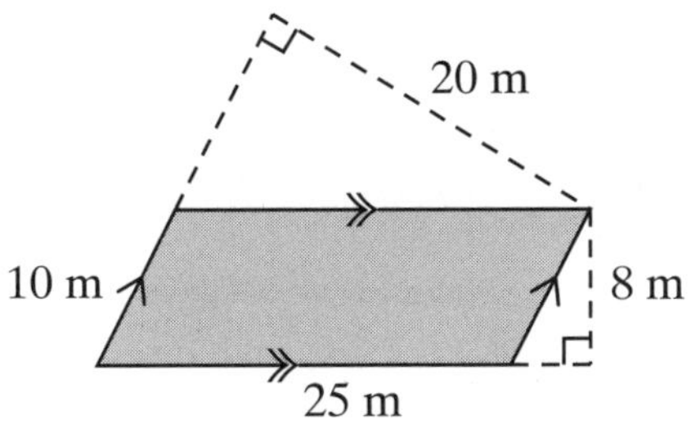

What is the area of this parallelogram? ____________ 1

25 What is the product of $4\frac{3}{5}$ and $3\frac{4}{5}$? ____________ 1

26 How many cubic centimetres are in 8 m^3? ____________ 1

27 What are the coordinates of a point that has been translated three units left and four units down from the origin? ____________ 1

28 What is $\frac{1}{40}$ as a percentage? ____________ 1

29 What is the lowest common multiple of 12, 18 and 20? ____________ 1

30 What is the difference between the complement and supplement of any angle? ____________ 1

Total marks /30

EXAM PAPER 5 : LEVELS 2 AND 3 — PART C

1 **a** Simplify $3a + 5b - 2c + b - 6c$. [1 mark]

b If $a = 7$, $b = 9$ and $c = 8$, find the value of $3a + 5b - 2c + b - 6c$. [1 mark]

2 135 people were surveyed about the way they had travelled to work. The results are shown in the sector graph.

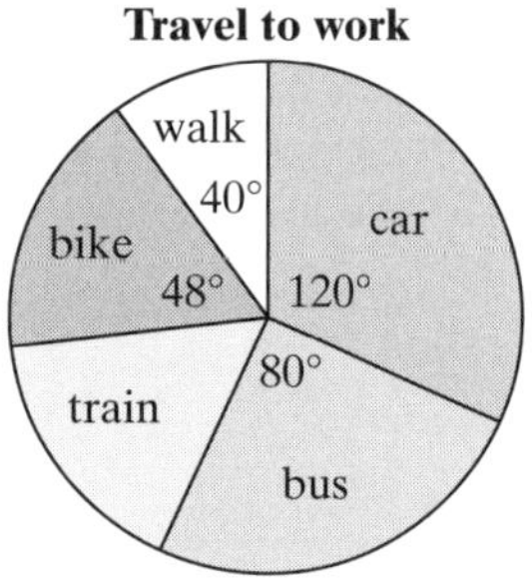

a What size is the angle for travelling by train? [1 mark]

b What percentage of those surveyed travelled by car? [1 mark]

c How many people rode a bike? [1 mark]

d If one of the people surveyed was chosen randomly, what is the probability that they walked to work? [1 mark]

3 Three-fifths of the squares in a crossword are black.

a What is the ratio of black to white squares? [1 mark]

b If there are 40 white squares, how many are black? [1 mark]

4 Jemma has $3\frac{3}{4}$ m of fabric. She uses $\frac{2}{3}$ of it to make a dress for her daughter.

a How much did Jemma use? [1 mark]

b How much fabric did she have left? [1 mark]

c Jemma uses $\frac{2}{5}$ of what is left to make a matching dress for her daughter's doll. How much more material did Jemma need for her daughter's dress than for the doll's dress? [1 mark]

d How much material did Jemma use altogether? [1 mark]

5 **a** Write 924 as the product of its prime factors. [1 mark]

b Find the highest common factor of 630 and 924. [2 marks]

6 When a certain number is divided by 14 and the result subtracted from 312 the answer is 81. Let the number be x.

a Write an equation showing this information. [1 mark]

b Solve the equation and find the value of the number. [2 marks]

7 The temperature in a freezer was –11 °C at 3 pm. At 8 pm the temperature had increased by 7°.

a What was the temperature at 8 pm? [1 mark]

b What was the average hourly rise in temperature? [1 mark]

8

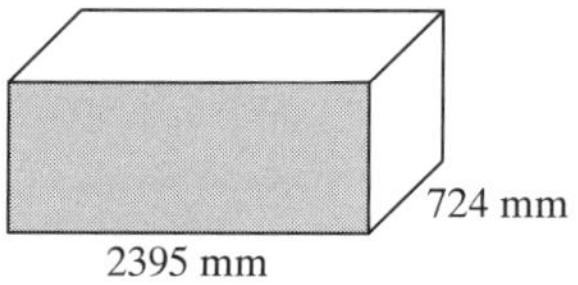

a The area of the shaded face of this rectangular prism is 3.353 m^2. What is the missing dimension, in millimetres? [2 marks]

b What is the volume of the prism in cubic metres? Give the answer to two decimal places. [2 marks]

c What is the capacity in litres, to the nearest 10 L? [1 mark]

9

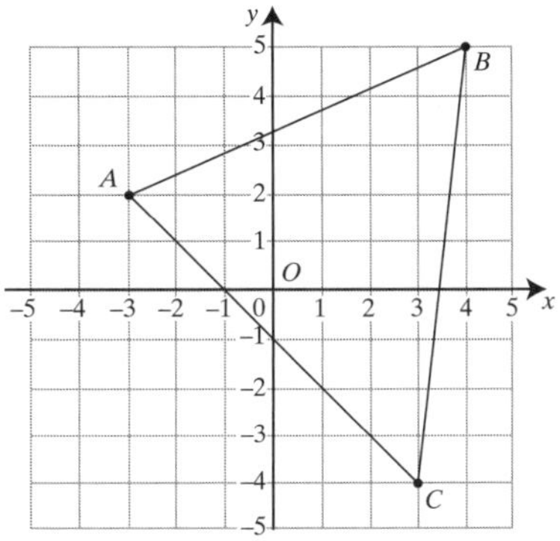

a What are the coordinates of *A*? [1 mark]

b If Δ*ABC* is rotated 180° about *O*, what will be the coordinates of *C'*? [1 mark]

10 a Fill in the missing values in this table. [2 marks]

x	0	2	5		12
3*x* – 2	–2	4		25	34

b Write a rule connecting *y* and *x* for this table. [1 mark]

x	0	1	2	3	4	5
y	1	7	13	19	25	31

11 *AB* is parallel to *FC*. ∠*BAD* = 64°, ∠*ABC* = 36° and ∠*AED* = 52°.

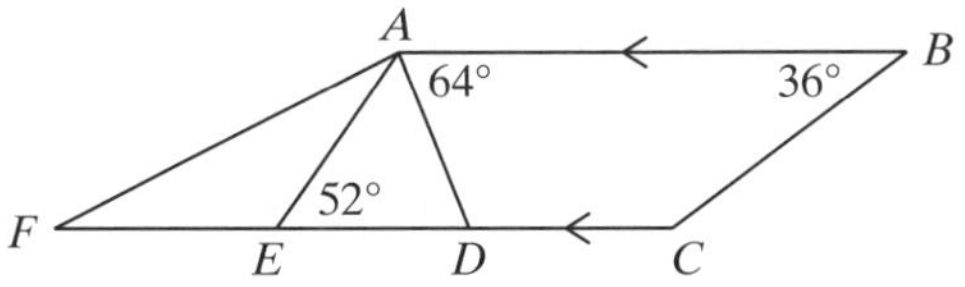

a What type of quadrilateral is *ABCD*? [1 mark]

b Find the size of ∠*EAD*, giving reasons. [2 marks]

c What type of triangle is Δ*ADE*? Justify your answer. [2 marks]

d If Δ*AEF* is isosceles, find the size of ∠*FAE*. (Give reasons.) [2 marks]

e Is *AF* parallel to *BC*? Justify your answer. [1 mark]

12 What fraction is found halfway between $\frac{1}{6}$ and $\frac{1}{8}$ on the number line? [2 marks]

13

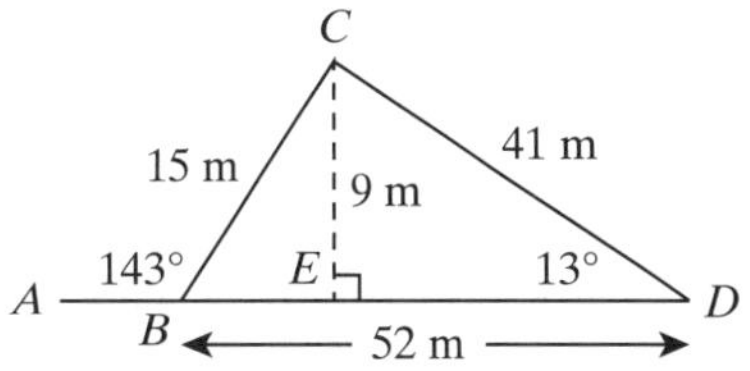

a What is the size of ∠*BCE*? [1 mark]

b What type of triangle is Δ*BCD*? [1 mark]

c What is the area of Δ*BCD*? [1 mark]

d If the area of Δ*BEC* is 54 m², what is the ratio of *BE* : *ED* in simplest form? [2 marks]

Total marks for PART C /45 **Total marks** /100

Answers

Squares and Index Notation

Page 1 **1** D **2** B **3** B **4** B **5** C **6** D **7** D **8** C **9** C **10** C **11** A **12** A **13** A **14** B **15** C **16** B

Page 2 **1** B **2** C **3** D **4** B **5** C **6** A **7** C **8** A **9** D **10** B **11** D **12** A **13** A **14** C **15** D

Page 3 **16** 36 **17** 10 **18** 7^6 **19** $11 \times 11 \times 11 \times 11$ **20** $2 \times 3 \times 7$ **21** 32 **22** 3 **23** $2^2 \times 3^3$ **24** 6 and 7 **25** 45 **26 a** It ends in 5. **b** 18 **c** The sum of the digits is divisible by 9. **d** As it is divisible by both 5 and 9 it must also be divisible by 5×9 as 5 and 9 have no common factors (other than 1). **e** $3 \times 3 \times 5 \times 587$ **27 a** $2 \times 3 \times 3$ **b** 324 **28 a** (see diagram; slightly different variations are possible) **b** 15 **c** 300

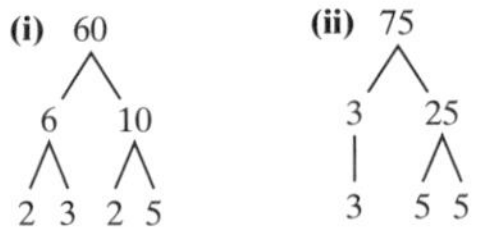

Page 4 **1** A **2** A **3** B **4** D **5** C **6** D **7** C **8** D **9** A **10** A **11** B **12** C **13** D **14** D **15** C

Page 5 **16** 81 **17** $2^3 \times 3 \times 5^2$ **18** 10 **19** 50 000 **20** 44 **21** 16 **22** 441 **23** 100 **24** 25 **25** 3 **26 a** $2 \times 2 \times 7$ **b** 784 **27** 21 609 **28 a** (see diagram) **b** $2^2 \times 3^4$ **c** 18 **29 a** $2^3 \times 3^3$ **b** 6 **30** 7560

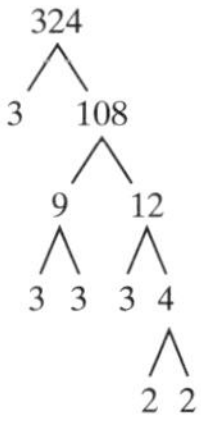

Page 6 **1** B **2** B **3** C **4** D **5** D **6** B **7** C **8** B **9** A **10** C **11** A **12** D **13** C **14** A **15** A

Page 7 **16** 4096 **17** 2401 **18** 83 **19** 43 **20** $2^2 \times 3 \times 7^2$ **21** 158 760 **22** 68 **23** 568 **24** 5 **25** $\frac{1}{6}$ **26 a** $2 \times 2 \times 2 \times 2 \times 2 \times 2 \times 2 \times 2$ **b** 2^8 **27 a** 27 **b** Yes, $\left(\sqrt{9}\right)^3 = 3^3 = 27$ **28** because $4 = 2 \times 2$, $4^3 = (2 \times 2) \times (2 \times 2) \times (2 \times 2) = 2^6$ **29 a** No, $\sqrt{1089 + 3136} = 65$ but $\sqrt{1089} + \sqrt{3136} = 89$ **b** Yes, both are equal to 1848. **30 a** $3^5 \times 2^3 \times 7^2$ **b** $3^4 \times 2^2 \times 7^3$ **c** 15 876 **d** 666 792

Computations with Integers

Page 8 **1** B **2** D **3** D **4** C **5** D **6** B **7** C **8** B **9** C **10** B **11** A **12** C **13** A **14** D **15** A

Page 9 **1** B **2** A **3** D **4** C **5** D **6** B **7** B **8** D **9** A **10** D **11** C **12** D **13** A **14** C **15** B

Page 10 **16** 790 **17** 6200 **18** 0 **19** $29\frac{1}{13}$ **20** 2772 **21** 1784 **22** 863 **23** 7300 **24** 2130 **25** 13 **26 a** true **b** false **c** true **d** true **27 a** 276 **b** $12\frac{8}{23}$ **c** 299 **28 a** 8874 **b** 8961 **c** 9744 **29 a** 93 753 **b** 92 806 **30 a** 5451 **b** 5304 **c** 5460

Page 11 **1** D **2** A **3** A **4** B **5** B **6** A **7** B **8** D **9** A **10** D **11** C **12** B **13** C **14** D **15** C

Page 12 **16** 4 **17** –4 **18** –14 **19** –12 **20** –16 **21**

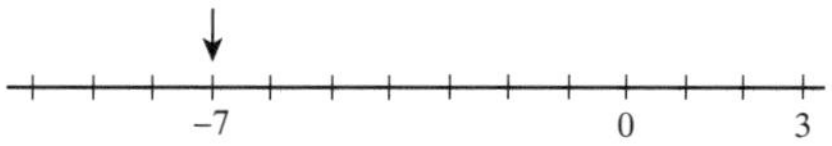

22 –10, –8, –6, –5, 0, 2, 4 **23** 10 **24** –11 **25** –2 **26 a** –7 **b** –15 **c** 0 **d** –24 **27 a** –3° **b i** –1° **ii** –9° **c** a rise of 11° **28 a** –8 **b** –1 **c** –1 **d** no **29 a** The bank is owed \$1200. **b** –\$1430 **c** –\$630

Page 13 **1** B **2** C **3** B **4** B **5** A **6** C **7** D **8** A **9** B **10** A **11** A **12** C **13** D **14** D **15** D

Page 14 **16** –11 **17** –8, –3, 0, 15 **18** –16 **19** –20 **20**

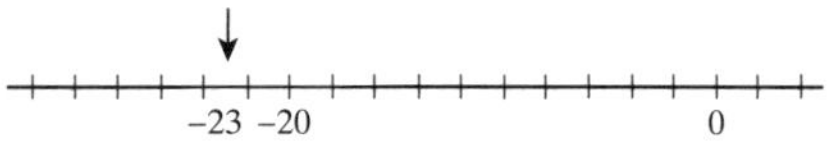

21 –11 **22** –13 **23** –4 **24** –18 **25** 29 **26 a** –25 °C **b** –20 °C **c** –5 °C **d** 11 °C **e** Yellowknife, 14° **f** 22° **g** It was 4° lower. **h** –2 °C **27 a** –\$894 **b** –\$462 **c** \$167 **28 a** –5 **b** 0 **c** 12

Page 15 **1** B **2** D **3** D **4** B **5** D **6** A **7** C **8** B **9** B **10** A **11** C **12** D **13** C **14** A **15** C

Page 16 **16** 439 **17** –97 **18** –101 **19** –35 **20** –424 **21** –915, –866, –728, –23, 57, 1004 **22** –2621 **23** 12 **24** –148 **25** 63 **26** –213 by 18 **27 a** yes **b** no **c** You can add numbers in any order but in subtraction order is important. **28** Both have the same value. Adding a negative number is the same as subtracting. **29** Yes, both are equal to –5 and as the inequality sign is 'greater than or equal to' the expression is correct. **30 a** 51° **b** 8 °F **c** The difference is 8° in both, but one is in degrees Fahrenheit and the other is in degrees Celsius. Fahrenheit degrees are not the same as degrees Celsius, so the difference is not exactly the same. **d** 50 °C **e** 37 °C **31 a** 37 **b** 25th

Fractions

Page 17 1 C 2 A 3 D 4 A 5 B 6 D 7 B 8 C 9 D 10 B 11 A 12 A 13 C

Page 18 1 C 2 B 3 A 4 C 5 B 6 A 7 B 8 C 9 C 10 D 11 B 12 D 13 A 14 D 15 C

Page 19 16 $\frac{2}{3}$ 17 $\frac{19}{7}$ 18 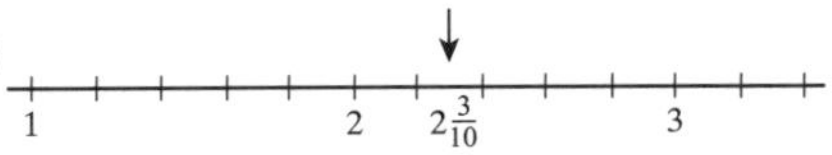

19 $3\frac{2}{3}$ 20 $\frac{4}{5}$ 21 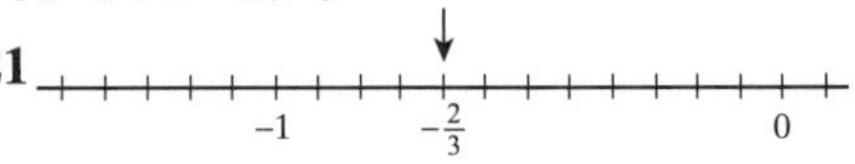

22 56 23 $7\frac{1}{2}$ 24 $\frac{7}{12}$ 25 $2\frac{3}{8}$ 26 a 80 b $\frac{9}{16} = \frac{45}{80}$ and $\frac{11}{20} = \frac{44}{80}$ so $\frac{9}{16}$ is larger. 27 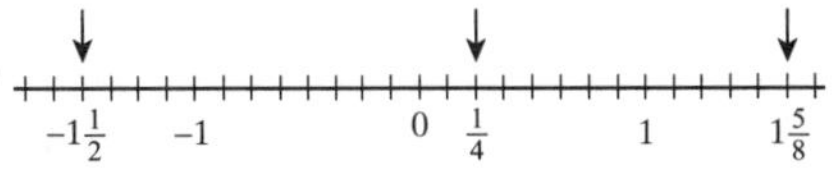

28 $\frac{7}{10}, \frac{5}{7}, \frac{26}{35}, \frac{4}{5}$ 29 a $\frac{17}{5}$ b $\frac{21}{9} = 2\frac{1}{3}$ c No, adding a number to both the numerator and denominator does not produce an equivalent fraction. 30 $\frac{7}{8} = \frac{21}{24}$ and $\frac{5}{6} = \frac{20}{24}$ 31 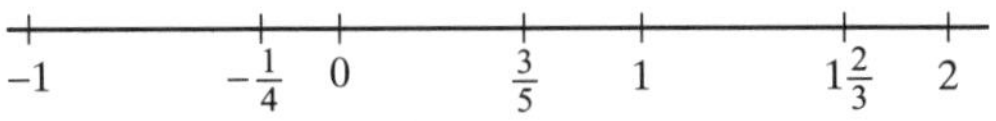

Page 20 1 B 2 A 3 A 4 B 5 C 6 D 7 B 8 A 9 C 10 B 11 D 12 D 13 C 14 D 15 C

Page 21 16 $\frac{3}{4}$ 17 $\frac{1}{8}$ 18 $\frac{3}{10}$ 19 $\frac{5}{8}$ 20 $\frac{1}{3}$ 21 $\frac{7}{8}$ 22 $\frac{3}{10}$ 23 $\frac{2}{3}$ 24 $\frac{3}{4}$ 25 $\frac{3}{5}$ 26 a $\frac{2}{3}$ b $\frac{4}{5}$ c $\frac{3}{4}$ 27 a $\frac{1}{3}$ b $\frac{4}{9}$ c $\frac{4}{5}$ 28 a $\frac{1}{5}$ b $\frac{1}{4}$ c $\frac{1}{2}$ d $\frac{1}{20}$ 29 a $\frac{2}{7}$ b $\frac{1}{3}$ c black

Page 22 1 B 2 D 3 C 4 A 5 C 6 A 7 C 8 A 9 D 10 D 11 D 12 B 13 B 14 C 15 A

Page 23 16 $\frac{7}{10}$ 17 $\frac{5}{8}$ 18 6 19 $5\frac{5}{8}$ 20 $\frac{5}{12}$ 21 $\frac{8}{9}$ 22 $4\frac{2}{3}$ 23 $\frac{37}{40}$ 24 $\frac{1}{56}$ 25 $1\frac{11}{36}$ 26 a $10\frac{11}{30}$ b $\frac{37}{60}$ c $3\frac{5}{6}$ d $\frac{23}{30}$ 27 a $14\frac{3}{4}$ b $5\frac{3}{4}$ 28 a $\frac{7}{12}$ b $\frac{5}{12}$ 29 a $\frac{13}{20}$ b $\frac{1}{60}$

Page 24 1 B 2 D 3 C 4 C 5 A 6 B 7 D 8 A 9 D 10 C 11 B 12 B 13 C 14 D 15 A

Page 25 16 $3\frac{1}{2}$ 17 6 18 $\frac{9}{20}$ 19 $\frac{1}{2}$ 20 $\frac{31}{40}$ 21 $4\frac{5}{7}$ 22 $1\frac{3}{10}$ 23 $8\frac{3}{8}$ 24 $6\frac{3}{5}$ 25 $6\frac{5}{6}$ 26 a $\frac{1}{36}$ b $8\frac{7}{15}$ c $3\frac{23}{36}$ 27 $12\frac{9}{20}$ ha 28 a $\frac{13}{20}$ b $\frac{7}{20}$ c Milly d $\frac{3}{20}$ 29 a $\frac{4}{15}$ b Tuesday

Page 26 1 D 2 B 3 C 4 C 5 C 6 C 7 D 8 A 9 D 10 D 11 A 12 A 13 B 14 B 15 A

Page 27 16 $\frac{1}{2}$ 17 $1\frac{11}{24}$ 18 $\frac{7}{20}$ 19 $5\frac{13}{20}$ 20 $10\frac{4}{11}$ 21 $\frac{2}{15}$ 22 $1\frac{1}{12}$ 23 $1\frac{5}{8}$ 24 $\frac{5}{6}$ 25 $14\frac{1}{8}$ 26 a $7\frac{53}{60}$ b $6\frac{8}{15}$ c $\frac{13}{24}$ d $\frac{29}{30}$ 27 $\frac{1}{24}$ 28 a $\frac{8}{15}$m b No, Sally does not have quite enough. She needs an extra $\frac{13}{60}$ m. 29 $\frac{59}{60}$

Page 28 1 C 2 B 3 B 4 C 5 A 6 D 7 C 8 D 9 A 10 A 11 C 12 D 13 A 14 D 15 B

Page 29 16 $\frac{1}{12}$ 17 $\frac{1}{5}$ 18 3 19 18 20 $1\frac{1}{4}$ 21 7 22 $\frac{1}{9}$ 23 $1\frac{1}{3}$ 24 $\frac{3}{10}$ 25 $\frac{10}{27}$ 26 a 1 b $7\frac{7}{8}$ c $20\frac{1}{4}$ d 16 e $1\frac{1}{20}$ 27 a 120 days b 14 28 30 m^2 29 a $2\frac{1}{4}$ h b 6 h

Page 30 1 A 2 D 3 B 4 D 5 A 6 A 7 A 8 B 9 D 10 C 11 D 12 B 13 C 14 C 15 C

Page 31 16 $\frac{1}{2}$ 17 $\frac{1}{25}$ 18 $\frac{3}{10}$ 19 6 20 18 kg 21 $1\frac{1}{35}$ 22 6 23 $\frac{1}{16}$ 24 $\frac{9}{10}$ 25 $4\frac{3}{8}$ 26 a 28 b $2\frac{1}{4}$ c $\frac{1}{10}$ d $1\frac{5}{16}$ 27 a 3 m b 1 m 28 a 36 b $2\frac{1}{4}$ cups flour, $\frac{1}{2}$ cup sugar, $\frac{3}{4}$ cup cream

Page 32 1 C 2 D 3 A 4 B 5 D 6 B 7 A 8 A 9 D 10 A 11 C 12 C 13 B 14 D 15 C

Page 33 16 $\frac{1}{4}$ 17 $\frac{5}{7}$ 18 $\frac{3}{7}$ 19 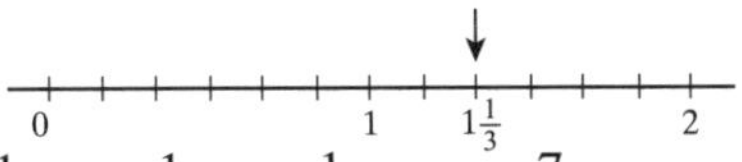

20 36 21 3 22 $\frac{3}{10}$ 23 $2\frac{1}{8}$ 24 14 25 $\frac{5}{12}$ 26 a 24 b $\frac{7}{12}, \frac{5}{8}, \frac{2}{3}$ 27 a $1\frac{5}{24}$ b $1\frac{1}{10}$ c $2\frac{1}{4}$ d $1\frac{1}{4}$ 28 a $\frac{7}{12}$ cup b $\frac{5}{6}$ cup c $\frac{5}{8}$ cup

Page 34 1 B 2 C 3 D 4 D 5 A 6 B 7 B 8 A 9 C 10 A 11 B 12 B 13 C 14 D 15 A

Page 35 16 $8\frac{7}{30}$ 17 $1\frac{7}{10}$ 18 $11\frac{2}{3}$ 19 $\frac{3}{8}$ 20 $\frac{8}{9}$ 21 625 000 22 $\frac{1}{12}$ 23 $\frac{1}{3}$ 24 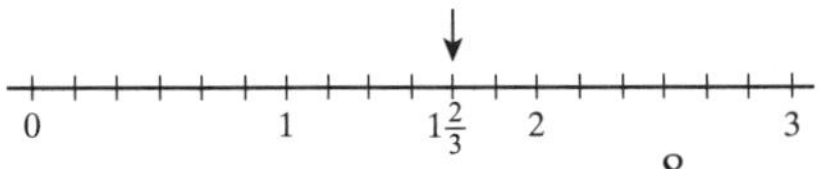

25 $2\frac{1}{4}$ 26 a 7 b $\frac{1}{4}$ bale 27 a $38\frac{1}{2}$ mm b $5\frac{1}{2}$ mm c $1\frac{3}{4}$ mm d $6\frac{1}{4}$ mm e $8\frac{3}{4}$ mm 28 a 144 cm b 96 cm c $\frac{8}{15}$ 29 a $1\frac{5}{6}$ h b 3 h 35 min c $6\frac{3}{4}$ h

Decimals

Page 36 1 A 2 D 3 C 4 D 5 C 6 A 7 A 8 B 9 B 10 D 11 A 12 B 13 C 14 C 15 D 16 D

Page 37 1 D 2 C 3 A 4 D 5 B 6 D 7 A 8 B 9 B 10 C 11 D 12 C 13 C 14 A 15 B

Page 38 16 0.000 0056 17 3 18 4.24 19 0.044 20 3140 21 1.5673 22 7.1 23 0.01 24 9 25 0.0003 26 a 0.26 b 0.084 c 86.94 d 17.15625 27 a 6 b 1.05 L 28 a 20 b 4 29 a 840 b 0.336 c 0.0004

Page 39 1 A 2 D 3 C 4 A 5 B 6 B 7 C 8 C 9 D 10 B 11 D 12 D 13 A 14 B 15 A

Page 40 **16** 3.3 **17** 64.58 **18** 218.3 **19** 56.403 **20** 111.89 **21** 6258.50 **22** 10.0 **23** 15.419 **24** 51 496.736 **25** 0.0035 **26 a** 0.04 **b** 0.038 **27 a** 14 **b** 14.0 **c** 13.99 **28 a i** 3.8 **ii** 19.9 **iii** 25.5 **b** 49.2 **c** 49.1425; 49.1 **d** b; Rounding the numbers off first creates a small rounding error. The rounding should be done last. **29 a i** 17.26 **ii** 17.265 **b** 17.27 **c** In the answer to part **ii** the number has been rounded off and then rounded again, introducing an error.

Page 41 **1** C **2** B **3** D **4** A **5** A **6** D **7** D **8** D **9** B **10** C **11** C **12** B **13** B **14** A **15** C

Page 42 **16** 1.5 **17** 0.012 **18** 630 **19** 48.0 **20** 0.056 2375 **21** 2.6 **22** 0.03 **23** 12.05 **24** 9 **25** 130 000 000 **26** 0.05 **27 a** 0.27 **b** 0.42 **c** 7.5 **28 a** 3 **b** 1 **29 a** 4.8 kg **b** 0.02 kg **30 a** 1.53 kg **b** 0.675 kg

Page 43 **1** D **2** D **3** C **4** B **5** C **6** B **7** B **8** C **9** A **10** B **11** C **12** A **13** A **14** D **15** B

Page 44 **16** 0.170 82 **17** 0.0072 **18** 17.24 **19** 6.35 **20** 3.822 51 **21** 0.1245 **22** 24.6 **23** 798 **24** 3.1 **25** 0.678 **26 a** 1.358 56, 1.4 **b** 0.059 773 828 76…, 0.1 **c** 14.582 976, 14.6 **27 a** 43.2 m **b** 7 **28 a** 270 kg **b** 225 **29 a** 2556.1821 **b** 696.8115 **30 a** 45 **b** 0.224 L

Page 45 **1** B **2** C **3** D **4** A **5** A **6** B **7** A **8** C **9** A **10** D **11** C **12** B **13** B **14** C **15** D

Page 46 **16** $14\frac{9}{20}$ **17** 204 **18** $8\frac{5}{8}$ **19** 0.009 375 **20** 6.568 **21** 40 000 000 **22** 0.001 **23** $\frac{3}{16}$ **24** 13 km/h **25** $\frac{2}{3}$ **26 a** 0.875 m **b** 0.385 m **27 a** 1111.9275 **b** 148.96 **c** $7\frac{1}{2}$ **28 a** $2\frac{1}{4}$ m **b** $\frac{2}{3}$ **c** No, she would need $\frac{1}{6}$ m more. **29 a** green **b** $1\frac{1}{30}$ buckets **c** $\frac{1}{15}$ of a bucket **30** $\frac{7}{10}$

Percentages

Page 47 **1** C **2** B **3** A **4** C **5** B **6** A **7** D **8** C **9** A **10** B **11** D **12** B **13** C **14** D **15** D

Page 48 **1** B **2** C **3** C **4** A **5** D **6** D **7** A **8** A **9** B **10** D **11** A **12** B **13** D **14** B **15** C

Page 49 **16** 32% **17** \$700 **18** 75% **19** \$9.60 **20** 35c **21** 68% **22** 1.8 kg **23** 11% **24** 10.8 **25** \$300 **26 a** 5% **b** 10 g **27 a** \$84 **b** 40% **28 a** \$120 **b** \$480 **c** 25% **29 a** 85% **b** The history mark was 80% so English was the higher score. **30 a** \$540 000 **b** \$21 600 **c** 86.4%

Page 50 **1** A **2** B **3** D **4** B **5** D **6** C **7** B **8** D **9** A **10** C **11** B **12** A **13** A **14** C **15** C

Page 51 **16** \$286.80 **17** $66\frac{2}{3}$% **18** 2.125 t **19** 85% **20** \$680 **21** \$72.54 **22** 87.5% **23** \$1800 **24** $6\frac{1}{4}$% **25** 20 **26 a** 176 **b** $18\frac{3}{4}$% **c** $28\frac{3}{4}$% **27 a** 7 680 000 **b** 4 920 000 **c** 64% **28 a** \$576 **b** 5% **c** 12.68% **29 a** 3.2% **b** 5 cents per litre

Page 52 **1** D **2** A **3** C **4** B **5** C **6** A **7** C **8** C **9** A **10** C **11** B **12** D **13** A **14** D **15** B

Page 53 **16** $0.\dot{3}$ **17** $\frac{7}{20}$ **18** 7.5% **19** 28% **20** $\frac{3}{50}$ **21** 1.5 **22** 0.625 **23** 125% **24** $\frac{12}{5}$ **25** $\frac{11}{25}$ **26 a** 72% **b** $\frac{18}{25}$ **27 a** 0.175 **b** $\frac{7}{40}$ **28 a** 0.025 **b** 0.02 **c** $\frac{1}{50}$, $2\frac{1}{2}$%, 0.28 **29 a** $0.08\dot{3}$ **b** $\frac{1}{2}$ **c** $0.58\dot{3}$ **30 a** 60% **b** 92% **c** 76% **d** $\frac{19}{25}$

Page 54 **1** C **2** A **3** B **4** A **5** A **6** C **7** C **8** B **9** B **10** D **11** A **12** C **13** B **14** D **15** D

Page 55 **16** 0.007 **17** $41\frac{2}{3}$% **18** $\frac{3}{8}$ **19** repeating **20** 105.5% **21** $\frac{136}{625}$ **22** $0.\dot{3}\dot{6}\dot{0}$ **23** 0.0175 **24** 34.375% **25** $\frac{1}{500}$ **26 a** $\frac{19}{20}$ **b** $2\frac{1}{4}$ **c** $\frac{1}{3}$ **27 a** $0.\dot{5}7142\dot{8}$ **b** $0.0\dot{6}$ **28 a** $0.2708\dot{3}$ **b** 27.1% **29** $\frac{1}{16}$ **30 a** $0.1\dot{7}$ **b** $0.\dot{1}\dot{7}\dot{6}$ **c** $0.17\dot{6}$ **d** $17\frac{2}{3}$%, $\frac{35}{198}$, $\frac{8}{45}$ **31 a** $12\frac{1}{4}$% **b** 12% **c** $\frac{1}{4}$%

Money

Page 56 **1** C **2** C **3** B **4** A **5** B **6** D **7** A **8** A **9** D **10** D **11** A **12** D **13** B **14** C

Page 57 **1** C **2** A **3** C **4** D **5** D **6** D **7** B **8** A **9** A **10** C **11** C **12** D **13** B **14** B **15** B

Page 58 **1** C **2** D **3** B **4** D **5** D **6** A **7** A **8** D **9** B **10** B **11** C **12** A **13** B **14** C **15** D

Page 59 **16** \$2.40 **17** \$1.60 **18** \$14 **19** \$2 **20** \$42 **21** \$4 per kg **22** 5 **23** \$4.30 **24** 30c **25** \$2.40 **26 a** \$21 **b** \$21 **c** All the packs cost \$21 for 24 rolls so it doesn't matter whether you buy four small packs, three medium packs, two large packs or any combination of the packs. **27 a** \$31.50 **b** \$3.50 **28 a** \$10.40 per kg **b** \$10.20 per kg **c** the 9 kg pack; \$10.10 per kg **d** \$1 **e** (possible answers) You might only need 5 kg. You might only be able to carry the 5 kg pack. **29 a** \$2.40 **b** the single cans; saving \$2.40

Page 60 **1** C **2** B **3** C **4** D **5** B **6** A **7** D **8** C **9** C **10** A **11** C **12** D **13** B **14** A **15** B

Page 61 **16** \$11.25 **17** \$0.55 **18** \$196 **19** \$12 **20** \$6.50 per litre **21** \$962.50 **22** \$537 **23** 39.6 L **24** \$23.50 **25** \$500 **26 a** \$0.42 **b** \$1.12 per litre **c** 12c **27** Both are the same: \$8.40 per kg. **28 a** \$7.27 **b** \$67.97 **c** They are cheaper. **d** You might only want one shirt. **29 a** \$825 **b** The second quote is cheaper if price is the only concern. **30** \$62.50

Ratio and Rates

Page 62 **1** B **2** D **3** C **4** B **5** C **6** D **7** C **8** B **9** B **10** C **11** D **12** A **13** A **14** A **15** D

Page 63 **16** 4 : 3 **17** 3 : 5 **18** 3 : 2 **19** 4 : 1 **20** 2 : 3 **21** 2 : 5 **22** $\frac{2}{9}$ **23** 81 **24** 27 : 2 **25** 18 **26 a i** 1 : 2 **ii** 8 : 3 **b** The first box. It has 6 blue pegs for every 8 green ones whereas the second box only has 5 blue for every 8 green. **27 a** 90 **b** 32 **c** 208 black, 312 white **28 a** 5 : 7 **b** 4 : 7 **c** No, Nova is not correct. Subtracting the same number from both parts of a ratio does not produce an equivalent ratio. The new ratio would be 2 : 3. **29 a** 2 : 1 **b** $500 more

Page 64 **1** B **2** D **3** C **4** A **5** B **6** C **7** D **8** A **9** B **10** A **11** C **12** C **13** D **14** B **15** A

Page 65 **16** 1 : 3 **17** 6 : 5 **18** 3 : 5 **19** 11 : 6 **20** 30% **21** 64 **22** 63 **23** 1 : 3 **24** 15 : 2 **25** 144 **26 a** 44 **b** 162 **c** 54 red, 243 white **27 a** 5:9 **b** Jill $2500, Kate $4500 **28 a** 12 **b** 9 : 26 **29 a** 3 : 2 **b** 3 : 7 **c** 2 : 3 **d** 18

Page 66 **1** B **2** B **3** D **4** C **5** B **6** C **7** C **8** A **9** D **10** A **11** B **12** C **13** D **14** A **15** B

Page 67 **1** A **2** A **3** D **4** B **5** B **6** C **7** C **8** C **9** D **10** D **11** B **12** C **13** A **14** D **15** B

Page 68 **16** 3 km **17** 10 min **18** 20 km/h **19** between 90 and 100 min **20** 20 km **21** 50 **22** 70 min **23** 32 km **24** 7 km **25** The graph only shows the distance travelled but not the direction taken. **26 a** (see diagram) **b** 390 km **c** 78 km/h **d** 30 min **27 a** 40 L **b** Petrol is being added to the tank. **c** The car is not using petrol. It is stopped. **d** 52 L **e** 1 L

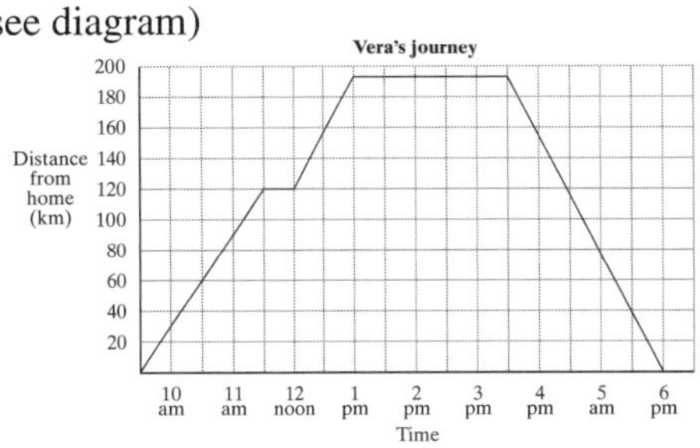

Algebra, Equations and Coordinates

Page 69 **1** C **2** B **3** D **4** C **5** C **6** B **7** C **8** B **9** A **10** A **11** D **12** A

Page 70 **1** D **2** A **3** B **4** A **5** D **6** A **7** D **8** C **9** C **10** B **11** C **12** A **13** C **14** B **15** B

Page 71 **16** $9x$ **17** 1 **18** $12a$ **19** $12m^2$ **20** $4n + 9$ **21** $x + y$ **22** $4z$ **23** $2x$ **24** 9 **25** $6a^2b$ **26** (top) 6, (bottom) 10, 35 **27 a** $10p$ **b** $16p^2$ **c** 4 **28 a** There is no value of y when the expression is simplified. **b** 570 **29 a** unlike terms **b** 23 **30 a** $100x$ **b** $7n$ **c** $y - 5$ **31 a** $8a$ **b** $5t + 9u$

Page 72 **1** D **2** A **3** B **4** B **5** D **6** C **7** C **8** C **9** B **10** A **11** D **12** A **13** B **14** A **15** B

Page 73 **16** $8x + 5y$ **17** $12p^2$ **18** 0 **19** $\frac{2t}{3}$ **20** $60x$ **21** $2a + 6b + 4$ **22** 14 **23** $12p^2q$ **24** $x - 8$ **25** $3x + 4y$ **26** $32x$ **27** (top) 10, (bottom) 17 **28 a** 4 **b** 48 **c** 4 **d** 200 **29 a** $10m + 3n + 5$ **b** 68 **30 a** $m = 3t + 2$ **b** 26 **c** 1, 5, 9, 13, 17, 21 **d** 17

Page 74 **1** B **2** A **3** C **4** D **5** C **6** A **7** A **8** D **9** A **10** A **11** D **12** B **13** D **14** B **15** C

Page 75 **16** $-a - 9b$ **17** $24x$ **18** –42 **19** $20x^2yz$ **20** $\frac{y}{3x}$ **21** $-5 - 4m$ **22** $-2x$ **23** $4x^2$ **24** 10 **25** $x^2 - x$ **26 a** $40x^2$ **b** $k + 16$ **27 a** $17pq - 12p$ **b** $-k$ **28 a** $2n$ **b** $10n$ **29** $x + 16$ **30 a** –7 **b** 1 **31 a** 1, 3, 5, 7, 9, 11, 13, 15 **b** 1, 9, 25, 49, 81, 121, 169, 225 **c** $z = y^2$

Page 76 **1** B **2** D **3** A **4** C **5** A **6** D **7** C **8** B **9** D **10** B **11** B **12** B **13** A **14** C **15** A **16** C

Page 77 **1** A **2** A **3** A **4** D **5** C **6** D **7** A **8** C **9** B **10** D **11** C **12** B **13** B **14** D **15** D

Page 78 **16** 22 **17** 21 **18** 46 **19** 98 **20** 14 **21** $y = 63$ **22** $n = 48$ **23** $t = 25$ **24** $k = 100$ **25** $z = 0$ **26 a** $x = 5$ **b** $x = 33$ **c** $x = 18$ **d** $x = 3$ **e** $x = 52$ **f** $x = 9$ **27 a** 7×8 is 56 and 3 more than that is 59 not 84. **b** $7x + 3 = 87$ **c** $x = 12$; the number is 12

Page 79 **1** B **2** A **3** B **4** C **5** A **6** B **7** B **8** C **9** D **10** B **11** D **12** B **13** B **14** C **15** C

Page 80 **16** $x = 4\frac{3}{4}$ **17** $x = 13$ **18** $k = 0$ **19** 5.6 **20** $x = 32$ **21** 6 **22** $k = 4$ **23** $x = 27$ **24** 5 **25** $d = 25$ **26 a** $x = 0.85$ **b** $m = 611\frac{5}{6}$ **c** $a = 25$ **d** $g = 8\frac{2}{3}$ **e** $n = 45$ **27 a** $x + 5$ **b** $x + 12$ **c** $3x + 17 = 44$ **d** 14

Page 81 **1** C **2** A **3** C **4** A **5** D **6** B **7** A **8** B **9** C **10** A **11** C **12** B **13** D **14** A **15** D

Page 82 **16** $x = 5.27$ **17** $x = -8$ **18** $g = \frac{1}{4}$ **19** 7 **20** $y = \frac{3}{4}$ **21** –1 **22** 8 **23** $c = 9$ **24** $a = 1$ **25** 2.8 **26 a** $h = 67$ **b** $x = 10.25$ **c** $n = -4.5$ **d** $k = -12$ **e** $x = 1\frac{2}{3}$ **27 a** $125 + 45h = 890$ **b** 17 **c** $60 **28** 12

Page 83 **1** D **2** A **3** D **4** B **5** B **6** A **7** B **8** C **9** D **10** A **11** B **12** C **13** C **14** C **15** A

Page 84 **1** B **2** B **3** C **4** D **5** D **6** C **7** A **8** A **9** A **10** B **11** C **12** C **13** D **14** A **15** A

Page 85 **16** (–3, 2) **17** *K* **18** (see diagram below left) **19** $(2\frac{1}{2}, 1\frac{1}{2})$ **20** (see diagram) **21** (5, 1) **22** It would return to the original position. **23** rotating about *O* through 180° **24** (4, –5) **25** (1, 9)

18, 20

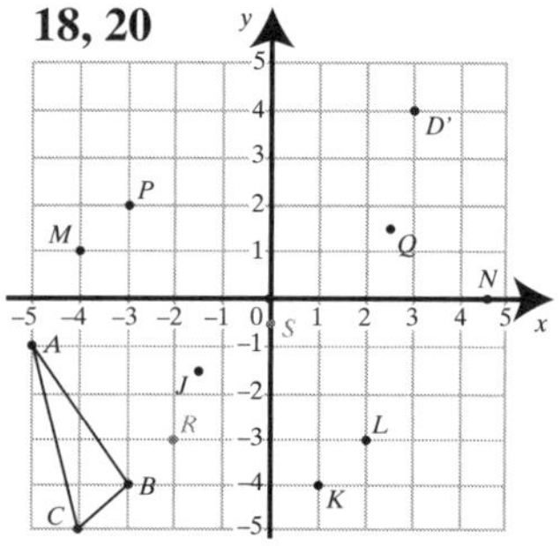

26 a, b

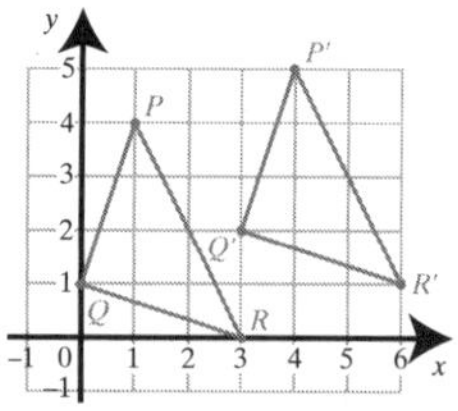

27 a

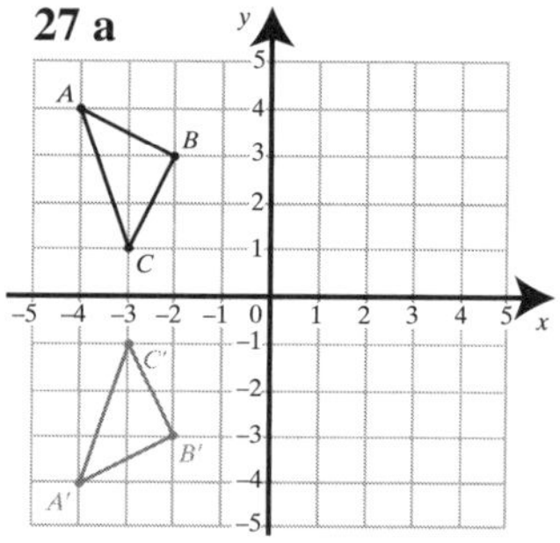

28 a

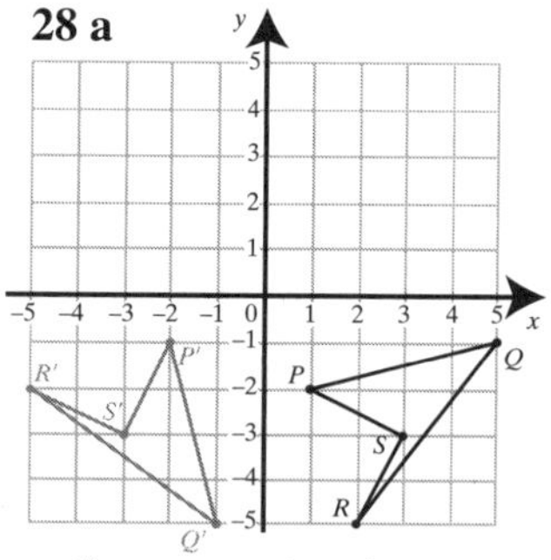

26 a (see diagram 2 above) **b** (see diagram) **c** (0, 1) **27 a** (see diagram 3 above) **b** The *x*-coordinate remains the same and the *y*-coordinate has the same magnitude but different sign. **c** (2, 3) **28 a** (see diagram above right) **b** The *x*-coordinate of the image is the *y*-coordinate of the point. The *y*-coordinate of the image is the negative of the *x*-coordinate of the point. **c** (3, 3)

Page 86 **1** B **2** C **3** D **4** B **5** A **6** C **7** C **8** D **9** A **10** B **11** A **12** A **13** D **14** B **15** C

Page 87 **16** $12ab^2$ **17** $5 \times p \times p \times q$ **18** $9n$ **19** 1 **20** $6x$ **21** 5 **22** $3t$ **23** $3a + 2b$ **24** 12 **25** $x = 421$ **26 a** $26x$ **b** $4ab$ **c** $x^2 + 15x$ **27 a** $7x + 7$ **b** 21 **28 a** $x = 4$ **b** $x = 12$ **29 a** (5, –1) **b** *A* **c** (see diagram) **29 c** **d** (4, –4) **e** (–4, –2) **f** (–4, –2)

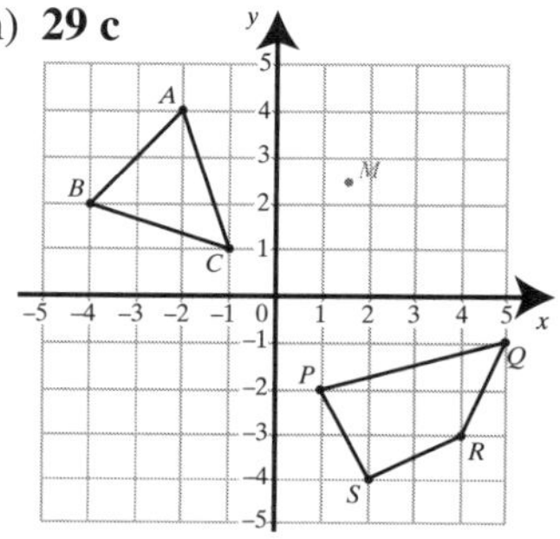

Page 88 **1** C **2** B **3** A **4** C **5** D **6** B **7** D **8** D **9** A **10** C **11** A **12** A **13** C **14** C **15** B

Page 89 **16** $y = 6$ **17** $\frac{4}{3}$ **18** 4 **19** $5x^2$ **20** 12 **21** 0 **22** $10x - 6$ **23** $y = 3x - 2$ **24** $x = 1.5$ **25** (–4, –2) **26 a** $6p + 7q - 6$ **b** $3a^2 + 4a$ **c** $24pq + 20p$ **27 a** $x = 71\frac{6}{7}$ **b** $x = 168$ **28 a** 1, 4, 7, 10, 13 **b** 18 **29 a** (0, 5) **b** (see diagram) **c** (4, 2) **d** reflection in the *x*-axis

29 b

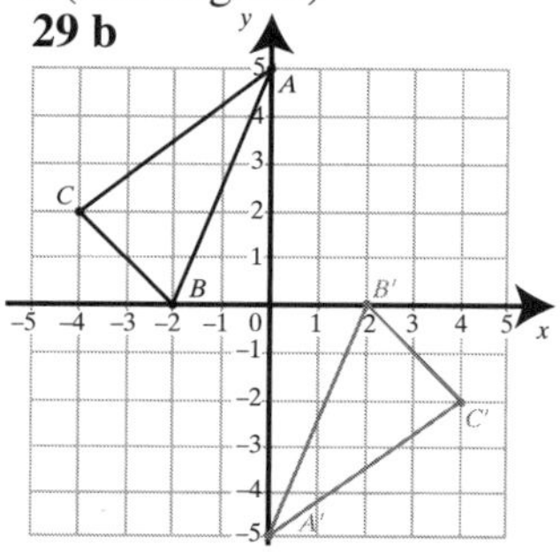

Length, Area and Volume

Page 90 **1** C **2** A **3** C **4** D **5** C **6** B **7** D **8** B **9** C **10** B **11** A **12** D **13** B **14** A

Page 91 **1** C **2** D **3** A **4** B **5** C **6** D **7** C **8** D **9** B **10** B **11** A **12** B **13** A **14** A **15** C

Page 92 **16** mm^2, cm^2, m^2, ha, km^2 **17** 121 cm^2 **18** 304 cm^2 **19** 132 cm^2 **20** 1776 cm^2 **21** $\frac{1}{2}$ **22** 18 **23** 32 m^2 **24** 9 **25** 669.26 m^2 **26 a** 100 000 m^2 **b** 10 **c** 8 **27 a** 40 m **b** 180 m^2 **28 a** 70 m^2 **b** 30 m^2 **c** \$2160 **29 a** 17 cm **b** 17 cm^2 **30 a** 54 m^2 **b** 12 m^2 **c** $\frac{2}{9}$ **d** 21 m^2

Page 93 **1** C **2** D **3** B **4** C **5** C **6** B **7** D **8** C **9** B **10** A **11** A **12** C **13** D **14** A **15** B

Page 94 **16** 58.5 cm^2 **17** 0.7569 m^2 **18** 21.6 m^2 **19** 9.165 ha **20** 17 cm^2 **21** 35 cm **22** 3456 m^2 **23** 340.75 ha **24** 83 cm **25** 114 cm^2 **26** smaller: a hectare is 100 m by 100 m. **27 a** 1.92 m^2 **b** 1.681 m^2 **c** 29.039 m^2 **d** 1 **28 a** 2.16 m^2 **b** $\frac{1}{5}$ **29 a** 3272.5 m^2 **b** 15 180 m^2

Page 95 **1** A **2** C **3** D **4** C **5** A **6** B **7** A **8** C **9** C **10** A **11** B **12** C **13** B **14** C **15** B

Page 96 **16** 2 350 000 **17** 46 cm **18** 102 **19** 9.2 cm **20** 49 cm^2 **21** 120 cm^2 **22** 53.5 m^2 **23** 125 m **24** 38 940.5 m^2 **25** 280 ha **26** The difference in length needs to be multiplied by the whole width and the difference in width by the whole length; 45.125 m^2. **27** no difference **28 a** 9600 m^2 **b** 96 **29 a** 20.96 m^2 **b** \$910.45 **30** $\frac{11}{49}$

Page 97 **1** B **2** A **3** D **4** A **5** C **6** B **7** C **8** D **9** B **10** D **11** A **12** B **13** C **14** C

Page 98 **1** C **2** B **3** D **4** B **5** D **6** C **7** A **8** B **9** A **10** A **11** B **12** D **13** C **14** A **15** B

Page 99 **16** 24 cm^3 **17** 6000 **18** triangle **19** 620 **20** 72 **21** ◯ **22** 36 m^3 **23** 72 cm^3 **24** 1 m^3 **25** 1000 L
26 a hexagonal **b i** 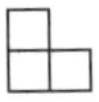 **ii**  **iii**  **iv** 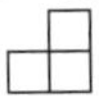 **c** 3 cm^3 **d** 3 mL **27** 300 000 L **28 a** They are all the same.
b 18 000 cm^3 **c** 252 000 cm^3 **d** 0.252 m^3

Page 100 1 B 2 D 3 A 4 B 5 B 6 C 7 A 8 C 9 C 10 C 11 A 12 C 13 B 14 D 15 D

Page 101 **16** 3500 **17** 3105 cm^3 **18** 2850 **19** 8 **20** triangular **21** rectangular **22** 6250 **23** pentagon **24** 64 cm^3
25 25.6 **26 a** 11 cm^3 **b i** 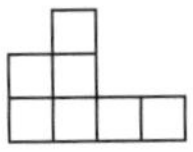 **ii** 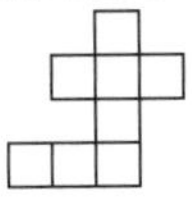 **iii** 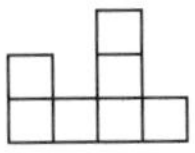 **iv** 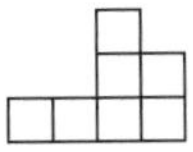 **27 a** 0.9 m^3 **b** 900 L **c** 3
28 a 0.88 m^3 **b** 0.81 m^3 **c** 70

Page 102 1 A 2 A 3 B 4 C 5 D 6 A 7 B 8 D 9 B 10 D 11 C 12 C 13 A 14 D 15 D

Page 103 **16** 11 cm **17** 50 **18** 144 cm^3 **19** 9 **20** 2184 cm^3 **21** heptagonal prism **22** 343 mL **23** 12 541.9
24 0.768 m^3 **25** 520 m^3 **26** No, a cube has all three dimensions the same whereas a square-based prism might have a different height than its length and width. **27 a** triangular **b** pentagonal prism **c i** **ii**  **28 a** 6.27 m^3 **b** 0.114 m^3
c \$2.85 **29 a** rectangular prism **b** 70 cm^3 **c** 1890 cm^3

Page 104 1 B 2 D 3 A 4 A 5 C 6 D 7 A 8 B 9 D 10 C 11 C 12 A 13 A 14 A 15 B

Page 105 **16** 60 m^2 **17** 200 m **18** 252 cm^3 **19** 40 cm **20** 2 040 000 L **21** 2.223 km **22** 1.386 m^2 **23** 40
24 1 mm^2, 1 cm^2, 1 m^2, 1 ha, 1 km^2 **25** 1000 kg (or 1 t) **26 a** 1 m **b** 576 cm^2 **c** 6912 cm^3 **d** 6.912 L **27** 0.18 m^2
28 a \$1078 **b** \$6162 **c** 2.34 m^3 **29 a** 3.724 km **b** 55.3 ha

Page 106 1 D 2 C 3 C 4 A 5 D 6 C 7 A 8 B 9 A 10 D 11 B 12 D 13 A 14 A 15 B

Page 107 **16** 27 m^3 **17** 350 **18** 84 m^2 **19** 26.318 m **20** 256 cm^2 **21** 1 L **22** 90 cm^2 **23** 1 000 000 **24** 8
25 $\frac{1}{1000000}$ **26 a** \$1522 **b** \$2040 **c** 90 m^3 **d** 90 000 L **27 a** 65.5 cm **b** 202 cm^2 **28 a** 600 m **b** 600 m^2 **c** 24 m **29** 4%

Geometric Reasoning

Page 108 1 B 2 C 3 A 4 D 5 B 6 C 7 D 8 D 9 C 10 B 11 D 12 D 13 B 14 B 15 A

Page 109 1 C 2 D 3 D 4 D 5 C 6 C 7 A 8 B 9 C 10 A 11 B 12 D 13 A 14 C 15 A

Page 110 **16** 31° **17** 78° **18** 152° **19** equal **20** supplementary **21** equal **22** 48° **23** 71° **24** 53° **25** 115°
26 a $\angle AQR$ **b** vertically opposite **c** arrow markings **d** 68°, corresponding angles, parallel lines **e** $\angle STB$ **f** $\angle QTU$
g 112° **27 a** parallel; Alternate angles are equal. **b** parallel; Co-interior angles are supplementary. **c** not parallel; Corresponding angles are not equal. **28** 36° ($\angle DEB$ = 126°, vertically opposite; $\angle BEF$ = 126° – 90°)

Page 111 1 B 2 D 3 A 4 C 5 D 6 B 7 C 8 A 9 D 10 D 11 B 12 A 13 C 14 C 15 D

Page 112 **16** $\angle ABE$ (or $\angle EBA$ or $\angle ABH$ or $\angle HBA$) **17** $\angle DEH$ **18** $\angle ABG$ or $\angle CBE$ **19** $\angle BEF$ **20** $\angle GBC$
21 $\angle BED$ **22** 125° **23** 152° **24** 45° **25** obtuse **26 a** $\angle DCE$ and $\angle ECA$ **b** $\angle DCE$ and $\angle ECA$ (or $\angle ECA$ and $\angle ACB$ or $\angle DCA$ and $\angle ACB$) **c** $\angle DCA$ and $\angle ACB$ (or $\angle DCE$ and $\angle ECB$) **d** Only one angle has a vertex at *E* but several different angles have a vertex at *C*. **27 a** (any 3 from) $\angle ATQ$, $\angle RVB$, $\angle AVW$, $\angle VWD$, $\angle UWS$, $\angle TUW$, $\angle CUQ$ **b** 105°
c (any 3 from) $\angle VTQ$, $\angle RVT$, $\angle BVW$, $\angle VWU$, $\angle DWS$, $\angle QUW$, $\angle CUP$ **28 a** No, the corresponding angles $\angle APE$ and $\angle PRG$ are not equal. **b** Yes, $\angle QSR$ = 180° – 87° = 93° so the corresponding angles are equal. **29 a** $\angle ADC + \angle BCD$ = 90° + 90° = 180° so the co-interior angles are supplementary. **b** 117° **30** 40°; $\angle PRC$ = 50° (corresponding angles, $AB \parallel CD$), $\angle PRC + \angle CRT + \angle TRS$ = 180° (angles in straight line)

Page 113 1 C 2 C 3 D 4 B 5 A 6 A 7 B 8 D 9 B 10 D 11 A 12 B 13 B 14 A 15 B

Page 114 **16** ⊥ **17** alternate **18** *R* **19** *KL* (or *LK*) **20** 36 **21** 108° **22** 34 **23** 56 **24** 124 **25** 149° **26 a** 61; $\angle EFC = \angle AFB$ (vertically opposite), $\angle EFC + \angle FCD$ = 180° (co-interior, $EB \parallel DC$) **b** 18; $\angle LMJ = \angle KLH$ (corresponding, $GH \parallel IJ$) **c** 65; $\angle PQT$ = 180° – $\angle QTS$ (co-interior, $PQ \parallel ST$, $\angle QUV = \angle PQT$ (alternate, $PR \parallel UV$) **d** 280; $\angle WZY + \angle XWZ$ = 180° (co-interior, $WX \parallel ZY$), angles in a revolution **27 a** not necessarily. If $AD \parallel EH$ the corresponding angles will be equal and $IJ \parallel KL$ but if *AD* and *EH* are not parallel then *IJ* and *KL* will not be parallel either. **b** Yes; $\angle CBF$ = 106° (vertically opposite) co-interior angles are supplementary. **28** 118°; $\angle CDF$ = 180° – 141° = 39° (co-interior, $CD \parallel EF$), $\angle BDC$ = 101° – 39° = 62°, $\angle ABD$ = 180° – 62° = 118° (co-interior, $AB \parallel CD$)

Page 115 1 C 2 D 3 A 4 B 5 D 6 D 7 C 8 A 9 C 10 B 11 C 12 C

Page 116 1 D 2 A 3 C 4 C 5 D 6 C 7 B 8 A 9 C 10 D 11 A 12 B 13 A 14 C 15 B

Page 117 **16** 60° **17** 4 **18** 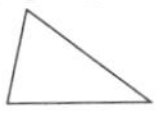 **19** rhombus **20** true **21** false **22** 360° **23** false **24** 50° **25** 65° **26 a** 90°
b 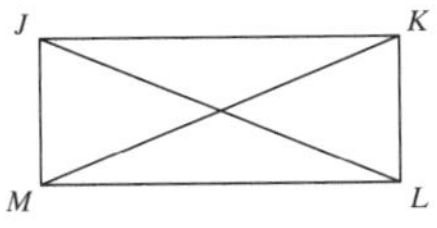

c yes **d** yes **e** no **f** no **27 a** angles opposite equal sides in isosceles triangle **b** 100°
c obtuse-angled isosceles **28 a** 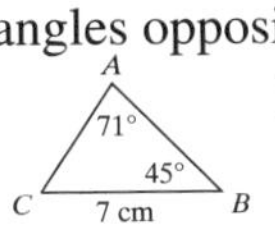

b 64° **c** acute-angled scalene **29 a** kite **b** 104° **c** 68°

Page 118 **1** D **2** D **3** A **4** D **5** D **6** B **7** A **8** B **9** C **10** C **11** C **12** A **13** B **14** C **15** B

Page 119 **16** square **17** 0 **18** trapezium **19** 155° **20** rectangle **21** 102 **22** 41° **23** 46 **24** 45 **25** 50 **26 a** true **b** false **c** true **27 a** 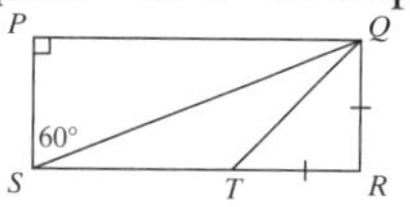

b right-angled isosceles **c** 45° **d** 15° **28 a** equilateral, $AB = BC$ (sides of rhombus), so $\angle BCA = \angle BAC = 60°$, and $\angle ABC = 60°$ (angle sum of triangle) **b** 30°, diagonals bisect the angles **29 a** 26° **b** 52° **c** 116° **d** obtuse-angled scalene

Page 120 **1** A **2** B **3** B **4** D **5** C **6** C **7** C **8** B **9** A **10** D **11** B **12** A **13** A **14** D **15** A

Page 121 **16** square **17** 1 **18** both 39° **19** parallelogram (or rhombus, square or rectangle) **20** 122 **21** 30° **22** 45° **23** false **24** acute-angled, isosceles **25** The angles of a triangle add up to 180° whereas a reflex angle is larger than 180°. **26 a** 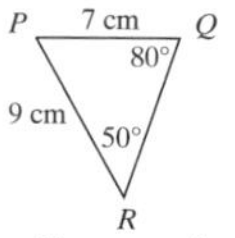

b 7 cm, $\angle QPR = 50°$ (angle sum of triangle is 180°) so ΔPQR is isosceles **27 a** 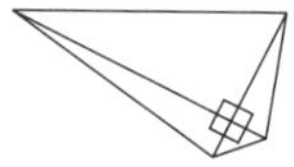
b One diagonal would also need to bisect the other. **c** The diagonals would need to bisect each other at right angles. **28** 147°; $\angle EDC = 114°$ (opposite angles of parallelograms are equal), $\angle CED = 33°$ (base angle of isosceles triangle), $\angle AEC + \angle CED = 180°$ (angles in straight line) **29 a** 30°; $\angle JKL = 90°$ (angle of square), $\angle JKN = 60°$ (angle of equilateral triangle), $\angle NKL = \angle JKL - \angle JKN$ **b** $KN = JK$ (sides of equilateral triangle) and $KL = JK$ (sides of square) **c** 75° **d** 150° **e** obtuse-angled isosceles

Page 122 **1** C **2** D **3** D **4** A **5** D **6** A **7** B **8** A **9** B **10** A **11** D **12** B **13** C **14** C **15** B

Page 123 **16** 100° **17** quadrilateral **18** 180° **19** $\angle ACB$ **20** 90° **21** 60 **22** 3 **23** false **24** 78 **25** rectangle **26 a** corresponding angles, $TQ \parallel SR$ **b** Opposite angles of parallelograms are equal. **c** 112°; $\angle TPQ = 68°$ (base angle of isosceles triangle), $\angle PQT = 44°$ (angle sum of triangle is 180°), $\angle PQR = \angle PQT + \angle TQR$ **d** trapezium **27 a** 65°; $\angle ABC + \angle CBD = 180°$ (angles in straight line) **b** 65° (base angle of isosceles triangle) **c** 130°; $\angle CDE = \angle CBD + \angle BCD$ (exterior angle of triangle) **28 a** vertically opposite **b** 108° **c** No, the corresponding angles are not equal.

Page 124 **1** D **2** D **3** C **4** A **5** C **6** D **7** A **8** B **9** C **10** C **11** B **12** A **13** B **14** C **15** B

Page 125 **16** square **17** rhombus **18** 120° **19** 120° **20** 121° **21** 3 **22** 101° **23** 30° **24** 37° **25** 150° **26 a** 4 **b** 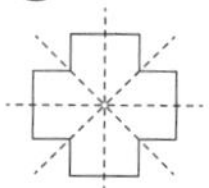
c trapeziums **27 a** 78 **b** 112 **c** No; Co-interior angles are not supplementary. **28 a** 20 **b** 80° **c** acute-angled scalene **29 a** corresponding angles $AB \parallel DC$ **b** alternate angles $AD \parallel BC$ **c** 62° **d** 31° **e** obtuse-angled isosceles

Page 126 **1** B **2** C **3** D **4** A **5** D **6** C **7** D **8** D **9** A **10** B **11** C **12** D **13** A **14** B **15** C

Page 127 **16** 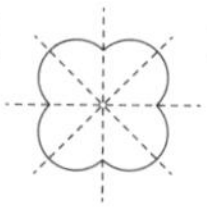
17 square **18** 900° **19** 90° **20** 16 **21** trapezium **22** 55 **23** Co-interior angles are supplementary. **24** 36 **25** trapezium **26 a** 35°; $\angle DEB = 110°$ (corresponding $AB \parallel DE$) so $\angle BDE = 35°$ (base angle of isosceles triangle) **b** $\angle ABE = 70°$ (angles in straight line) so $\angle ABD = \angle DBE = 35°$ **c** Yes, $\angle FEH = \angle DEB$ (vertically opposite), $\angle EFH = \angle EHF = 35°$ so alternate angles are equal. **27** $\angle ADQ = \angle PBC$ (opposite angles of a parallelogram). Both triangles are isosceles so as the base angles are the same so must the vertex angles be equal. **28 a** 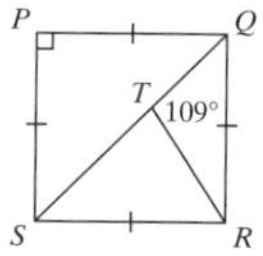

b angle of square is 90°, diagonals bisect the angles **c** obtuse-angled scalene **d** 64°; $\angle TRQ = 26°$ (angle sum of triangle is 180°), $\angle TRS = 90° - 26° = 64°$ **29** 117°; $\angle ACB = \angle ABC = 54°$ (base angles isosceles triangle ABC), $\angle CDE = \angle DEC = 63°$ (base angles isosceles triangle CDE), $\angle DEB = 180° - 63°$ (angles in straight line)

Statistics

Page 128 **1** B **2** D **3** C **4** C **5** B **6** D **7** C **8** D **9** A **10** C **11** C **12** D **13** D

Page 129 **1** A **2** C **3** C **4** C **5** B **6** D **7** B **8** B **9** C **10** D **11** D **12** D **13** A **14** C **15** B

Page 130 **16** 23 **17** 167 cm **18** 41 cm **19** 4 **20** 6 **21** Rose **22** 4 **23** Blake **24** 2 **25** $\frac{3}{10}$

26 a

Score	Tally	Frequency
1	卌 II	7
2	卌	5
3	IIII	4
4	IIII	4
5	II	2
6	卌 III	8
Total		30

b 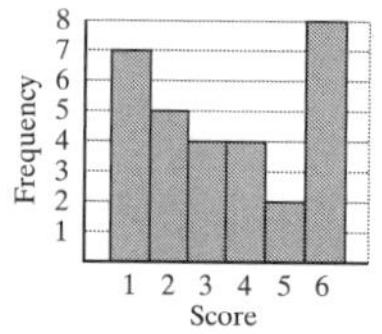

27 a 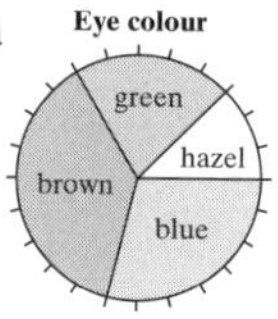

b 75° **28 a** 7 **b** 14%

c No, only the percentage of students present is shown. There is no information about actual numbers of students.
d It allows comparisons between the years.

Page 131 **1** B **2** B **3** B **4** C **5** C **6** C **7** D **8** D **9** D **10** C **11** B **12** A **13** C **14** C **15** D

Page 132 **16** 7 **17** 0 **18** 8 **19** 2 **20** 6 **21** 60 **22** 135 **23** 20% **24** $\frac{1}{20}$ **25** There are not enough houses. The sample would be too small. **26 a** \$480 000 **b** end of 2014, beginning of 2015 **c** \$60 000 **d** 2015 **e** The scale on the vertical axis does not begin at 0. It makes the differences between points on the graph appear larger than they actually are.
27 a (below) **b** 36% **c** Easier to see the spread of the scores or any patterns **d** The range of scores is too large and most scores only occur once. **28**

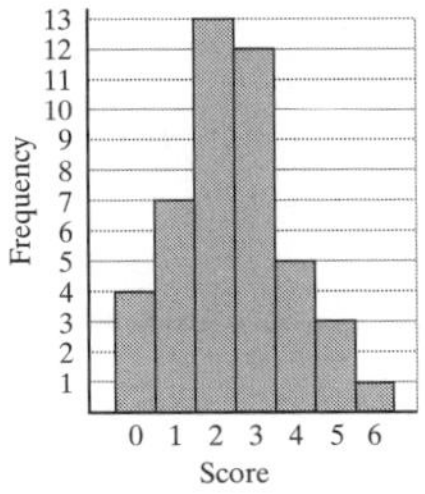

27 a **Exam marks**

5	6 7 9
6	0 2 4 4 5 8
7	1 3 3 6 7 7 8
8	2 2 2 4 5 6 9
9	1 5

Page 133 **1** B **2** C **3** D **4** A **5** D **6** C **7** B **8** A **9** D **10** C **11** B **12** A **13** D **14** C **15** D

Page 134 **16** 8 **17** 20 **18** 12 **19** 18 **20** 8 **21** 10 **22** 22.7 **23** 849 **24** 8 **25** 19.5 **26 a** 75.75 **b** 76 **c** 16 **d** Kitty performed just slightly less than average. Her mark was slightly less than both the mean and the median. **27 a** 6 **b** 20 **c** 159 **d** 17.4 **e** 17 **28 a** 165 cm **b** 163 cm **c** 19 cm **d** The median decreased to 160 cm and the mean decreased to 160 cm, but the range did not change.

Page 135 **1** C **2** A **3** C **4** B **5** D **6** B **7** A **8** A **9** A **10** C **11** D **12** A **13** D **14** B **15** D

Page 136 **16** 13 **17** 9 **18** 29 **19** 3 **20** 30 **21** 14.75 **22** 31.5 **23** 19 **24** 63 **25** 30 **26 a** 73.2 **b** 33 **c** 73 **d** 78 **e** 73.4; Darby was not correct because Xavier's mean mark was slightly better than Darby's. **f** 13. So the range of Xavier's marks is much less than that of Darby so there is a smaller spread. Xavier is more consistent. **27** 74.5% **28** 169 cm
29 a 9 **b** Although the sum of the scores doesn't change there are more scores so the sum is divided by a larger number and the mean will decrease. It would change to 7.5. **c** 9

Page 137 **1** D **2** B **3** B **4** B **5** B **6** A **7** C **8** B **9** B **10** C **11** C **12** C **13** C **14** A **15** D

Page 138 **16** 17 **17** 9 **18** 17 **19** 30 **20** 8 **21** 卌 III **22** chocolate **23** 80° **24** 25% **25** $\frac{1}{9}$ **26 a** 3 **b** 11 **c** 76 **d** 40 **e** 11 **f** 11 **g** 10.5 **27 a** **Cricket scores** **b** 59 **c** 171.5 **d** 167 **28 a** 92 **b** 12

13	7
14	1 4 8
15	5 9
16	0 7 7
17	1 2 4 5
18	0 2 3 6 7 9
19	6

Page 139 **1** C **2** B **3** A **4** C **5** B **6** C **7** D **8** C **9** C **10** B **11** B **12** C **13** D **14** B **15** D

Page 140 **16** 25 kg **17** 20 kg **18** 24 kg **19** 25 kg **20** 22.9 kg **21** 12 °C **22** 22 °C **23** at around 11:30 am and at 7 pm **24** 6.5 **25** 2.8 km **26** There are only three scores and at least two of those must be 32 so the middle score must be 32.
27 a It is misleading because it is not completely round and uses depth so distorts the proportions. It seems that the sector for wages, for example, is much larger than those for rent and other when they should all be the same. **b** 60°
c Allocation of costs **28 a** 15% **b** 198° **c** (below) **d** The sample is small. The free samples may cause the results to be biased.

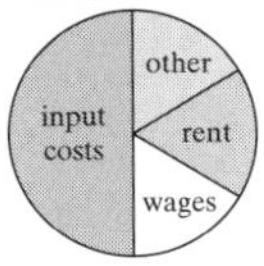

28 c

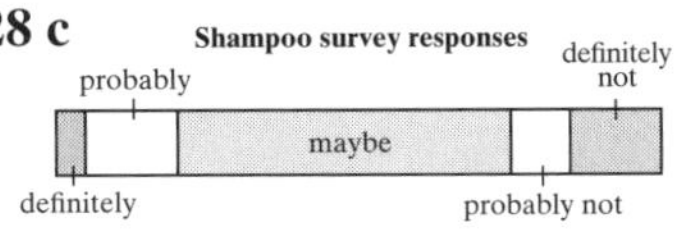

Probability

Page 141 **1** D **2** B **3** D **4** B **5** A **6** B **7** D **8** B **9** B **10** C **11** A **12** C **13** B **14** A **15** C

Page 142 **1** C **2** D **3** D **4** C **5** D **6** D **7** B **8** B **9** A **10** A **11** B **12** A **13** D **14** D **15** A

Page 143 **16** $\frac{1}{6}$ **17** $\frac{1}{7}$ **18** $\frac{7}{12}$ **19** {4, 5, 6, 7} **20** $\frac{1}{2}$ **21** $\frac{4}{15}$ **22** 60 **23** 0 **24** 1 **25** $\frac{3}{5}$ **26 a** $\frac{5}{12}$ **b** $\frac{1}{4}$ **c** $\frac{1}{3}$ **27 a** $\frac{1}{3}$ **b** $\frac{5}{12}$ **c** $\frac{1}{4}$ **28 a** {∇, •, ∗, ⊗} **b** ∇ and ⊗ **c** 25% **d** 0.5 **29 a** {1, 2, 3} **b** $\frac{1}{2}$ **c** fifty-fifty **30** false. The outcomes are not equally likely.

Page 144 **1** A **2** B **3** C **4** D **5** C **6** C **7** D **8** B **9** B **10** B **11** D **12** A **13** A **14** D **15** C

Page 145 **16** 50% **17** $\frac{1}{13}$ **18** 1 **19** 0 **20** 25% **21** {1, 3, 5, 7, 9} **22** 24 **23** $0.\dot{3}$ **24** 8 **25** $\frac{4}{11}$ **26 a i** $\frac{1}{5}$ **ii** 0 **iii** $\frac{13}{25}$ **b** 32% **c** 40% **27 a** $\frac{1}{3}$ **b** The outcomes are not equally likely. $\frac{1}{6}$ **28 a** $\frac{3}{5}$ **b** $\frac{1}{5}$ **c** $\frac{1}{3}$ **29 a** $\frac{1}{5}$ **b** $\frac{1}{10}$ **c** $\frac{1}{2}$ **d** $\frac{3}{5}$

Page 146 **1** B **2** C **3** B **4** A **5** C **6** D **7** A **8** A **9** D **10** C **11** B **12** D **13** A **14** B **15** B

Page 147 **16** $\frac{2}{5}$ **17** 0 **18** $\frac{5}{6}$ **19** $\frac{1}{8}$ **20** 30 **21** 14 **22** $\frac{1}{12}$ **23** The probability of an event cannot be greater than 1. **24** 133 **25** The outcomes are not equally likely.

Page 148 **26 a** $\frac{7}{60}$ **b** 9 **c** $\frac{5}{9}$ **27** No; the probability would be $\frac{1}{5}$ if the outcomes were equally likely, but the probability could be different if the outcomes were not equally likely. **28 a i** $\frac{1}{20}$ **ii** 0.15 **iii** 10% **b** unlikely **29 a** 4 **b** impossible **c** 8 **d** 4

Exam Paper 1

Page 150 **1** C **2** D **3** B **4** A **5** D **6** C **7** A **8** C **9** C **10** A **11** D **12** D **13** B **14** B **15** A **16** B **17** C **18** D **19** C **20** B **21** A **22** D **23** A **24** B **25** D

Page 152 **1** $\frac{1}{2}$ **2** 60 **3** $150 **4** $2 \times 3 \times 5$ **5** 12 m^2 **6** 2 : 3 **7** $6x + 8y$ **8** $0.\dot{3}$ **9** –2 **10** $3.70 **11** 6 **12** 180° **13** 12 **14** 4 **15** $\frac{1}{4}$ **16** 6 **17** trapezium **18** 35 mL **19** $\frac{37}{10}$ **20** (3, –2) **21** 20 **22** 20 **23** $\frac{1}{4}$ **24** 40 m^2 **25** 75% **26** 6 **27** equilateral **28** $3m$ **29** 2 **30** $\frac{1}{8}$

Page 154 **1 a** 3 **b** 30 **2 a** $x = 4$ **b** $x = 64$ **3 a** 68 m **b** 55 m **c** 25 m **4 a** $3\frac{13}{15}$ **b** $\frac{1}{2}$ **c** $1\frac{2}{3}$ **5 a** 300 m **b** 1500 m **c** 150 m **d** 3000 m^2 **e** 0.3 ha **6 a** (see below left) $2^2 \times 7^2$ **b** 14 **7 a** acute-angled, isosceles, $AB = BC$ adjacent sides of a rhombus **b** 90° **c** 50°, alternate angles AB is parallel to DC **8 a** $75 **b** the first shop by $5 **9 a** $\frac{3}{5}$ **b** 40 **c** $\frac{2}{5}$ **10** (see below centre) **11 a** 80 **b** No; the co-interior angles add to 175° not 180°. **12 a** 1000 cm^3 **b** trapezoidal prism **c** (see below right) **d** 1.5 L

6 a

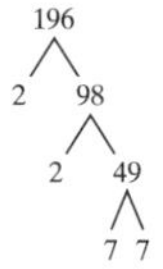

10

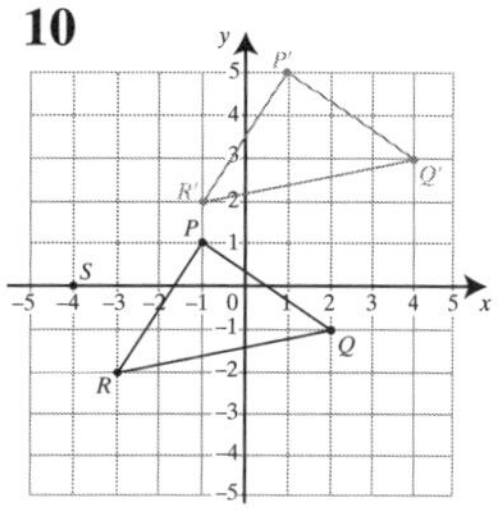

12 c

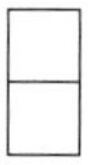

Exam Paper 2

Page 156 **1** A **2** D **3** C **4** C **5** D **6** B **7** C **8** A **9** C **10** C **11** D **12** B **13** A **14** D **15** D **16** B **17** B **18** A **19** C **20** D **21** D **22** A **23** B **24** B **25** A

Page 158 **1** 7 **2** $5x + 5y$ **3** $\frac{8}{15}$ **4** 9 : 11 **5** 25 cm^2 **6** $\frac{1}{6}$ **7** 23.8 **8** 7300 **9** –38 –23, –6, 0, 7, 19 **10** corresponding **11** 72 **12** 750 000 **13** –3 **14** 40 **15** 26% **16** 10 **17** 9 **18** $\frac{2}{3}$ **19** $\frac{47}{8}$ **20** 40 **21** $1\frac{9}{10}$ **22** $m - 7$ **23** 8000 cm^3 **24** $0.\dot{6}$ **25** 100 **26** $2\frac{2}{5}$ **27** 6 **28** 5000 **29** 600 cm^3 **30** 50 m

Page 160 **1 a** right-angled, scalene **b** 53° **c** 6 m^2 **2 a** Kim **b** 25% **c** 100° **d** $\frac{1}{9}$ **e** $\frac{1}{6}$ **f** 14 **3 a** $6\frac{1}{4}$ **b** $2\frac{13}{20}$ **4 a** (see one possibility below left) **b** $2^2 \times 3^2 \times 5$ **5 a** trapezium **b** 117°, alternate angles parallel lines **c** No; the co-interior angles add to 190°, not 180°. **6 a** 6° **b** 5 °C **7 a** (see below centre) **b** (4, 2) **c** (see below centre) **d** (4, –1) **8** $x = 4$ **9 a** hexagonal prism **b** 120 m^3 **c** 8 m **d** 184 000 L **e** (see below right) **10 a** $48 **b** $1152 **c** $1267.20 **11 a** 21 **b** 158 cm **c** 41 cm **d** 135 cm **e** 132 cm **12 a** 84 m **b** 0.108 m^2

4 a

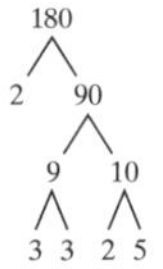

7 a, c

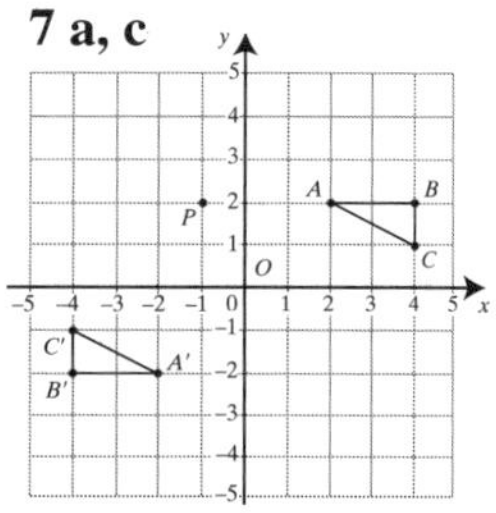

9 e

Exam Paper 3

Page 162 1 A 2 C 3 B 4 D 5 A 6 D 7 D 8 A 9 B 10 A 11 D 12 D 13 C 14 C 15 A 16 B 17 C 18 B 19 D 20 D 21 B 22 C 23 B 24 C 25 A

Page 164 **1** 5.10 **2** 4 **3** –14 **4** 1.8 **5** \$84 **6** $x = 6$ **7** 11 **8** 4 **9** 0.0251, 0.03, 0.215, 0.3 **10** $13 - 3p$ **11** \$480 **12** $2\frac{3}{4}$ **13** \$2398 **14** $\frac{16}{25}$ **15** –15 **16** 25 ha **17** $\frac{3}{25}$ **18** $-9m$ **19** $\frac{1}{2}$ **20** 7 **21** 10 **22** 9 **23** $\frac{9}{20}$ **24** 1 **25** 45 **26** $\frac{1}{10000}$ **27** $x^2 + 9x$ **28** 3 **29** 0.0625 **30** $\frac{1}{7}$

Page 166 **1 a** (see below left), $2^2 \times 3^2 \times 7^2$ **b** 42 **2 a** $x = 28$ **b** $x = 265$ **3 a** $14\frac{7}{40}$ **b** $14\frac{4}{5}$ **c** $\frac{1}{20}$ **d** $\frac{15}{22}$ **4 a** 80 **b** $33\frac{1}{3}$% **c** 40 **d** $\frac{2}{15}$ **5 a** –17 **b** 24 **c** –26 **6 a** \$1280 **b** 1.5 m **7 a** 510 km **b** $6\frac{1}{2}$ hours **c** 70 km/h **8 a** 34 **b** 143 **c** 138 **d** 10% **9 a** \$51.00 **b** \$50.00 **10 a** 57°, $\angle CBE = 33°$ (alternate angles, parallel lines), angle sum of ΔBCE is 180° **b** 308 cm² **11 a** (see below right) **b** (–2.5, –0.5) **c** reflection in the x-axis **d** reflection in the y-axis and rotation through 180° about O **12 a** 10.72 m² **b** 67

1 a

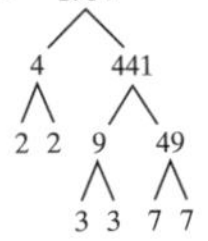

11 a

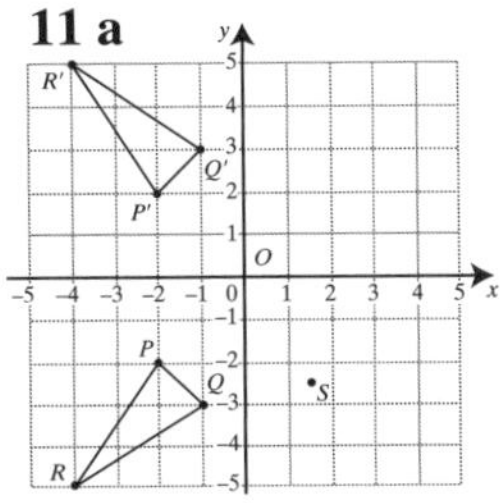

Exam Paper 4

Page 168 1 B 2 A 3 D 4 D 5 A 6 B 7 C 8 D 9 D 10 B 11 D 12 B 13 B 14 A 15 B 16 C 17 A 18 A 19 C 20 A 21 C 22 C 23 C 24 D 25 C

Page 170 **1** 10 **2** $9x + 1$ **3** 13 000 **4** obtuse-angled isosceles **5** 8 **6** 8, 0, –2, –5, –11, –17 **7** $\frac{4}{5}$ **8** 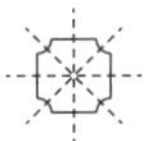 **9** 63 **10** $\frac{1}{3}$ **11** $30ab$ **12** 518 cm² **13** $0.\dot{5}$ **14** 4 : 9 **15** 64 **16** 210 m³ **17** 197.6 **18** y **19** $x = 252$ **20** (–2, 3) **21** (–4, –2) **22** $11\frac{17}{60}$ **23** 85 **24** 1.6 m² **25** 0 **26** $2^3 \times 5$ **27** 33 **28** 75% **29** 51 **30** 253 cm²

Page 172 **1 a** (see below left) **b** 8 **c** 4 **d** 7 **e** 8 **f** $7\frac{7}{9}$ **g** $33\frac{1}{3}$% **h** $\frac{1}{9}$ **2 a** $\frac{2}{5}$ **b** 40 **3 a** 6.5% **b** \$5526 **4 a** {1, 2, 3, 4} **b** 1 **c** 25% **5 a** $x = 7$ **b** $x = 455$ **6 a** The bank is owed \$723. **b** \$194 **c** –\$299 **7 a** 0.72 **b** $\frac{18}{25}$, 0.7225, $72\frac{1}{2}$% **8 a** 5544 L **b** 3234 L **c** 9 h **9** (see below right) **10 a** $\frac{2}{3}$ can **b** $5\frac{1}{4}$ cans **11 a** rhombus **b** 56°, co-interior angles add to 180°, QR is parallel to PS **12 a** 1, 3, 7, 13, 21 **b** $x = 51$ **13** 17.5 ha

1 a

Score	Tally	Frequency
6	||||	4
7	~~||||~~ ||||	9
8	~~||||~~ |	6
9	||||	5
10	|||	3
Total		27

9

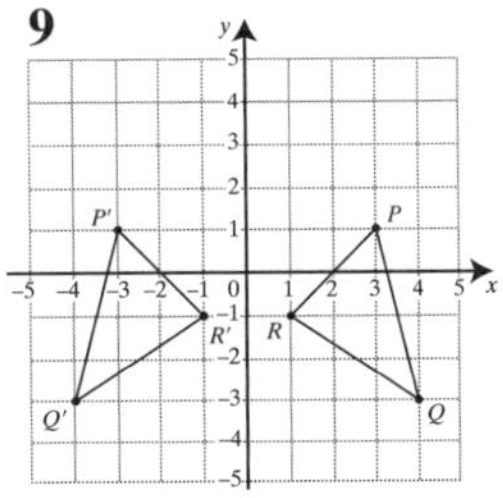

Exam Paper 5

Page 174 1 D 2 D 3 B 4 C 5 B 6 B 7 D 8 C 9 C 10 C 11 B 12 A 13 D 14 A 15 C 16 A 17 B 18 A 19 A 20 A 21 D 22 B 23 C 24 D 25 D

Page 176 **1** 20 **2** 14 **3** 3.90 **4** 2 **5** $3xy$ **6** square **7** $11x - 9$ **8** \$1386 **9** 2187 **10** 14 **11** 43 500 **12** $0.41\dot{6}$ **13** $3x$ **14** 1.0 **15** 8 : 9 **16** $x = 32$ **17** $\frac{1}{6}$ **18** $\frac{5}{14}$ **19** 26 cm **20** \$5.75 **21** 4.525 **22** $\frac{1}{3}, \frac{7}{20}, \frac{3}{8}, \frac{2}{5}$ **23** $\frac{2}{5}$ **24** 200 m² **25** $17\frac{12}{25}$ **26** 8 000 000 **27** (–3, –4) **28** $2\frac{1}{2}$% **29** 180 **30** 90°

Page 178 **1 a** $3a + 6b - 8c$ **b** 11 **2 a** 72° **b** $33\frac{1}{3}$% **c** 18 **d** $\frac{1}{9}$ **3 a** 3 : 2 **b** 60 **4 a** $2\frac{1}{2}$ m **b** $1\frac{1}{4}$ m **c** 2 m **d** 3 m **5 a** $2 \times 2 \times 3 \times 7 \times 11$ **b** 42 **6 a** $312 - \frac{x}{14} = 81$ **b** 3234 **7 a** –4 °C **b** 1.4° per hour **8 a** 1400 mm **b** 2.43 m³ **c** 2430 L **9 a** (–3, 2) **b** (–3, 4) **10 a** 9 (top line), 13 (bottom line) **b** $y = 6x + 1$ **11 a** trapezium **b** 64°, $\angle BAE + \angle AED = 180°$, co-interior angles ($AB$ is parallel to FC) **c** acute-angled, isosceles, $\angle ADE = 64°$ (alternate angles, parallel lines) **d** 26°, $\angle AEF$ is obtuse so the equal angles are $\angle AFE$ and $\angle EAF$ and $\angle AFE + \angle EAF = \angle AED$ (exterior angle of triangle) **e** No; $\angle FAB + \angle ABC = 154° + 36° = 190°$ so the co-interior angles are not supplementary. **12** $\frac{7}{48}$ **13 a** 53° **b** obtuse-angled scalene **c** 234 m² **d** 3 : 10

NOTES